THE JEWS IN PALESTINE IN THE EIGHTEENTH CENTURY

JUDAIC STUDIES SERIES
Leon J. Weinberger, General Editor

The Jews in Palestine in the Eighteenth Century

Under the Patronage of the Istanbul Committee of Officials for Palestine

Jacob Barnai

Translated by Naomi Goldblum

Copyright © 1992
The University of Alabama Press
Tuscaloosa, Alabama 35487–0380
All rights reserved
Manufactured in the United States of America

∞
The paper on which this book is printed meets the minimum requirements of American National Standard for Information Science-Permanence of Paper for Printed Library Materials, ANSI Z39.48-1984.

designed by zig zeigler

Library of Congress Cataloging-in-Publication Data

Barnai, Y.
  [Yehudey Eretz-Yiśra'el ba-me'ah ha-18. be-ḥasut 'Peḳidey Ḳushṭa'. English]
  The Jews in Palestine in the eighteenth century : under the patronage of the Istanbul Committee of Officials for Palestine / Jacob Barnai : translated by Naomi Goldblum.
    p.   cm. — (Judaic studies series)
  Translation of: Yehudey Eretz-Yiśra'el ba-me'ah ha-18. be-ḥasut 'Peḳidey Ḳushṭa'.
  Includes bibliographical references and index.
  ISBN 0-8173-0572-6
  1. Jews—Palestine—History—18th century. 2. Hasidim—Palestine—History—18th century. 3. Halukkah. 4. Jews—Turkey—Istanbul—Charities. 5. Palestine—Ethnic relations. I. Title. II. Series: Judaic studies series (Unnumbered)
DS124.B2813   1992
305.892'405694'09033—dc20   91-31051

British Library Cataloguing-in-Publication Data available

Contents

Contents

TABLES

vii

PREFACE

THE HISTORY OF PALESTINE is a topic that has attracted the attention of modern historiography since the nineteenth century. During the past 150 years many historical studies of Palestine have been written, from a variety of viewpoints. Perhaps it can be said that there are many "histories" of Palestine as a consequence of the variegated history of the land—its many rulers and its diverse population—and of the unique place held by Palestine in the three religions of Judaism, Christianity, and Islam. A significant factor in the development of research on the Jews in Palestine during the Middle Ages was the Zionist movement, which searched for its roots in Palestine even in periods when the country was not under Jewish rule. We are now witnessing a similar phenomenon in the development of Arab-Palestinian historiography of this country. This connection between nationalism and historiography is a well-known phenomenon occurring in many nationalist movements. Although this connection leads to an expansion of growth in historical research, it also brings with it grave dangers of apologetics and distortion arising from ideological and political considerations.

This study, which deals with the history of the Jews in Palestine during the eighteenth century, is intended to cover a period in the history of Palestine that has not been fully dealt with in historical research. The study began as a Ph.D. dissertation, which I wrote at the Hebrew University of Jerusalem under the supervision of my late teacher, Prof. Shmuel Ettinger. I then broadened the dissertation into a more comprehensive study, which was published in Hebrew by Yad Ben-Zvi Publications in Jerusalem in 1982.

In the present English edition I inserted changes, corrections, and updates—some deriving from further research on this subject and some intended to make things clearer for the English reader.

In transliterating the Turkish and Arabic terms appearing in the book the translator and I followed the most important scholars in this field, Bernard Lewis and Amnon Cohen.

It is a pleasant obligation to thank Yad Ben-Zvi Publications for their permission to publish this edition of the book in English. I owe special

ix

thanks to Naomi Goldblum, who translated the book from the Hebrew, for her excellent and dedicated work. Thanks are also due to Yitzhak Zisk for calling my attention to certain documents and to Yosef Ofek for assistance in the preparation of the index. I would also like to thank two anonymous readers of the English manuscript whose important advice helped greatly in shaping and editing the book in its present form. Finally, I am grateful to The University of Alabama Press and especially to its director, Malcolm M. MacDonald, and to Prof. Leon J. Weinberger, who put in much effort to ensure the publication of this book.

The cover illustration and frontispiece, published courtesy of the Collection Israel Museum, Jerusalem, is "Jaffa, Looking South, 1839," a lithograph from *The Holy Land* by David Roberts.

This book was completed when I was a member of the Institute for Advanced Studies at the Hebrew University of Jerusalem.

THE JEWS IN PALESTINE IN THE EIGHTEENTH CENTURY

Introduction: The Sources

In recent years there has been an increasing amount of research on Palestine and on Jewish settlement there during the Ottoman period. Until now, however, the attention of historians has been centered mainly on the eventful nineteenth century, although there has also been some consideration of the sixteenth century, the first century of the Ottoman conquest of Palestine. When I began studying the Jewish settlement in Palestine in the eighteenth century, there were relatively few studies of this topic.

The sources for the history of the Jewish settlement in Palestine during the Ottoman period may be divided into several types: Moslem, European Christian, Jewish, and archaeological.

Moslem Sources

The principal Moslem sources for the history of Palestine (including the history of the Jewish settlement there) are Moslem chronicles, biographies, geographical literature, monographs, collections of various traditions, Moslem juridical literature,[1] government archives, the archives of the Shariʿ courts,[2] and genealogy books.[3]

The Ottoman and Arab archives concerning the history of Palestine have been increasingly available for inspection in the present generation and especially in this decade. The official Ottoman archives, written in Ottoman Turkish (in Arabic letters), are found in Istanbul. They include population censuses, lists of taxpayers, and orders of various kinds connected with the history of the Jews in Palestine. In Jerusalem almost the entire archive of the Shariʿ (Moslem) court in the city has remained from the Ottoman period, and there is also much important documentary material concerning the history of the Jews in Palestine. All the juridical activities of the area took place in the Shariʿ courts, as did the registration of all administrative procedures. Thus archives such as these contain not only the protocols of trials but also notarized registrations (e.g., of wills), called *Sijill*, and copies of official documents that were sent from Istanbul or other cities (in Arabic and Turkish).

1

Besides these official sources there are also private archival materials that remained with Arab families in Palestine and with the *Ulema*, the Moslem religious figures in Palestine. Here, too, one may find historical material concerning the Jews of Palestine.

EUROPEAN CHRISTIAN SOURCES

The European Christian sources for the history of the Jews in Palestine are many and varied. As with the Moslem sources, there are greater quantity and variety of documentary sources than ever before, and there is an especially large number of sources from the nineteenth century.

European-Christian travel books[4] form one important type of source material. The travel books of Crusaders, tourists, and scholars are rich in historical material. There are thousands of such books that were written from the beginning of the Middle Ages until modern times. The main focus of this literature is not on the Jews of Palestine, who constitute a marginal factor in it, but on the Christian aspects of the Holy Land. One of the serious problems with using this travel literature for research purposes is its lack of reliability as a historical source. There are many repetitions in this literature (material that was copied over and over from previous books) and various stereotypes, such as the image of the Jew.[5] The facts transmitted in these books are selective and frequently based on hearsay. There are also problems of plagiarism and falsification, as some of the "travelers" never visited the places they describe. Nevertheless, some books among this travel literature are excellent historical source material. As for the rest, it is possible to use them only after careful distillation. There are some useful bibliographies that allow the scholar direct access to this type of source.[6]

Christian churches and monasteries in Palestine as well as those in other countries contain a great deal of historical source material, and only a small fraction of this material has so far been used for research purposes. In these archives there are, to be sure, documents concerning mainly the history of the Christians and the Christian churches in Palestine. Yet aside from their brief, and occasionally more extensive, pieces of information about the Jews in the land, these documents have great importance in that they can serve as historical sources permitting comparison between the Jews and the Christians in Palestine. Interesting examples of the use that can be made of this material may be found in the scholarly edition of the book *Hurvoth Yerushalayim* (The Ruins of Jerusalem).[7] This Hebrew chronicle, which was first published in Venice in 1631, describes the harsh events that occurred to the Jewish community in Palestine at the beginning of the seventeenth century, during the period of Muhammad Ibn Farukh's rule. Alongside the new edition of the original, the editor added a Christian version of the episode of Ibn Farukh's rule, drawn from the archives of the Franciscan monastery in Jerusalem of the same period. If this comparison, which tells us of the tyranny of this ruler not only over the Jews but also over the Christians, is not enough, there are also Moslem sources from the Shar'i archives in Jerusalem (discussed above) that shed light on his harsh attitude toward the Moslem population as well.[8]

Other examples of the richness of these sources, which reflects their importance to the Jewish settlement in Palestine, are the diaries of the missionary Nicolayson, who was the founder of the Anglican church in Jerusalem at the beginning of the nineteenth century and left diaries of the years 1826–42. In these diaries there is a great deal of material about the history of the Jews in the first half of the nineteenth century, and they have already been used in historical research in recent years.[9]

Another rich source that is of incalculable importance for the present topic is the consular and diplomatic source material. As is well known, the European powers intensified their activities in Palestine in the nineteenth century, both by establishing consulates and by extensive intervention in events there. Some anthologies describing the activities of the consuls and their connections with the Jewish settlement in Palestine have already been published and more are being published at present.[10]

Important European sources are the archives of economic groups that traded with Palestine during the Middle Ages and of European Levant-companies that were founded in the sixteenth century and continued to operate during the Ottoman period. The archives of Venice are outstanding for important material about the economic life of the Mediterranean area in general and the Jews in particular during the Middle Ages. Eliyahu Ashtor has used this source extensively in many studies.[11] The material of the European Levant-companies (especially those of England, France, and Holland) has been used so far only partially for research connected with the Palestine economy,[12] although these archives in general have been studied in the past and important new sources have been discovered there in recent years as well.

We also have the many journals that were published in Europe in the nineteenth century, which contain important material on the history of the Jews in Palestine. The journals of the missionaries are especially noteworthy.

JEWISH SOURCES

Whereas the Moslem and Christian sources provide us with an external viewpoint on the history of the Jews in Palestine, the Jewish sources complete the historical picture from an internal point of view. Just as there are Moslem and Christian travel books and chronicles, there is a similar Hebrew literature, though of limited scope.[13] In a number of cases Jewish travelers repeated material in earlier Jewish and Christian travel books.[14] We therefore find the same flaws in the Jewish travel literature that we listed for the Christian literature: lack of precision, repetitions, stereotypes, use of earlier books as models for travel descriptions, and so on. The main interest of the Jewish travelers was, of course, the Jewish settlement and holy places in Palestine, which are of importance for our topic. The Jewish rabbinic literature and chronicles are superior to the travel literature, even though they also contain exaggerations in the descriptions of troubles and a certain one-sidedness in the description of facts.

Official community sources, such as the community record books, official correspondence, and account books from the Jewish communities in Palestine during the Middle Ages and the Ottoman period are almost nonexistent. Thus, we do not possess even one community record book from Palestine during any period at all, and what we do have is very fragmentary. To cite just one example, in the early 1840s the Book of Regulations of Jerusalem was published,[15] in which the earliest regulations collected were from the eighteenth century, and even these are not continuous and represent only what was found in the offices of the Sephardic community at the time of publication.

We have many documents from emissaries who were sent to the Diaspora by the Jewish communities in Palestine over the generations. These have survived and reached us from their addressees, that is, from the Jewish communities in the Diaspora.[16]

Such misfortunes as earthquakes, expulsions, and the destruction or abandonment of communities account for the loss of most of the records of the Palestine communities. The lack of material reflects the lack of organic continuity in these communities during the late Middle Ages and the Ottoman period.

The various types of rabbinic literature, especially the responsa literature, serve as important sources for understanding the internal life of the Jewish community. We have in our possession a considerable body of printed rabbinic literature written by scholars in Palestine from the sixteenth century on, as well as a great deal of historical information in the rabbinic literature written by scholars in the Jewish communities in the Diaspora. In addition, respectable collections of responsa literature exist in manuscript. Here, too, one finds methodological problems in using this type of literature for historical research. There is the quantitative problem: to what extent the examples found in the rabbinic literature reflect the general situation. Moreover, identifying details, such as the name of the city, the names of the interested parties, and even the dates, generally were omitted from the responsa.[17] These are some of the problems that face investigators who attempt to use the rabbinic literature as historical source material.

The following summary of archival collections gives examples of additional collections and individual documents that exist in various archives, some of which have been published and studied in part.

The most important collection concerning the Jews of Palestine in the Middle Ages is the Cairo *geniza*.[18] This important collection of documents was discovered at the end of the nineteenth century in the attic of the ancient "Ezra" synagogue in Cairo, and it contains thousands of documents from the ninth to the nineteenth centuries. At present these documents are dispersed among various libraries and archives throughout the world, although the most important documents are at Cambridge University in England. These documents give us a picture of the spiritual, social, and economic life of the Jews in the Mediterranean countries. There is no doubt that the discovery of the Cairo *geniza* has completely changed our knowledge and understanding of the history of the Jewish settlement in Palestine during the Middle Ages.

The main sources I used for this investigation were the letters and manuscripts of the Jerusalem Officials in Istanbul, especially the *Pinkas* (Book of Letters). On this source is based the central thesis of this book, which claims that the Istanbul Officials for Palestine filled a central role in the history of the Yishuv (Jewish settlement in Palestine) at that time. The *Pinkas* is preserved at the Jewish Theological Seminary in New

York,[19] and it contains more than five hundred letters from the years 1741–71 (plus one letter from 1729) that the Jerusalem Officials in Istanbul sent to the Jerusalem community and other Jewish communities. Of the various numbering systems in the *Pinkas*, I have used the numbers at the top in the center of the left-hand side of each folio page.

Much material is preserved in the archives of the Jewish Theological Seminary of New York, the Ben-Zvi Institute in Jerusalem, and the Institute of Microfilmed Hebrew Manuscripts of the Jewish National and University Library, Jerusalem. We have abundant source material concerning the middle of the eighteenth century, whereas there is much less historical material on the beginning and end of the century. These periods therefore require additional investigation.

In recent generations many studies have been published about the Yishuv in the eighteenth century, in journals and in other publications, most of them in Hebrew and a few in European languages. I have made much use of these as well as of the dozens of Ottoman documents that have been published in various places.

A much larger collection houses the books of letters of the Amsterdam Officials and Administrators from the nineteenth century. Presently found in the archives of the Ben-Zvi Institute in Jerusalem,[20] this collection serves as one of the important sources for the history of the Jewish settlement in Palestine during the nineteenth century. The main disadvantage of these books of letters is that they present an image only of the side that wrote them, that is, the officials in Istanbul and in Amsterdam. We do not have the complete answers to these letters, nor do we have similar books of letters written by officials in Palestine.

An additional type of source is the nineteenth-century Montefiore censuses and the Montefiore collection, the major portion of which is found in the Montefiore archives in Ramsgate, England. This collection is a result of Sir Moses Montefiore's seven visits to Palestine and his extensive activities on behalf of its Jewish inhabitants. The collection also includes the diaries of Montefiore and his wife and many other writings connected with him.[21]

To these must be added the *Igronim*, that is, collections of authentic documents that served as models for scribes and communities, and which we can use in our research only after careful study,[22] inasmuch as identifying details such as names, dates, and place names have often been omitted.

Other types of archival materials are family collections that have survived, especially in some families from the ancient Sephardi Yishuv and in Ashkenazi families from the "old Yishuv." One example of such a collection is the "Elyashar collection," a catalog of which has been printed.[23]

As mentioned, much information about the Jewish settlement in Palestine and on the relationship of Diaspora Jewry to the Promised Land has survived in literary and community material, in print and in manuscript, which originated in the communities of the Diaspora. To these must be added the Jewish periodicals of the nineteenth century both in Palestine and in the Diaspora.

MATERIAL SOURCES

Palestine is noted for its many important archaeological sites. The many changes that took place in the country, the wars that occurred, and the powers that ruled over it left a variety of archaeological remains. Christian and Jewish archaeologists were especially interested from the beginning, each group for its own reasons, in the ancient periods of the land. Only more recently have remains from later periods—Byzantine, Crusade, and even later—begun to be uncovered. Because the Jewish settlement in Palestine during these periods was very small, very few Jewish sites remained from the early Middle Ages.

On the other hand, many more Jewish finds remained on the surface, especially from the Ottoman period. Among these are public and private buildings, synagogues, and cemeteries. Most of the monuments in the cemeteries were inscribed in the nineteenth century, but many of the inscriptions have been erased or blurred.

CONCLUSION

Among the important studies examined, several are especially noteworthy: Azriel Shohet's paper, "The Jews in Jerusalem in the eighteenth century," which was published more than fifty years ago and broke new ground in this area (*Zion* 1 [1936]; for an expanded and amended version see *Cathedra* 13 [1980]: 3–46); two important studies by Meir Benayahu, "The Holy Brotherhood of R. Judah Hasid and their settlement in Jerusalem" (*Sefunoth* 3–4 [1960]) and "The Ashkenazi community of

Jerusalem 1647–1747" (*Sefunoth 2* [1958]), which made a decisive contribution to our understanding of the history of the Yishuv at the beginning of the eighteenth century; and Amnon Cohen's important book, *Palestine in the Eighteenth Century* (1973), which is fundamental for the history of Palestine in that century. The present work constitutes a complement to it from the Jewish perspective.

This book deals not only with the history of the small, poor Jewish settlement in Palestine, but also with the immigrations to Palestine, the connections between the Yishuv and the Jewish communities of the Diaspora, and the economic support it received from them. This broad perspective is not accidental, but derives from the view that the Jewish settlement in Palestine, in the period under discussion just as at other times, was nourished by the communities of the Diaspora and nourished them in turn, so that it is impossible to see its history as a separate one.

In a book that summarizes such a long period and is based on sources and studies containing thousands of details, there are probably topics that have not received sufficiently detailed description. Many of the personalities are described very briefly, and it is hoped that they will eventually be given separate attention.

PART I

The Ruling Authority in Palestine in the Eighteenth Century and Its Relationship to the Jewish Population

1

HISTORICAL BACKGROUND

WHEN THE OTTOMANS conquered the Balkans and Anatolia from the Byzantines (in the fourteenth and fifteenth centuries) and Syria and Palestine from the Mamelukes (1516–17), they found ancient Jewish communities in these countries. In the previously Byzantine areas there were communities of Jews called Romaniotes, while in the previously Mameluke areas there were Jews called Musta'riba. These ancient Jewish communities were joined by Sephardi (Spanish) Jews during the fifteenth century and especially after the expulsion of the Jews from Spain in 1492. The Sephardim were welcomed with open arms by the Ottoman authorities, and during the sixteenth century they became the dominant force in the majority of the Jewish communities in the Ottoman Empire.[1]

The legal status of the Jews in the Moslem Ottoman Empire was determined from the beginning on the basis of the legal status of the *dhimmis* (non-Moslems) in Islam.[2] Within this legal framework Christians and Jews enjoyed a rather extensive autonomy[3] as well as the protection of the government. Nevertheless, they were subject according to Moslem law to a series of regulations that were limiting, discriminatory, and sometimes even degrading.

Non-Moslem religious groups in the Ottoman Empire—Greeks, Armenians, and Jews—were officially recognized by the central and local Ottoman authorities, although scholars disagree about the development of the frameworks of the various groups, which are known as *millet*.[4]

The Ottoman Jews were quickly integrated into the Ottoman Empire, which was growing and flourishing in the sixteenth century. Many Jews acquired key economic positions and were active in different areas of industry, trade, and finance. These were mainly the Spanish Jews, who had brought with them from the Iberian Peninsula their long tradition of a high cultural level and progressive technology in the areas of medicine, printing, arms manufacture, textiles, and other industries.

Within the flourishing economic and cultural milieu of the Jews in the Ottoman Empire in the sixteenth century, the religious creativity reached a peak in the centers of Torah study that were established by the Sephardim in Safed, Istanbul, and Salonika. In the Safed center two important areas of Jewish religious creativity, which greatly influenced Jewish communities throughout the world, were developed: Kabbala (mainly the teachings of R. [Rabbi] Isaac Luria) and Halakha (mainly R. Joseph Karo's work, the *Shulhan Arukh*). In the middle of the seventeenth century the entire Jewish world was agitated by the appearance of Sabbetai Zevi and his announcement in Palestine in 1665 that he was the Messiah. He drew crowds of people who accepted his announcement, and in spite of his immediate conversion to Islam after he was arrested by the Ottomans in 1666, the Sabbatean movement continued to influence various streams and groups in the Jewish world. The present work will discuss several aspects of this influence in the eighteenth century. The gradual political and economic decline of the Ottoman Empire in the seventeenth and eighteenth centuries also influenced most of the Jewish communities in the empire.

Palestine was conquered by the Ottomans in 1516. From an administrative and political standpoint the regime in Palestine was similar to that in other countries of the Ottoman Empire. During most of their rule Palestine was not particularly important to the Ottomans, for they received a very small income from it. The area known as Palestine was not a separate unit, but was divided into two subunits of the Syrian province. The northern part of the country was subject to the *eyalet* (*vilayet*) of Sidon, which included Safed and Tiberias, whereas the central and southern parts were subject to the *eyalet* of Damascus, which included Jerusalem and Hebron. In each *eyalet* there were several *sancak* in which certain changes occurred during different periods: during the seventeenth century the Ottomans separated Mount Lebanon and the Galilee from the Damascene sector and included them in the Sidonian sector; and in the middle of the eighteenth century Jerusalem was apparently an independent region for some time, directly subject to the central authority in Istanbul.[5]

In the Ottoman Empire in general there was an accepted attitude toward non-Moslems, who were called "Ahl al-Dhimma," that is, the protected ones. Each non-Moslem community was organized separately and enjoyed a certain amount of autonomy. Following the weakening of the central authority in Istanbul the power of the local rulers in the provinces grew, and the corruption of the appointed officials spread. This also influenced their relationship with the Jews of Palestine.[6]

Contacts between the local authorities and the Jewish community were conducted through the chief rabbi, whom the authorities saw as the formal leader of the Jews, and also through the officials of the community, the *pekidim*, mainly well-to-do Jews who had entry to the courts of the rulers. What was special about the Jewish communities in the cities of Palestine was that the central authorities in Istanbul often intervened in what took place between the local authorities and the Jewish communities.[7] This phenomenon, which was caused by the dependence of the communities of Palestine on the Jews of the Diaspora and the large sums of money which the latter sent to the former, reached its peak in the eighteenth century as a result of the activities of the Palestine Officials in Istanbul. One may say that the relations between the communities of Palestine and the local authorities were conducted, in practice, in two directions: heavy pressure from the side of the authorities, and counter-pressure from Jewish factors in the Diaspora in an attempt to moderate their attitude.

Arab and Turkish documents support what is written in Jewish sources about the plight of the Jews. It seems likely that the central authority in Istanbul was aware of the difficult situation of the Jews of Palestine, and in spite of laws discriminating against the Jews—such as prohibitions on buying land, on building houses and synagogues, and on riding horses, and restrictions in matters of dress and inheritance—the Istanbul authorities tried to act fairly toward the Jews. Indeed, ever so often the authority sent *firmans* (imperial orders) to settle the debts of the Jews. In these *firmans* the accumulated interest was cancelled and it was established that the principal should be returned in installments.[8] The Turkish documents also attest that in quarrels between the local rulers and the Jewish communities concerning exorbitant sums demanded by the rulers—for example, for the right to bury the dead on the Mount of Olives—the central authorities generally intervened on the side of the Jews.

From court judgments that have survived it is apparent that justice was done fairly, and the Jews were not taken advantage of in the courts. In several important court judgments in the Shar'i courts the Jews won, and their evidence was accepted against the evidence of the Moslems; this fact contradicts the accepted assumption about Ottoman court procedures.

The Jews of Palestine were included in the economic flourishing of the Ottoman Empire and of Palestine itself during the sixteenth century. In Safed a large Jewish community with thousands of members grew up, and there was a well-developed textile industry there, similar to the one in Salonika. In Jerusalem as well the Jews were included in the development of the city and in its economic life during the sixteenth century.[9]

In the seventeenth century the gradual decline of the Ottoman Empire continued, a process that had already begun during the second half of the sixteenth century. During the first stage it was most evident in the remote provinces and in the economy. The provincial rulers, who were replaced frequently, showed little interest in the development of the region, and all their efforts went into making profits and amassing power. It is no wonder, therefore, that they oppressed the local population, especially the Jews. Consequently, the economic situation in the provinces deteriorated, and road security was endangered. In Syria and Palestine local factions—such as the Bedouins, the Druzes, the Maronites, and the Metoualis—rose up and rebelled against the central authority, and occasionally even fought one another. In general the Jews were caught in the middle and suffered severely. The Ottoman authorities tried to fight the disorder and the rebellions with a show of power, on the one hand, and by appointing administrative rulers loyal to them, on the other. In the end the Ottomans were forced to make peace with the situation, and as the seventeenth century wore on they gave the local rulers considerable autonomy in return for the systematic collection of taxes in the region.

In the middle of the seventeenth century Tiberias was destroyed as a result of the incessant wars, and its Jewish community was dispersed. In the second half of the seventeenth century the Jewish presence in Palestine dwindled, and the Jewish presence in the Galilee also shrank. Only in Safed was there a small community. The main community was that of Jerusalem, and even in this city there were no more than a thousand people (about ten percent of the population).

In 1658 the English Christian minister Henry Jessie described the situation of the Jerusalem Jews in these words:

> The state of the Jews at Jerusalem of late was such, that they could not live and subsist there, without some yearly supply and contribution from their Brethren abroad, because the place doth yield them little or no trading, whereby to maintain themselves; but their love to the place doth oblige them to remain there, although with great poverty and want; And their Brethren abroad among the Nations, have been willing to uphold them there at Jerusalem, that the place should not be left destitute of some considerable number of their Nation, to keep as it were possession, or at least some footing in it, and to show their hopes, till a full restitution come.[10]

The situation of the Jews of Palestine in the eighteenth century was dependent on the province to which they belonged. In the Sidonian *Eyalet*, which was the more developed and important, their situation was a little better.

The Galilean Rulers and Their Attitude
toward the Jews

In the 1720s the Zaydan family, from a Bedouin tribe that came from the Arabian peninsula,[11] established rule over the Galilee, and from the thirties to the seventies the head of this family, Dahir al-ʿUmar, was the most important figure in Palestine. He established his rule over the Galilee in the accepted fashion by leasing the right to collect the taxes in the region, and he gradually became an almost autonomous ruler. It is true that he continued to send taxes to the Sublime Porte and to the *Vali* of Damascus, but in his own territory he was master. At first he settled in Tiberias, after rebuilding and fortifying it. In the forties and fifties he moved to Acre, which was beginning to develop at this time owing to the export of Galilean cotton to France.

Dahir al-ʿUmar appointed his sons to be the rulers of the subprovinces in the Galilee. In his efforts to develop the Galilee economically he took care of the security of the region and strove to increase its population. To this end he also turned to the Jews and asked them to take part in the resettling of Tiberias. As a result of his positive attitude toward the Jews, which was expressed in lowering taxes and helping to build the community in Tiberias, some growth began to take place in the Jewish population of the region.[12]

Dahir al-ʿUmar's firmly established rule over the Galilee and the center of the country was a thorn in the side of the central authorities in Istanbul, but it especially provoked the displeasure of the ruler of Damascus, Süleyman al-ʿAzm, who had control over most of the country. The ruler of Sidon, whose position was not very strong, did not interfere with Dahir al-ʿUmar's interests.

Süleyman went to war three times against Dahir al-ʿUmar. In 1737 he attempted to capture Tiberias for the first time and failed.[13] After this attempt he was deposed, but in 1741 he was reappointed ruler of Damascus and tried to renew the war with Dahir al-ʿUmar. In 1742 Haim Farhi and Joseph Lutzati, Süleyman's two Jewish bankers, wrote to

R. Haim Abulafia and informed him that Süleyman intended to besiege Tiberias again and that it would be advisable for all the Jews to move immediately to Safed and send their property to Acre.[14] Rabbi Abulafia informed Dahir al-ʿUmar about this, but the latter thought that it was only a trick by Süleyman to get the residents of the city to flee. After some time R. Abulafia received another letter from Farhi and Lutzati,[15] and it became clear that Süleyman was really about to appear at the gates of the city. The Jews of Tiberias wanted to leave the city, but R. Abulafia prevented them. His reasons were that he did not want to leave the synagogue and the houses that he had built; the other residents of the city were likely to destroy them with the complaint that the Jews had brought about a demoralization "since when they fled the city the hearts of the residents would melt like their hearts."[16] It would also not be possible for the Jews to take their possessions out of the city, because the roads were dangerous. Another reason was that he was already eighty-two years old and did not have the strength to travel.

Thus R. Abulafia was in Tiberias when the second siege began. In the middle of the campaign Farhi and Lutzati tried to influence him to save his two sons at least by sending the sons to them. R. Abulafia refused this offer as well and influenced the Jews to remain in the city in spite of the attacks.[17] This second siege was suddenly ended when Süleyman received an order from Istanbul to take care of the caravans of pilgrims to Mecca that were about to pass through the area of his rule.[18]

In 1743 Süleyman besieged Tiberias for a third time. This time R. Abulafia intervened on Dahir al-ʿUmar's behalf and wrote a letter to the officials in Istanbul in which he praised the man, and he tried to send this letter to the central authorities and to the ambassador of France in Istanbul. The Istanbul officials answered him through the rich men of Damascus, who wanted to leave the city.[19] It seems that the Istanbul authorities were cooperating with Süleyman against Dahir al-ʿUmar. Because of this letter many of the Jews of Tiberias fled, but R. Abulafia and some of his men remained in Tiberias in spite of the danger.[20] This episode also ended uneventfully because of the death of Süleyman.

From these events it appears that the Jews were instruments in the hands of the local rulers, who exploited the Jews everywhere in order to advance their own interests in their battles with their rivals. R. Abulafia was faced with a difficult decision, and fortunately his decision to remain in Tiberias did not harm him.

In other parts of the Galilee as well the Jews were dependent on the mercy of the local rulers, and more than once they became a target for extortion. In Safed, where Dahir al-ʿUmar's son was the ruler, the situation of the Jews was particularly bad. There are many attestations to extortions and expulsions. Documents describing the mission of the emissary R. Raphael Israel Kimhi in the years 1728–30 mentioned a prohibition on the burial of the dead in Safed and attempts to extort money.[21] Safed was less safe than the other holy cities. Jerusalem and Tiberias were surrounded by walls, and in Hebron the Jews lived in an inner court. But Safed was an open city, and the peasants in the area could easily enter the city to rob and persecute the Jews.[22] During the 1740s the situation of the Safed Jews became even worse, as is attested by the words of R. Haim ben Attar: "There are many fears and many troubles in the city."[23] His student, R. Abraham Ishmael Hay Singuineti, described the assessment of high taxes for the army of Dahir al-ʿUmar.[24] During these years some of the Jews in Safed had to flee to the surrounding hills because of the pressure of the authorities. And R. Ezra Malkhi wrote: "Because of the rage of the tormenter . . . the siege of the holy city of Safed . . . terrors have overwhelmed us . . . we had to climb high mountains and hills to flee the wickedness of the Gentiles."[25]

The most difficult period was the time of the great earthquake of 1759, in which many Jews were killed.[26] In the wake of the earthquake there were plagues, and the debts of the Jews increased. But even at this time the rulers insisted on the taxes being paid and extorted more money.[27] The relatively better situation of the Jews in Tiberias, and their closeness to Dahir al-ʿUmar, induced many of the Jews of Safed to move to that city.[28] In 1763 there were battles between Dahir al-ʿUmar and his son, the ruler of Safed, and the Jews of that city were required to pay large sums to cover the battle expenses.[29] In 1767 the sages of Safed wrote to Pisa in Italy about "the rage of the tormenter . . . because the enemy has the upper hand and is causing Israel many troubles."[30]

In the 1770s Dahir al-ʿUmar's position was weakened, and various rivals appeared. During this time the ruler of Egypt, Ali Bey, rebelled against Turkish rule, and his armies reached Damascus. These were years of war between Russia and Turkey, and the rebels were helped by the Russians, who were attacking the government powers from the shore. This war, in which Ali Bey made a treaty with Dahir al-ʿUmar, brought great troubles upon the Jews of Safed.[31] In 1775, after many turns of battle, the Turks succeeded in putting down the rebellion of Ali Bey and killing Dahir al-ʿUmar in a battle near Acre.

17

After the death of Dahir al-ʿUmar the Sublime Porte in Istanbul decided to take advantage of the opportunity and bring order to the *Eyalet* of Sidon. To this end the Bosnian officer Jezzār Aḥmed Paşa, who was known for his cruelty, was appointed *Vali* of Sidon. At the end of the century, when he had amassed a great deal of power in Palestine and Syria, Jezzār was also appointed *Vali* of Damascus.[32]

Jezzār—in contrast to Dahir al-ʿUmar—was not a local sheik who had risen to power and become an autonomous ruler, but a governor who was appointed by the central administration for the purpose of increasing its involvement in Palestine. The reason for this appointment was that at this time the economic importance of the country, and especially of the Galilee, was growing. The cotton trade was very intensive and increased the incomes of the rulers. There was also the problem of the lack of security at the end of Dahir al-ʿUmar's reign, which disturbed the caravans of the hajj to Mecca.

The period of Jezzār Aḥmed Paşa's rule in Palestine, which lasted until 1804, was not essentially different from the period of Dahir al-ʿUmar. He too was not replaced for an entire generation, which was unusual, and in practice was an almost entirely autonomous ruler. He continued the economic development of the Galilee and took advantage of his income, and he acted in Palestine as master.

His attitude to the Jews as well was similar to that of Dahir al-ʿUmar. It is true that he displayed a hostile attitude toward non-Moslems,[33] but his desire to develop the region caused him to act fairly to them as long as he gained some advantage from them.

At the time of his appointment he moved the capital from Sidon to Acre. As his economic adviser he appointed Haim Farhi,[34] who helped the Galilean Jews as much as possible. After the great immigration of Hasidim in 1777 Farhi acted as agent between the Jews and the authorities in various financial matters.[35] However, in Farhi's relations with Jezzār and his heirs there were ups and downs, and in 1820 he was executed by Abdullah, the servant of Jezzār's son Süleyman.

When he became ruler Jezzār took a step similar to that of Dahir al-ʿUmar in Tiberias and called on the Jews to settle in Safed, which had been almost completely destroyed in the earthquake of 1759.[36] Some residents, among them Jews, had indeed returned to the city in the sixties, but the city was still in ruins. The heads of the Jewish community described the ruined state of the city in a letter of 1783: "Some terrible tales about . . . upper Galilee . . . that the mouth cannot speak [!] or the copyist with his pen. A fire was sent by God and it destroyed the land, it fell apart, it broke into pieces, until the land was laid waste, wrenched away from the Jews, and their homes were destroyed . . . also the synagogues and houses of study . . . became ruins."[37]

Jezzār decided to rehabilitate the city, and to this end he turned to the Jews and offered them reductions in taxes and customs duties. In a letter of 1778 the leaders of the Hasidim wrote:

> In the great mercies of God, who influenced the heart of the king and his officers to make things easier and to increase their mercy . . . and to rebuild the ruins of Safed . . . and great freedom for the Jews . . . it is impossible to speak of the great welfare of Safed. The place is now broad and it is possible to support oneself [there] when [the place] will be settled, but we do not know the language and the customs of the state. . . . Only wheat is expensive because of the many wars that there were, and the locusts that were here until now.[38]

In a letter from the beginning of the 1780s R. Jacob Elyashar wrote to the HiDA (R. Haim Yosef David Azulay) "that all that evil family of Dahir al-ʿUmar and his sons are ended and finished . . . and the above-mentioned Paşa has been good to [the Jews] and has issued *firmans* on all the taxes and the *cizye* (poll tax) . . . so that they have to pay only two thousand *kurus* (Turkish piasters) per year."[39]

Additional evidence is included in the above-mentioned letter of the community leaders in Safed from 1783: "The new ruler . . . has said who is among you from all his nation . . . he should go up to the good land . . . the ruins have been rebuilt and each day another family comes and is added."[40]

Jezzār actually did grant the Jews many reductions in taxes and customs duties, but the war with Napoleon at the end of the century brought about a severe crisis in his relations with the Jews; in this period he needed a great deal of money and he consequently extorted large sums from the Jews.[41] In the end he was able to expel Napoleon from Palestine with the help of the British.

The Ruling Authorities of Jerusalem and Hebron and Their Attitude toward the Jews

The position of the Jews in Jerusalem and Hebron was somewhat different from that of the Galilean Jews. The Jewish community of Jerusalem, the largest community in the country, was subject to the *Sancak* of Jerusalem, which was included, as mentioned above, in the *Eyalet* of Damascus.

The position of the Jewish communities of Jerusalem and Hebron did not improve during the entire eighteenth century, and they suffered from expulsions and hostilities during the whole period. Because of the weakened state of the empire each local ruler tried to get as rich as possible during his short period of rule, which generally lasted a little longer than a year. The Jewish residents of Jerusalem bore the heavy burden of the taxes and the huge debts from the days of the crisis in the Ashkenazi community at the beginning of the century.

Nevertheless, it would be a mistake to say that the problems of the Jews in Jerusalem and its surrounding area during the eighteenth century reflect the central core of their lives; despite the problems the community developed and remained secure after the crisis at the beginning of the century, and was under the protection of the Istanbul Officials. It seems that the life of the community was conducted with some uncertainty. The Jewish, Arab, and Turkish documents in our possession generally reflect not the routine life of the community but rather the problems that arose from time to time and required the intervention of the authorities.

The beginning of the century was a difficult period for the Jewish community of Jerusalem from the viewpoint of its relations with the local rulers. The growth of the community and its involvement in debt brought about confrontations with the local rulers. Many of the community leaders were arrested, and many fled the city. Therefore, there was added disquiet in the city, which was expressed in rebellions of the local residents against the Paşa and in the rebellion of the Paşa of Jerusalem against the Paşa of Damascus.[42] The problems that arose at this time led to the intervention of the Kadi of Jerusalem in the affairs of the Jerusalem community. From a judicial deliberation that took place in the Shariʿ court of Jerusalem in 1719[43] it appears that the leaders of the community asked the Kadi to help them depose the community leader and appoint another in his stead. This points up the weakening of the conduct of the community affairs that led to the intervention of the authorities in the appointments of the community.

The problem of the debts that the Jews owed the Moslems required judicial and political intervention during the entire eighteenth century. It appears that the authorities tended to help the Moslem creditors obtain payment of the debts by occasionally waiving the interest and allowing the repayment of the principal in installments. In the thirties, when the community was rehabilitated by the Istanbul Officials, extensive growth occurred in the Jerusalem community, and yeshivas and synagogues were built. This growth was appreciated neither by the local rulers nor by the Moslem residents.

The early forties were critical for the community, and it was feared that the tragedy of 1720 (burning the synagogue) would be repeated. In 1741 the emissaries R. Abraham ben Asher and R. Isaac Zerahia Azulai were sent with a letter saying that there had been attempts to expel the Jews from Jerusalem because of the growth of the city's Jewish population. The Jews were also prohibited from buying food with the excuse that because of the increase in the number of Jews, "the Arabs had nothing to eat." To avoid expulsion the Jews had to pay a large bribe.[44] In 1744 the Istanbul Officials wrote that the increased number of Jews in Jerusalem was the cause of the libels and the heavy taxes that the authorities were assessing.[45] And indeed, in 1752 R. Moses Bula, one of the sages of Jerusalem, wrote that the increase in the number of immigrants had led to the greed of the local residents: "Because the cries of the poor people who sigh and suffer from the gentiles, from the robbers, the bold nations have increased . . . due to [the gentiles'] accusations . . . because they say that too many [Jews] are coming."[46]

The local rulers extorted money with many excuses (for example, giving a *firman* for the construction of a cemetery).[47] One of the problems that disturbed the Jews most during the Ottoman period was the prevention of Jewish burials, in order to extort money from them. The residents and the local authorities acted in an especially hostile manner when they attempted to expropriate Jewish burial plots on the Mount of Olives and disturbed the transfer of Jews to the cemetery. Every few years it was necessary for the central authority in Istanbul to intervene in order to settle the matter.

In the sixties, when the controversy among the leadership of the Jerusalem community reached its peak, the authorities took advantage of the situation to extort money. These were crisis years for the community, and many Jews fled the city, at their head some of the important sages. The German Jew Simon de-Gilderin, who was living in Jerusalem at the time, described the situation: "More than two hundred . . . left the city . . . to flee in the night because it is difficult to live in the city . . . every moment there are libels and harmful decrees . . . every day they take a person or a sage or a rich man and beat him until he gives them what they want."[48]

Various problems plagued the Jewish settlement in the latter part of the century. In the seventies, at the time of the rebellion of Ali Bey, it is true that Jerusalem was not directly harmed, but it was besieged and the authorities exploited the Jews of the city. In 1781 a Jerusalem synagogue collapsed because of heavy snows, and in order to rebuild it was necessary to pay large sums to the Paşa of Damascus.[49] During the Napoleonic invasion the Jews were accused of collaborating with the enemy, and the Jerusalem community was forced to pay huge bribes to the local authorities.[50] Other problems that arose from time to time, which may be seen in Turkish and Arab documents, were illegal taxes that were assessed by the local authorities from Jewish and Christian immigrants and from pilgrims who came to Jerusalem.[51] Thus we see that throughout the eighteenth century the Jews of Jerusalem were forced to pay taxes and various other payments to the local authorities.

Besides the strong day-to-day contact between the leadership of the Jerusalem community and the rulers of the city, there was at the same time contact with the central authorities in Istanbul. These latter contacts frequently served as an alternative when relations in Jerusalem were strained. This situation, caused by the great dependence of the Jerusalem community on the Istanbul Officials, was taken into consideration by the authorities. They knew that if they wanted to collect taxes from the Jews of Palestine in an orderly way, they had to compromise not only with the Jewish communities there, but also with the Istanbul Officials. Two factors were added to these: First, during part of the century Jerusalem was subject directly to the Ottoman regime in Istanbul, which strengthened the connection with the Istanbul Officials. Second, there was frequent turnover among the officeholders and their staffs in Jerusalem, among them many who came from Istanbul, and before they set out for Jerusalem contacts were established between them and the Istanbul Officials, which included bribes and gifts.

Business between the Jews and the authorities was thus conducted on several dimensions, involving (1) the leadership of the Jerusalem community and the local authorities in the city; (2) the Istanbul Officials and the Sublime Porte; (3) the Istanbul Officials and administrators who went to Jerusalem; and (4) the Jews who were close to the courts of the Pashas of Damascus and Sidon, also under the influence of the Istanbul Officials.

An important area in which there was cooperation between the Jewish community and the authorities was in the assessment of estates without heirs.[52]

In Hebron the position of the Jews did not differ from that of the Jerusalem Jews. We have evidence in our possession concerning the extortion of money by the rulers and repeated attempts to expel the Jews.[53] The situation is described in a question sent to one of the sages of Jerusalem: "And troubles are multiplied by the wars that have been renewed between many nations that are fighting one another within the city."[54]

In a letter sent by the Hebron Jews to the Diaspora in 1744, they wrote: "We were delivered to cruel gentiles . . . and the creditor comes to collect his debt . . . and we do not have [the money to pay] . . . and he raises his hand against [the Jews] with whips, and beats and wounds, and called together a meeting to arrest all of the community . . . because all the Christian gentiles have taken counsel together and our enemies have said, 'Let us destroy that people' . . . and they plotted against us with religious plots."[55]

Thus the Hebron Jews were persecuted by the local rulers as well as by the Christian population of the city. This complex system of relationships, in which the Hebron Jews were caught between the Moslems and the Christians, also appears in a letter sent by the officials of Hebron in Istanbul in 1765: "Let us replace the Jews by another nation so that the name of Israel will no longer be remembered in the hills of Hebron, let us expel them and bring in idol-worshippers [i.e., Christians] in their place."[56]

The difficult situation in Hebron also is described in documents from the end of the century, although it is clear that the exaggerations in documents of this type must be moderated. Nevertheless one should not take lightly what is said in these letters, because they undoubtedly reflect a harsh reality. To give an example of the difficulties that confront us in ascertaining the situation of the Hebron Jews in this period, compare the sources above with a letter written in 1748 from R. Abraham Gerson of Kuty to his brother-in-law, the Baal Shem Tov:

In this holy city in which there is one Jewish courtyard it is closed on the Sabbath and on holidays and no one comes in or out and at night there is almost no fear of the gentiles, the doors are left open . . . and when there is a feast of circumcision or other festivity all the important people come and everyone is happy and moreover the important people among the gentiles like the Jews very much. . . . When I came here the most important official of the city came to greet me . . . and other officials came and they were clapping and dancing just like the Jews and singing praises in their language, the Arabic language, and they go around here in green and other colors and no one says anything.[57]

Should one perhaps distinguish between the attitude of the Ottoman rulers to the Jews and the attitude of the local population? At any rate, when the son of the sheik of Hebron disappeared in the seventies the Jews were accused of murdering him.[58]

Part II

Immigrations to Palestine in the Eighteenth Century

2

THE INFLUENCES OF PILGRIMAGES AND IMMIGRATIONS ON THE JEWISH SETTLEMENT

THE PILGRIMAGES AND THE IMMIGRATIONS in the eighteenth century preserved the existence of the Jewish settlement. If not for the never-ending stream of Jews to the country, the settlement would have been almost completely wiped out because of the high mortality rate, the large number of emigrants, and the low birth rate due to the high average age of the Jewish population.

THE PILGRIMAGES

In the eighteenth century, which is known in the general history of Europe as a century of traveling and tourism,[1] pilgrimages became more widespread in the Christian world, and the Jews were certainly influenced by the surrounding society. Jewish pilgrims arrived in Palestine either independently or in ships that were chartered by various communities during the summer months. Evidence that such ships arrived in Palestine as early as the 1730s[2] suggests the renewal of the settlement at that time.

The pilgrims—mostly from Turkey, the Balkans, and Italy, with a few from North Africa and eastern Europe—tended to visit the holy cities and to travel to the graves of holy men in all parts of the country. In general they remained in the country until after the early fall holidays and then returned to their own countries, but some settled in Palestine. Every year many hundreds of pilgrims arrived, and sometimes there was no room in the synagogues during the holidays.[3]

In 1726, at the beginning of the activities of the Istanbul Officials, the pilgrimages increased and they also became more organized. The book *Tzach Ve-Adom* (Clear and Ruddy) by R. Raphael Treves provides evidence for the increase in the pilgrimages. In this book, which includes prayers for immigrants and pilgrims, there is a clear distinction between the prayers for "immigrants to Eretz Israel" (this is the Hebrew name for Palestine used in all the traditional sources) and the prayers for "pilgrims." In one of the prayers the pilgrims apologize because they are forced to leave the country and return to the Diaspora: "It is clear and known to You how my heart is poured out and my spirit is in dread, my hands are weak and my knees fail because I have to leave the place of the inheritance of my forefathers, holiest of all lands. . . . Please, our God, hear our prayer, listen to our entreaty in Your faith, answer us in Your charity for our welfare, so that we may return at the time of the ingathering of Your sons with joy in the land."[4]

The book *Zichron Yerushalayim* (Memorial of Jerusalem) by R. Judah Poliastro, which was printed three years after the book *Tzach Ve-Adom*,[5] also attests to the large number of pilgrims in the 1740s. It too contains instructions for pilgrims to Palestine, sections of the book *Tzach Ve-Adom*, and touring routes for pilgrims. The booklet was reprinted many times in the Jewish communities of the world.[6]

R. Simha of Zalozce, who immigrated to Palestine from eastern Europe in 1764, together with some friends of the Baal Shem Tov, gave this nice description:

> [W]e had to wait for the ship which the community of Istanbul hires every year . . . since every Sephardi Jew who fears God and has the means goes to Eretz Israel once in his lifetime, and goes around to the graves of our forefathers, to the righteous and the pious men, and also the women go around, and devote themselves with all their heart and soul. And it should be counted for them as an atonement of sins, as it is said, "And the land will atone for its people," and they return to their cities and their houses, and there are some who go to settle there until the day of their death. Therefore even though there are other ships to be found which go to Egypt and from there to Eretz Israel . . . we waited for them . . . and when they hire a ship, they announce it in all the synagogues.[7]

The Jewish communities of Palestine obtained a small income from the pilgrims, as the latter brought gifts, gave money when they were called up to make the blessing over the Torah in the synagogue, and paid various taxes. But first and foremost the local authorities profited from them, as they taxed the pilgrims, and certainly encouraged the pilgrimages of both Christians and Jews.

The cost of a pilgrimage was 200–400 *kurus*. Half of the sum served for the expenses of the journey; the other half went for board and taxes in

Palestine.[8] According to the instructions of the Istanbul Officials, important pilgrims were entitled to credit in the Jerusalem community if their money ran out.

IMMIGRATIONS AND THEIR EFFECT ON THE SETTLEMENT

The crisis in the Jerusalem community at the beginning of the eighteenth century led to a cessation of immigration to Palestine, but in the thirties, in the wake of the rehabilitation of the Palestine communities by the Istanbul Officials, the immigrations were renewed, and at the beginning of the forties there was already a large Jewish community in Jerusalem.

It is possible that many people were deterred from immigrating to Israel because of the difficulties of the journey, as the roads were quite dangerous at that time, pirates ambushed ships, and many ships sank. The political situation in the region was also a deterrent. The local wars between the sheiks in Palestine and in Syria and the wars between Russia and Turkey prevented passage on both sea and land routes. To these must be added the difficult economic situation in Palestine, which did not particularly encourage immigration, and in many cases actually caused Jews to leave the country.

Nevertheless there was a constant movement of immigrants from the 1730s until the end of the century.[9] There were three main reasons for this: anticipation of the arrival of the Messiah, traditional motives, and economic and personal problems. Immigration to Palestine in order to pray and be buried there took place throughout the generations, but in the eighteenth century it increased, because of the activities of the Istanbul Officials.

On many occasions Jews immigrated to Palestine when their economic situation in the Diaspora was difficult, and they hoped to benefit from the fixed yearly support given to Jews in Palestine. Personal problems also led occasionally to the immigration of individuals.

The Istanbul Officials not only enabled the immigration of thousands of Jews to Palestine, but also organized it. Every year they made an exact listing of the immigrants and the potential immigrants from other countries, and every summer they hired a ship, sometimes several ships, for the immigrants and the pilgrims.[10] From two contracts (in English) for the hiring of boats in 1775, which were signed by the Istanbul Officials and English ship captains and which were later published, we learn how the system worked. The Istanbul Officials would hire a ship from a captain and obligate themselves to pay a fixed sum for it even if it would not be filled. Afterwards they collected the money for the costs of the rental from the immigrants and the pilgrims.[11] In general the ship sailed close to the Jewish New Year—in September or toward the end of August—but occasionally additional ships were hired during the summer. Sometimes individual immigrants went with the regular ships that sailed to Palestine.

The boats that sailed from Istanbul generally contained about 100–200 people.[12] But boats did not sail only from Istanbul. We know that toward the end of the summer boats set out from Izmir,[13] Salonika,[14] Leghorn (Livorno),[15] and even Amsterdam.[16] It seems likely that hundreds of Jews went to Palestine every year, some of them in order to settle there and others for a pilgrimage:

> There has never been anything like this from the time we were exiled from our land; like birds that fly from the four corners of the world everyone is coming to Eretz Israel and the increase in the people has been a cause for the redoubled increase in expenses.[17]

> They are gathered from East and West, some by boat in the heart of the sea and some from the desert and the mountains in order to go up to [Jerusalem], which is surrounded by hills.[18]

This large number undoubtedly attests to a trend within certain groups, which were prepared to immigrate to Palestine in spite of the dangers on the roads and the difficult conditions prevalent on the boats and at their destination. The journey to Palestine from Turkey, the Balkans, and Italy took between ten and twenty days, whereas from eastern Europe it took many months.

The journey itself was very expensive. In the middle of the eighteenth century the voyage from Turkey or Italy cost about 100 *kurus*, at least, for each person.[19] To this it was necessary to add an immigration tax of 10–20 *kurus* and various expenses, such as equipment and food. R. Isaac Hacohen Rapoport, who returned to Palestine from Izmir in 1749, spent about 300 *kurus* for travel expenses,[20] that is, twice the yearly expenses of an individual in Palestine.

The rental of boats cost a great deal of money, as most of the immigrants were poor people: "Two boats have arrived in Eretz Israel from

Istanbul and one from Salonika, and they are mostly wretchedly poor people."[21] The immigrants were not always able to pay for the voyage, and the Istanbul Officials had to carry the burden of the expenses. Incidents are known of immigrants who were not able to pay, and out of great despair forced their way onto the boat.[22]

Sometimes the taxes due to the authorities in Palestine were not paid, especially during the 1740s, when the number of Jewish residents in Jerusalem increased. In these cases the Turkish authorities prevented the boatloads of immigrants from leaving, and only after great efforts and the payment of bribes were the Istanbul Officials able to arrange the sailing.[23] In 1750, when the number of immigrants to Jerusalem increased, the Istanbul Officials imposed a tax on each immigrant, and did not allow every poor person to immigrate.

There were many delays in the departure of the ships during the years of the wars between the Turks and the Russians. In 1767–68, only after wearying negotiations with the authorities did the Istanbul Officials succeed in obtaining a ship for the immigrants.[24] Indeed, a year later this war brought about the complete cessation of immigration for at least five years, and perhaps even for a longer period. In a letter sent from Jerusalem to Pisa, Italy, in 1774 we find:

> The height of the tribulation, the sadness and sorrow of heart, the city is desolate as it sees that the gates of Jerusalem are locked; the roads to Zion are mourning because there are no pilgrims for the holidays or immigrants for five years now; the taste of going to the land [Eretz Israel] has been taken away because of the rage of the oppressor; the kings [Turkey and Russia] are fighting with one another and all the gates are locked; no one leaves and no one enters; it is a very bitter trouble.[25]

In the wake of the war between Turkey and Russia the movement of immigrants and pilgrims to Palestine was completely stopped. It is possible that after the treaty of Küçük-Kaynarcı, which was signed by the two countries in the year the letter above was written, this movement was renewed; at any rate, in 1777 immigrations of Hasidim from eastern Europe began. The cessation of the immigration in those years made things difficult for the settlement, because the immigrants brought with them monetary support from the Diaspora. Explicit evidence on this point is found in the continuation of the letter quoted above: "Because all the people who live in Zion are waiting anxiously for the arrival of the ship

. . . who bring their sacrifice for the sake of the holy city Jerusalem . . .
the assistance for the expenses of our holy city, and the wells have dried
up . . . there is no money."[26]

Among the immigrants were well-known rabbis and rich Jews, who
donated much money to Palestine and entrusted considerable sums to the
Istanbul Fund.[27] These enjoyed the privilege of a special relationship,
and the Jerusalem officials were asked to take their standing into consideration and to give them special attention. Occasionally the Jerusalemites
were asked to appoint immigrants of good family as officials in the communities of Palestine or to allow them to join one of the yeshivas.

The increased immigration of Torah scholars led to the building of
yeshivas in various places, especially in Jerusalem, in which several hundred Torah scholars were concentrated. It is difficult to speak of a spiritual
blossoming in the country, but the yeshivas did have some influence both
in Palestine and in the Diaspora, as they drew attention to the settlement
and helped in the acquisition of donations.

The immigration of R. Haim Abulafia to Tiberias and the great immigration of Hasidim in 1777 had some effect on the development of the
settlement of the Galilean Jews. Other immigrations also contributed to
the establishment of the settlement and affected the relationship between
Palestine and the communities of the Diaspora to some degree.

In spite of the continual immigration in the eighteenth century the
number of Jews in Palestine did not increase. The poverty and the lack of
opportunities for earning a living not only dissuaded many people from
immigrating, but also caused many others to leave the country. The
earthquakes, droughts, and plagues also did their share and, aside from
heavy mortality, brought about emigration from the country. R. Haim
ben Attar did not settle immediately in Jerusalem because of the plague
that was raging there during the years 1741–42; R. Moses Haim Luzzatto
and his family died of the plague in Acre in 1744; and R. Abraham Gerson of Kuty describes a great plague in Jerusalem in 1747, in which many
people perished. In 1759–60 strong earthquakes occurred in Safed and
caused the dwindling of the Jewish community in the city. Various prohibitions, the ban on bachelors under sixty years of age from settling in
Jerusalem, the continual wars in the forties and in the seventies, and the
libel in Hebron in 1773 also caused many people to leave the country.
The continual friction between the Sephardim and the Ashkenazim in
the Jerusalem community and leadership also occasionally brought about
the emigration of Jewish residents from Eretz Israel.[28]

Influences on the Jewish Settlement

It is difficult to say that economic development resulted from the immigrations, as most of the immigrants lived on donated money. The Jews who went to live in the Galilee during the eighteenth century had no intention of creating an agricultural settlement. They generally settled in the villages only in the wake of transitory events, such as the wars in Tiberias in the forties, the earthquake in Safed in 1759, plagues, and the oppression of the rulers. Some of them did indeed engage in trade or act as agents, and occasionally they even grew some agricultural produce, but even these people lived on donations from the Diaspora.

Most areas of life in the settlement were completely static, and unlike the Jewish communities of Europe during the eighteenth century, there were no changes in its economic, social, or spiritual life. From an economic viewpoint the settlement in Palestine was different from most of the Jewish communities of the Ottoman Empire, where the Jews supported themselves by their own work. These communities also differed socially from the settlement in Palestine, although from the viewpoint of religious ideology there was not much difference.

3

IMMIGRATIONS AT THE BEGINNING OF THE EIGHTEENTH CENTURY

IN 1700 AN EVENT OCCURRED that led to widespread changes in the Jewish settlement in Palestine: the immigration of R. Judah Hasid and his followers from Eastern and Central Europe. Such immigrations at the first of the century had a considerable effect on the history of the Jewish people in general, and on the history of the Jewish settlement in Palestine in particular.[1] Not only did these immigrations, with their messianic fervor, capture the imagination of many Jewish communities in Europe, but they also led to a greater involvement of the communities in the Diaspora with the small settlement in Palestine and to the extension of the protection of the Istanbul Officials to the Yishuv.

The failure of Sabbateanism had led to a severe crisis in the Jewish communities in the form of the despair that overtook the communities, and had resulted in a search for ways to relieve the subsequent great tension. One of the ways was immigration to Palestine. Indeed, at the end of the seventeenth and the beginning of the eighteenth centuries several caravans of immigrants were organized, first and foremost that of the Sabbatean R. Judah Hasid and his followers in 1700.[2] In 1702 another group with a Sabbatean flavor, with the Kabbalist and Sabbatean R. Abraham Rovigo of Modena at its head, immigrated to Palestine from Italy.[3]

These were not the only groups that immigrated to Palestine during these years. For example, in 1703 a group of Ashkenazi immigrants passed through Plovdiv (in Bulgaria) on their way to Palestine.[4]

These immigrations failed because they were disorganized and underfunded; organization and financing were neglected in the desire to immigrate. In addition, internal wars between the local rulers in Jerusalem caused chaos in the city at the beginning of the eighteenth century[5] and contributed to the deterioration of the situation of the Jewish community in the city.

34

4

IMMIGRATIONS DURING THE MID-EIGHTEENTH CENTURY

IN THE WAKE of the disintegration of the Jewish community in Jerusalem at the beginning of the eighteenth century there was, as mentioned, an almost total cessation of immigration to Palestine,[1] and only during the thirties, after the rehabilitation of the Jewish settlement by the Istanbul Officials, was the immigration renewed. During these years several important persons immigrated, together with their followers.

The activities of the Istanbul Officials led to a great increase in the number of Jewish immigrants and pilgrims to Palestine, beginning at the end of the 1730s. As a result a permanent yearly event came into being, in which ships were leased, mainly during the summer months, in Istanbul, Izmir, and Salonika, to take the many Jewish immigrants and pilgrims to Palestine.[2] The immigrants in the mid-eighteenth century came from various ends of the Diaspora: from Yemen, Morocco, Turkey, Greece, Poland, Italy, and western Europe. These were generally immigrations of groups numbering several dozen people, headed by a rabbi-leader. What characterized these immigrant leaders was that most of them were Kabbalists and that one can find in their writings a clear messianic tension. Some of them even had connections with the groups of the last Sabbateans. It should be stressed that during the 1730s there were strong messianic expectations owing to the approach of the year 5500 of the creation of the world according to the Jewish calendar (1740 C.E.). In general messianic expectations were aroused at the approach of each new century in the Jewish calendar, and these expectations motivated many of the immigrants at the end of the thirties and in 1740 C.E.

Among these immigrants were a group of rabbis from Izmir who arrived in Palestine during the thirties and forties, after they published the book *Hemdath Yamin*, which was replete with Sabbatean motifs. This group included R. Jacob Israel Algazi, R. Haim Abulafia, R. Isaac Hacohen Rapaport, R. Raphael Treves, and R. David Hazan.[3] In 1747 two of the chief rabbis of Istanbul, R. Abraham and R. Isaac Rozanes, immigrated to Palestine.[4] The Polish-born rabbi of the Ashkenazi community of Amsterdam, R. Elazar Rokeach, immigrated in 1740. He settled in Safed and headed the small Ashkenazi community in that city.[5] R. Moses Haim Luzzatto also immigrated to Israel from Amsterdam, in 1743. Luzzatto, who was born in Italy, had agitated the Jewish world in the thirties with his mystical and Sabbatean books and activities, and his books had been banned. He was forced to move to Amsterdam and not to engage in the activities that had led to his exile, and after a few years he decided to immigrate to Palestine with his family, settling in Acre.[6] During the thirties the Kabbalist R. Shalom Shar'abi-Mizrahi immigrated to Palestine from Yemen. He became the head of the Kabbalist yeshiva Beth-El in Jerusalem.[7] In 1741 R. Haim ben Attar immigrated to Palestine from Morocco, accompanied by dozens of his students, and established the yeshiva Knesseth Israel in Jerusalem with the assistance of wealthy Italian-Jewish donors.[8] In 1747 the brother-in-law of the Baal Shem Tov, R. Gerson of Kuty, immigrated to Palestine from Poland. He first settled in Hebron and later headed the small Ashkenazi community in Jerusalem.[9] During the fifties as well both groups and individuals continued to immigrate to Palestine from all parts of the Diaspora. The immigrants mentioned by name, as well as others, were well-known rabbis in their Diaspora communities, and their immigration greatly strengthened the connections between the Jews of Palestine and the Jewish communities in the Diaspora.

5

THE HASIDIC IMMIGRATION

DURING THE EIGHTEENTH CENTURY there was a continuous stream of Jewish immigrants to Palestine from all parts of the Diaspora: from Turkey, Greece, and other countries in the eastern basin of the Mediterranean Sea, from North Africa and Italy, from central and eastern Europe. There were almost no immigrants from western Europe. Until 1760 the immigrants and pilgrims came mainly from the countries of the Ottoman Empire and belonged to the Sephardi communities, whereas only a few were Ashkenazim.

In the 1760s a change occurred, and the number of Ashkenazi immigrants began to grow. During the sixties these were still only small groups of about twenty immigrants, but during the seventies there began the great immigration of hundreds of Hasidim of the Baal Shem Tov, which brought about a demographic change in the Jewish settlement in Palestine.

During 1764–65—that is, after the death of the Baal Shem Tov in 1760—a group of immigrants from eastern Europe arrived in Palestine. This group became famous mainly because of its travelogue, the book *Sippurei Eretz Hagalil* (Travels in the Galilee), which was written by the preacher R. Simha of Zalozce.[1] At the head of the group, which included about thirty immigrants from eastern Europe as well as immigrants from Turkey and the Balkans, were two of the most famous of the Baal Shem Tov's friends, R. Nahman of Horodenka and R. Menahem-Mendel of Premyślan, with several people who were close to them.[2] We do not know if the other immigrants were Hasidim, but the two Hasidim in the group determined its character, and it was called "the immigration of the Hasidim." It is worth stressing that this was only one of a series of immigrations from eastern Europe, yet it cannot be ignored that the other immigrants in the group, though not counted among the Hasidim, were close to them geographically and personally. These included R. Simha of Zalozce,[3] who describes the journey from eastern Europe to Palestine and the hardships on the ship and at the destination;

from his account we learn the prices of various products and the problems of the immigrants during this period. Concerning the way R. Nahman of Horodenka and R. Menahem-Mendel of Premyślan reached this group we have good evidence in the form of a Hasidic legend. This may be one "praise" that was not included in the book *In Praise of the Baal Shem Tov*, which contains other legends about the immigration of these two men.[4]

This group of Ashkenazim, like those who had immigrated to Palestine from the middle of the eighteenth century, settled in the communities of Tiberias and Safed, and so established another foundation stone for the development of the Jewish settlement in the Galilee. During this period there were few Ashkenazim in Jerusalem; it seems that in those years they still tended to keep their distance from Jerusalem because they remembered the destruction of the Ashkenazi court in Jerusalem at the beginning of the century. The economic development of the Galilee by Dahir al-ʿUmar and Jezzār Aḥmed Paşa also increased the flow of immigrants to this region. The immigrants settled in Safed, where they found a Jewish community of several hundred people and even a small community of several dozen Ashkenazim.

The immigration of Hasidim in 1777 was relatively large and consisted of several hundred people who arrived at the same time. At its head were three Hasidic leaders of White Russia: R. Menahem-Mendel of Vitebsk, R. Abraham of Kalisk, and R. Israel of Plock. The caravan set out in March 1777 from eastern Europe and arrived in Palestine, via Istanbul, in September of the same year.[5]

The Hasidim constituted only a small fraction of these immigrants, because hundreds of people joined them who took advantage of the departure of the caravan and did not have the slightest connection to Hasidism.[6] The leaders of the Hasidim were not happy about this and they called them names such as *erev rav* (the rabble). There was indeed much justification for their displeasure because before their immigration the Hasidim had provided for orderly economic support from their brothers in the Diaspora, as was accepted in those days, whereas the *erev rav* had no means of support and became a burden to the Hasidim, especially to the leaders of the group.

This immigration differed somewhat from the other immigrations in the eighteenth century, both of the Sephardim and of the Ashkenazim, in that it was an immigration resulting from a new movement within Judaism that led to a turning-point in the modern history of the Jewish people: Hasidism. The immigration was organized in the Diaspora on the initiative of charismatic leaders and established a foundation for further emigrations from Europe. Nevertheless, the influence of this immigration on the Yishuv was much smaller than has been described by historians.

Historians have different opinions about the causes of this immigration: (1) the establishment of a Hasidic center in Palestine;[7] (2) bringing the redemption closer, that is, a messianic immigration;[8] (3) flight from the increasing persecution of the Hasidim in eastern Europe in the 1770s;[9] and (4) prayer and Torah study in Palestine.[10]

The main sources for the history of this immigration are a few dozen letters sent by the immigrants to their rabbis and their Hasidic followers in the Diaspora. Halpern was correct in his argument that it is difficult to draw conclusions from these sources, because the immigrants were given to messianic moods.[11] On the other hand, there is some weak evidence that the persecutions by the opponents of Hasidism were among the causes of the immigration,[12] and that the traditional reason of Torah study and prayer also played a role in the immigration. There is no clear proof for the hypothesis concerning the desire to establish a Hasidic center in Palestine. R. Menahem-Mendel of Vitebsk, R. Abraham of Kalisk, and R. Israel of Plock continued to view themselves as part of the Hasidic center in White Russia. Only in 1788, after the death of R. Menahem-Mendel of Vitebsk, did R. Abraham of Kolyszki try unsuccessfully to separate from the leadership of R. Shneur-Zalman of Lyady in White Russia. Similarly, the leaders of the Hasidic immigrants in Palestine did not continue to lead those of their Hasidim who remained in eastern Europe. Thus the road was paved for the immigration of local Hasidic leaders from eastern Europe, and especially the leadership of the founder of Habad Hasidism, R. Shneur-Zalman of Lyady.[13]

Besides the ideological causes of this immigration—which remain in dispute—there were also some political reasons. The situation of the Polish Jews in those years was particularly difficult, and prohibitions and pogroms caused many Jews to flee Europe.

Another factor is associated with the timing of the immigration. At that time the war between Turkey and Russia, the country of origin of most of the immigrants, had stopped, and in 1774, after several years of warfare during which the shores of Palestine were bombarded and the Black Sea was dangerous to cross, the treaty of Küçük-Kaynarcı was signed between the two powers.[14] In 1775 the rebellion of Ali Bey was put down and Dahir al-ʿUmar was killed, and with the rise to power of Jezzār Aḥmed Paşa under the auspices of the central Ottoman authorities, the years of unrest in the Galilee ended.[15]

6

THE ATTITUDE TOWARD PALESTINE AND IMMIGRATION THERE

THE QUESTION OF MESSIANIC TENSION and messianism in the Jewish world during the eighteenth century is fraught with controversy among historians, mainly concerning what is involved in the background of the growth of Hasidism. G. Scholem believes that at the beginning of the eighteenth century messianic tension in the Jewish world weakened, and this allowed the development of the Hasidic ideology. Ben Zion Dinur sees in Hasidism a movement aimed at redemption, and he believes that the messianic tension remained as it was even after the failure of Sabbateanism, and that the longings for the redemption and the immigrations to Palestine expressed this tension. On the other hand, Isaiah Tishbi argues that it is indeed possible to find messianic tension in the writings of those contemporaries who were on the fringe of the growth of Hasidism, but he challenges Dinur's view about messianism in Hasidism.[1]

In discussing the background of the immigrations to Palestine in the eighteenth century one should consider the trends in attitudes toward Palestine and immigration there that were widespread at that time. Within the framework of this book it is obviously impossible to examine the question of messianic tension in all the writings of the period, as that would necessitate a separate investigation. Therefore I will limit myself to the writings of the acknowledged great men of the generation, the immigrants themselves and those who advocated immigration, and those who had reservations about it. It is worth emphasizing that in the period under discussion Palestine was not the main Jewish focus of interest. Spiritual and social thinking was directed mainly at the great changes that had occurred in Jewish life in the Diaspora. Nevertheless there was something special about the limited group that turned its attention to Palestine and immigration there, and in order to understand the events it is worth discussing this attitude at length.

In the Jewish world of the eighteenth century there was no visible unity in attitudes toward messianism, Palestine, and immigration to Palestine, and one can only point to a few trends in thought: (1) a concept of clear messianic tension—whether ordinary messianic tension or that derived from metamorphoses of Sabbateanism—with practical expressions that were calculations of the date of the redemption, advocating immigration to Palestine, and actual immigration; (2) a concept that opposed the idea of redemption and the importance of Palestine in the life of the nation, or opposed immigration to Palestine for practical reasons; and (3) a concept in between, without expectations of redemption in the near future and not acting to bring the redemption closer, either by immigration to Palestine or by advocating it. This concept nevertheless fostered abstract hopes for redemption in the distant future.

MESSIANIC TENSIONS

Despite the fact that decades had gone by since Sabbetai Zevi's conversion to Islam in 1666, echoes of this great movement still reverberated in the Jewish world. Remaining Sabbateans, Kabbalists, and Torah scholars continued to foster messianic hopes for a speedy redemption, and from time to time they set a new date for it. First 1700 and later 1706— that is, the fortieth anniversary of Sabbetai Zevi's conversion to Islam— were considered in some circles to be the year of redemption, and after that the years 1740, 1768, 1775, 1782,[2] and others. Great disappointment following the nonrealization of the redemption drove many to despair and led to a decrease in the number of believers in a speedy redemption.

It seems possible to point to certain circles, both in the East and in the West, in which great messianic tension prevailed at that time. What many of them had in common was a wish to immigrate to Palestine as a direct consequence of their beliefs. Among the remaining Sabbateans were R. Judah Hasid, R. Abraham Rovigo, Nehemiah Hayyun, Dr. Cantarini, R. Moses Haim Luzzatto, R. Jacob Israel Algazi, and R. Raphael Treves. People who tended toward messianic tension without any connection with Sabbateanism were Kabbalists and Torah scholars such as R. Haim Abulafia in Turkey, R. Haim ben Attar in North Africa, and R. Peretz ben-Moses and R. Simha of Zalozce among the Hasidim in Poland. Even in Germany there were people who calculated the date of the redemption in those days.[3] Some of the more important sages who immigrated to Palestine during the eighteenth century (R. Jacob Israel Algazi, R. Haim Abulafia, R. Raphael Treves, R. Abraham Rozanes, R. Isaac Hacohen Rapaport, and even R. Elazar Rokeach) kept up strong ties with the Sabbateans and their followers, and their attitude to Sabbateanism was ambivalent.

It is worth noting the connection between the circle of Kabbalists in Brody and its surroundings, in which there were conspicuous messianic hopes,[4] and the fact that from this area dozens, if not hundreds, of Jews immigrated to Palestine during the eighteenth century. It becomes clear that governing elements of Hasidism—for example, the theory of the *tzaddik* (holy man)—and frequent expressions in the writings of the early Hasidim also appear in the writings of Kabbalists with messianic hopes among the Sephardim, such as, R. Haim ben Attar and R. Raphael Treves, both of whom immigrated to Israel at the time when the Baal Shem Tov's activities in Podolia were beginning.

Dinur[5] has already dealt at some length with the role of the *tzaddik* according to the ideology of R. Haim ben Attar,[6] which is similar to that of R. Jacob Joseph of Polonnoye and other early Hasidim. But it is also possible to find elements very similar to those of Hasidism in the writings of R. Raphael Treves. He wrote: "Our redemption and the liberation of our souls is dependent on this: That we should leave behind our own sorrows and sorrow about what concerns His honor, and this is something that not everyone can achieve but only the select . . . in such a way that when the Jewish people will cling to their God they will achieve this virtue, and then their paths will become straight in all their affairs and everything will be prepared for them."[7]

Besides the expressions from the theory of the *tzaddik*, one can find in his words other expressions that the early Hasidim used frequently, for example: "It is well known that aside from the all-embracing fear that it is necessary to feel for God . . . because His glory fills the world so that there is no place that is free of Him . . . it is forbidden to walk proudly erect . . . because this is the gateway to God and holy men shall enter therein."[8] Likewise, "Eretz Israel is like a ladder that is based on the ground while its top reaches the heavens . . . when I am standing in Jerusalem this is the gateway to God."[9]

The distinction between the redemption "in its time" and the redemption in the style of "I will hasten it"—which already appears in the writings of R. Haim ben Attar—can also be found in the writings of R. Raphael Treves: "And now because of our sins the redemption will take much longer and we and Jerusalem are in disgrace . . . and even if we understand that we will have no recovery except 'in its time' we are obligated to . . . act, perhaps the God of Hosts will have mercy on the ruins."[10]

In the circle of Kabbalists in Brody two trends of thought developed. The view that was more extreme in its conception of messianism turned to Palestine and sought to hasten the redemption through practical steps. Among the prominent advocates of this trend were some of the most famous immigrants to Palestine of the eighteenth century, and it would not be an exaggeration to say that they were among the designers of the Jewish settlement in Palestine. The more moderate view sought a different type of road to redemption: the redemption of the individual, which precedes the general redemption. Perhaps this constitutes an explanation for the fact that only a few early Hasidim immigrated to Palestine.

The immigration of R. Judah Hasid and his group was undoubtedly messianic-Sabbatean. Rabbi Hasid was filled with messianic expectation and believed in Sabbetai Zevi. Recently a sermon of his from about 1695 was published in which he said, among other things: "Amira (Sabbetai Zevi) is the redeemer and there is no redeemer except him."[11] He also kept up connections with Sabbateans such as R. Abraham Rovigo and R. Haim Malach.

R. Haim Abulafia saw in the renewal of the settlement in Tiberias a sign of the coming redemption. It seems that the expressions of messianic tension in his writings are not empty metaphors. The sentence "The messiah will soon arrive and will emerge from the Sea of Galilee," which attributes an Arabic source to R. Abulafia,[12] and expressions such as "the time of the nightingale has come" and "it is now the messianic time," which are scattered about the book *Zimrath Ha-Aretz* (The Fruit of the Land), written by his son-in-law, R. Jacob Berav, unquestionably attest to messianic tension in his group.[13] It is possible that the date of his immigration, 1740, also attests to this.

An outstanding representative of the above-mentioned trend was R. Raphael Treves, who immigrated to Palestine before 1740.[14] In his writings he set aside a central place for mourning the ruin of the Holy Land. His two books, *Tzach Ve-Adom* (Clear and Ruddy) and *Dagul Me-Revava* (Outstanding of Myriads), are full of longings for the redemption. *Tzach Ve-Adom* was written for pilgrims to Palestine as a guide to their behavior, to prayers, and to study of the Zohar.

43

In his sermons he spoke a great deal about the privilege of immigrating to Palestine, but he warned against those who saw in this period the time of the Messiah: "And if someone will say . . . that our days are the longed-for days, that the time of the nightingale has come . . . we must not make calculations [of the time of redemption] in this period but we should rather mend our ways."[15]

The possibility of hastening the redemption was in the hands of the nation. Those who lived in Palestine were on a higher level because of the holiness of the land—"It is well-known that Eretz Israel is the palace of God, the king of kings"[16]—and he warned against slandering the land: "Whoever harms it, it is as though he has harmed the pupil of the eye of God . . . and concerning those who live there one should remember in his heart that they are mighty angels."[17]

The importance of Palestine, according to R. Treves, was especially great at that time because of the difficult exile and the difficult situation involving the Holy Land. Against those who argued that the exile had already ended he said: "Woe unto us that it has happened in our time that it is necessary to bring proofs that we are in the crucible of exile."[18]

Against the opponents of immigration to Palestine he argued that in earlier times—such as the time of Nahmanides—the situation in Palestine was much worse, and nevertheless it was never said that living there is not a religious obligation. At the time of Nahmanides there were hardly any Jews living in Palestine, "which is not the case, thank God, in these generations."[19] The rules he established for the behavior of the pilgrims all show the stamp of the Kabbala, such as immersions, midnight prayers, and mortification of the flesh. Only Palestine was "The place of perfection, the place of holiness and purity, the place which is prepared for the observance of the commandments, the place which is prepared for the inspiration of the Shekhinah and the attainment of the Holy Spirit, the place of happiness and atonement, the place of rebirth and redemption."[20]

In the immigration of R. Haim ben Attar and his group in 1741 it is also possible to find signs of messianic strains, even though there were other motives for his immigration as well. Rabbi ben Attar was one of the calculators of the year of redemption in his generation and once even expressed the opinion that 1740 would be the year of redemption. In his letters as well there are expressions of messianic expectations.[21]

Kabbalists and calculators of the year of redemption also immigrated to Palestine during the eighteenth century. Thus, for example, R. Simha of Zalozce and R. Peretz ben-Moses, who were also filled with messianic expectancy, immigrated from eastern Europe. Obviously, not all the immigrants we know about from this period left behind writings from which it is possible to discover whether or not their immigration was connected with messianic tension—for example, R. Abraham of Kuty and some Sephardi sages. The clear connection between the region where Hasidism developed and the region from which most of the Ashkenazic immigrants to Palestine in the eighteenth century started out points to a messianic mood on the periphery of the development of Hasidism. Nevertheless it seems that the great Hasidic immigration in 1777 was not distinguished by messianic tension and that it differed from the earlier immigrations only in its greater size. At any rate, it is hard to find any hint in the writings of the immigrants that messianism was a reason for their immigration. Reading their letters produces the impression that the reasons for their immigration were the traditional motives of Torah study and prayer in Palestine, and perhaps the wish to escape from persecution by the opponents of Hasidism.

The common denominator of the immigrations headed by several of the more important immigrants to Palestine in the eighteenth century— R. Judah Hasid and R. Abraham Rovigo at the beginning of the century, R. Haim Abulafia and R. Haim ben Attar in the middle of the century, as well as some of the Eastern European immigrants—was that strong messianic hopes were to be found among them. All of them came from circles of Kabbalists in the East and in the West, and this fact is evidently important because the connection between the Kabbala and the messianic-Sabbatean movement is one of the foundation stones in the study of this movement. [22]

In one way or another some of the immigrants mentioned above were connected with the remnants of Sabbateanism, even though not all of them belonged to that movement. On the other hand, it seems that the great Hasidic immigration of 1777 was in a different category, and that it was the product of the new movement which had just arisen.

Do these immigrations reflect the mood of the time? We do not possess precise data, but it seems to me that it is very hard to decide who is right in the great debate among historians concerning the messianic tension of those days. On the one hand, there was a weakening of messianism, but on the other, there were circles in the East and in the West, even if diminished, in which there was strong messianic tension, and these generally immigrated to Palestine. It seems possible to speak of a thread connecting the Kabbalists of Brody, Istanbul, and Morocco, which caused them to meet in Jerusalem, and especially in the Kabbalist yeshiva Beth-El.

It is clear that the immigrations of R. Haim Abulafia and R. Haim ben Attar and the Hasidic immigrations in the second half of the century were not without influence in the Jewish world, and certainly spurred others to follow in their footsteps. The circle of connections within Palestine through relatives or people who came from the same city probably also increased the sphere of influence of these immigrations. It is true that one cannot speak of immigrations that drew large numbers of people with messianic urges, but nevertheless these immigrations influenced the continuation of immigration to Palestine in the following generations.

Opponents of Immigration

The Denial of the Redemption

It is customary to divide the remnants of Sabbateanism in the eighteenth century into two groups: the moderates and the extremists.[23] The more moderate group did, it is true, keep its Sabbatean belief, but it generally did so in secret and remained within the mainstream of Judaism. The more extreme group partly left this mainstream.

In the attitudes toward Palestine it is also possible to discern two main groups among the remainders of Sabbateanism. One group, as mentioned above, was nourished on Sabbatean teachings, and its goal was Palestine. The other group denied the redemption, reduced the importance of Palestine, and stopped mourning its ruin. To this latter group belonged the Frankists, who sought physical and spiritual redemption in Europe and held up Poland as the chosen land for the Jewish people, and also the Dömme sect in Turkey and Greece. Other groups did not actually reach such great extremism and did not leave the mainstream of Judaism, but in the wake of the teachings of Sabbetai Zevi they abolished the fast of the Ninth of Ab, and thus aroused a fierce controversy.

Opposition to settling Palestine and mourning the destruction of the Temple was also found in that period among the descendants of Marranos and the Sephardim, the first *maskilim* (members of the Haskala, or Enlightenment, movement), who lived mainly in Amsterdam.[24]

The view expressed in these circles was that the holiness of Palestine no longer obtained, and that its settlement was not vital. They also expressed doubts about the reliability of the emissaries and the letters from Eretz Israel concerning the difficult situation in the Yishuv. Obviously, in order to oppose the settlement of Palestine they needed clear apologetics. Thus they argued that it was the will of God that Palestine should remain desolate, and that it was wrong to nullify this will. In these circles as well there was a widespread tendency to leave the traditional mainstream of Judaism, which was expressed in the increasing integration of the descendants of the Marranos into the surrounding society.

Another group that dissociated itself from the traditional concept of the redemption and from the settlement of Palestine began to grow in the middle of the eighteenth century among the *maskilim* in Germany, and toward the end of the century this group's ideas became more entrenched. The members of this circle, whose ideological father was Moses Mendelssohn, [25] spent much time considering the problems associated with the redemption, the religious commandments, the Hebrew language, and the concept of the return to Zion. The growth of the Enlightenment in Germany strengthened the anti-Palestine trend among the German Jews, and the abolition of prayers for the return to Zion in the nineteenth century was merely a symbolic step expressing this trend.

The Opponents of Immigration for Practical Reasons

In those days there was also opposition to immigration in totally different circles and for completely different reasons: the difficult situation in Palestine, the danger on the roads, the poverty of the immigrants, and the fear that it would not be possible to support oneself in Palestine. The Istanbul Officials, the guardians of the Yishuv, limited the number of immigrants and levied immigration taxes, with the intention of preventing economic crises in the country. [26]

In Jerusalem itself they reestablished the regulations that forbade bachelors—and probably all young people—under the age of sixty from living there, in order to limit the population of the city and prevent treacherous behavior on the part of the authorities.

Letters and writings by members of the older generation tell of the fears associated with immigration to Palestine. Rabbi Yakir, the son of R. Abraham Gerson of Kuty, wrote in a letter to his father-in-law in Brody that because of the difficulties of supporting oneself it would be better for him not to immigrate to Palestine before the age of seventy. According to Scholem, one cannot find in this letter the enthusiasm for immigration that modern literature has tried to ascribe to people of that generation.[27]

R. Jacob Emden, it is true, approved of the settlement of Palestine, but he had reservations about the rashness of immigrating without assuring oneself of appropriate economic means: "But it is nevertheless a great matter for a person to leave his homeland and move to a new place"[28] A study of Rabbi Emden's writings shows that he was unable to decide between the two positions. Not only did he argue that "as long as the Jewish people, and especially the Torah scholars among them, will not give thought to their land their Torah study will not endure,"[29] but also he even considered immigration, according to his own words. It is true that, for reasons that are unknown to us, he himself did not immigrate to Palestine, but he commanded his sons to do so. Rabbi Emden even accused his bitter opponent, R. Jonathan Eybeschütz, of opposing Palestine and immigration there.[30]

R. Joseph Sofer of Beresteczko, one of the immigrants from eastern Europe in the middle of the century, also warned: "Whoever comes here must bring money with him."[31] Even the Hasidic immigrants at the end of the century warned their friends in the Diaspora against immigration in the face of the difficult conditions that reigned in Palestine.

It appears true, that besides the extreme group, which approved of the settlement of Palestine, there were also those who rejected immigration for ideological reasons. In these circles one can see the forerunners of the modern age in Jewish history, that is, the pioneers of the departure from the traditional camp. At the same time there were also groups that had reservations about immigration to Palestine for fear of an economic crisis.

The Intermediate Trend

In the writings of many of the important rabbis of that period one cannot find any messianic strain. The redemption and the Messiah were mentioned, it is true, but a study of the sources reveals that they were mentioned only on the title pages of books, at the ends of prefaces, and sometimes in particular sermons as well. It seems that expressions such as "When will the messiah arrive and we will go to Eretz Israel,"[32] "Send us, our Father, the priest, the messiah,"[33] "God in His mercy will hasten to redeem us from the four corners of the Earth . . . and He will build our glorious Temple,"[34] or "And the time of the redemption will call

. . . . and the Temple as it will be built and the palace for judgment . . . and so [the son of] Jesse at the head, the praised king, the messiah of the God of Jacob"[35] were only routine metaphors, the fruit of an extended tradition of quoting biblical verses and verse fragments indicating a faint longing for the Messiah. The concept of settling Eretz Israel, which was accepted in many circles, was not an expression of messianic tension, and it is important to distinguish between the two.

The leaders of the generation and the heads of the movements that were developing among the Jewish people in the eighteenth century did not immigrate to Palestine and did not conspicuously advocate such immigration. The Baal Shem Tov and the Gaon of Vilna, R. Jacob Emden and R. Jonathan Eybeschütz, R. Aaron Amarillo and R. Jacob Saul were not among those who immigrated to Palestine; rather, they dedicated themselves to shaping the lives of the Jewish communities in the Diaspora. The trend toward immigration to Palestine was stronger among the rabbis of the East than among the rabbis of Europe.

One may say that the connection to Palestine was particularly strong in Kabbalist and Sabbatean circles, but it was also possible to find it among many levels of ordinary people—mainly in the Ottoman Empire and in eastern Europe—who went to Palestine to live or who made pilgrimages there. But even those who opposed immigration or who were undecided about the position of Palestine did not make light of the deep relationship with that land which filled the hearts of the scattered Jewish people in the eighteenth century.[36]

Part III

Economic Support for the Yishuv and the Istanbul Committee of Officials for Palestine

7

The Pattern of Economic Support for the Yishuv from the Diaspora

The Ideological and Historical Basis of the Support

During the time of the Second Temple there was already a widespread tradition within the Diaspora of helping the Yishuv, the Jewish settlement in Palestine.[1] The Halakhic justification for this support was based primarily on the giving of charity and the commandment to settle Eretz Israel (the name for Palestine used in Halakhic sources), and in this spirit were written most attempts at persuading the Diaspora to support the Yishuv. But even though it is possible to find historical continuity in the support itself, this is not true of its ideological basis. The axis about which the Halakhic discussions revolved was the biblical verse "And if there be a poor person among you, one of your brothers in one of the cities of your land, harden not your heart" (Deut. 15:7), which was interpreted by Midrash Sifrei to imply: "The poor of your city take precedence."[2] According to the Halakha there was thus a preference for the poor of one's own city, and it was necessary to provide a special argument to exempt Eretz Israel from this rule. Therefore it was established by Midrash Sifrei—and later in the Shulchan Aruch as well—that Eretz Israel took precedence over the poor of the Diaspora, although not over the poor of the city in which one actually lived.

After the Moslem conquest (634–638) there occurred a gradual decline in the Jewish settlement in Palestine, and interest in it waned.[3] The Karaites, who settled in Jerusalem,[4] showed some interest in Palestine and its settlement during the tenth century. During the Crusades the Jewish settlement of Palestine stopped almost completely.[5]

A change in the attitude toward Eretz Israel, both ideological and practical, occurred during the thirteenth century. A clear expression of this may be found in the writings of R. Judah Halevi, who emphasized the centrality of Eretz Israel and immigrated there, and of Nahmanides, who included the commandment of settling Eretz Israel in his listing of the commandments and also relocated there. It is also possible to find an expression of this trend in the immigration to Palestine of the French rabbis in 1211. It is true that this was not an immigration of the masses, but its influence was felt, and it seems that this suggests a strengthening of the ties to Palestine in the Diaspora.[6]

A revival of the immigrations to Palestine and of the economic support for its settlement occurred in the fifteenth century, when the persecution of the Jews began in Spain. In the Jewish communities, and especially in Italy, funds were established and collectors were appointed to send donations regularly to the Yishuv. The immigrations of R. Ovadiah of Bartenura[7] and of Meshullam of Voltera[8] reflect the strengthening of the ties between Palestine and the Diaspora, and it is possible to see in them the background for the development of the Yishuv and its ties with the Diaspora after the expulsion from Spain.[9]

Three successive historical events contributed to the rise in importance of Eretz Israel in the Jewish world and to the development of economic support for the Yishuv: the Ottoman conquest of Constantinople in 1453, the expulsion of the Jews from Spain in 1492, and the conquest of Palestine by the armies of the Ottoman Empire in 1516. The trend of immigrating to Palestine and organizing economic support for the Yishuv began to take shape among the Jews of Spain even before the expulsion, but it grew with the dispersion of the Spanish Jews among the communities of Turkey, the Balkans, and western and central Europe. Among these communities strong ties began to form, both on economic and on familial grounds. The Sephardim began to stand out both in the economies of the countries in which they settled and in international economics. The conquest of Palestine by the Turks led to a strengthening of these ties, as Palestine and the strong Sephardi communities of Istanbul, Edirne, and Salonika were now all under one rule, making it possible to organize support of the Yishuv more efficiently. The growth in importance of Safed and Tiberias in the sixteenth century was probably connected, among other things, with their closeness to centers of Jewry such as Damascus and Aleppo, which had strong ties with the Istanbul community, and of course with economic factors as well.[10]

In the seventeenth century the Jewish settlement in Palestine did indeed decline,[11] but nevertheless the importance of that land in the

consciousness of the Jewish people increased enormously. The causes of
this were the Kabbala and the messianic elements that arose at this time
among the Jewish people, of which Sabbateanism was first and foremost.
In this movement Eretz Israel held a central place,[12] and even after the
failure of the movement the centrality of Eretz Israel continued to grow
in certain circles. The Sabbatean movement left such a deep impression
on the Jewish people that many of the most important rabbis continued
to nurture messianic hopes, some in secret and some in public. Among
the masses as well the episode did not simply disappear. Computations of
the year of redemption and immigrations to Palestine of neo-Sabbateans
and of ordinary Jews all strengthened the ties with Palestine in the years
after the Sabbatean movement and increased the basis for economic support from the Diaspora for the Jewish settlement there.[13]

At the same time enlightened movements began to arise in the seventeenth century among the Spanish exiles and the Marranos, and the
status of Eretz Israel was undermined. These circles, whose center was in
Amsterdam, began to scorn the importance of Eretz Israel and the neces-
sity of supporting the Jews there.

The support for the Jewish settlement in Palestine in the eighteenth
century was connected with the spiritual and social transformations that
occurred within the Jewish nation, so it is worth considering the movements that unified the great concentrations of Jews in the Diaspora: first,
the turning away from Jewish society toward the outside world, as found
among the descendants of the Marranos, the various types of *maskilim*,
the court Jews, the Frankists, and other groups that began to come into
contact with the surrounding society; and second, the trend among those
circles whose activity was turned inward to the Jewish camp, such as the
remnants of Sabbateanism, the Kabbalists, the calculators of the year of
redemption, and the founders of other movements in Judaism (for example, the Hasidim and their opponents, the Mithnagdim).

In the beginning of the eighteenth century there arose a tendency—
first among the Jews of Palestine and later also among the sages of the
Diaspora—to give the residents of Eretz Israel precedence over the poor
of one's own city. It seems that the first to do this was R. Moses Hagiz,
who wrote sharp words against the neglect of the Yishuv and those who
scorned Eretz Israel.[14] R. Haim Joseph David Azulay[15] and R. Raphael
Treves[16] followed in his footsteps, and later well-known European rabbis,
such as R. Moses Sofer,[17] also interpreted the Halakha in this manner. It
seems to me that in this question of the poor of one's city and the poor of

Eretz Israel there indeed occurred a change at the beginning of the eighteenth century, and perhaps even at the end of the seventeenth. These are the reasons for it:

First, there was the growth of sentiment denying the commandment of settling Eretz Israel and its ideological and practical importance. Elements supporting this sentiment, who came mainly from the circles that turned away from Jewish society toward the outside world, were precisely the targets of R. Moses Hagiz's polemics.[18] This provides evidence that this trend was not a marginal one, but rather a trend that probably had many echoes among the Jewish people. Second, one must consider the difficult position of the Jewish settlement in Palestine as a result of its growth and its burden of debts. Third was the Sabbatean crisis, whose echoes were still being heard during the eighteenth century. A result of this was the strengthening of the debate about the redemption and how to attain it, and this was the source of the sharp controversy on the matter of the poor of Eretz Israel. Finally, there was the tendency of the laymen of the communities, who were responsible for the poor and the institutions within the province of their activities, to reduce support for the Yishuv. Incidentally, the debate turned only on the poor of one's own city; on the precedence of the poor of Eretz Israel over the poor of other cities there were no differences of opinion, as the formal Halakha did not deny the precedence of the poor of Eretz Israel.

When the debate concerning support became stronger, discussions of the mutual relationship between the Diaspora and Eretz Israel also increased—namely, giving money in return for spiritual gains, which included prayer and Torah study in Eretz Israel and the commandment of settling Eretz Israel.

It seems that in the eighteenth century Amsterdam was the principal meeting place for all the contradictory trends that were prevalent among the Jewish people in connection with Eretz Israel and its support: the Sephardi *maskilim* who were descended from the Marranos, and the Sabbateans and their followers, on the one hand, and the famous rabbis who supported the Yishuv and immigrated there, such as R. Elazar Rokeach, on the other. Amsterdam was also a meeting place for the emissaries from Palestine and for people from Palestine who had emigrated from there for one reason or another. The economic support of the Amsterdam community for the Yishuv was very substantial, and at the initiative of its donors several yeshivas in Palestine were even established.

There were, as mentioned, many circles in which Eretz Israel occupied a position of great importance and so its settlement was supported: famous rabbis, Kabbalists and calculators of the year of redemption, and also the moderate group among the remnants of Sabbateanism. R. David Oppenheim, the rabbi of Prague, was the "president of Eretz Israel" at the beginning of the eighteenth century and did much for R. Judah Hasid's group in Jerusalem. [19] R. Ezekiel Landau, one of the most important ages of the generation, was also "president of Eretz Israel"[20] and kept up strong ties with the immigrants from among the Jews of eastern Europe and even offered them financial assistance. Hakham Zevi and his son R. Jacob Emden were at the head of the collectors of money for Eretz Israel. Rabbi Emden conducted a debate with the groups that had forgotten Eretz Israel and pleaded with them to support its settlement. [21] R. Jonathan Eybeschütz, one of the most important rabbis in central Europe in the eighteenth century, also had a strong attachment to Eretz Israel, as can be clearly seen from his writings. [22] This group also included Kabbalists and rabbis from Turkey, such as R. Haim Abulafia, whereas R. Raphael Treves, whose books are filled with calculations of the year of redemption, called for support of the Yishuv and wrote polemics against the opponents of the settlement of Palestine.

Among the Marranos one could also find great interest in and support for the Yishuv. Baron D'Aguilar, a close associate of the royal court in Vienna in the middle of the eighteenth century, did much for the Ashkenazi settlement in Palestine, in coordination with Jewish groups such as the Istanbul Officials. It is true that this is the only example known to us, but it has great importance because of the standing of this individual. Could it perhaps have been precisely these circles, which had distanced themselves from traditional Jewish society, that sought their own path to redemption? At any rate, among the Marranos and the Sephardi communities there was a strong Sabbatean element. It is nevertheless possible that in the case of persons such as Baron D'Aguilar there was rather a Christian influence. In the eighteenth century various Christian groups demonstrated great interest in Palestine and the return to Zion, [23] and it is not impossible that it was precisely the Jews who had become part of the surrounding society who had absorbed the views that were destined to penetrate the Jewish world in the nineteenth century and increase interest in Palestine and its settlement.

Support for Palestine never came easily, and people from Palestine and community leaders in the Diaspora were forced to fight for it continually. There is much exaggeration in the idyllic description of the support and enthusiastic welcomes that greeted the emissaries. In actuality, there was a constant tension between the solicitors and the donors of the money.[24] The Jewish communities in the Diaspora and their institutions did indeed see support for the Yishuv as an indispensable part of their task, but frequently problems arose at the time of implementation of the decisions and regulations, because of the difficult economic situation and legal standing and because of the exaggerated demands for contributions on the part of the people from Palestine.[25] There is much evidence of continual battles concerning the collection of funds. In eastern Europe often the money in the funds for Palestine was used to serve the needs of the eastern European community because of the difficult economic situation.[26] The protocol books of the communities of Berlin[27] and Hamburg[28] also attest to this phenomenon.

On the other hand, there is evidence of the important position that Eretz Israel held—at least symbolically—in the consciousness of the Jewish communities, from the many regulations for the collection of money for Eretz Israel and the many personages who were involved.

THE INTERNATIONAL SITUATION

The extent of the economic support for the Yishuv and the orderly transfer of funds to Palestine were closely connected with the international situation and with the political situation of Palestine and Syria. In the eighteenth century the economic situation of the Ottoman Empire was unstable, and this prevented regularity in the collection of funds for the Yishuv.[29] The funds were transferred from many distant places to key cities, and the Yishuv was thus dependent on the various avenues of distribution. About a year before the immigration of R. Judah Hasid's group one of the wars between Turkey and the European states ended with the signing of the Karlowitz treaty. During the entire eighteenth century there were wars between Turkey and Russia, and the gradual decline of the Ottoman Empire began.[30] In the middle of the eighteenth century the Seven Years' War took place in Europe. It is clear that there were delays in the transfer of funds to Palestine because of all these wars, and especially the wars in Turkey, which greatly disturbed the activities of the Istanbul Officials and even led to devaluations of the currency.

Difficulties of transportation and disorders in the postal system also delayed the transfer of funds to Palestine. It was sometimes difficult to obtain a boat for the transfer of the money because of pirates in the waters of the Mediterranean and all along the coast of Palestine; often boats were lost, and the money with them. The slower land routes were not any safer.

The local rebellions that occurred at the beginning of the century in Jerusalem and afterwards in Hebron also led to delays in the transfer of funds.[31] Moreover, the wars between Dahir al-ʿUmar and the Pasha of Damascus in the 1740s and the rebellion of Ali Bey in the 1770s led to the intervention of the powers and prevented free access to the coasts of Palestine.

There is no doubt that the delays in the transfer of the funds caused great damage to the Jewish settlement in Palestine. A prime example is the collapse of the Jewish community in Jerusalem at the beginning of the century because of funds that arrived late.[32]

THE ECONOMIC AND LEGAL STANDING OF THE DIASPORA

One of the important factors for understanding the support for the Jewish settlement in Palestine is the economic and legal standing of the Jews in the various countries.

In the Ottoman Empire each Jewish community was organized in the framework of a *millet*, as were the communities of the other religious minorities. The richest and most important communities were those of Istanbul, Izmir, Edirne, and Salonika, and at their head were the communities of the Spanish exiles. The Jews were well integrated into the economy of the empire, and many of them filled important roles in international trade and financial matters. Often they achieved senior positions in the courts of the rulers, both in the Sublime Porte and in the provinces.[33] These Jews were links between the Jewish communities of the empire and those outside it, and they helped the Jewish settlement in Palestine in many ways, such as in the collection and transfer of funds, money changing, providing credit, and especially intercession with the rulers.

In the eighteenth century the importance of the Istanbul community for the rulers increased in all matters connected with the funds sent by the communities in the Diaspora to the Jewish settlement in Palestine, and the establishment of the Committee of Officials for Palestine in Istanbul further strengthened this position and drew the communities in Palestine closer to the heart of the Ottoman regime.

In North Africa, the most remote part of the Ottoman Empire, the situation of the Jews was undermined in the eighteenth century, and only a few donations arrived from there for the Jewish settlement in Palestine.[34]

The communities in Italy enjoyed a special status.[35] In the eighteenth century this was a country of small states and city-states, which had a special status in international trade, because Italian ports connected the Mediterranean lands with western and central Europe. Cities like Leghorn and Venice had flourished, it is true, mainly in the previous centuries, but extensive economic activities still existed there. The Jews also took part in this activity, and some of them even enjoyed a respected status.

In their communities in Italy the Jews were also organized on the basis of their countries of origin. In each city there were several communities, with the community of Spanish exiles at the head. During the eighteenth century Italy was one of the countries through which money was transferred to Palestine from the Jewish communities of Europe and North Africa. The immigrants to Palestine from these countries also passed through the ports of Italy. The Jewish communities of Italy themselves also donated large sums for Palestine, and in various cities committees for the support of the Yishuv were established, as mentioned above.

The states with absolute regimes in central and western Europe adopted the mercantile economic system, which faced the Jews with a new reality. On the one hand the regimes did not accept the special status of the Jews, as they saw in it a contradiction of the principle of centralization, but on the other hand they prevented the integration of the Jews in the society and in the economy by means of various regulations. Nevertheless, the court Jews helped the regimes with credit by utilizing their connections with merchants in other countries. The governments solved the paradoxical situation that was thus created by giving the Jews permission to maintain a separate framework, although imposing severe limitations and curtailing the internal autonomy of the Jews. At times the Jews were even expelled from their places of residence. For example, the Jews were expelled from Vienna in 1670, and in 1744–45 there was an attempt to expel them from Prague.[36]

One of the basic principles of the mercantile economy was that the power and wealth of the state depended on the amount of money in its possession. This principle led the states to curtail imports and increase exports, and as a result controls were imposed on taking money out of the country. Obviously, collecting money for Palestine stood in opposition to this principle, and the absolute regimes frequently imposed limitations in this matter.

At the beginning of the eighteenth century enormous sums were gathered in all the Jewish communities of central Europe in order to rescue the Ashkenazim of Jerusalem from their crisis. One day a Jew from Palestine arrived in Prague and asked for R. David Oppenheim, the rabbi of the city, in order to repay the debt that the Ashkenazim in Jerusalem owed him. The matter reached the court of the city, and as a result an order was proclaimed throughout the Hapsburg Empire that forbade the collecting of money for Palestine. The order also promised a reward to anyone who informed on those who disobeyed the order. The official justification for this order was that in any case the Jews were late in paying their taxes. The proclamation also denigrated the honorary titles of Rabbi Oppenheim, such as "president of Eretz Israel." Until the end of the 1820s, at least, the authorities enforced this order.[37]

A similar incident is known from the principality of Hessen Kassel in Germany.[38] In 1737 an emissary from Jerusalem visited this principality, and the local prince forbade his subjects to give money to the emissary. From that time the community leaders were forced to ask special permission whenever an emissary arrived. In 1740 the emissary R. Petahia Katzenellenbogen visited this place on behalf of the Ashkenazim of Jerusalem and went to the authorities to ask them for permission to collect money. After negotiations this permission was obtained. The authorities of the region also placed another obstacle in the path of the emissaries and required a special payment from them for their stay in the place.

At the beginning of the eighteenth century several German principalities imposed a control on the appointment of collectors for Palestine and on the collection of money in the synagogues. In 1726 the accounts of the Jewish community of Metz were inspected.[39] During the century these communities were burdened with heavy debts, and their economic situation was very bad.

The role of the court Jews in the economic support for the Jewish settlement in Palestine is also of great interest. Until recently historians stressed the importance of the court Jews as liaisons between the Jewish communities and the governments and dwelt upon their role in the economy of Europe, but they did not pay attention to the assistance these Jews offered the Jewish community in Palestine. Good examples are R. Samson Wertheim and his son, and Baron D'Aguilar, member of a family of Marranos in Vienna, who held the tobacco franchise in Austria and was at the head of the Sephardi community in Vienna. He not only played an important part in the attempts to prevent the expulsion of the Jews from Prague in 1744–45 but also did much for the Ashkenazim in Palestine. It seems that in the 1750s he gathered together each year the donations that had been collected from the various communities for the Ashkenazim in Palestine and transferred this money to the Istanbul Officials. He also tried to bring about a general concentration in Vienna of all the money from Europe in cooperation with the Istanbul Officials, but in this effort he was not successful.[40]

In the eighteenth century there was a gradual decline of the central royal government in Poland, and the power of the nobles gradually increased. The legal and economic status of the Jews became very weak, and in 1764 the Council of the Four Lands (*Vaʿad Arba Aratzot*) was disbanded.[41] This fact affords an explanation for the small number of emissaries who arrived in Poland during the eighteenth century and the small amounts of money that the Jewish communities there donated to the Yishuv. Jewish institutions did indeed take care of the collection of money for Eretz Israel, but the difficult conditions did not allow for extended support. In Poland as well the authorities frequently prevented the transfer of funds to the Jews of Palestine. For example, they prevented the transfer of funds at the time of the great Hasidic immigration in 1777, probably because they feared a loss of income as a result of the emigration of the Jews.[42] At the time of the bitter controversy between the Hasidim and the Mithnagdim at the end of the eighteenth century, the Mithnagdim informed on R. Schneur Zalman of Lyady, and as a result the authorities accused him of smuggling funds to Palestine. The transferring of funds to the Yishuv is also mentioned in a memorandum about the Jews presented by the official Derjavine to the Russian government.[43]

INSTITUTIONALIZATION OF THE SUPPORT

The Establishment of Hevroth *(Societies) and Funds*

In the Jewish communities of Egypt there were already beginnings of organized support for the Yishuv at the start of the sixteenth century,[44] but it seems that the honor of being the first to organize support for the Yishuv goes to the Jewish community in Venice. Around 1532 there was an attempt there to collect money for Palestine in a systematic way,[45] and funds from Germany for the support of the Yishuv started to be sent there.[46] This is also the first time that we hear of special committees for this purpose in the other Jewish communities of Italy, and from the last third of the sixteenth century we have knowledge of Societies for Eretz Israel in Istanbul,[47] Poland, and Rome.[48]

A strong incentive for the organization of the support for the Yishuv was provided by the emissary from Palestine, R. Bezalel ben Abraham Ashkenazi, who established a certain amount of regularity in the donations at the end of the sixteenth century, most especially the custom of donating "half a shekel" on Purim.[49] Around 1600 an additional development took place in Venice as a result of the mission of the emissary R. Moses Alshech, who described the difficult situation in the Yishuv and brought about the establishment of the Fund for the Support of the Residents of Eretz Israel.[50] In 1601 official authorization was given in Venice for the establishment of a fund and its organization on a permanent basis. The decision of the community was that on the week of Parashat Shekalim (when a portion from the Torah prescribing the donation of money to the Temple is read in synagogues) every Jew over the age of twenty who had an income was obligated to donate "half a shekel" to Palestine. If someone refused to do so, it was permitted to bring him to court and even to hand him over to the authorities. At the head of the fund were three collectors, and a code was established for dividing the money among the Jewish communities in Palestine.

At the beginning of the seventeenth century the pasha of Jerusalem had oppressed the population with harsh decrees, and as a result in 1623 the community leaders in Venice turned to the Jewish communities of Europe and announced the establishment of a central fund in their community. Gradually funds, collectors, and collection systems were organized, and by the middle of the seventeenth century all the Jewish communities had established various regulations that systematized the collection and transfer of funds for Palestine.[51] These regulations were not confined to a limited geographic area, but covered Turkey,[52] Italy,[53] North Africa,[54] central Europe,[55] and eastern Europe.[56]

From the middle of the seventeenth century the collection of funds for the Yishuv was accomplished in an organized manner, which continued to develop during the eighteenth century. The matter was apparently connected with the events mentioned above: the expulsion from Spain and the dispersion of its Jews on the one hand, and the Ottoman conquest on the other. There were also other causes of the organization of the support for the Yishuv, first and foremost the difficult situation of the Jewish settlement. Starting from the second quarter of the seventeenth century a number of severe catastrophes occurred to the Palestine Jews, one after another, and at the beginning of the seventeenth century the Galilee declined and the Jewish communities of Tiberias and Safed dwindled. As a result there was a growth in the Jewish community in Jerusalem, which began at that time to suffer from the harsh government of the local rulers.[57]

Another cause of the organization of support for the Yishuv may be found, as mentioned, in the messianic ferment in the Jewish world in the seventeenth century, which reached its peak in Sabbateanism. This movement caused increased interest in Palestine and motivated many Jews to immigrate there. The immigrations of the seventeenth century[58] strengthened the ties between the Diaspora and Palestine and made the collection of money easier for the emissaries. At the end of the seventeenth century and the beginning of the eighteenth the number of immigrants to Palestine grew, mainly from European countries,[59] and as a result the support of the European communities for the Yishuv also grew.

An important cause of the organization of support for the Yishuv was the organization of the Jewish communities in the East and in the West into the framework of societies.[60] In the sixteenth century various societies for free loans and the study of the Torah were growing, and the number of societies of various craftsmen increased. There were several reasons for this phenomenon, especially the tradition of forming societies that the Spanish exiles brought with them and the influence of the charitable societies of the Christians. There are those who believe that the societies spread in Italy in the wake of the individualistic trend that flourished after the Renaissance, which led to widespread social activity not sanctioned by the authorities. The cooperative trend in European society probably also influenced the form of the organization in the framework of societies. The *Hevroth* (Societies) for Eretz Israel were thus the contemporary embodiment of the desire to contribute to the Yishuv. In 1659 the Society of Assistance for the Holy Land was founded in Frankfurt-am-Main,[61] and in 1673 the Society for Jerusalem, which was still operating in the eighteenth century, was founded in Rome.[62]

Support from the Diaspora

The Collectors for Eretz Israel

In the middle of the seventeenth century, at the start of the organization of the collections, people who were appointed to collect this money began to operate in the Jewish communities; they were called "collectors for Eretz Israel" or "treasurers for Eretz Israel" in the Ashkenazi communities,[63] and "officials for Eretz Israel" in the Sephardi communities. In Breslau the title was "treasurer of Jerusalem";[64] in Berlin, "trustee and official of Hebron."[65] Another title was "rabbi of Jerusalem."[66]

In the large communities in which the money for Palestine was gathered together the person appointed to collect the money was called "president of Eretz Israel," for example, R. David Oppenheim, rabbi of Nikolsburg and later rabbi of Prague, who was appointed to this position by the sages of Jerusalem;[67] R. Samson Wertheim in Vienna; R. Jacob Josha of Cracow in Frankfurt-am-Main; R. Ezekiel Landau in Prague; R. Simha Menahem in Lvov; and R. Moses ben-Elazar Rokeach in Brody.[68] At times the title "president of Eretz Israel" remained with its bearer even after his immigration, as was the case with R. Elazar Rokeach.[69]

Persons in these positions, who are mentioned in regulations of the various Jewish communities together with the other officials of the communities, were chosen every year or every three years together with the holders of other positions. At times the collectors for Eretz Israel were chosen on the recommendation of the emissary from Palestine who was staying in the community. Thus, for example, the officials in Salonika were appointed with the intervention of the Jerusalem emissary R. Jacob Ashkenazi de-Corona.[70] In general honored members of the community served as collectors for Eretz Israel, which attests to the importance of the position. At times the care of the funds for Palestine was inherited, especially among the titled Sephardi families. For example, the following was written about the Agiv family of Leghorn: "The sons of the rich man, the official of our yeshiva 'Hesed le-Avraham u-Vinyan Shlomo' in the holy city of Jerusalem whose shelter is spread over the holy cities of Safed and Hebron . . . Señor Solomon Agiv."[71]

The Pereyra family in Leghorn, Amsterdam, and London supported yeshivas in Palestine. In Venice the Abuhab family had been at the head of the fund for Palestine since the seventeenth century.[72] In Modena the Singuineti family was at the head of the fund for Palestine and supported the yeshiva Knesseth Israel, at which one of the sons studied.[73] In Ancona the Morpurgo family took care of the money for Palestine;[74] in Leghorn, the Franco and Rakah families;[75] in Venice, the Padova family;[76] in Padua, the Rakah family;[77] and in Ferrara, the Mepronti family.[78] In Egypt R. Solomon Algazi, the rabbi of Cairo, took care of the transfer of funds to Palestine,[79] and in Metz, Rabbi Falk.[80] Some court Jews were also involved in this, such as Baron D'Aguilar in Vienna.

A study of the regulations of the various Jewish communities reveals that from the middle of the seventeenth century there was a development of the institutions of the collectors. During the eighteenth century collectors were appointed not only for funds for all of Palestine but also for the individual cities: Hebron, Tiberias, Safed, and first and foremost, Jerusalem.[81] Separate collectors were also appointed for the Ashkenazi and Sephardi communities. In the Jewish community of Hamburg the Sephardi community appointed special officials to collect money for the Sephardim, whereas the Ashkenazim of the city appointed collectors for the Ashkenazi community in Jerusalem.[82]

Times and Forms of the Collections

The times of the collections for Eretz Israel were not uniform, but there were certain days on which it was customary to collect money: (1) on Fridays, and sometimes also on Sundays, when the collectors for Eretz Israel visited the households;[83] (2) at the time of going up to the *bima* for the Torah reading on holidays, with the saying of special blessings in which one pledged to give charity;[84] (3) on fast days, in the synagogue;[85] (4) on the eves of Rosh Hashanah and Yom Kippur, both at the synagogue and at the cemetery;[86] (5) on Purim;[87] (6) at a feast of circumcision; or (7) at the time of saying "Yizkor" (a special prayer in which one pledges to give charity in honor of one's departed relatives).

The donations were generally voluntary, and so the sums were not fixed. In the regulations of the communities only the dates of the collections and how to obtain them more quickly are mentioned, but there were also communities that imposed a minimum on the donations for Eretz Israel, or even established special taxes on behalf of Eretz Israel. In Hamburg in 1659 all the members of a certain society were obligated to pay one *reichstaler* per year for Eretz Israel.[88] In the Jewish community of Yassi it was decided in November 1781 to require every head of a household to give "half a shekel" in the sum of two *paras*; it was also decided to give a yearly sum of five *paras* per person for the Ashkenazi yeshiva in Jerusalem and one percent of the presents received at every wedding, in addition to the regular collection, which was voluntary.[89] The Jewish communities of Lithuania and the Council of Four Lands in Poland decided that on Fridays, when the collectors visited the households, each head of a household would give no less than one *gulden*.[90]

In addition special emergency collections were arranged from time to time, and special taxes were imposed on behalf of the residents of Palestine. In 1710 the Jewish communities in Germany were called together to arrange a special fund-drive in order to rescue the Ashkenazi community in Jerusalem from its crisis. The fund-drive was organized by R. Samson Wertheimer, who succeeded in mobilizing very large sums for this purpose. He also succeeded in getting many Jewish communities in Germany to sign pledges that they would pay fixed sums for ten years, but the communities did not keep the pledges.[91]

Often indirect taxes were imposed for Palestine. In 1761 the Sephardi community in Venice imposed a special business tax.[92] In 1763 the Jewish community of Istanbul imposed indirect taxes on wine on behalf of the Jewish community of Hebron.[93] In Salonika as well a special tax on behalf of Palestine was imposed.[94]

At times the communities imposed fines on transgressors, and the money was set aside for the Jewish communities in Palestine. For example, in 1717 an official of the Jewish community of Kastoria in the Balkans was deposed, everyone who came into contact with him was fined, and the resulting sums were donated to Palestine.[95]

Concentration of the Funds in Various Countries and Their Transfer to Palestine

The money that was collected in the Jewish communities of the Diaspora, whether in an organized manner or privately, was transferred to Palestine in several ways: (1) by means of the Jewish communities that collected the money for Palestine from their immediate surroundings and transferred them to a larger center; (2) by means of emissaries who circulated among the communities; and (3) by means of individuals such as immigrants and pilgrims. Later on most of the money was transferred through the Istanbul Officials, the central institution for the concentration of donated funds in the eighteenth century.

In most of the countries there was a uniform method for collecting the money. The small communities transferred the money they had collected to a central community in the region, and this community sent the money to a central city in that country. From there the money was transferred to Palestine through other countries or through emissaries. Often the emissaries came themselves to the small communities. Generally the funds for Palestine were sent through port cities, but at times changes occurred in the methods of transfer, depending on the economic status of the cities involved.

The collection of funds in Italy. In the seventeenth and eighteenth centuries large sums of money from Germany[96] and North Africa[97] passed through Italy, although the money from North Africa was sometimes transferred through Egypt, where there were a number of wealthy Jews who donated much money for the Jewish settlement in Palestine and who were very active on its behalf.

The communities of Italy also donated considerable sums for the Jewish settlement in Palestine. Venice was the central city in Italy for the transfer of funds until the middle of the eighteenth century, when it began to decline.[98] The center then shifted to Leghorn, in which the richest Jews lived, and during the second half of the eighteenth century ramified activities on behalf of the Yishuv took place there. In addition to the collection of funds from all parts of Italy, the Jewish community in Leghorn supported the establishment of yeshivas and assisted immigrants to Palestine from North Africa, such as R. Haim ben Attar and his group.[99] The Jews of Leghorn even made an offer to Ali Bey to buy Palestine for the Jews. With the renewal of the settlement in Tiberias its emissaries established special funds in Leghorn and in other Italian cities.

The money for Palestine was also concentrated at times in Modena, where there was one of the most important branches of the committee for the yeshiva Knesseth Israel in Jerusalem.[100]

The collection of funds in western and central Europe. The Jewish communities of Holland, Germany, France, Bohemia, and Moravia all donated very large sums of money for the Yishuv. The foundations for the collections in these countries were laid in the seventeenth century.

One of the key cities for the collection of the money in western Europe was Amsterdam, where the support was very well organized. During the seventeenth and eighteenth centuries the Jewish community in Amsterdam had very strong ties with Palestine, and many emissaries visited there and received a warm welcome. In Amsterdam were concentrated the funds from northern Germany—mainly Berlin—and from London and France. The important Portuguese community in Amsterdam was especially outstanding in its activities on behalf of the Yishuv. This community and some of its rich members offered much help to the Yishuv, especially to the yeshivas.[101]

In the first decade of the eighteenth century the Jewish community of Frankfurt-am-Main was at the forefront of the rescue activities on behalf of the Yishuv. Through regulations and letters this community obligated all the German Jewish communities to contribute on behalf of Jerusalem. The communities of Hamburg, Altuna, Metz, and others responded to the call and pledged to eliminate the debts of the Jerusalem community, but they did not persist in this.[102] The Jewish community of Metz was very active on behalf of the Yishuv from the time of the crisis in the Jerusalem community at the beginning of the century, and afterwards it also supported the Yishuv in a systematic way, especially the Ashkenazim in Jerusalem.[103]

In southern Germany the contributions were concentrated in the smaller cities like Fürth and Heidingsfeld,[104] and from there they were transferred to Frankfurt-am-Main. Funds from eastern Europe[105] and also from nearby cities in France, such as Metz, were also transferred to Frankfurt at times. Funds from the Ashkenazi community in Hamburg were frequently sent to Frankfurt-am-Main and transferred on to Venice or Leghorn, and from there to Istanbul and to Palestine. The Sephardi community in Hamburg generally sent the money directly to Italy.[106]

In northern Germany the money was concentrated in Berlin, mainly from cities such as Frankfurt-am-Oder.[107] From Berlin the money was usually transferred to Amsterdam, and from there it made its way to Palestine, either directly[108] or through Italy.[109]

From the regulations of the state of Moravia we learn that the foundations of the collection of funds for the Yishuv were laid also in the seventeenth century. These regulations were similar to those of eastern Europe.[110] The money was transferred from secondary centers (for example, Nikolsburg) to Vienna, where there was a "president for Eretz Israel." An extensive fund-raising effort was conducted in Vienna after the immigration to Palestine of R. Judah Hasid's group and its involvement in debt in Jerusalem. Large sums of money were collected in Vienna and were frozen there by the authorities.[111] The importance of Vienna was inherent in the fact that it was a city of passage between the Austrian Empire and Turkey, and the mail was also sent through it.[112] In

1750 Baron D'Aguilar attempted, as mentioned, to concentrate the funds from various countries in Vienna in order to avoid duplication in the collection, but did not succeed. Nevertheless he persisted in sending the money to Jerusalem via Istanbul.[113]

The funds for Palestine from the Jewish communities in Bohemia were concentrated in Prague, which also served at times for the transfer of money from eastern Europe via Breslau. In Prague there was an important Jewish community, and there was also a "president for Eretz Israel" there. From 1740, when Schlesia was separated from Austria and annexed to Prussia, there was a decline in the donations, because in Prussia the authorities intervened in the visits of the emissaries and in the collection of funds for Palestine.[114]

The collection of funds in eastern Europe.   In the seventeenth and eighteenth centuries the Jewish communities of Poland and Lithuania did not contribute large sums for the Yishuv because of their difficult situation.[115] The regulations established by the Council of Four Lands for the systematization of the methods of collecting the donations are mainly from the seventeenth century; in the eighteenth century only a few regulations were established.[116] The money from the donations was collected twice a year during the great fairs in Lublin and Jaroslaw, and from there it was transferred to the "president of Eretz Israel" in Lvov; from 1750 to 1760 the "president of Eretz Israel" resided in Brody.[117] From Lvov or Brody the funds were transferred via Istanbul to Palestine, or sometimes also through Frankfurt-am-Main, Breslau, or Egypt.[118]

In 1705 and 1750 regulations were established in Lvov for the appointment of the "presidents of Eretz Israel."[119] In 1739 proclamations were issued to the Jewish communities to appoint collectors for Eretz Israel,[120] and in 1742 proclamations were issued forbidding the use of the funds for Eretz Israel for other purposes.[121] Another matter that was discussed was the establishment of a special fund for Hebron and Safed.[122]

The Council of Lithuania followed the regulations of the Council of Four Lands, and its regulations are also mainly from the seventeenth century. The regulations deal with these matters: the establishment of a special fund for Hebron,[123] the prohibition of using the money for Eretz Israel,[124] the appointment of collectors for Eretz Israel, and the times and manner of the collections.[125] The money of the donations was concentrated in Vilna and Brisk, and from there it was transferred to the great fairs in Lublin and Jaroslaw.

Support from the Diaspora

After the great Hasidic immigration of 1777 the flow of donations from eastern Europe increased, especially from the land of origin of the immigrants. When the caravan of Hasidim reached the Galilee one of its leaders, R. Israel of Polotsk, was sent immediately to eastern Europe in order to "create a status and situation for the collection of donations."[126] After him additional emissaries were sent, and thus the economic support for the Yishuv from eastern Europe became institutionalized.

SUPPORT AMONG OTHER MINORITIES IN PALESTINE

In a general way one could say that in the seventeenth and eighteenth centuries there was a great similarity between the Christians and the Jews in Jerusalem, not only in their judicial status but also from the standpoint of their economic and social problems and their solutions. At any rate, the Christians in Jerusalem also received economic support from other countries. It seems that in this matter they followed the Jews, who had had this custom for generations, even though there is reason to assume that with the passage of time, when the methods of support were developed, the Jews also learned from the Christians.

In an essay from the end of the seventeenth century R. Raphael Mordecai Malkhi, one of the rabbis of Jerusalem, complained about the poor sums that the Jewish community of the city was receiving and described with envy the large sums received by the Christian sects in Jerusalem—the Catholics, the Greeks, and the Armenians—from their brothers in other countries.[127]

Many times the Istanbul Officials were assisted by the ambassadors and consuls of France in Istanbul, Acre, and Sidon, who were accustomed to help in the transfer of funds to the Catholics in Palestine. The Istanbul Officials were also assisted by the Armenians—whom they occasionally called "Amalekites"[128]—and transferred money to the Jews in Palestine via boatloads of Armenian pilgrims.

Armenian sources also attest to the amazing similarity between them and the Jews in the matters of economic problems and economic support.[129] In 1670 the Armenian patriarchate in Istanbul extended its patronage to the Armenian community in Jerusalem in the wake of unending battles between the three Christian sects in Jerusalem and the relationship of the local authorities to the Armenians, which consisted mainly of the extortion of money.

In 1702 a complete unification of the patriarchates was established, and the patriarchate of Istanbul completely dominated the one in Jerusalem, which aroused much bitterness in the Armenian patriarchate in Jerusalem.

From 1703 to 1706 the fights between the local authorities and the residents of Jerusalem increased, and as a result the Armenian community was mired in heavy debts, which reached the sum of 400,000 *kurus*—a much larger amount than the debts of the Jews, which amounted to about 60,000 *kurus*. These were the years of the great economic crisis of the Ashkenazi community in Jerusalem, and there is reason to assume that there was a connection between the two. The Armenian sources tell that the Armenians owed money to the Moslems and the Jews, and when the creditors did not receive their money they broke into the Armenian monastery and looted it, an action that reminds one of the looting of the Ashkenazi court.

In 1713 the Armenian patriarchate in Istanbul sent a special messenger to Jerusalem to find out the reasons for the crisis. The conclusion of the messenger was that it was necessary to abolish the unification of the two patriarchates, and in 1711 it was decided to return to the old system of patronage and economic support and to appoint "officials" who would be responsible for the Armenian community in Jerusalem. Later the Armenian community in Istanbul reached an agreement with the creditors and obtained *firmans* for the cancellation of the debts and the rehabilitation of Armenian holy places in Jerusalem. It is interesting that the source of power of the Armenian patriarchate in Istanbul in the seventeenth and eighteenth centuries—like the power of the Jewish community in Istanbul—was the immigrants from the provinces, who did well in business and banking and reached important positions in the economy and the administration of the Sublime Porte.

The similarity between the Armenians and the Jews was thus expressed in the following areas: (1) a similar judicial status and a negative attitude on the part of the local authorities toward minorities; (2) immersion in heavy debts and involvement with the local authorities. The Armenians lent money to the Jews and the Jews also lent money to the Armenians, probably for fear that in an economic crisis they would not receive their money from the members of their own groups; (3) battles with a financial background, both among the various Christian sects and between the Sephardi and Ashkenazi Jews; (4) the method of treating the crises: the establishment of a committee in Istanbul, the attainment of *firmans* cancelling the debts and rehabilitating the buildings, and the domination of the people of Istanbul over the people of Jerusalem as a result; and (5) the strength of the Armenian patriarchate in Jerusalem and the Jewish community of that city thanks to the rich merchants and bankers who settled in the imperial capital.

Probably there were also other similarities, and it is not impossible that the Armenian example is precisely what led to the establishment of the Committee of Officials for Palestine in Istanbul. And might the central authorities in Istanbul perhaps have spurred both the Armenians and the Jews to establish this method of supporting their brothers in Palestine? At any rate, without the *firmans* it would not have been possible to rehabilitate the communities.

8

THE DISTRIBUTION OF
SUPPORT MONEY

THE MONEY COLLECTED in the Diaspora was divided among the Jewish communities in Palestine according to a certain formula, which was changed from time to time and was not the same in different parts of the Diaspora.[1] In the sixteenth century the money was divided into twenty-four parts as follows: Hebron—3, Safed—10, Jerusalem—7, Tiberias—4.[2]

After the destruction of Tiberias in the middle of the seventeenth century the communities of Jerusalem and Safed demanded an increase in their incomes at the expense of Tiberias, and in the last quarter of the century the formula was as follows: Jerusalem—12, Safed—8, Hebron—4.[3]

According to an agreement of 1700, which remained in force until the 1740s, the division was as follows: Jerusalem—11, Safed—7, Hebron—6.[4] In 1728 the agreement of 1700 was reaffirmed.[5]

When its settlement was renewed in 1740, Tiberias fought for the right to receive part of the money, but only in the 1770s, after difficult struggles, were its efforts crowned with success, and the formula was modified to include twenty-eight parts as follows: Jerusalem—11, Safed—7, Hebron—6, Tiberias—4.[6]

It is surprising that, on the one hand, the Istanbul Officials supported the renewal of the settlement in Tiberias, but on the other hand they opposed its incorporation in the formula for the distribution of the support money. Was this perhaps an action of the Jerusalem officials, who did not consult the umbrella organization of the Istanbul Officials? At any rate, only in 1771 did the Istanbul Officials write to the Jewish communities in Germany: "To return the crown to its former state . . . that the fund for Eretz Israel should be divided into 28 parts, 11 parts . . . Jerusalem . . . and 7 parts for the emissaries of Safed . . . and 6 for the emissaries of Hebron and 4 for the emissaries of Tiberias."[7]

However, changes took place even in this formula because of the fluctuations in the populations of the various cities in Palestine.[8] Jerusalem received the lion's share of the donations, because of its status and the number of its residents.

In addition to the share that it received according to the formula, each community tried to increase its income by the establishment of special funds, particularly during the eighteenth century. Thus, for example, the Jewish community of Berlin established a special fund for Hebron at the beginning of the century,[9] and other communities followed in its footsteps,[10] such as Istanbul,[11] Leghorn,[12] and the Jewish communities of Moravia.[13] At times this led to rivalry between the communities.

After the renewal of its settlement Tiberias also established separate funds, especially in Italy and Turkey, and so it received an income in addition to what it got from the Istanbul Officials.[14] Tiberias also established funds in the Jewish communities of North Africa and in Gibraltar.[15]

The small Jewish community of Safed received an income from the funds it established in North Africa and in Italy,[16] in addition to the money it received from the Istanbul Officials.[17] The Ashkenazim in Jerusalem sent special emissaries on their own behalf, which led to fierce quarrels with the Sephardim.

QUARRELS AMONG THE COMMUNITIES OVER THE SUPPORT MONEY

Despite the agreements friction arose among the emissaries of the various cities. In 1742 the Istanbul Officials complained about the rivalry between the emissaries of Safed and Jerusalem in the cities of Turkey, the Balkans, and Europe. In several places the emissaries of Safed preceded the emissaries of Jerusalem and collected all the funds for Eretz Israel.[18] In 1744 the Jerusalem emissary R. Abraham ben Asher complained to the Istanbul Officials that the formula for Jerusalem, Hebron, and Safed was not being followed properly in several of the Jewish communities of Europe, and the funds were being divided equally between the settlements. In the wake of this complaint the Istanbul Officials sent a letter of protest concerning this matter.[19]

The most bitter quarrel we know of from that time broke out between the Jewish community of Tiberias and the cities of Jerusalem, Hebron, and Safed. Despite the renewal of the settlement in Tiberias, the formula had not been changed and this city had not been given money from the existing funds. Therefore Tiberias also began to send emissaries to the Diaspora and to establish separate funds for itself. An emissary of Tiberias—apparently R. Haim Ventura—went around in Italy at that time and emptied all the funds for Eretz Israel, and when the emissary of Jerusalem—R. Abraham ben Asher—arrived, he found no funds. He immediately presented a bitter complaint to the Istanbul Officials, and the latter sent letters to the Jewish communities of Europe and pleaded with them to maintain the existing distribution, according to which only the cities of Jerusalem, Hebron, and Safed were to receive donations. They also turned to the communities of Jerusalem, Hebron, and Safed to renew the agreement about the formula.[20]

Incidentally, in Morocco in 1791 a completely different formula was in use that allotted half of the money to Jerusalem and half to the other three holy cities in equal parts.[21]

QUARRELS BETWEEN THE SEPHARDIM AND THE ASHKENAZIM OVER THE SUPPORT MONEY

At the end of the seventeenth and during the eighteenth centuries there was no end to the quarrels between the Ashkenazim and the Sephardim in Palestine concerning the collection of the donations in Europe and the manner of their distribution. The Sephardi community, which was dominant in Palestine, was responsible to the authorities for all the Jews in the country and was required to pay the many taxes imposed on the Jews in general. Therefore the Sephardim believed that they were entitled to collect all the funds for Eretz Israel in the Diaspora and to distribute them according to their judgment and needs. The Ashkenazim did not agree to this, as they saw themselves being discriminated against, and they protested to the communities of Europe. These communities apparently did not know what the money was for, and the only result of the protests of the Ashkenazim was a decline in the amount of the contributions. It is true that the Ashkenazi community received only a small part of the sums that arrived at the Yishuv from Germany and eastern Europe, and even this only with the agreement of the Sephardi leadership, but the money served mainly for the needs of the community—such as taxes, bribes to the authorities, interest and the repayment of loans—and only a small amount was given to individuals. This was indeed the counterargument of the Sephardim.

Under pressure from the Ashkenazi community regulations were established from time to time stipulating that the money from the European countries should be given only to the Ashkenazim. The first regulation of this kind that is known to us was in force from 1645 to 1673.[22] The Council of the Four Lands decided to set aside all the funds for Eretz Israel for the Ashkenazim in Jerusalem and to give nothing to the Sephardi emissaries. In those days the Ashkenazi community in Jerusalem was beginning to flourish, and at its head was a leader of stature, R. Moses Cohen, at whose initiative many emissaries were sent and the above regulation was established.

In 1689 the Ashkenazi community in Venice decided to send the money that had been collected in the city "all to the holy city of Jerusalem, to the Ashkenazi community there";[23] a similar decision was taken by the same community in 1697.[24] Even stricter regulations were established by the rabbis of Egypt in 1691. R. Moses Cohen went on a mission to Europe, and on his way back he stayed in Egypt, where he succeeded in obtaining the following court judgment: "To strengthen and authorize the *taqana* (regulation) which was made by the leaders of Polonia and its rabbis a long time ago . . . that in the next three years they should not give their donations to any emissary from the Sephardi community."[25]

About two years afterwards the rabbis of Egypt again intervened in a quarrel between the Ashkenazim and the Sephardim. In a letter to the rabbis of Venice they admitted having established the above-mentioned regulation in 1689, and they claimed that the emissaries of Hebron and Safed had been taking some of the money of the Ashkenazim.[26]

Another regulation on this matter is mentioned only indirectly. It is from the year 1729, that is, after the destruction of the Ashkenazi court in Jerusalem. In a court document from 1770 in the city of Fürth it is mentioned that the emissary R. Haim Aaron Kotover, son of R. Abraham Gerson of Kuty, presented the problem of the money of the Ashkenazim to the court and brought "several Halakhic decisions from earlier sages from 1694 to 1729 . . . that all the donations . . . in all the regions of Poland and Germany, all of it . . . should be specifically for the Ashkenazi community in Jerusalem."[27]

In the 1730s several additional attempts were made to rehabilitate the Ashkenazi community in Jerusalem, and for this purpose emissaries were sent to the Jewish communities of Europe, some of them by the Sephardim. One of the most important of the emissaries was R. Pethahia Katzenellenbogen.[28] In the communities he visited he obtained large sums of money for the Ashkenazim, and there are documents of the Istanbul Officials which attest that he took care to establish regulations in the Ashkenazi communities specifying that the money for Eretz Israel should be transferred only to the Ashkenazim. This led to quarrels with the Sephardim, and the Istanbul Officials nicknamed him "Pethahia the confuser."[29] At this time the Ashkenazim made efforts to collect large sums in Europe even though there were only a few dozen Ashkenazim in Jerusalem. It is possible that this resulted from the desire to pay back part of their debts, in spite of the *firman*.

At the end of the 1740s many emissaries went around Europe at the same time, both Ashkenazi and Sephardi, and competed for the money in the funds for Eretz Israel. The Jerusalem emissaries R. Mordecai Rovio and R. Abraham Israel and the Hebron emissary R. Isaac Zedaka went to Europe on behalf of the Sephardim. As a result of the quarrels R. Isaac Zedaka did not succeed in collecting any money, and he had to return empty-handed. News of the quarrels came to the attention of the Istanbul Officials, who denigrated the Ashkenazi emissaries "Pethahia . . . and the last one was even worse, R. Yeruham Vilna . . . and the instigator R. Judah Yeruham."[30] It is probable that the Ashkenazi emissaries relied on the regulation of the Istanbul Officials of 1742,[31] which included the obligation to support the Ashkenazim and find places for them in the yeshivas. The emissaries argued that this had not been done, and so they demanded that the money from the European communities should be given directly to the Ashkenazim. The Istanbul Officials demanded that the Ashkenazi communities and emissaries should stop their quarrels, because this was damaging the collection of money in general. They asked the Jewish communities in Palestine to write to the European communities about this.[32]

But the appeals of the Istanbul Officials did not help, and the quarrels persisted. During the first mission of R. Haim Joseph David Azulay to southern Germany in 1754, it became clear to him that the local communities were unwilling to give money to the communities in Hebron, because they had "a regulation from the Istanbul rabbis and the Istanbul Officials who agreed that they should not give any money to any emissary because all of it should be for the poor of the Ashkenazi Jews in Jerusalem."[33]

The agreement mentioned here was apparently the above-mentioned regulation of 1742, which was not preserved. Rabbi Azulay blamed the above-mentioned Ashkenazi emissary R. Judah Yeruham for the difficulties he encountered.

The complaints of the Ashkenazim continued during the following years as well. In a letter that they sent from Jerusalem to the Jewish community of Metz in 1757 they wrote that the Sephardim were receiving all the money from the Diaspora, "and we are very few . . . our devastation and calamity is very great."[34] Their argument was that the money from Germany belonged to them according to the regulations, "which were established a long time ago with the agreement of the great rabbis of Germany." They repeated this argument in letters that they sent to Metz in 1763.[35]

In the 1750s the Ashkenazi emissary from Jerusalem, R. Shneur Feivish, went to Germany and aroused the anger of the Sephardim by collecting all the money for Eretz Israel from many communities and establishing a center for the donations of the Ashkenazim in Metz.[36] Documents from 1763 state that the emissary Jacob de-Corona was received with difficulty by the Ashkenazi community in Amsterdam because they had found out about the discrimination against the Ashkenazim in Jerusalem.[37] It is possible that the contents of the letter that was sent at the time from Jerusalem to Metz had been brought to their attention.

The conflict reached its peak during the mission of R. Haim Aaron Kotover, who went out on behalf of the Ashkenazi community in Jerusalem at the end of the 1760s and reestablished the above-mentioned regulations in all the Jewish communities of Europe. This aroused great anger among the Sephardi emissaries and led to the intervention of the Istanbul Officials as well as the sages of the generation, such as R. Ezekiel Landau. In 1771 it was finally decided that the regulations should be abolished, and that the Sephardim would support the Ashkenazim in Palestine and would be permitted to collect money in the German Jewish communities.[38] But this did not end the quarrels, and in the 1780s some of the Jewish communities in Germany and eastern Europe still expressed opposition to donating money for the Sephardim.[39] This occurred after the great Hasidic immigration of 1777, which undoubtedly increased the tension regarding the donations, and indeed the quarrels continued even more fiercely in the nineteenth century.

The small Ashkenazi community in Safed, on the other hand, cooperated with the Sephardim in the collection of money in the Diaspora. In

1770, at the time of the severe strife in Europe, the Ashkenazim in Safed even signed a letter to the Sephardi emissary R. Abraham Memran, in which the following was written, among other things: "The Sephardi sages and rabbis, may God protect and redeem them, love us like themselves . . . and they help us with their money in spite of their distress and pain."[40]

This letter was printed on a single sheet of paper and distributed in the European communities. There is reason to believe that it was part of the attempt of the Istanbul Officials to bring about a change in the regulations concerning the donation of the money for Eretz Israel to the Ashkenazim alone. R. Abraham Memran was also involved in the conflict with R. Hiam Aaron Kotover.

9

THE JEWISH COMMUNITY OF ISTANBUL AND THE ESTABLISHMENT OF THE COMMITTEE OF OFFICIALS FOR PALESTINE IN ISTANBUL

THE CENTRALITY OF THE ISTANBUL COMMUNITY

In the sixteenth century the Jewish community in Istanbul already fulfilled an important task in the history of the Jewish settlement in Palestine,[1] but only in the eighteenth century did it become the patron of the Yishuv and the deciding factor in most of its concerns. The Committee of Officials for Palestine in Istanbul (referred to throughout this book as the Istanbul Officials), which was established in order to organize the economic support for the Yishuv, was not only responsible for collecting the donations in the Diaspora, concentrating them, and transferring them to Palestine, but also represented the Palestine Jews in practice before the central authorities in Istanbul and before the authorities in the provinces of Damascus and Sidon, and even in the cities of Palestine itself. It was this committee that was dominant in the Jewish communities of Palestine, and the Jews were obligated to obey its commands. It acquired its great power precisely at the time when the Jewish communities of the Ottoman Empire—including the Istanbul community— were in decline, like all of the Ottoman Empire, after its peak period in the sixteenth and seventeenth centuries.

The main reason for this was apparently the need for more efficient organization of the support for the Jewish settlement in Palestine after the destruction of the Ashkenazi community in Jerusalem at the beginning of the eighteenth century and the crisis that it brought about in the other Jewish communities in Palestine.

In Istanbul there were all the conditions for the establishment of an

81

inclusive institution for the support of the Yishuv. Many of the immigrants and pilgrims from the Balkans and from eastern and central Europe passed through Istanbul, and a lively economic trade was conducted there. From a political standpoint it had great importance, as it was the capital of the Ottoman Empire. Descendants of the Spanish exiles had constructed an extensive network of trade and banking connections between the Ottoman Empire and the Christian world, and many Jews achieved key positions in the Sublime Porte. Their connections with the Sublime Porte on the one hand and with the Jewish communities on the other formed a powerful lever for the collection of funds. The authorities also derived great benefit from this, as their income grew with the growth of the donations for the Yishuv. Many appointments of officials and army officers for the provinces took place in Istanbul, and not infrequently the Istanbul community formed ties with the candidates for immigration to Eretz Israel.

In the Istanbul community there was also a publishing house, which made possible the distribution of the writings of the emissaries and of propaganda material for the collection of funds.[2]

It is nevertheless worth stressing that the success of the Istanbul Officials in organizing was due to the great importance that the Jewish communities in the Diaspora ascribed to Eretz Israel, and that the ideological side was no less important than the practical side.

It is worth dwelling briefly on the structure of the Jewish community in Istanbul, as the processes taking place in this community are likely to explain why the establishment of an institution like the Istanbul Officials became possible precisely in the eighteenth century, and not previously. We do not possess much information about the structure of the Jewish communities in the Ottoman Empire and the changes that took place in them, but the small amount of information that we do have about the Jewish community in Istanbul is capable of opening a door to the understanding of these matters.

In the sixteenth century and the beginning of the seventeenth most of the Jewish communities in Turkey and the Balkans were divided into two main groups: the Romaniotes, the long-standing residents of the empire, on the one hand, and the Spanish and Portuguese exiles and their descendants, on the other. In Palestine, Syria, and Egypt, where the Mamelukes had reigned previously, the long-standing Jewish residents were called Mustʿariba ("being mixed" in Arabic). Besides these there were also Ashkenazim and Karaites. In each group there were many congregations, according to their countries of origin.[3] However, with the passage of time the Sephardi communities began to gain the upper hand, both because of their greater numbers and because of their economic and cultural superiority. In the second half of the seventeenth and in the eighteenth centuries all of the groups were assimilated into the Sephardi communities, and they gradually abandoned their original customs and gave up their separate institutions.

This occurred in the Istanbul community as well. Both Jewish and Turkish sources tell us that in the sixteenth and seventeenth centuries the Jewish population of the city was divided into dozens of small communities.[4]

It is true that in 1572 a uniform leadership was established for the Istanbul community in a celebrated agreement between the Romaniotes and the Sephardim.[5] The distintegration of the old organizational structure according to country of origin was felt only in 1633 and in 1660, when great fires broke out in the city. These fires completely destroyed the old Jewish quarters, especially the dwellings of the Romaniotes, and led the long-established Jewish population to resettle on the shores of the Bosporus. This completely changed the traditional structure of the communities, as the residents became mixed together and neighborhood communities were established. Within a short time the Romaniotes and the Ashkenazim were assimilated within the Sephardi communities, which were mostly near the shore, and so the unity of the community increased. It seems that it was this unity that made possible the establishment of the Istanbul Officials. At any rate, among the Jews in Istanbul during the sixteenth and seventeenth centuries—who were divided into dozens of communities—it would have been impossible to establish this type of institution. It was possible to collect money from the Diaspora, to maintain contacts with the authorities, and to impose obedience on the Jewish communities only after a strong spiritual and social leadership was stabilized at the head of the Istanbul community, which had authority both in the community itself and in other communities of the Diaspora. An exhaustive study of the leadership of the Istanbul community during this period has not yet been carried out, but it is known that it was headed by three or four "chief rabbis,"[6] who represented the neighborhoods, the congregations, and the large synagogues. At their side were officials who took care of material concerns and maintained contact with the authorities. There was also the institution of the *Maʿamad*—an elected meeting of the representatives and the holders of important positions—

which met for the purpose of establishing regulations about various matters, including matters concerning the Jewish settlement in Palestine.

THE ESTABLISHMENT OF THE COMMITTEE OF OFFICIALS FOR JERUSALEM IN ISTANBUL

Already during the years 1701 and 1702, at the beginning of the crisis in the Ashkenazi community in Jerusalem, many emissaries went to the Diaspora to collect money. The assistance of the Jewish community in Istanbul in getting the money out of the Austrian Empire increased its importance and this established the foundation for the committee of the Istanbul Officials. It is possible that the Armenian patriarchate in the city served as an example of such a committee, as it had solved the crisis of the Armenian church in Jerusalem at the end of the seventeenth and the beginning of the eighteenth centuries in a similar manner. It is plausible that the Armenian and the Jewish institutions for assisting their brothers in Palestine were established with the agreement of the central authorities, who were interested in the stability of the provinces and tried to prevent friction of the kind that was the lot of the Armenians and the Jews in Jerusalem. Besides, part of the sums transferred to the provinces reached the cellars of the treasury or the pockets of the government officials, whether in the form of taxes or of bribes and gifts. Thus the organized economic support for the Jewish communities in Palestine enabled a higher income from taxes, and moreover part of the donations came from European communities outside the Ottoman Empire.

During the second decade of the eighteenth century the community leaders in Istanbul tried to obtain a preliminary "agreement" for the debts of the Jewish community in Jerusalem, in cooperation with leaders of European Jewry, with R. Samson Wertheim at their head. The tense relationship between Austria and Turkey and the confiscation of the donations by the Austrian authorities delayed the achievement of the "agreement" and increased the activities of the Istanbul community.[7] During these years the Istanbul community tried to mediate between the Moslem creditors in Jerusalem and the Jews of the city, and to this end turned to the central authorities, but the attempt failed. The creditors demanded payment of the debts from the Sephardi community in Jerusalem, which in their eyes was responsible for the Ashkenazi community as well. The Istanbul community even tried to organize a fund-drive "from all the nations, from the cities of Turkey and the cities of Europe,"[8] but in spite of all its efforts the Ashkenazi court was destroyed and the Jerusalem community disintegrated.

These events did indeed have widespread repercussions in all the Jewish communities of Europe, but the center of gravity of the activities on behalf of Jerusalem was in Istanbul. In 1723, when Jerusalem's troubles increased, a special messenger was sent to Istanbul, R. Moses Becher Samuel Meyuhas.[9] The leaders of the Jewish communities in Europe, headed by R. Simon Wolf, the son of R. Samson Wertheim, maintained contact with the Istanbul community and requested the assistance of the Austrian ambassador in Istanbul to help the Jerusalem community.[10] The active force in the activities on behalf of the Jewish settlement in Palestine was R. Mordecai Alfandari, one of the leaders of the Istanbul community, who had good connections with the authorities and about whom the verse was quoted: "And the man Mordecai was great in the house of the king."[11] In 1727 two messengers were sent to Jerusalem, one on behalf of the central authorities and one on behalf of the Istanbul community, to investigate the demands of the Moslem creditors in Jerusalem: "And at the same time was sent from here . . . a great officer who is called Kapıcı Başı in their language and with him a knowledgeable Jew."[12]

Because of this activity an "agreement" was achieved and a *firman* was issued for the settling of the debts in Jerusalem. According to the "agreement" the interest was cancelled, and the debt of 60,000 *kurus* was to be paid out over ten years in fixed installments.[13] The achievement of the "agreement" was the first activity of the Committee of Officials for Jerusalem in Istanbul.

Until now, on the basis of the documents we had,[14] we believed that the committee of Jerusalem Officials was established in 1727, the year in which the "agreement" was achieved and the first emissaries were sent out under the auspices of the Istanbul Officials. However, from a letter that the Istanbul Officials gave the emissary R. David Ashkenazi in 1737[15] it appears that the committee had already been established in 1726, a year previously. This is what was written in the letter: "We the undersigned have been appointed to this holy task from the year 1726 until now and our obligation is to strengthen Jerusalem and to serve the community."[16]

It thus seems likely that the formation of the committee of Jerusalem Officials preceded the achievement of the "agreement" by a year. The first messengers were sent only in 1727.[17] The obligation of the Jewish communities in the Diaspora to participate in the support for the Yishuv by yearly payments began in 1727–28.[18] The initiator of the establishment of the committee was Mordecai Alfandari, one of the rich men of Istanbul. One of the first activities of the committee was the securing of the collection of the yearly allotments from the communities, the imposition of "the *para* collection" (the *para* was the smallest Ottoman coin in this period), and supervision of the sending of emissaries.[19] Because of the importance of the committee of Jerusalem Officials in the history of the Yishuv in the eighteenth century it is worth quoting in full two documents that describe the procedure of appointing the officials in the 1740s.

The Appointment of the Officials for Jerusalem in Istanbul by the Rabbis of Istanbul[20]

A copy of the letter of the honored rabbis of Istanbul to the honored officials according to all the conditions that the authorities in Istanbul established.

We, the undersigned, who constitute the rabbinical court, because in this great city of Istanbul, it is customary to appoint officials every year in the city congregations in order to [. . .] and they will supervise the income and the outlay of the community. These officials have the power to collect money and to take large loans in time of need. At the end of their service they may appoint officials under them. Whatever signed obligations the officials of the previous year still have may be collected by the creditors from the officials coming after them. This is the policy of this city and this is also the halakhic ruling. Now the Officials of the holy city of Jerusalem have resigned due to the great burden of work and the sages and patrons of the city have appointed seven officials in their place who will supervise all the affairs of the holy city of Jerusalem. And indeed the community of the holy city of Jerusalem owes large sums to creditors by the signature of the previous officials. Therefore we, the undersigned, the rabbinical court, have obligated the new officials that any time any creditor comes to collect a debt that the community of Jerusalem owes him, with the signature of the officials, they must pay the debt within three days, without exception, as that is the letter of the law that obligates us to pay the debts which the previous officials had incurred, as they took out the loans for the needs of the holy city. And the new officials are also obligated to give a cancellation certificate to the previous officials and when they give them the cancellation certificate the previous officials will hand over all the documents and bills and account books which were in the possession of the previous officials to the new officials who were appointed in their place. And in order that this should be evidence we have signed this document on the twelfth of Tammuz in the year of the Creation 5606 [1746] in Istanbul.

In the week in which the portion "Balak" (Num. 22:2–25:9) is read and it is legally valid.

Abraham son of Joseph Rozanes[21]

Abraham son of Judah Meyuhas[22]

Isaac son of David, may God save and redeem him[23]

Document Appointing the Officials of Jerusalem in Istanbul on the Authority of the Leadership of the Jerusalem Community[24]

Copy of the authorization of the honored Officials sent from the holy city.

We, the undersigned, the sages and elders and patrons and officials and leaders of the holy city of Jerusalem, attest a complete and valid attestation, as one who attests before a high court, that we voluntarily and with full agreement, without any trace of coercion, have appointed and authorized seven fully authorized [persons],[25] the eyes of God who stand before the Creator of the Earth, the city of praises, Istanbul, may God bless her and guard her, the official and scribe who performs justice to all, the noble patron of all blessings and praise, R. David Zonana; and the wise, perfect patron R. David Kimhi; and the wise, perfect patron R. Shabbetai Alfandari; and the wise, exalted R. Jacob Alfandari; and the wise, exalted patron R. Moses Asseo; and the wise, exalted patron R. Moses Ashkenazi; and the exalted patron R. Joseph Baruch, may God save and redeem him, fully authorized by means of four cubits of land that we transferred to them from our property. *We have given them appropriate power and sufficient authority to be supervisors of all our affairs, to conduct our work, to coordinate the communities of our city, to take care of the poor of our locality, and no man may do anything without their permission.* We obligate ourselves totally in a manner that is legally binding and halakhically valid, accepting their authority, following their decrees, listening to their words and acting according to their leadership, according to the path on which they direct us in the force of their wisdom, and keeping all their agreements, whether in matters concerning the expenses of the city for the taxes of the king and officers, or concerning other expenses and the payment of debts, or concerning the arrangements of the income of the holy city and its collection. *We have given them appropriate power and sufficient authority to impose and collect and take whatever is needed for the benefit of our community in general and in particular, from all the cities of Rumelia [Greece] and Anatolia [Turkey], from the East and from the West, all the lands of the Moslems [Arabs] until the cities of Yemen, from the Christian countries, Eu-*

rope and its borders, until the remote islands—the fixed donations, such as the
"*para*" collection, which is famous throughout the Diaspora, for the redemption of the holy city, and the other allotments, funds, pledges, legacies, and collections; and the occasional donations, from anyone who gives a gift of money or a voluntary donation to our community of Jerusalem, and whatever belongs to the benefit of the Torah scholars and the sages in the yeshivas, and from now on, now that the above-mentioned noble officials have been appointed, their powers are like ours and their authority is like ours . . . so that whatever will be done and decided or a collection or gift from all the Jewish communities by the above-mentioned noble officials will be accepted by us as if it had been done and decided and imposed and collected by us ourselves, without our being able to say to them that we sent them to improve matters and not to make them worse.

And this is what we said to the above-mentioned noble officials: "Go and benefit yourselves and others, and whatever opportunities arise, act according to your understanding."

It seems likely that the rabbis of Istanbul who composed the document of appointment of the Officials for Jerusalem in Istanbul then sent it to Jerusalem for authorization. The document indeed attests to the status of the Istanbul Officials, but it is nevertheless significant that they required official authorization, even if only formal, from the Jewish community in Jerusalem. The Istanbul rabbis distributed the document throughout the Diaspora.

The attempt to rescue the Ashkenazi community in Jerusalem indeed failed, but the new institution succeeded in preventing the total destruction of the Jewish community in Jerusalem by reorganizing its leadership. In theory the Istanbul Officials took care of all the material concerns of the Jerusalem community, but in practice they controlled its leadership and held a decisive position in all the Jewish communities in Palestine.

THE ESTABLISHMENT OF COMMITTEES FOR THE OTHER HOLY CITIES

As a result of the success of the activities of the Jerusalem Officials similar committees were established for the support of the other holy cities, but we do not have concentrated information about them as we do for the Jerusalem Officials. In 1733, after preparations begun in 1729, the Committee of Officials for Hebron in Istanbul was established. This

is what was written in the document of the mission of R. Gedalia Hayyun: "And also the patrons of the nations gathered together in 1729, the
officials of Istanbul and the rich men of Izmir . . . they benefitted themselves and others and gave a donation for the redemption of Hebron from
their money."[26]

The Jewish community of Hebron had also had great difficulties with
its budget in the 1720s, and the community's debt swelled from 12,000
kurus in 1717 to 19,000 *kurus* in 1727 and to 46,000 *kurus* in 1729.[27]
The number of Jews in Hebron was much smaller than the number in
Jerusalem, and thus this was a huge debt. It is no wonder, then, that the
Jewish community in Istanbul, which was probably encouraged by the
success of its first activities in Jerusalem, decided to establish a committee
for Hebron as well. We possess two interesting documents concerning the
Committee of Officials for Hebron. The first was written in 1733, and it
is the above-mentioned document for the mission of R. Gedalia Hayyun,
the founder of the study-house for Kabbalists called Beth-El in Jerusalem. In this document the Hebron Officials reveal the reasons for the
establishment of the committee and review their activities on behalf of
the community. It appears that between 1729 and 1733 they succeeded in
mobilizing 20,000 *kurus*, which covered part of the debts of the Hebron
community. Some of the most respected people in the Istanbul community were members of the committee, and at their head was R. Abraham
Rozanes, one of the rabbis of the Istanbul community, who immigrated
to Palestine in 1747. The second document is the document of appointment of the committee under the auspices of the Istanbul community.[28]

A document that the Hebron Officials wrote in 1764 tells us about a
series of activities they undertook to ease the difficult situation of the
Hebron community: "Besides the thousand *kurus* we send you from the
community of our city every year for the expenses of the city as a fixed
donation, we have obligated all the residents of our city to give one *para*
per person once a week for the redemption of the holy city of Hebron and
a new *gabiela* [an indirect tax] of half an *akce* for each liter of wine and
liquor, and we have obligated the sexton of each synagogue and study-
house to give eight *kurus* per year."[29] The Hebron Officials, like the
Jerusalem Officials, sent emissaries to all the Jewish communities of Europe and the Ottoman Empire.[30]

The Committee of Officials for Tiberias was established in 1740, with
the renewal of the Jewish settlement there. It is plausible that the Committee of Officials for Safed in Istanbul also began its activities at that

time, even though we do not have clear information about the start of its activities. Our first piece of information about the Safed Officials is from 1742, when three members of the committee took care of the emissaries from Safed.[31] The Safed Officials were especially active after the earth-quake that hit the city in 1759, and they played a large role in the rehabilitation of the Jewish community in Tiberias[32] by R. Haim Abulafia.[33] The Istanbul Officials played an active role in the contacts between Dahir al-ʿUmar and the renewers of the Jewish settlement in Tiberias, and they assisted the renewed community afterwards as well.

In addition to the four committees for the holy cities an umbrella organization called the Committee of Officials for Palestine was estab-lished as well. This committee took responsibility for matters that were common to all the Jewish communities in Palestine, coordinated the other committees, and intervened in the quarrels that broke out between the Jewish communities in Palestine, mainly concerning the collection of funds in the Diaspora.[34] Within a few years an unprecedented mecha-nism for the support of the Yishuv was thus established. Because of the size and status of the Jerusalem community the Jerusalem Officials were the most important of the committees that were established.

The Committee of Officials for Jerusalem generally consisted of seven of the most important and richest men of the Istanbul community, among them several who were close to the government. At their head was the "head of the Officials."[35] The other committees consisted of between three and seven members. Often there were members who served in sev-eral committees at the same time.[36] The committees were chosen once in several years, together with the other institutions of the Istanbul com-munity.

The Istanbul Officials had a permanent information network in the Jerusalem community, which transferred updated information about the manner of the administration of the community by the officials and the rabbis.[37]

THE GRADUAL DECLINE IN THE INFLUENCE OF THE ISTANBUL OFFICIALS

It is difficult to judge when the intensive activity of the Istanbul Of-ficials as practical rulers of the Jewish communities in Palestine came to an end. Just as the establishment of the institution occurred in stages, so did its gradual decline.

At the beginning of the 1770s the activities of the Istanbul Officials were still in full force. This is clear both from the *Pinkas* (book of letters) of Istanbul[38] and from the fact that it was within their authority to render a decision, along with the great men of the generation in Europe, in the controversy between the Sephardim and the Ashkenazim concerning the collection of money in Europe. In the 1780s and 1790s their activities still continued,[39] as is attested by their recommendations for emissaries for Palestine.[40] At the same time there was a growing number of emissaries who no longer passed through Istanbul on their way to and from their missions in the Diaspora.

At the beginning of the nineteenth century, with the establishment of the Committee of Officials and Administrators in Amsterdam, the Istanbul Officials' exclusive authority was taken away from them and a sharp decline in their status began.[41]

This decline had several causes. The growth of the Ashkenazi base in the Yishuv from the time of the great Hasidic immigration in 1777 until the immigration of the Perushim at the beginning of the nineteenth century[42] led to the shifting of the center of gravity of the economic support for the Yishuv to central and eastern Europe. At the same time the decline of the Jewish community in Istanbul and the other important Jewish communities of the Ottoman Empire—such as Izmir, Salonika, and Edirne—continued as a result of the economic and political crisis taking place throughout the Ottoman Empire.[43] The interminable wars between Turkey and Russia, Napoleon's campaign in the East, and the wars in Palestine[44] made it difficult for the Jews to maintain their ties with Palestine through Istanbul, and so they sought alternative routes for the transfer of funds, whether directly from Europe or through Egypt. The great improvements in transportation—for example, the first steamboats, which began to travel at the beginning of the nineteenth century[45]— opened up many more possibilities for the transfer of funds directly from Amsterdam and the coasts of Italy to Palestine.

It is worth mentioning that the foundations of the support that were laid by the Istanbul Officials in the eighteenth century were transferred to Europe, and from the end of the eighteenth century centers for the support of the Jewish settlement in Palestine (organized in the same way as the center in Istanbul) were established in various cities, such as Amsterdam, Vilna, and Brody.

Moreover, at the beginning of the nineteenth century the center of gravity of interest in Palestine shifted to Europe, as a result of the increasing activities of Christian elements—especially Protestant groups—in the return to Zion and in Palestine in general.[46] This influenced enlightened Jewish groups, and from the first half of the nineteenth century they turned their energies to activities on behalf of Palestine. The establishment of the Committee of Officials and Administrators in Amsterdam by the representatives of orthodoxy in western Europe is associated with the orthodox war against the Reform movement and the Enlightenment and was intended to fight against innovating groups, so that the Liberals and Reforms would not be the only ones engaged in support for the Jewish settlement in Palestine.

Thus the center of support for the Yishuv moved from Istanbul and the other cities of the Ottoman Empire to Europe, and there it came into contact with the new trends that shaped Jewish history in the nineteenth century.

10
AREAS OF ACTIVITY
OF THE ISTANBUL OFFICIALS

MAINTAINING CONTACT WITH THE
OTTOMAN AUTHORITIES

One of the most important and sensitive areas in the sphere of activities of the Istanbul Officials was the contact with the Ottoman authorities. In the Ottoman Empire contacts with the local rulers were not sufficient, but it was essential to operate in the Sublime Porte as well. Thus, for example, difficult problems arose in the contacts with the authorities of the *sancak* of Jerusalem, which was subordinate to the pasha of Damascus, but which was sometimes ruled directly from Istanbul. The problems were doubly severe because of the difficult economic situation of the Jewish communities in Palestine and the extensive support they received from the Jews of the Diaspora, which enabled the local authorities to put strong pressure on the Jewish population. An additional problem was the unstable administrative structure of the Ottoman Empire, in which local rulers frequently revolted and acted in the provinces as masters.

From the extensive correspondence in the *Pinkas* of Istanbul we learn about the nature of the ties with the authorities in Istanbul, with the authorities in Damascus and Sidon, and with the rulers of the districts in Palestine.[1]

The central authorities in Istanbul were interested in the establishment of a body of the type of the Istanbul Officials, as this assisted them in the collection of taxes and in the maintenance of peace in the Jewish communities of Palestine. Many of the officials of the government in Palestine—such as army commanders, Mufti, Mula,[2] Mütesellim,[3] and others—were appointed to their positions from Istanbul, and the Istanbul Officials came into contact with them before they left for their positions. The ties of the Istanbul Officials to the authorities in everything that was connected with the Palestine Jews thus had decisive weight in their practical domination of the affairs of the Jewish communities in Palestine.

Several of the activities of the Istanbul Officials were performed at the request of the Jewish communities in Palestine or of the local rulers there. For example, from time to time the residents of Jerusalem asked the Istanbul Officials to obtain *firmans* from the Sublime Porte for the settlement of their taxes and debts.[4] The Istanbul Officials also obtained *firmans* for the construction of public buildings in Jerusalem, such as synagogues and study-houses.[5] At the end of the 1730s Dahir al-ʿUmar turned to the Istanbul Officials with the request that they help him bring in Jews for the renewal of the Jewish settlement in Tiberias.

In other areas the Istanbul Officials took the initiative in turning to the authorities by such means as gifts and bribes to the government officials who had been appointed to various posts in Palestine and were about to set out.[6] With a few of the officials and army officers ties were formed even before their appointments became known, which helped at the time they left for Palestine. Obviously, the best way to establish ties was through bribery, which in the sources is called "gifts." At times the Istanbul Officials provided these officials and officers with letters of recommendation from the Sublime Porte and from "Sheik al-Islam" and took care to distribute these letters among the rulers of Palestine.[7]

Another area that brought the Istanbul Officials into contact with the authorities was immigration to Palestine, as the ships required licenses from the central government in order to set sail.

In their connections with the authorities the Istanbul Officials were assisted by the foreign embassies in Istanbul, particularly those of Austria and France. At the time of the crisis of the Ashkenazic community in Jerusalem at the beginning of the century they were helped by the services of the Austrian ambassador Von Dirling, and later on they were assisted by a "representative of the foreign nations," whose name was not always mentioned. They also benefited from the assistance of English and French merchants of the Levant companies.[8]

The Istanbul Officials also had strong ties with the courts of the pashas in Damascus and Sidon, and in this activity they were assisted by respected Jews who were close to the courts of the pashas, such as the families Farhi[9] and Lutzati in Damascus and Acre,[10] who were especially active during the war between Süleyman and Dahir al-ʿUmar, and the Asseo family in Sidon.[11]

The Istanbul Officials also maintained ties with the Christian churches in Istanbul, whose standing in the Ottoman Empire was similar. Their treatment of their congregants in Palestine also had a similar form. They had especially strong ties with the Armenian patriarchate, both in financial matters and in the transfer of mail to Palestine.[12]

This wide variety of connections may explain why not only respected and wealthy members of the community were chosen for the Istanbul Officials, but also businessmen with daily connections with the Sublime Porte in economic and other matters, such as the families Zonana,[13] Cammondo, Aluf, and Kimhi.[14]

ACTIVITIES IN THE COMMUNITIES OF THE DIASPORA

The committee of the Istanbul Officials was established for the purpose of collecting money in the Diaspora and transferring it to Palestine. In doing so it established connections with many communities in the Jewish world, both in the East and in the West, and it is thus worth examining the activities of this institution not only from the philanthropic standpoint, but also from the standpoint of the connections it established with the Jewish communities.

The activities of the Istanbul Officials in the communities of the Diaspora began in the area of organization. In order to facilitate the collection of funds, they appointed "officials for Eretz Israel" in these communities or asked them to appoint such officials, and thus increased the institutionalization of support for the Yishuv. These representatives, who received letters of recommendation from the Istanbul Officials, took care of the collection of donations for Eretz Israel in their regions and the transfer of this money to Istanbul.[15] At times the rabbis of the communities agreed to serve in this position, but in general it was the wealthy men who engaged in this, and their extensive influence in the community helped quite a bit in the collection of donations.

Even though the activities of the Istanbul Officials took place in all of the Jewish communities, Ashkenazi as well as Sephardi, their main power was in the areas of Turkey, the Balkans, and Italy. The territorial authority of the Istanbul Officials was defined in a letter of authorization given to them: "the cities of Rumelia [Greece] and Anatolia [Turkey], from the East and from the West, all the land of the Moslems [Arabs] until the cities of Yemen, from the Christian countries, Europe and its borders, until the remote islands."[16] As the distance from Istanbul became greater—whether from a geographical or a political standpoint (that is, countries that were not part of the Ottoman Empire)—the influence of the Istanbul Officials became smaller. From the sources—for example, the *Pinkas* of Istanbul—it appears that the Sephardi communities in Europe maintained a stronger connection with Istanbul than did the Ashkenazi communities.

The Istanbul Officials had an especially strong connection with the Jewish community in Izmir, one of the largest Jewish communities in the Ottoman Empire. In the middle of the 1740s the community numbered about 7,000 and played an important role in the economic life of the Ottoman Empire.[17] Between the Izmir community and the Jewish settlement in Palestine there were strong ties, which were expressed both in immigrations and in donations. The funds for Eretz Israel in Izmir were headed, at different times, by R. Isaac Hacohen Rapaport, R. Jacob Saul, and R. Abraham ben Ezra.[18] The Istanbul Officials even appointed the Jewish community in Izmir to the position of collecting the donations for Eretz Israel from the small communities in the region, and particularly from the surrounding islands.[19] During the eighteenth century there was a noticeable decline in the economic situation of the community, and this had a negative influence on the size of the donations for Eretz Israel and the procedures for their transfer.

The Istanbul Officials also had connections with the Jewish community of Edirne. The "officials for Eretz Israel" in this community were headed by R. Abraham Geron, the chief rabbi of the community.[20] At the head of the collections in Salonika and its surroundings were the rabbis of the community, R. Benveniste Getenio and R. Moses Amarillio.[21]

The Jewish communities in Arab lands also had strong ties with the Istanbul Officials. There were representatives of the Istanbul Officials in Egypt,[22] North Africa,[23] Aleppo,[24] Damascus,[25] Basra, Baghdad,[26] and Yemen.[27]

The Jewish communities of Italy donated a great deal of money, which was transferred to Palestine via the Istanbul Officials. In 1746 the Istanbul Officials appointed the merchant-banker Solomon Rakah of Venice to be an "official for Eretz Israel" and to be responsible for the transferral of the money that arrived from Germany. The document of appointment they sent him stated: "We, the Officials of the holy city of Jerusalem here in Istanbul . . . have appointed and authorized . . . Solomon Rakah . . . a fully authorized official . . . that we have given him from our estate and from the power which has been handed to us by all the rabbis and sages of the holy city of Jerusalem."[28]

In Leghorn members of the Franco family and other families were appointed as responsible for the collection of the funds.[29]

The Istanbul Officials also had connections with the Jewish community in Amsterdam, which did much for the Yishuv and for the yeshivas that its rich members had established in Palestine.[30] The money donated from Amsterdam was also transferred through the Istanbul Officials.

In their efforts to increase the support for the Yishuv the Istanbul Officials did not neglect even the smallest communities, such as Old Anatolia,[31] Larissa,[32] Tokat,[33] Bosnia,[34] Rodoscuk,[35] Gallipoli,[36] Borgaz,[37] and Iznimit.[38]

The Istanbul Officials also conducted a correspondence with the Ashkenazic communities in Europe.[39] Their representative in Europe was, as mentioned, Baron D'Aguilar of Vienna, who transferred to them the money he collected for the Ashkenazim in Palestine. The Istanbul Officials also received funds from the rabbis of central and eastern Europe—such as R. Ezekiel Landau of Prague and R. Jacob Landau of Tarnopol—and they even succeeded in collecting money for the Yishuv from as far away as North America.[40]

An extensive and controlled network of collecting money for Eretz Israel was thus created, the likes of which had never existed before. In spite of the problems that arose in the collection of the money it is possible to say that the establishment of the center in Istanbul enhanced both the mutual connections among the Jewish communities and their connections to the Jewish settlement in Palestine.

ORGANIZATION OF THE FUND-DRIVES

The Para *Fund-Drive*

The *para* fund-drive,[41] which was conducted by the Istanbul Officials at the beginning of their activity, was intended to collect one *para* once a week from each and every person in the communities of the Diaspora, including paupers who lived on a stipend from the community.[42] The collection of the *para* caused difficult problems throughout the period under discussion, and from time to time it was necessary to renew the regulation and to put pressure on the communities to collect the money for the fund-drive regularly.[43]

We have in our possession the text of the *para* regulation from the 1740s with the signatures of R. Isaac Behar David and R. Isaac Rozanes, members of the rabbinical court in Istanbul, which stated: "We, the undersigned, the rabbinical court, the patrons came to us . . . the Officials of the holy city of Jerusalem and they brought us bad news . . . troubles have befallen the holy city of Jerusalem and expenses have increased . . . they complain that most of the worthy men of the city [Istanbul] have closed their fists so as not to let the money out . . . often we have announced in the synagogues that they should pay what they owe from the assessment of the *para*."[44]

It seems that the fund-drive was not very successful, and in the end the Istanbul Officials turned it into a sort of tax on the whole community. The communities were responsible for the collection of the money from individuals, and they had to make up the difference from their own funds. We know, for example, that the Istanbul Officials imposed the *para* "tax" on the communities of Izmir[45] and Rodoscuk[46] precisely like the fixed yearly assessment.

The Fixed Yearly Assessment

In their attempt to increase the donations, in 1728 the Istanbul Officials imposed a yearly tax on all the Jewish communities in Turkey and the Balkans,[47] according to their economic situation and their size. The amount of the tax was fixed every ten years.[48] Not infrequently there were harsh disagreements between the Istanbul Officials and the various communities about the size of the assessment, and generally a compromise was achieved for a smaller sum than had been requested originally.[49]

In 1748 the Istanbul community donated the following amounts for the Jewish settlement in Palestine: 1,800 *kurus*—assessment, 2,000 *kurus*—*para* fund-drive, and 200 *kurus*—supplement, for a total of 4,000 *kurus*. The sums of the donations from Istanbul remained the same in 1773 as in 1748 and constituted about six percent of the debit in the budget of the community.[50]

The Jewish community of Izmir was generally requested to give about a quarter of the total amount paid by the Istanbul community; at first it paid 250 *kurus* per year, and later the sum was raised to 1,000 *kurus*.[51] On the smaller communities yearly taxes amounting to only tens of *kurus* were imposed.

Activity of the Istanbul Officials

The *Pinkas* of the Istanbul Officials includes many letters to the Jewish communities, both large and small, who had fallen behind in their payments, such as Leghorn;[52] Ankara;[53] Skopje;[54] Salonika;[55] Kandia, Kania, and Ritimo;[56] Nikopol, Buda, and Sofia;[57] Edirne;[58] Rodoscuk; Iznimit[59] and other small communities in Turkey;[60] Baghdad;[61] and first and foremost the Izmir community; "because they said that if the city of Izmir has turned its back on Israel . . . how will we gather strength to force the villages and the small towns [to pay]."[62]

There were undoubtedly objective reasons for the difficulties in the collection—such as the plague in Izmir,[63] the fires in Edirne[64] and Izmir,[65] earthquakes, economic decline—but it is also possible that the leadership of the communities did not accord the assessment sufficient importance. R. Haim David Azulay describes in his diary the difficulties in collecting the donations in the important Jewish communities of Italy, such as Mantua and Modena; the reasons were the difficult economic situation and the large number of emissaries.[66] Rabbi Azulay also encountered difficulties in the towns and villages of southern Germany. In many communities he was treated with great disrespect,[67] and in a few communities he was not even permitted to enter.

One-time Donations, Dedications, and Legacies

Individuals frequently gave large sums of money for the establishment of yeshivas in Palestine or for the various general funds. The initiative for these donations generally came from the Istanbul Officials, who also engaged in collecting them and concentrating them in Istanbul.[68] They usually lent out the money at interest and used the profits to support Torah scholars and communities of Torah scholars in Palestine. The goal of the Istanbul Officials was indeed the concentration of the support for the Yishuv, but they were not always successful, and frequently quarrels arose between them and the custodians of the money—both individuals and communities—in the matter of dedications and legacies.[69]

Another form of support for the Yishuv was the sending of clothes to the Jewish settlement in Palestine. For example, the Jews of Salonika sent clothing to their brothers in Jerusalem.[70]

The Istanbul Officials also supervised the budget of the Jerusalem community and demanded an itemized account of all its income and expenses.

COORDINATION OF THE CONCERNS OF
THE EMISSARIES

Sending and Supervising the Emissaries

Until the end of the 1720s the emissaries went to the Diaspora on the responsibility of the Jewish communities in Palestine,[71] but with the establishment of the Istanbul Officials a fundamental change occurred. One of the first activities of the Istanbul Officials was to impose supervision on the sending of emissaries. Thus an important economic power was taken away from the leaders of the Yishuv. From then on, only the Istanbul Officials had the authority to initiate the departure of an emissary to the Diaspora. They generally turned to the Palestine communities and asked them to send an appropriate person, but sometimes they also chose the candidate and even dictated the contents of the letters they supplied to the emissary.

The Istanbul Officials also set the criteria for the selection of the emissaries. For instance, they demanded from the rabbis of Jerusalem that the emissaries should be "worthy and respectable, good speakers, and they should be able to get along with people."[72] The Istanbul Officials also determined the area to which the emissary would be sent and coordinated between the emissaries of the various cities. Each emissary had to pass through Istanbul and be supplied with authorizations and recommendations from the Istanbul Officials, who also sent letters to the Jewish communities to inform them of the arrival of the emissary. On their way the emissaries often collected the money of the *para* fund-drive and the assessment, emptied the funds for Eretz Israel, and collected individual donations.

The choice of emissaries was very limited because many of the rabbis and Torah scholars in Jerusalem were old and did not want to go on missions, in spite of the income of the emissary, which was generally thirty percent of the sum collected. Many of them also shied away from the task because it involved separation from Palestine and from their families, dangers on the roads, wandering about on long journeys— sometimes for years—and also problems encountered in the various Jewish communities. This is probably the reason why there were often emissaries who went out two or three times on missions, such as, for example, R. Azulay and R. Haim Isaac Karigal.

Not all the emissaries returned from their missions. Often an emissary settled in one of the communities visited after being appointed rabbi there. The mission was a good opportunity to form ties with the various communities and to receive an appointment as rabbi. The arrival of an emissary from Palestine certainly increased his chances of receiving an appointment. In this way, R. Azulay was appointed rabbi of Leghorn, and R. Moses Israel was appointed rabbi of Rhodes. Sometimes the Jerusalem rabbis also took advantage of their missions in the Diaspora to publish their books there.

Besides the official emissaries frequently "emissaries for themselves" pretended to be emissaries of the communities but kept the money for themselves.[73]

In the eighteenth century more than 250 emissaries went to the Diaspora.[74] It seems that the first emissary sent by the Istanbul Officials was R. Moses Israel, the rabbi of Rhodes, who went out on his mission in 1727.[75] These emissaries came from the holy cities and from Kafr Yasif. Separate emissaries were also sent on behalf of the Ashkenazim in Jerusalem and on behalf of the various yeshivas in Jerusalem and Hebron. The emissaries were sent to almost every country, but most of them went to the rich Jewish communities in Germany and Italy. Many emissaries also visited Turkey, the Balkans, and North Africa. Only a few visited eastern Europe, Yemen, Egypt, and Kurdistan and neighboring countries.

The international situation had a great effect on the areas of the missions and on the routes of the emissaries. The wars in the East and in Europe prevented safe passage on the roads and affected the movements of the emissaries. Because of the Seven Years' War in the middle of the century Rabbi Azulay did not succeed in reaching the regions of the battles in Prussia.[76] The wars in Palestine and the battles between Russia and Turkey in the 1770s made it difficult for the emissaries to leave Palestine via Egypt or the port of Jaffa.[77]

Highwaymen also increased the dangers. R. Emanuel Hai Raphael Riki, an emissary for himself, was murdered in Italy.[78] And Rabbi Azulay tells in his diary of robbers who ambushed the caravan in which he was making his way from Palestine to Egypt.[79]

The supervision the Istanbul Officials imposed on the emissaries was very strict, as there were many complaints about their activities in the communities, their excessive profits, and the disorder of their account-books. It was therefore decided that on his return from his mission each emissary had to pass through Istanbul and present his account-books to the Officials.[80] We have evidence of the investigation of the accounts of the emissaries R. Nissim Berakha;[81] David Ashkenazi, who hurt the mission and led to the "destruction of Eretz Israel";[82] Elijah Zevi;[83] Yakir, the son of R. Abraham Gerson of Kuty; Jacob Ashkenazi;[84] and Mordecai Rovio.[85] We also have a letter in which the Jerusalem community is requested to refrain from sending any more emissaries on behalf of the yeshiva Yefa'er ʿAnavim, lest the patrons close it.[86]

At the end of the century the supervision over the emissaries was weakened, and many of them bypassed the Istanbul Officials.

The Influence of the Emissaries on the Jewish World

It is my opinion that the emissaries played no role in the great changes that occurred in the Jewish nation in the eighteenth century and that they had no influence on the various trends in the Jewish world. At the beginning of the century R. Moses Hagiz debated with the assimilationists in Amsterdam concerning their attitude toward Eretz Israel, but one cannot generalize from this event. Nevertheless the emissaries did intervene in several controversies that were raging in the European Jewish world, particularly between the remnants of the Sabbateans and their persecutors. This intervention came about at the request of both sides in the controversy, each of which had used the name of Eretz Israel in order to strengthen its position. A good example is the controversy aroused by R. Moses Haim Luzzatto.

A second controversy in which emissaries from Palestine were involved occurred in the middle of the century between R. Jacob Emden and R. Jonathan Eybeschütz, who was also suspected of Sabbateanism. It is interesting that the three emissaries from Palestine involved in the controversy—among them R. Haim Yeruham Vilna, the son of R. Jacob Vilna—all supported Rabbi Eybeschütz. As a result Rabbi Emden heaped abuse on the emissaries and called for caution in the giving of donations to Eretz Israel.[87]

In the days of the growth of Hasidism in eastern Europe almost no emissaries visited there because of the difficult economic situation of the Jewish communities in Poland, and the few emissaries who reached the area did not take part in the battles between the Hasidim and their opponents, the Mithnagdim. Only after the Hasidic immigration of 1777 did the number of emissaries who visited that region increase.

The emissaries also did not intervene in the Enlightenment movement that had begun to grow in Germany in the second half of the eighteenth century. In general they were satisfied to collect the donations and ignored the beginnings of the disintegration of the Jewish communities in Germany.

The slight role of the emissaries in shaping the image of the Jewish world derived not only from the fact that they were not always great enough for their intervention to be justified, but probably also from their wish to avoid entanglement, as their goal was the collection of the money.

The emissaries did intervene occasionally in the daily life of the communities, particularly in the settling of local quarrels, but it nevertheless cannot be said that they had a real influence on the community life.[88] One of the important contributions of the emissaries was that they brought with them information about the lives of the other communities of the Diaspora. They also distributed books and Torah teachings and strengthened the connection between the Jewish settlement in Palestine and the Jewish communities in the Diaspora.

SUPERVISION OF THE IMMIGRATIONS TO PALESTINE

The good organizational arrangements of immigration to Palestine from the end of the 1730s led to an unprecedented rush of ordinary folk, among them many elderly people, who tried to take advantage of the hiring of boats by the Istanbul Officials to get to Palestine. The Istanbul Officials were afraid that a large, uncontrolled immigration of poor people without any financial support would create another crisis in the Jerusalem community, and so they began to supervise and thus regulate the immigration. Their first step was to require that the immigrants furnish a written obligation from their relatives in the Diaspora to send them yearly support, whether directly or through the Istanbul Officials.[89] At the appropriate time the Istanbul Officials turned to these relatives and importuned them to pay the stipend on time, but often the families refused to continue the support.[90]

When the immigrant did not furnish an obligation, the Istanbul Officials tried to prevent his or her immigration, but they did not always manage to do this, and many immigrants succeeded in entering Palestine without this obligation.[91] At times, when the number of poor immigrants increased and the financial situation was particularly bad, the Istanbul Officials prevented the boats from setting out and froze immigration to Palestine.[92]

When an immigrant had property, he or she would leave a fund with the Istanbul Officials, and the interest on the money would serve for his or her sustenance in Palestine. Therefore the Istanbul Officials also paid the taxes that the immigrant was required to pay to the Jewish community in Palestine, including burial taxes. This arrangement did not include the payment of the head tax in Palestine. With the death of the immigrant the deposit—or part of it—became community property; the rest of it was given to the heirs.[93]

Poorer immigrants, who were not able to leave a fund, received an exemption from the payment of taxes in exchange for 50–100 *kurus* per person. The Istanbul Officials worked hard to increase the amounts of the funds; from wealthy immigrants they collected hundreds and even thousands of *kurus* per person.[94] A good example is that of an elderly couple who left a fund of 1,500 *kurus* at an interest rate of nine percent; it was agreed that the couple would receive a stipend of 140 *kurus* yearly, and in the event of the death of the husband the wife would receive 80 *kurus* per year.[95] We have evidence of funds of 5,000 to 10,000 *kurus* and even more, and of interest rates of seven to nine percent.[96]

Every year the Istanbul Officials transferred the money to Jerusalem, accompanied by a list of the immigrants and the stipends that each was to receive, with detailed instructions concerning when to pay out the money.[97]

At that time there was indeed a marked improvement in the support for the immigrants, but it seems that this was not sufficient. At any rate, in 1750 the Istanbul Officials initiated a most important regulation in the area of immigration to Palestine, the "regulation of the payment for the immigration license," which was intended to regulate the immigration and increase the income of the Jerusalem community. According to this regulation every immigrant to Palestine from the port cities of Turkey and Greece had to pay ten *kurus* for an immigration license to the Istanbul Officials for taking care of his immigration.[98] Every year several boats full of immigrants and pilgrims set sail from Istanbul, Izmir, Salonika, and other places, and so the new regulation brought in a substantial income. The first information we have about this tax is included in a letter sent in May 1750 from Jerusalem to Istanbul, in which the regulation is authorized.[99] The regulation is also mentioned in other letters. For example, the Istanbul Officials informed the Jewish community of Salonika that they should collect the tax as the sages and officials of Jerusalem had established it.[100] The Istanbul Officials also sent letters to the Jewish community in Salonika in the matter of the payment for the immigration license, but they missed the collection of 1750, as the boat from Izmir had already set sail.[101] In 1760 the tariff for immigrants from Izmir was raised to twenty *kurus* per person, as the Izmir community had decreased its contributions to Jerusalem and had not fulfilled its obligations.[102]

The increase in the number of immigrants created difficulties in the collection of the tax. The Jews of Salonika wanted to show mercy to the immigrants, most of whom were poor people, and to exempt them from paying the tax. The Istanbul Officials opposed this strongly with the argument that if immigrants did not have the ten *kurus* for the payment of the tax, they would also not be able to support themselves in Palestine. In the end they ruled that any person who did not have a receipt for paying the tax in the Diaspora would have to pay twice the amount when he or she disembarked at the Palestine port. At the same time they allowed the Salonika community to pay the tax from its community fund.[103]

In Jaffa the Istanbul Officials appointed Solomon Gabbai to be responsible for matters relating to the tax, and they instructed him to check the receipts and to collect the taxes and the fines from those who had not paid before their departure.[104] After some time they asked the Jerusalem Officials to fire him, because he took advantage of his position to collect excessive sums.[105]

The tax was also imposed on the Karaites who immigrated to Palestine from Istanbul, and its collection also created difficulties.[106]

We can deduce the number of immigrants and pilgrims from the income derived from the tax. In 1755 the Izmir community transferred the sum of 1,100 *kurus* to the Istanbul Officials from the collection of the immigration tax for 1754, that is, in that year there were 110 immigrants from Izmir alone.[107] In 1760 two hundred immigrants went to Palestine from Istanbul, mostly poor people who did not pay the immigration tax, and the Istanbul Officials paid it for them. Many of them did not have enough money for the expenses of the journey, and the Istanbul Officials were afraid an increase in their number would lead to extortions and bans on the part of the rulers of Jerusalem.[108] According to the evidence of R. Simha of Zalozce, in 1764 as well about two hundred immigrants went to Palestine from Istanbul,[109] and that was the situation almost every year.

Part IV
JEWISH COMMUNITIES IN PALESTINE

11
THE JEWISH COMMUNITY OF JERUSALEM AND ITS LEADERSHIP

HISTORY OF THE JERUSALEM COMMUNITY

In the second half of the seventeenth century the Jerusalem community was the largest and the most important of the Jewish communities in Palestine, after the decline of the center in Safed and the destruction of the Tiberias community. In Hebron and in the villages as well, especially in the Galilee, there were only small Jewish communities.[1]

The centrality of Jerusalem in the second half of the seventeenth century was reflected in the large number of its great sages, such as R. Jacob Hagiz, R. Hezekiah de-Silva, R. Moses ben Haviv, and R. David Itzhaki. These sages, whose influence went beyond the borders of Palestine, were concentrated around the yeshiva Beth Jacob founded by the Vega family, which was the spiritual center of the community.

In the city there were three communities with separate organizational frameworks. The Ashkenazi community numbered a few hundred and the Karaites numbered only a few dozen, whereas the central community—which is called *kollel* in Jewish sources—was that of the Sephardim.

The crisis brought about in Judaism by Sabbateanism was not particularly noticed in Jerusalem, as most of the sages of the city opposed Sabbetai Zevi and his teachings. Nevertheless there was a trace of a controversy among the sages of the community at the end of the century.[2]

At the end of the seventeenth century there was a great decline in the Jerusalem community, especially from a spiritual viewpoint. In the 1690s many of the sages of the city died, apparently from the great plague that had broken out there.[3] The Jerusalem doctor R. Raphael Mordecai Malkhi, the author of a Torah commentary, wrote: "And now in the year 5458 of the creation [1698] the land has been almost completely destroyed. There was a Torah scholar who dreamed that 36 sages would die, and so it was. And within another two years even more than that number died, and the land has been left without any Torah scholars."[4]

The yeshiva Beth Jacob disbanded—apparently because the water pipes were stopped up[5]—and at the start of the eighteenth century the Jerusalem community was deprived of its sages and open to extortions by the local rulers, who succeeded one another at frequent intervals and often incited the residents to revolt.[6]

We possess a number of descriptions of the changes that occurred in the community at the end of the seventeenth century. R. Isaac Hacohen Rapaport, who lived in Jerusalem in his youth, wrote: "There were never such good days for the Jews who lived in Jerusalem as the days in which the Jews were at peace. . . . Happy is the eye that saw the great study-house of the Talmud . . . everything has disintegrated, until lamentations remain in Jerusalem."[7]

In a letter that was sent through the Jerusalem emissary R. Moses Sasportas, R. David Itzhaki, R. Moses Hagiz, and others told about the troubles of the community at the end of the seventeenth century:

> Trouble upon trouble, and distress after distress, there is no moment free from affliction . . . our holy city has gone down a slope of disasters, it owes the Gentiles the sum of 25,000 *kurus* . . . a new trouble that has arisen in the past five years at the command of his majesty, the king, on all the lands in his reign is to change the value of head-tax . . . and every person must pay five and a half *kurus* . . . even though the holy community loses more than two hundred *kurus* every year in bribes so that they will not be punished . . . and so, for our sins, some of us are killed by them, and the lives of many people depend on this, besides the many different kinds of damages within this disaster.[8]

The Beginning of the Eighteenth Century and the Decline in the Wake of the Immigration of R. Judah Hasid

The arrival of hundreds of immigrants[9] in Jerusalem at the beginning of the eighteenth century changed the structure of the Ashkenazi community in the city, which was, as mentioned, not particularly large and which since the end of the seventeenth century had been confronted with many economic difficulties.

The arrival of such a large group of Sabbateans did not arouse great enthusiasm in the community. In a letter written in 1704 R. David

Oppenheim, the rabbi of Prague, thanked the Ashkenazi leaders in Jerusalem for their suggestion that he serve as Ashkenazi rabbi of Jerusalem. Rabbi Oppenheim, who had offered much assistance to the Ashkenazi community in Jerusalem, attacked mainly the Sabbateans (apparently the extremists) who arrived with Rabbi Hasid's group and the severe controversy that they aroused in Jerusalem. This had caused the discontinuation of support for the community, and the Sabbateans had to be excommunicated. He wrote: "My heart is sad to hear this news, why there is such a loud outcry in the city. . . . The rich men in all the Jewish communities . . . are closing their fists in order not to contribute . . . to those people who act with contempt . . . and even in public turn the days of mourning for the destruction of the Temple into holidays . . . and they do not observe the customs of mourning."[10]

But in addition to their reservations about the Sabbateanism of the immigrants, the community had serious fears about their shaky economic and social situation. Indeed, these fears soon proved quite well founded. The members of Rabbi Hasid's group had in fact secured for themselves systematic financial support from the European Jewish communities before their immigration, but when they arrived in Palestine the immigrants needed a large amount of money for renting apartments, for buying food and other necessities for daily living, and for paying taxes and bribes to the local authorities. The money from Europe did not arrive on time, and the immigrants found it necessary to borrow large sums of money from moneylenders, mainly Moslems, who charged very high interest. When the arrival of the money was delayed, the creditors began to dun the Sephardi community as well. The Ashkenazi and the Sephardi communities were actually run separately, but the creditors understood that they had to put pressure on the Sephardi leadership if they wanted to get their money. The leaders of the Sephardi community were young and inexperienced,[11] and there was much friction among them. It is also known that there were incidents of embezzlement and corruption in the leadership, and the matter even went as far as informing the local authorities.[12] During the first decade of the century the heads of the Sephardi community were arrested, and many people—including important rabbis—were forced to leave the city for fear of the authorities and because of the great poverty. In the first year of the century there was great chaos in Jerusalem in the wake of the battles between the Ottomans and the local ruler, and this increased the suffering of all residents of the city.[13]

The Sabbatean core in Rabbi Hasid's group soon broke up, and many of them went back to the Diaspora as official emissaries or emissaries for themselves and did not return. Others were driven out of the city because of their overt support of Sabbateanism or fled the city during the crisis. There were even some who converted to Islam or Christianity or went to Mannheim in Germany, where there was a study-house for Sabbateans.

R. Abraham Rovigo's group had a different character, even though it also had clear Sabbatean motives.[14] This was a small group, which joined the Sephardi community. We do not have any information on conversions within this group, and it seems that they were more moderate Sabbateans. Besides, Rabbi Rovigo was sent out several times as an emissary on behalf of the Sephardi community in Jerusalem[15] (apparently they were unaware of his Sabbatean beliefs).

When the severe economic crisis erupted after the death of Rabbi Hasid, attempts began within the Yishuv itself, in Istanbul, and in the European Jewish communities to rescue the Jerusalem community. Dozens of emissaries were sent to the communities of Europe and the Ottoman Empire,[16] and the large sums of money that were collected eased the pressure somewhat.[17] However, there was no fundamental improvement, and in the second decade of the century the crisis in the community became even more severe. Here is evidence from that period: "They have laid it [the city] waste like a stream of burning sulphur; because it was burning half the city has gone into exile and their king [leaders] in front of them."[18]

In a document describing the situation at the beginning of the eighteenth century we read:

There is serious trouble at the time of burning . . . and their land, which is their inheritance, has been given over in this bitter and bad exile to harsh masters and all its cities are their dwelling-places. At the decree of the king . . . the righteous have gone to their reward, they have gone to their rest in Paradise and left the remainder in anger and fury and reproofs, to be slaves in the land of their captivity . . . the poor nation that dwells in Zion [suffers] from the burden of the king and the enemies. They have put tax-collectors over them in order to torture them in their sufferings. A cruel nation which will not give account to anyone . . . and they have flayed them alive and carried them in their [shirts?]. From day to day and from month to month they have established new restrictions . . . and a mob has come upon those who from poverty and want have been forced to borrow at interest from the strong ones of the land and the crawlers in the dust, at forty percent, which is like the bite of a snake . . . and when they saw that there was no more money and they were not able to collect their debts they punished them and the leaders of the Jews were put in irons. An arrow pierced their souls; suddenly they were beating them. The Jews were oppressed as they saw that the suffering had increased greatly. They have put bars on their houses and locked their doors. . . . They have come into the streets of the city and God has sent them out from their land. And the news arrived that the flock of God had been captured and the daughter of Zion had been left like a hut in a vineyard. . . . This was in the year 5471 [1711].[19]

The situation in the Sephardi community in Jerusalem was also worsening, and intensive efforts were undertaken in the Istanbul community to ease the pressure. In 1711 a special fund-drive was announced, and the first steps were taken for the establishment of the Committee of Officials for Palestine in Istanbul.[20]

Among the people who strove to save the Jerusalem community were R. David Oppenheim, R. Samson Wertheim, and Berman Segal. In a letter sent by the sages of Safed to Segal, the connection with R. Wertheim and with Segal in previous years was mentioned explicitly: "And the strength of the actions that this distinguished person is performing, both in his holy camp, to provide sufficient income for the Torah scholars and the great sages in his study-house, . . . and also with the Askhenazi community in the holy city of Jerusalem, with His wings may he protect them and give them strength and salvation as the hand of God is on him for good."[21]

The efforts in Europe to save the Jerusalem community were concentrated mainly in the communities of Vienna, Prague, Metz, Breslau, and Venice. Large sums of money were collected, but they were not transferred to their destination because of the difficulties in the execution of the "agreement" with the creditors at the beginning of the second decade of the century. The efforts to achieve the "agreement" were performed by persons in the Istanbul community who were close to the court of the sultan, with Joseph the physician at their head, as is attested by his correspondence with Rabbi Wertheim and the community leaders in Europe from 1711 to 1717.[22] At the beginning of this decade Joseph the physician succeeded in achieving a draft of an "agreement," but in the end the matter failed. In his last letter[23] Joseph the physician laid the blame on the European communities, which did not succeed in mobilizing the enormous sum of 60,000 *reichstaler* (about 60,000 *kurus*). The situation became more and more severe, and the Jerusalem sages sensed that ruin was to be expected, as appears from two letters that were sent from Jerusalem in 1717 and 1719. This is what was written in a letter that was sent to the emissary R. Joseph Barki in 1717: "But what shall we do for our sister [Jerusalem] . . . when God will speak to her in His anger and fury and will make them like the dust to be trodden with an earthen vessel . . . and her foundations will be destroyed and the Jews will be eaten by every mouth . . . because the flock of God has been captured, some will be killed by the sword and some will be taken into harsh captivity."[24]

In a letter to the emissary R. Yekutiel David in 1719 they wrote:

> that Jerusalem . . . is bereft of her veil, like a burned ship and a person pushed into a corner . . . and the traitor has betrayed and the robber has robbed and the oppression is cursed, and they have stretched out their hands [to beg], from the suckling to the infant, and all the Jews are groaning and crying. . . . Moreover . . . the officer who is the enemy of the land stands over us in anger and fury to despoil us. . . . For our troubles have increased and all the inhabitants of the land are finished because there is no more money. It is a generation of only poor people and the land is the pasha's, the roads of Zion are mourning because of the fury of the oppressor and the intrigues of the wicked and the spirit of confusion . . . our debts to the Gentiles have exceeded 25,000 *kurus* . . . and there is great mourning in Jerusalem because of these wicked men . . . we fear that the wicked will continue in their wickedness . . . and Jerusalem will be taken away from the Jews and there are no words in our language to mourn this.[25]

All the efforts to save the Ashkenazi community came to naught. In November 1720 the creditors burned the Ashkenazi court and its synagogue, and the Ashkenazi community was dispersed. Ruin was also in store for the Sephardi community.

The Years of Decline

The years 1720–26, between the destruction of the Ashkenazi court and the establishment of the Istanbul Officials, were years of decline. The leadership of the Jerusalem community had disintegrated, as some leaders were arrested and some fled to safety, and the Jews of the city were faced with a severe economic and social crisis.

During the years of the crisis many of the sages of Jerusalem were forced to leave the city. There were some who went to the Diaspora as emissaries and did not return. One of these was R. Ephraim Navon, who settled in Istanbul and who together with the other rabbis of the city was active in the establishment of the Committee of Officials for Jerusalem in Istanbul. His son Judah, who returned to Palestine, described his father's departure from Jerusalem in 1720 in these words: "And half of the city went into exile . . . and he alone remained from the rest of the giants, carrying the burden of the community . . . and he could not bear the toil of the traitorous time . . . and he got up and left."[26]

In the 1720s additional disasters occurred to the Jerusalem community. In 1722 the city was attacked by a severe drought, and in 1723 a new ruler arrived from Istanbul, who made many false accusations and extorted much money.[27] For example, he demanded a payment of 91,000 *kurus* from the community within ninety-one days and arrested the community official R. Moses Meyuhas. The community quickly sent his grandson, R. Raphael Meyuhas Bechar Samuel—later chief rabbi of the city—to Istanbul on a rescue mission. With the assistance of the rich men of Istanbul the emissary succeeded in influencing the central authorities to arouse the mercy of the ruler.[28]

These years saw intensive activity in Istanbul in an attempt to rescue the Jerusalem community from its severe crisis, and in the wake of these activities the Committee of Officials for Jerusalem in Istanbul was finally established.

The Rehabilitation of the Community

In the middle of the 1730s and in the 1740s the Yishuv grew, thanks to the activities of the Istanbul Officials, whose influence on the leadership of the community became increasingly strong. Instead of one official, three or four officials now took care of financial matters. Many new regulations were also established.

In the 1750s and 1760s there were already established patterns, and the administration was conducted in a standard way. During this period a stronger leadership arose in Jerusalem, with the official Rahamim Hacohen at its head, who was trusted by the Istanbul Officials and the Turkish authorities in Jerusalem. Hacohen enjoyed the support of Raphael Meyuhas, the chief rabbi of Jerusalem, who was also a strong personality with much influence in Jerusalem and in the Jewish community of Istanbul. This had paradoxical results, it seems, because in spite of the basic dependence on the Istanbul Officials, who explicitly supported these two men, the autonomy of the leadership in Jerusalem increased.

The forcefulness of the leadership aroused opposition, headed by several officials who did not accept the authority of Hacohen, and also several Torah scholars—apparently youths[29]—who complained against the authority of the chief rabbi and his associates. The quarrels in the leadership of the community became sharper, and there were frequent dismissals and counterdismissals. The intervention of the Istanbul Officials did not always help, and the controversy even reached the courts of the gentiles and led to arrests. In the 1760s the community was divided into two camps, and many people fled the city, among them R. Haim Joseph David Azulay.[30]

At the end of the sixties and in the seventies the status of the householders and the Torah scholars became stronger, and they were allowed to join the leadership.

THE LEADERSHIP OF THE JERUSALEM COMMUNITY

In the seventeenth century the leadership of the Jewish community in Jerusalem was similar to that of the other Jewish communities in the Ottoman Empire. It is true that the Jerusalem community's budget—like that of the other holy cities—was financed by the Jewish communities of the Diaspora, but it nevertheless had an independent leadership, headed by rabbis and laymen-officials. The organizational life of the community was concentrated around the synagogues of the immigrants from different parts of the Diaspora, mostly Sephardim and Ashkenazim with a few Italian and Mugrabi Jews.[31]

During the second half of the seventeenth century the standing of the rabbis in the leadership of the community became much stronger, first and foremost because well-known rabbis with spiritual authority were concentrated in the city. In the last years of the seventeenth century many of these rabbis died—for example, R. Hezekiah de-Silva, R. Moses ben Haviv, and R. Jacob Hagiz—and the leadership of the community declined. Their place in the community leadership was filled by young rabbis whose authority was not as great.[32]

In the wake of the crisis in the Ashkenazi community at the beginning of the eighteenth century many of the rabbis who had remained in the city then left it. Some of them—for example, R. Haim Abulafia—went to other cities in Palestine, mainly Safed. This phenomenon was the reverse of what had occurred in the seventeenth century, when many of the sages of Safed went to Jerusalem. Others left for the Diaspora and served in the rabbinate of important communities. Thus, for example, R. Isaac Hacohen Rapaport was appointed rabbi of Izmir, and R. Moses Israel was appointed rabbi of Rhodes.[33] Yet others went to the Diaspora as emissaries and did not return. During the twenty years after the immigration of R. Judah Hasid the community leadership was bereft of important personalities. The attempt to offer the position of rabbi of the Ashkenazi community of Jerusalem to R. David Oppenheim of Prague, a wealthy man and a well-known Torah scholar, did not succeed.[34]

In the wake of the disintegration of the leadership the importance of the Istanbul Officials and their patrons increased. Not only did they control the money that was sent to Palestine, but also they formed ties with the authorities and began to capture first place in community leadership. The rabbis and community leaders in Palestine and the Diaspora were very angry about the embezzlements by some of the officials in the beginning of the eighteenth century and about their arbitrariness in their division of the funds.[35]

After 1721 only an impoverished Sephardi community without any leadership and a few unorganized Ashkenazi Jews remained in Jerusalem.[36] The few that remained tried to save whatever they could, and to this end they turned to the Istanbul community,[37] which responded to them and began to concentrate the collection of money on behalf of Eretz Israel from all parts of the Diaspora. Indeed, the leaders of the Jerusalem community were aware of the fact that the Istanbul Officials had saved Jerusalem from ruin:

> Our brothers, who have redeemed us, the rabbis and officials of the Jewish community in Istanbul have given their attention to repairing the destroyed altar of God.[38]

> They have entered deeply into the matter to fence in the breach . . . the crown has been restored to its former condition.[39]

> The officers of Judah and the leaders of the nation . . . who are in the important Jewish community of Istanbul, . . . God has aroused . . . so that they acted and succeeded in benefiting Jerusalem and putting her first in the land.[40]

Within a few years the Istanbul Officials succeeded in rehabilitating the community, gaining control over most of the affairs of the Jerusalem leadership. They were the ones who appointed the local officials, intervened in the appointment of the chief rabbi, staffed the yeshivas that were established in the city, established regulations, conducted negotiations with the authorities, and supervised the collection of taxes, the budget, and the immigrations. In practice, very little authority was left to the leadership of the Jerusalem community.

It is true that the rabbis of Jerusalem still had authority in matters of Halakha and in the appointment of religious officials—for example, ritual slaughterers[41]—but even in these matters the Istanbul Officials did not hesitate to intervene. Nevertheless some space remained for the rabbis to have a few independent activities.

The great influence of the Istanbul Officials derived not only from the fact that the Istanbul community had saved the Jerusalem community from its severe financial situation, but also from the frequent changes in the social composition of the Jews of Jerusalem. Many of them arrived in Jerusalem in their old age and died soon after their arrival, whereas those who were born in the city were often forced to leave it for economic and security reasons. As a result a stable leadership of stature did not arise in the community, and patterns of leadership did not crystallize.[42] That the community included Jews coming from different parts of the Diaspora and that besides the controversies about the support from the Diaspora there were also many controversies about customs and traditions also contributed to the lack of unity. For these reasons the Istanbul Officials succeeded in gaining control over the Jerusalem community without arousing fundamental opposition. Moreover, this control was even accepted gratefully. From time to time differences of opinion did, of course, arise between the Istanbul Officials and the Jerusalem community, but in the end the Jerusalem community generally followed the instructions of Istanbul.

The influence of the Istanbul Officials on the Jerusalem community was expressed on two principal planes: first, strict supervision of the funds that were sent to Jerusalem and rigorous inspection of the activities and accounts of the emissaries to the Diaspora; and second, the organization of the Jerusalem community itself and the appointment of officeholders. Besides, the Istanbul Officials took care to obtain a power of attorney from the people of Jerusalem, by which the latter authorized them to conduct all the affairs of the community. In a letter that they sent to the rabbis of Jerusalem in 1746 the Istanbul Officials reported the selection of new Officials for Jerusalem in Istanbul and gave these officials power of attorney. The Jerusalem rabbis and officials were obliged to sign this document, but their signing was only a formality. In this

power of attorney the relationship between the Istanbul Officials and the
leadership of the Jerusalem community, and the authority and tasks of
the Istanbul Officials, were only a formality. In this power of attorney the
relationship between the Istanbul Officials and the leadership of the
Jerusalem community, and the authority and tasks of the Istanbul Officials, were specified with rigorous precision. Among other things, they
wrote:

> Without the slightest hint of duress we appointed and permitted these seven
> men to be totally authorized . . . to supervise all our affairs, to conduct our
> business, to direct the communities of our city . . . and without their permis-
> sion no one is to do anything. . . . [Everyone must] accept their discipline
> . . . and obey all their agreements both in matters of the expenses of the city
> in taxes to the king and the officers . . . and in other expenses and the pay-
> ments to creditors . . . and in the arrangement of the income of the holy city
> and its collection.[43]

This document of appointment has great importance as a historical
source. We learn from it that the authority of the Istanbul Officials in
financial and administrative matters was very extensive and included supervision of the ongoing activities of the Jerusalem community, including the payment of debts and taxes to the authorities and to the
community. It seems that in the eighteenth century the Jerusalem community turned into a kind of branch of the Istanbul community, and its
leadership only carried out the instructions from Istanbul. Moreover, the
influence of the Istanbul Officials was not confined to political direction
but was sometimes extended to include the realm of application.

From the *Pinkas* of the Istanbul Officials it is difficult to discover the
exact nature of the relations between the Istanbul Officials and the
Jerusalem leadership, as only one side is reflected in it. There is reason to
assume that activities approved by the Istanbul Officials are not reflected
in the *Pinkas*. The style and content of the letters that the Istanbul Officials sent to Jerusalem show that in spite of the authority of the Istanbul
Officials there was almost continuous conflict between the two sides,
which probably arose from the difference between the approach of the
initiators of the policies and the approach of the executors, who saw the
daily requirements from close up and were not prepared to obey blindly.
It is clear that the Jerusalem leadership did not protest in principle against
the authority of the Istanbul Officials to decide organizational and finan-

cial matters in Jerusalem, but the local leaders were often forced to act on their own because of the pressure of time. At any rate, throughout the eighteenth century the Istanbul Officials complained that the Jerusalem community disobeyed instructions or acted irregularly. The complaints of the Istanbul Officials were mainly in two areas: the conduct of community affairs,[44] and corruption among the officials and the community workers, and even among the Torah scholars.

It is worth mentioning that the complaints in the first area do not always attest to disorders, but rather point to the different priorities of the two sides because of the differences in their policies. Thus, for example, the Istanbul Officials complained about the waste of public money in building various structures without sufficient coverage or guarantees, such as the building of R. Raphael Emanuel Hai Riki's home. In one of the letters the Istanbul Officials reprimanded the Jerusalem leadership for its attempt to build another synagogue at a time when its budget barely sufficed for ongoing expenses.[45] Another example of waste in the eyes of the Istanbul Officials was a payment of 500 *kurus* to the local ruler in an attempt to fix a wall in Rachel's tomb.[46]

The Istanbul Officials complained bitterly about the people of Jerusalem because they did not invest their money in the community, but preferred to lend it to the gentiles because of the security of the investment.[47] They reprimanded the Jerusalem officials mainly because they lent the money to the community at exorbitant interest rates. For example, Elijah Rolo gave the community a loan at fifteen percent interest, even though according to the Istanbul Officials the accepted interest was twelve percent.[48] Rahamim Hacohen wanted to lend the community 4,000 *kurus* at an interest rate of ten percent, while the Istanbul Officials claimed that the accepted rate was only seven percent.[49]

The Istanbul Officials also complained about the faulty treatment of legacies.[50] During this period (from the 1740s to the 1770s) the collection of taxes also was not conducted properly,[51] and the community paid the head tax for some members of the community, in opposition to the instructions from Istanbul.[52] In this as well one can see an expression of the differences of approach between the Jerusalem residents and the Istanbul Officials.

The Istanbul Officials raised strong complaints about the community budget: it was not balanced, and the deficit was increasing.[53] According to the Istanbul Officials the expenses of the community were exorbitant, the administrative staff was inflated, and the salaries of the officials and the community workers were too high.[54] They also complained that the account-books were not kept properly and that the officials were taking loans from the Moslems and the Christians at high rates of interest in the secure knowledge that the Istanbul Officials would pay the debts, and in a sarcastic tone they added that they did not have a printing-house for printing money to pay the exorbitant expenses of the Jerusalem residents.[55]

There is much evidence concerning deficits in the funds, sometimes due to embezzlement, but in general it is hard to determine who was to blame.[56] It seems that one of the causes was the exorbitant interest that the community paid the officials for the loans it took from them.

Frequently the Istanbul Officials were forced to threaten resignation[57] in order to put pressure on the Jerusalem leadership to accept their views, and it seems that this threat was really effective. It even happened that the Istanbul Officials stopped their activities for some time.[58] The threats of resignation generally arose when the debts of the Jerusalem community increased and the Istanbul Officials had difficulty in collecting the required funds.

The Istanbul Officials did not express the same attitude to the various groups in the Jerusalem leadership. When they turned to the chief rabbi they expressed honor and respect, even though they sometimes addressed him aggressively. Their attitude to the officials was more authoritative, as we see from the letters in the *Pinkas*. Nevertheless they did not relate equally to all the officials. This probably depended on the personality of the official and his status in the Jerusalem community.

In the quarrels that broke out among the various groups in the Jerusalem community the Istanbul Officials generally acted diplomatically. In the Istanbul *Pinkas* one can find almost identical letters that were written on the same day to several factors in Jerusalem. The fine differences between one letter and the next attest to the great caution with which the Istanbul Officials treated situations of this type. For example, they wrote four almost identical letters concerning the deficit in the budget: one to R. Isaac Hacohen Rapaport, the second to "the elders and patrons and leaders of Jerusalem," the third to the rabbis of Jerusalem, and the fourth to the Jerusalem Officials.[59] When news of quarrels was received—generally after much delay because of the mail difficulties— the Istanbul Officials tried first of all to ascertain the facts and to get information from objective sources in Jerusalem, as each side blamed the other in their letters, and without independent sources it was impossible to discover the truth. At times the Istanbul Officials needed to make use of their own information network in Jerusalem in order to obtain an objective report. From time to time delegations went from Jerusalem to Istanbul to explain what was happening,[60] and at times important people were sent from Istanbul—such as Jacob Zonana, one of the community leaders in Istanbul—in order to report on the situation in Jerusalem.

In the eighteenth century there were four centers of power in the Jerusalem community: (1) the officials and community workers, (2) the chief rabbi, (3) the rabbis and Torah scholars in the yeshivas, and (4) the householders. The fact that the Jerusalem community existed mainly on donations from the Diaspora led to a great amount of centralization in its leadership and to the ambition of all the groups to become part of it in order to benefit from the sources of income. Indeed, later the community leadership was extended, and two rabbis and householders joined the officials.

The Officials

This group, which was the ruling group in the community leadership in the eighteenth century, drew its power from the Istanbul Officials. They granted it wide authority and gave it great responsibility, especially in contacts with the Turkish authorities in the city and control of the community funds, both of the donations that arrived from the Diaspora and the legacies and of taxes that the community collected.

A short time after the establishment of the Committee of Officials for Jerusalem in Istanbul in 1726, an official—apparently Joshua Calev[61]—was sent to conduct the material affairs of the community, but within a short time the number of officials reached three or four.

In the 1740s there were three officials in Jerusalem: Meir Benveniste, Elijah Rolo, and Joseph Tzalmona.[62] In the fifties there were four: Rahamim Hacohen, Elijah Samnun, Dr. Isaac de-Bilasco, and Abraham Alhadef.[63] In the sixties there were only three: Abraham Bechar Menahem, Isaiah Isaac Shani, and Ezra Papula.[64]

The officials were not elected, but were appointed by the Istanbul Officials. We have in our possession the document of appointment of Rahamim Hacohen,[65] one of the most important officials in Jerusalem in the eighteenth century, who was appointed in 1754. He not only benefited from a particularly sympathetic attitude on the part of the Istanbul Officials and was accepted by the local authorities but also succeeded in gaining the trust of the chief rabbi and most of the rabbis of Jerusalem.[66] Nevertheless he threatened more than once to turn to the gentile courts and to hand people over to the local authorities.[67]

There were officials who served all their lives without being elected, which was very different from what was customary at the time in most of the Jewish communities in Europe and the Ottoman Empire. Generally well-to-do Jews, who also donated or lent money to the community, were appointed as officials in Jerusalem. Rolo had business dealings in Turkey,[68] and Hacohen had business dealings in Izmir.[69] The Istanbul Officials tried to appoint to this position individuals who had acquired administrative experience in the Diaspora, and they also considered immigrants for this purpose, but they did not always find anyone suitable. Some of the officials, however, had filled key positions in their communities before their immigration to Palestine. We know of officials who immigrated from Babylonia, Istanbul, Izmir, Salonika, and Rhodes, such as Alhadef, Samnun, Hacohen, and Dr. Isaac de-Bilasco.[70]

The position of official brought power and honor, and so occasionally one of the immigrants made the amount of his payments dependent on obtaining an appointment, and the Istanbul Officials were forced to appoint him against their will. One of these was Elijah Samnun, who immigrated to Palestine from Salonika in 1749 and demanded to be appointed as an official. The Istanbul Officials accepted him against their will because they were trying to collect the maximum amount from him as payment for burial charges and other taxes even before his immigration.[71]

Some of the officials were sent to Palestine specifically for this purpose, such as Meir Benveniste, whom the Istanbul Officials appointed because they were not satisfied with the administration of the city's affairs.[72] Other officials were immigrating to Palestine anyway, and they were appointed to their positions because they were known to the Istanbul Officials. In 1742 Abraham Alhadef, who immigrated to Palestine from Rhodes, was asked to become an official, but at first he refused.[73] Only after three years did he accept the position. In 1753 the Istanbul Officials added Moses de-Boton and Abraham Fintz to the staff of officials, as they knew them well from Istanbul.[74] Fintz died soon after his appointment, and in his place Judah Pisanti was appointed and served as the "informer" of the Istanbul Officials in Jerusalem.[75]

The appointment of the officials, which was sometimes made under pressure or out of obvious personal preference,[76] not infrequently aroused quarrels in Jerusalem and stirred up the officials who were already serving in Jerusalem, but in the end the Istanbul Officials always imposed their will.[77]

The Istanbul Officials did not stop at the appointment of officials, and when they discovered disorders in administration or in finances, they did not hesitate to remove a particular official from his post[78] or to limit his authority. In 1741 they ruled that Meir Benveniste should be responsible for keeping the accounts and should oversee communications with the authorities, that is, that he should be the chief official instead of Rolo. In this way the Istanbul Officials punished Rolo, whom they accused of administering the affairs of the city badly, wasting money, and causing harm to the community.[79] In 1745 the Istanbul Officials asked the sages of Jerusalem to appoint assistants for Benveniste to take care of legacies and other matters,[80] and for this purpose they invited Alhadef to join the officials and be responsible for the legacies, together with six other Torah scholars.[81]

It is thus probable that the areas of activity of the officials were not permanent. Nevertheless it may be that in general the following division of labor was customary. The chief official was responsible for the contacts with the authorities in Jerusalem, in the language of the period, "to go to the gates of the officers."[82] For this position a well-to-do man was generally appointed who already had good ties with the rulers and knew the language of the country. One of these was the aforementioned Rahamim Hacohen, who had all of these characteristics.[83] At times he was assisted by others.

The official who was second in importance was the treasurer—in the language of the period; "in charge of the funds"—who was responsible for the collection of the head tax and the community taxes. He also took care of the collection of the legacies, sometimes with the help of several Torah scholars, and he was responsible for the distribution of donations to individuals.

The third official, the scribe, was responsible for writing letters and especially for keeping the account-books of the community.

The fourth official was the secretary. The person in this position, which was not permanent, was responsible for the office.

The most detailed division of the responsibilities took place in 1755, after irregularities were discovered in the administration and in the funds. According to the suggestion of the Istanbul Officials, the responsibilities were divided as follows: (1) the cash-box was to be in the hands of Elijah

Samnun; (2) connections with external authorities and the petty cash were to be in the hands of Rahamim Hacohen, assisted by Elijah Rolo and Dr. de-Bilasco, who was still in Istanbul; (3) the sale of the effects from estates there was to be in the hands of Judah Pisanti, Eliezer Farhi, and Joseph Gerson; (4) the scribe Joseph ben Mayor was to be removed from his post, and in his place Moses Saporta was to be appointed because the former had been accused of embezzlement; (5) the comptroller of the community was to be R. Israel Bechar Jacob, who was to examine the account-books twice a week and supervise what was done in the community; and (6) the court assistants who were to remain were Elijah Obadiah and Elijah Meir, and Moses Algazi was to be fired.[84]

It is probable that the main cash-box was taken away from Hacohen, and Samnun was appointed in his place. Hacohen was left in charge only of the petty cash, in which there were 200 *kurus* for his running expenses in contacts with the authorities. The new treasurer was asked occasionally to take care of the petty cash.[85] Incidentally, when Samnun died his position was given to his son.[86]

From time to time, when the need arose, the Istanbul Officials appointed individuals to various positions for a short period. In 1755 an embezzlement of 10,000 *kurus* from the community fund was discovered, and the Istanbul Officials appointed an investigating committee consisting of three rabbis.[87]

The phenomenon of embezzlement was prevalent at that time. Several of the Jerusalem officials continued with their own private business dealings, and often they used the community funds as well. When they lost money, the creditors or their heirs seized the money from the community cash-box. Abraham Alhadef "mixed his money with the community money," that is, he took from the community cash-box. After his death it was discovered that there was a large deficit in the cash-box, and an attempt was made to seize his possessions, but without success.[88] This example and many similar ones in the documents throughout this period attest that this phenomenon was not a minor matter, but clearly left its mark on the community.

Among the officials themselves there were unending quarrels throughout the entire eighteenth century, and in many cases the Istanbul Officials appointed arbitrators on their own behalf. The main battle was over areas of authority.[89] Despite their ambition to enjoy at least a minimum of freedom of activity, the Jerusalem officials apparently had very little authority because of their total dependence on the Istanbul Officials. Two positions were the main sources of the quarrels: that of the liaison between the community and the authorities, and that of the person responsible for the cash-box. The person who acted as liaison with the authorities often took advantage of this connection to threaten his opponents and to impose his will on them, but control over the financial resources also conferred great power. The benefits that were involved in the positions aroused quarrels, as each new appointment was liable to deprive the others of part of their income.

In 1741 a quarrel broke out between Elijah Rolo and Meir Benveniste, who complained to the Istanbul Officials about Rolo's bad character traits.[90] About a year later an attempt was made to remove Joseph Treves, the aged scribe of the community, from his position.[91] In 1746 a severe quarrel broke out among the officials, which went so far as to involve the authorities.[92] Concerning a quarrel that broke out in 1749, the Istanbul Officials wrote angrily that this was endangering Jerusalem "and it is this that destroyed our Temple . . . enough already, officials of Israel."[93] In 1751 Meir Benveniste was removed from his post, and in a quarrel that broke out between him and Elia Meir the latter turned to the gentile courts. The Istanbul Officials were very angry with him about this; they called him "Elia the persecutor" and commanded that he be treated harshly in order to "break" him, and they even threatened to expel him from Palestine! The Jerusalem rabbis also tried to save the honor of the deposed official Benveniste, as he had been acquitted.[94]

The most severe quarrels that we know about occurred between 1756 and 1764, during the administration of Rahamim Hacohen. In the financial balance of 1755 there was a deficit of about 10,000 *kurus*, and the officials accused one another of embezzlement. The quarrel did not die down even after the investigating committee appointed by the Istanbul community ruled that Hacohen was not guilty. From then until 1764 the city was divided into two camps. Officials were removed from their positions and returned to them under the pressure of the warring groups, who even found it necessary to turn to the local authorities. Delegations of rabbis went to Istanbul; others fled to Egypt.[95]

The quarrels among the officials continued during the 1770s as well, and the Istanbul Officials were unable to stop them, principally because of the distance and the poor communications, which prevented their immediate intervention.

The Jewish Community of Jerusalem

Community Workers

The community workers were subject to the authority of the officials. In general they were appointed at the instruction or intervention of the Istanbul Officials.[96] The workers who performed activities connected with religious matters—such as, ritual slaughterers—were appointed by the Jerusalem rabbis, although at times according to suggestions from the Istanbul Officials.

These were the main types of workers in the community: the one in charge of the merchandise of the community,[97] the charity collector, the yeshiva officials, the scribes, and the ritual slaughterers.

The charity collectors—or "treasurers appointed for the charity fund"[98]—were responsible for the charity fund for poor people, as was accepted in every Jewish community: "As there is a custom in the city for every man or widow to give so much money each month for the charity fund."[99] One of the charity collectors was R. Jacob Ashkenazi, the collector for the food fund, who resigned in 1746 to protest that he was not given sufficient means. In a letter that they sent to Jerusalem the Istanbul Officials offered to give the fund 100 *kurus* and to ask R. Ashkenazi to return to his position.[100]

There were also several "servants" working in the community—sometimes up to seven—who were employed as guards or sent on errands. The Istanbul Officials frequently complained about the extra expense for the salaries of these servants and demanded a reduction in the staff.[101]

The Chief Rabbi

The chief rabbi of the Jerusalem community was, it is true, first in the hierarchy, but in practice the power of the officials was somewhat greater. The chief rabbi was the president of the Supreme Court and the head of one of the yeshivas. He did not take part in battles between the officials and the rabbis, the two warring factions in the leadership, and at times he served as a balancing factor.[102]

Starting in 1726 the selection of the chief rabbi was dependent on the Istanbul Officials on the one hand, and on the Jerusalem community on the other. Concerning this matter we have in our possession the explicit evidence of R. Raphael Meyuhas Bechar Samuel, the chief rabbi of Jerusalem: "The rabbi and leader of the city who was accepted by this holy city [Jerusalem] and particularly by the Istanbul community, may

God protect her, with the signature of its rabbis and patrons and officials and collectors."[103]

The formal appointment did indeed take place in Jerusalem,[104] but it seems that the initiative came from Istanbul. This is also apparent from the fact that frequently the person appointed for this position was someone who had just immigrated to Palestine on the initiative of the Istanbul Officials, who even took care to ensure his economic support. This is what occurred in the appointment of R. Eliezer Nahum,[105] who immigrated from Edirne, and it also occurred in the appointment of R. Isaac Hacohen Rapaport, who immigrated from Izmir after he had been away from Palestine for decades.[106] The letters that the Istanbul Officials sent him before his immigration to Palestine are evidence that they supported his candidacy.[107] Nevertheless they did not give him an explicit promise, which perhaps tells us that the final decision was in the hands of the Jerusalem community. The strong support of the Istanbul Officials for the appointment of Rabbi Rapaport is also shown by the fact that they financed his immigration,[108] increased his salary, and informed the Jerusalem officials that he had been appointed head of the new yeshiva Hesed le-Avraham u-Vinyan Shelomo.[109]

It seems that the Istanbul Officials sought a faithful and forceful person for this high position, one who could stand up to the authorities and bring peace to the warring factions in the community. At times they succeeded in their difficult choice, and several of the chief rabbis in the eighteenth century were indeed authoritative, such as R. Raphael Meyuhas Bechar Samuel. Sometimes the Istanbul Officials preferred a candidate from the Diaspora who wanted to immigrate to Palestine or was asked to do so. When there was no choice one of the elder rabbis of the city was occasionally chosen, although generally he died soon after his appointment. This is the reason for the short periods of office of some of the people in this position: R. Nissim Haim Moses Mizrahi served about four years (1746–49); R. Jacob Israel Algazi served about a year (1755–56), as did R. Abraham ben Asher (1771–72) and R. Raphael Moses Bula (1772–73). These were only interim periods and naturally these rabbis did not make a lasting impression on the community. This is not true of the chief rabbis who served for a long time, who strengthened their positions and earned respect and admiration both in and outside of Jerusalem.

It is worth mentioning that all the chief rabbis of Jerusalem in the eighteenth century—except for R. Abraham Itzhaki—died in office.[110]

We do not have any evidence about depositions, and this fact attests to the high status of the chief rabbi. This stability stands out with increased force against the background of the many quarrels in the community leadership and the large number of depositions relevant to them. Only in one case do the sources hint of a battle that occurred before the selection of the chief rabbi: after the death of R. Raphael Meyuhas in 1771, several rabbis served for short periods, until the selection of R. Yom-Tov Algazi, who served for a long time: "Our rabbi and teacher Yom-Tov Algazi who was king of Jerusalem for twenty-six years, the first in Zion."[111]

Rabbi Algazi died in 1802, and thus it seems that he was chosen in 1776, while he was still on a mission to the Diaspora. There is reason to believe that until his return from his mission in 1782 his position as chief rabbi and head of the rabbinical court was temporarily filled by R. Raphael Tzemah ben Simon, who is the first signer of the letter about the emissaries of 1774[112] and the regulation of 1776.[113] This rabbi was also the head of the yeshiva Hesed le-Avraham u-Vinyan Shelomo, and during the same period he apparently also served as head of the officials.[114] There are those who believe that after the death of R. Raphael Meyuhas his son, R. Moses Joseph Mordecai Meyuhas, was supposed to have been chosen, but he was actually chosen for this position only in 1802, after the death of Rabbi Algazi.[115]

The main power of the chief rabbi derived from his position as president of the rabbinical court and the leader of the Jewish community. From a formal standpoint he also represented the Jews before the local authorities as leader of the community, even though in practice the officials maintained the contact with the authorities. One of the factors that strengthened the status of the chief rabbi was his task of negotiating between the officials and the Torah scholars. In the many quarrels between the two factions he always filled the position of negotiator and arbitrator, with the encouragement of the Istanbul Officials, or even according to their explicit request. In a quarrel that broke out in 1752 between the rabbis and the officials concerning the appointment of the "seven benefactors of the city" and the payment of taxes by the Torah scholars, the Istanbul Officials asked Chief Rabbi Rapaport to intervene and put an end to the conflict, which had even reached the gentile courts and was costing a lot of money.[116] In a quarrel that broke out, as mentioned above, in 1756 among the officials, Chief Rabbi Algazi was asked to intervene and find out who was to blame in the matter, and to supervise the establishment of the investigating committee that had been appointed for this purpose. [117] In a controversy that arose between the rabbis and the officials in 1762 Chief Rabbi Raphael Meyuhas was asked to use his authority to stop the quarrel. [118]

The chief rabbi had a solid economic status, as he received his salary from Istanbul. The salary of Rabbi Rapaport was 504 *kurus* per year—a quite respectable amount for this period. To the salary of the chief rabbi was added as well the salary that he received as head of the yeshiva. R. Eliezer Nahum[119] was the head of the Pereyra yeshiva, and so was Rabbi Raphael Meyuhas. [120] Rabbi Rapaport was head of the yeshiva Hesed le-Avraham u-Vinyan Shelomo, [121] Rabbi Abraham ben Asher was head of the yeshiva Yefaʾer ʿAnavim, and Rabbi Bula was head of the yeshiva Neveh Shalom. [122]

The attitude of the Istanbul Officials to the chief rabbi was of honor and respect, and the salutations and style of the letters attest to this. It seems to me that this attitude was not just verbal and external. At any rate, on only a few occasions did the Istanbul Officials write harsh words to the chief rabbi or reprove him. [123]

It seems that in the eighteenth century the influence of the chief rabbi did not go beyond the boundaries of Jerusalem. In the whole Ottoman Empire there was no central authority in the spiritual realm, and in the documents in our possession from that period there is no hint that the Jerusalem rabbis intervened in the affairs of the other Jewish communities in Palestine or in the Diaspora.

Torah Scholars and the Rabbinical Courts

In the eighteenth century there were dozens of Torah scholars, that is, members of yeshivas, in Jerusalem. Learned men who were not members of yeshivas were considered householders. In 1758 there were about 180 Torah scholars in the city. [124]

The main task that the Torah scholars performed in the community leadership was deciding what was forbidden or permitted according to religious law, although in the 1760s their position became stronger, and they also penetrated the offices of the community, which then included two officials, two Torah scholars, [125] and two householders. In addition the Torah scholars assisted the officials in the collection of legacies that were left to the community from the relatives of the departed. [126] It is also possible that they served as witnesses at the time of the writing of wills and at deaths or handed down decisions as to what belonged to the community.

We do not have detailed descriptions of the rabbinical courts and their procedures in the eighteenth century, but from the small bits of evidence in various sources it is possible to draw a few outlines. It seems that in Jerusalem there were two or three rabbinical courts with three members and one with seven members.

The list of yeshivas and their scholars from the year 1758 shows the existence of several small rabbinical courts. Two of these are mentioned explicitly: one in the Pereyra yeshiva and one in the yeshiva Neveh Shalom. Concerning the Pereyra yeshiva, it says: "The sage Rabbi Meyuhas Bechar Samuel . . . the sage Rabbi Jacob Ashkenazi . . . the sage Rabbi Isaac Azulai . . . and they constitute the rabbinical court."[127] Concerning the yeshiva Neveh Shalom, it says: "The sage Rabbi Moses Bula . . . the sage Rabbi Nissim Berakha . . . and the sage Rabbi Yom-Tov Algazi . . . and they constitute the rabbinical court."[128] From this list it also appears that Chief Rabbi Raphael Meyuhas Bechar Samuel was at the head of one of these rabbinical courts. The list also tells us about the connection between the yeshivas and their heads, on the one hand, and the rabbinical courts, on the other. Benayahu suggests that at that time there were at least three rabbinical courts in Jerusalem.[129] His opinion that there was a rabbinical court in the yeshiva Damesek Eliezer, which had R. Judah Navon at its head, seems plausible, as in 1743 R. Haim David Azulay called him "the president of our rabbinical court."[130] From 1759 to 1760 Rabbi Azulay also served on the rabbinical court of Rabbi Samuel, together with R. Solomon Hiyya Mizrahi,[131] whose signatures together are found on three rabbinical decisions, two from 1759[132] and one from 1760.[133]

Evidence concerning the varying compositions of the rabbinical courts within three years' time hints that there were several courts at the same time. It seems that the rabbinical courts did not always have the same composition; at any rate, Rabbi Azulay served in at least two different panels, and Rabbi Samuel was also at the head of two different courts. It is known that at a later time there were four three-member rabbinical courts in the Sephardi community of Jerusalem, and each panel sat for one-quarter of the year,[134] and so possibly in the period under discussion matters were conducted in a similar manner.

From the evidence in our possession it appears that in addition to the

Jewish Communities in Palestine

three-member rabbinical courts there was also a seven-member court, with the chief rabbi at its head. This court was called "the great court" or "the proper court."[135] This rabbinical court met, it seems, in order to decide difficult cases, to establish special regulations, and to impose authority in cases of friction in the community, as in other parts of the Ottoman Empire.[136] R. Israel Mizrahi, one of the Jerusalem rabbis, wrote in 1742 about "a great rabbinical court and a small rabbinical court which sit at the head of our land and the inheritance of our fathers."[137]

From the signatures on the regulations that are included in the book of regulations it is difficult to determine whether all the rabbis who signed them were members of the rabbinical court or whether there were among them also rabbis who were not serving as judges at that time. At any rate, from an investigation of the signatures it appears that the chief rabbi and several officials almost always appeared at the head of the signers. The number of signatory rabbis—three, six, or nine—is likely to reveal the composition of one or several rabbinical courts. It is hard to find a connection between the type of regulation and the number of signers. Perhaps the matter is connected to the character of the gathering of the sages and officials—whether it was a general meeting or a more limited gathering.

The signatures of twelve men, with that of Chief Rabbi Eliezer Nahum at their head, can be found on a regulation from 1737.[138] The signatures of nine men, again with that of Chief Rabbi Nahum at their head, can be found on another regulation of the same year.[139] The signatures of three men—including at least three officials—with that of R. Nissim Haim Moses Mizrahi at their head, can be found on a regulation from 1749.[140] The signatures of eleven men—nine rabbis, headed by Chief Rabbi Rapaport, and two officials—can be found on a regulation of 1755.[141] The signatures of six rabbis, headed by that of R. Raphael Tzomach ben Simon, who was head of the yeshiva Hesed le-Avraham u-Vinyan Shelomo,[142] are found on a regulation from 1776.[143] The signatures of six rabbis, headed by that of Chief Rabbi Algazi, are found on a regulation of 1781.[144]

It seems that Benayahu was right when he asserted that a meeting of all the rabbinical courts was called together for the establishment of special regulations.[145] Some support for this opinion may be found in the activities of R. Isaac Hacohen Rapaport a short time after he was appointed chief rabbi in 1749:

This is what occurred in the holy city of Jerusalem, may she be speedily rebuilt in our days, when the wonderful rabbi, the Chief Rabbi Isaac Hacohen, came from Izmir. . . . At that time he published several agreements in matters in which he was an expert and he did not want to renew them [himself] but rather he sent word to all the rabbis and the rabbinical courts that they should study the permissibility of the agreements and they should be prepared for the day of the meeting. And so it was that they all agreed to permit [the agreements] and they all gathered together in his house and they all agreed together to permit [the agreements] and they permitted them [the regulations]; it occurred in public. [146]

The signatures of the members of the seven-member rabbinical court appear occasionally in the approvals given for books. For example, the list of the members of the seven-member court headed by Chief Rabbi Nahum appears in the approval given by the Jerusalem rabbis to the book *Admath Kodesh* (The Holy Land). In the approval given by the Istanbul rabbis they state explicitly "the great rabbinical court in Jerusalem."[147]

Householders

The householders played almost no role in the leadership of the city, in spite of their large number in the eighteenth century. The Jerusalem and Istanbul Officials dominated the material realm, while in the spiritual realm the chief rabbi and the other rabbis had the upper hand. The householders were mostly elderly people without means who were supported by a meager yearly stipend from their relatives in the Diaspora or by the Jerusalem community.

In the 1740s some well-to-do householders began to arrive in the city. For example, the wealthy Isaac di-Mayo of Salonika, who was close to the leaders of the Istanbul community, immigrated to Jerusalem in 1742, as it appears from the request of the Istanbul Officials to the Jerusalem officials to act respectfully toward him and to give him credit in time of need, as the money was guaranteed. [148]

In the 1760s the number of householders increased, and they turned to the Istanbul Officials with the complaint that the Torah scholars were enjoying high incomes, but in spite of this they were not paying any taxes, and the public burden was on the shoulders of poorer people. Moreover, the Torah scholars were taking from the funds large sums of money that had been set aside for the repayment of debts. In the face of the difficult situation of the community the Istanbul Officials could no longer find justification for giving a tax exemption to any group whatsoever, and so they instructed the rabbis and officials of Jerusalem to formulate a "regulation" (*Haskama*) for ten years, which was to state that the Torah scholars would no longer receive their ten percent of the money from the missions of the emissaries, as was accepted, and from now on they would share the burden of the taxes "because some of the householders have complained . . . the Torah scholars are not sharing the burden with them."[149]

The Istanbul Officials also decided to make changes in the structure of the leadership, which would now include not only officials but also Torah scholars and householders. There is no doubt that this change in the material leadership of the community resulted from the ascendancy to power of different groups.[150]

Friction between the Torah Scholars and the Officials

The division of authority between the rabbis and the officials was generally clear, as was customary in other Jewish communities. However, often quarrels broke out in matters that were connected both with religious law and with financial considerations, such as the appointment of ritual slaughterers, as there was a special tax—the *gabela*—on the slaughtering and selling of meat.[151] In this matter the Istanbul Officials decided in favor of the rabbis and authorized the rabbis to appoint or depose ritual slaughterers. Nevertheless, they made the rabbis' authority dependent on the condition that these appointments would not harm the community fund. The handing over of the decision in this matter to the Istanbul Officials is evidence, it seems, of the great power of the Istanbul community.

Other quarrels broke out when the rabbis attempted to limit the role of the officials and establish an institution called the "seven patrons of the city," which would have consisted of rabbis and would have supervised the work of the officials. The first attempt to appoint the "seven patrons of the city" was made in 1752, but the Istanbul Officials dissociated themselves from the matter.[152] The quarrel reached the authorities, and it cost the community 650 *kurus*. The Istanbul Officials complained angrily about the quarrel and the loss of money and wrote sharp letters to the Jerusalem officials and rabbis and to Chief Rabbi Rapaport. They demanded that the rabbis rescind the appointment of the seven and restore the status quo,[153] and they asked the chief rabbi to effect a compromise between the two sides. The Istanbul Officials naturally sided with the Jerusalem officials, as any change in the status quo in Jerusalem was an undermining of the arrangements instituted by the Istanbul Officials. They even threatened deposing people from their positions if the situation of the leadership were not returned to its previous state. Nevertheless, the rabbis attempted from time to time to establish such an institution, and it always led to a rift between them and the officials.[154] Another attempt was made, for example, in 1760, when several Torah scholars tried to "be judges for themselves," that is, to establish an additional rabbinical court of their own. As a result the seven-member rabbinical court headed by Chief Rabbi Raphael Meyuhas Bechar Samuel convened and established that it was not permitted to set up private rabbinical courts, and the Jerusalem officials were given permission to hand over to the gentile courts anyone who violated this prohibition.[155]

The appointment of the "seven patrons of the city" also had economic motives, as it was meant to prevent the implementation of the plan of the officials to require the Torah scholars to pay taxes like the rest of the householders in the community. Similar controversies had occurred in previous centuries in various communities of the Ottoman Empire, but in the second half of the seventeenth century, when the economic situation of the empire deteriorated, there were communities that imposed the taxes even on Torah scholars who did not do any other work.[156] In other communities a compromise was reached, and the Torah scholars paid only part of the taxes.

The earliest evidence of a controversy about this question in Palestine is found in letters from 1750.[157] According to a previous decision, Torah scholars in Jerusalem who did not do any other work were exempt from taxes. Even in the sixteenth and seventeenth centuries opinions on the matter in the Jerusalem community had been divided,[158] and in the other Palestine cities as well acrimonious debates were conducted on this question.[159] In 1750 the Istanbul Officials did not succeed in annulling the decision of the Jerusalem rabbis that the community must carry the burden of the taxes of the Torah scholars. However, when the controversy was renewed in 1752 the Istanbul Officials did not hesitate to decide that everyone must pay taxes, including Torah scholars.[160] In 1754 the Istanbul Officials determined most clearly that the attempt of the Jerusalem rabbis to exempt the Torah scholars from the payment of taxes was not justified because of the difficult situation of the Jerusalem community, and that the Torah scholars must pay taxes as they did in the other Jewish communities. In their words, "It is not right to establish their words upon a Torah decision,"[161] (upon the previous Halakhic decision). Moreover, sometimes the Torah scholars took more money than they were entitled to from the community fund, in spite of the difficult situation of the community.[162] The Istanbul Officials threatened dismissals if the regulation were not changed, and they demanded that two Torah scholars be sent to Istanbul to conduct the affairs of the Jerusalem community there. They admitted, it is true, that they were speaking of a Halakhic decision, but they added sarcastically that the pasha and the Turkish authorities did not recognize Halakhic decisions and were demanding money.[163]

It is impossible to know if the Torah scholars accepted the demand of the Istanbul community in this basic matter, but in the 1760s quarrels broke out again on this subject, and the Istanbul Officials reprimanded the Torah scholars because they were not participating in the expenses of the city. In their words, "There is no one who is poorer than the community," and whoever gives a donation to Eretz Israel does so in order that the land should be settled, and not for the Torah scholars.[164] At any rate, the quarrels between the officials and the rabbis did not stop even in the 1770s.[165]

THE JERUSALEM REGULATIONS

The regulations and decisions of Jewish communities and regions are among the most important sources for Jewish history. Reading these regulations conjures up a vivid picture of Jewish social and economic life and relations with the authorities. It is no wonder, then, that historians have always attempted to gather together the regulation books (*Pinkasim*) that were preserved, to publish them in scholarly editions, and to present them as tools for investigators. But while we possess many such books from the European communities, the material from the Jewish communities of the Ottoman Empire is very sparse. Here and there a few community regulations have remained, some in manuscript and some in books of responsa and other collections. We have a few regulations from Salonika[166] mainly from the period of its greatness in the sixteenth century, from Istanbul,[167] from Izmir,[168] and from other communities both large and small.[169] From the communities of Palestine some scattered regulations survived,[170] which were concentrated mainly in the book of regulations of Jerusalem.[171] Publication of this book was undertaken by the first Hakham-Basi (chief rabbi who was appointed by the Ottoman authorities) in Jerusalem, the Rishon Le-Zion (chief Sephardi rabbi of Jerusalem from the nineteenth century) R. Haim Abraham Gagin in 1842. Before long the book went into a second edition, to which was added an important introduction by the Rishon Le-Zion R. Solomon Moses Suzin.[172] In the Jerusalem Regulations are concentrated the regulations of the community from the eighteenth and nineteenth centuries, which rely in part upon earlier regulations. A second part, containing the customs of Jerusalem, has been added to this book. A book in which mainly customs of Eretz Israel and some regulations were collected is the book *Shaʿar Hamifkad* (The Gate of the Counting) by R. David ben-Simon, the founder of the Mugrabi community in Jerusalem in the nineteenth century. To this book were added the interpretations of his son, R. Raphael Aaron ben-Simon, one of the rabbis of Egypt, who published the book.[173]

Not a single, complete *Pinkas* has remained that would illuminate in its entirety even one period in the life of the Jewish communities in the Ottoman Empire. All the material in our possession is fragmented and random, and the question may be asked: How did it happen that the protocol books of the large and important communities were not preserved, or even those of the small communities with a tradition of organization, in which there was a busy social and economic life?

It seems that the notebooks were already lost completely in the generations in which they were written. The people of the Ottoman period were aware of this and mentioned it several times. According to information in our possession, the protocol books disappeared as a result of natural disasters and catastrophes that occurred in the communities of the Ottoman Empire. For example, there were great fires in Istanbul in 1660[174] and 1729.[175] In Izmir there was an earthquake in 1688,[176] and in the eighteenth century two great fires broke out. The following was written about the fire in that city in 1742: "And the fire burned every great building, the holy synagogues and study-houses . . . thirteen in number; they were all consumed by fire."[177]

Fires broke out in Edirne as well.[178] In the eighteenth and nineteenth centuries two violent earthquakes occurred in Safed,[179] and likewise in Salonika, which also suffered from harsh wars in the nineteenth and twentieth centuries.[180] During these catastrophes many of the buildings of the community were destroyed, and with them also their protocol books.

In the Jewish communities of Palestine, and particularly in Jerusalem, there were additional causes for the loss of the protocol books, especially the great turnover in the Jewish population and the frequent changes in the city's demographic composition, so that the Jews of Palestine were prevented from establishing a clear tradition of the transfer of leadership. Inspection of the names of the sages of Jerusalem in the middle of the eighteenth century reveals that only a few of them had lived in the city at the beginning of the century and that only a few isolated individuals were descendants of Jerusalemites.[181] It is even possible that there was no continuity in the regulations because the immigrants from different countries each had different customs. The following was written by R. Raphael Mordecai Malkhi, one of the rabbis of Jerusalem at the end of the seventeenth century: "I have already said that in Jerusalem at this time there is no established agreement or fixed custom and there is no law and order for anyone, but rather everything goes according to the luck of the individual."[182]

The loss of the protocol books also shows that people in those days did not attach great importance to them. When R. Isaac Hacohen Rapaport returned to Palestine in 1749, he searched for the old book of regulations of the community, which he remembered from the days of his youth in the city, but in vain.[183] Since he was unable to find the old *Pinkas*, he filled in from memory and established new regulations, some of which were undoubtedly customary in the city while others derived from his experience in Izmir.

The Jerusalem regulations of the eighteenth and nineteenth centuries that have reached us are more numerous because of the gradual improvement in the community due to the activities of the Istanbul Officials and the demographic stabilization that occurred as a result.

The sources for the regulations discussed in this volume are the books mentioned above and manuscripts. I will not describe all the regulations in my possession, as some of them are outside the framework of this discussion. Undoubtedly I have missed some of the regulations due to their being widely scattered.

It is important to keep in mind that (1) the Istanbul Officials played a large part in the establishment of the regulations, and (2) many of the regulations are based on earlier regulations, but they have not reached us in their original form, as they were reestablished or altered because of changing times. An analysis of the development of the regulations is a matter for a separate investigation, and so I will not describe their development from a chronological or Halakhic standpoint.[184] Rather, I will discuss their importance in the historical context.

The Istanbul Officials had a great influence in the area of the regulations as well as in other areas. It is true that theoretically this area was not included among the tasks they were supposed to fulfill, but nevertheless they considered themselves obligated to deal with it, as they considered themselves responsible for the fate of the Jewish settlement in Jerusalem. In practice this was no more than an effect of their great influence on what was done in the Jerusalem community. From the regulations established in Istanbul and in Jerusalem in the eighteenth century it appears that in principle and in practice the authority to establish regulations was in the hands of both the Istanbul Officials and the leaders of the Jerusalem community. However, with the passage of time the freedom of action of the people of Jerusalem in this area decreased, and many of the regulations in matters of taxation came from Istanbul or were established in Jerusalem with some sign that the Istanbul Officials had taken the initiative in establishing them. "The sages and leaders and supervisors and officials and patrons of the holy city of Jerusalem," noted "the power given us by the officers and assistants of the Istanbul Officials."[185]

Nevertheless some freedom of action still remained in the hands of the Jerusalem community in the area under consideration. Indeed, the community had the authority—even if not exclusively—to establish regulations in all matters concerned with the Jewish way of life, and the leadership even amended some of the regulations regarding community taxes. The initiative for other regulations—such as in matters of dress and ornaments—was in the hands of the Istanbul Officials exclusively.

A study of the regulations reveals that the Istanbul Officials intervened in the regulations when there was a decline in the income of the Jerusalem community and there was a danger to the legal and physical state of the Jews there. In ordinary times, on the other hand, the people of Jerusalem established regulations as they saw fit. It seems that the Istanbul Officials did not take unfair advantage of their status, and only established regulations when the situation demanded it. Moreover, even the regulations that were actually established in Istanbul were afterwards endorsed in Jerusalem. This fact too proves that the local leadership still retained some independence. Nevertheless, it is worth noting that this method of establishing regulations had no precedent in Jewish history, as we are dealing with two apparently independent communities. It is clear that the Jerusalem community could not behave as it wished, but it nevertheless established many regulations without consulting the Istanbul Officials.

Regulations in Matters of the Relations between the Jews and the Gentiles

The status of Jews in the framework of minority groups required the regularization of their relations with the Ottoman authorities, at least from a legal standpoint. We know that from a practical standpoint the Ottoman laws that forbade extortion of money, oppression, and arbitrariness were not always kept. Nevertheless, one cannot ignore the fact that the central government in Istanbul tried to enforce the rules that were established in the laws, which expressed a reasonably tolerant attitude toward the minority.[186]

Jewish sources tend to emphasize the arbitrariness of the local authorities and the local population in Palestine, but Ottoman sources reveal that the Sublime Porte generally tried to prevent excessive arbitrariness toward the *dhimmis* (non-Moslems). Jewish historical research has also emphasized precisely those sources that mention the arbitrariness of the authorities in Palestine,[187] and not always those that dwell on the constant tension that existed in this matter between Istanbul and the provincial rulers. It would be desirable to compare the status of the Jews in the Ottoman Empire with their status in Christian countries. If this were done, a somewhat different picture would undoubtedly emerge.[188] The Jews all over the empire enjoyed normal economic relations with their Moslem neighbors; moreover, they were organized with them in guilds.[189] It appears from various sources that many judgments between Jews and Moslems were tried in Moslem courts, and often the Jews won in these cases. This fact is especially important in the face of the legal inferiority of the Jews to the Moslems.[190]

We possess very few regulations from the eighteenth century that deal with the relations between the Jews and the gentiles. One of them deals with the prohibition against selling wine to a Moslem. It is true that drinking wine is prohibited to Moslems, as is well known, but probably there were many who violated the law and bought wine from Jews. Jews who were caught were liable to be punished and became a target for extortions.[191] Rabbi Gedalia of Siemiatycze, who immigrated to Palestine with R. Judah Hasid at the beginning of the eighteenth century, related: "The Jews do not have any income from this as the Ishmaelites [the Turks] and the Arabs [the local residents] do not drink either wine or whiskey."[192]

It seems that in spite of this the phenomenon was widespread in the eighteenth century. At any rate, in the book of regulations there is a regulation of 1754 that says: "Moreover, no woman, whether widowed or married, may sell wine or whiskey and no person and no Jew may sell wine or whiskey to any gentile [Moslem] or uncircumcised person [Christian]. Also no Jew may sit in a place of winesellers to eat and drink there."[193]

We have in our possession several pieces of evidence about the background for this regulation. This is what Rabbi Gedalia of Siemiatycze related: "If a Jew sells an Arab or any Ishmaelite a little wine . . . then they catch that Jew and beat him, besides monetary fines."[194] A source from the beginning of the eighteenth century tells of an Ashkenazic woman who sold wine to gentiles and became involved in a trial, as one of her customers became drunk and killed his friend.[195]

There were two reasons for the prohibition regulation, one internal and one external: to prevent drunkenness and immodesty, on the one hand, and to prevent trouble for the community on account of the violation of a Moslem law, on the other. Incidentally, it is not clear why the regulation forbade the selling of wine to Christians. The reason for the violation of this law by the Jews of Jerusalem apparently derives from the immigrations from countries in which such laws either did not exist or else were not strictly enforced. The Jews of eastern Europe, for example, were not aware of this law, as the leasing of taverns was an important source of income for them during this period.[196] The Jews who arrived from Turkey also did not always abide by this prohibition. At any rate, it appears from the documents of the Istanbul community that the phenomenon was widespread there in the second half of the eighteenth century.[197]

Other regulations dealt with purchases by Jews from gentiles. One regulation addressed a special problem: "milk that was milked by a gentile on a Jewish holiday under the supervision of a Jew is customary to be forbidden in the holy city of Jerusalem."[198] Another regulation permitted "buying water from gentiles who bring it from the well of *Ayub*, which is called the well of Joab, a known well within the [Halakhically defined

Sabbath] boundary."[199] Other regulations dealt with the employment of gentiles in construction work for Jews, in a situation that apparently occurred frequently at times of much immigration, as is attested by this source from the seventeenth century: "To build by means of gentiles on our houses . . . occurs every day in the holy city, [but] the rabbis of Jerusalem prevent the Jews who own the houses from building [on the Sabbath]."[200]

Another regulation concerned the buying of monuments from the gentiles. In 1729 the Istanbul Officials ruled that the monuments, which until then had been bought by a Jew who leased this privilege, should from then on be bought by the community, as this increased its income. Four of the Istanbul Officials were signatories to this regulation,[201] which, incidentally, was only an attempt to restore the status quo.

From the few regulations in our possession it appears that in the economic sphere there was cooperation between the Jews and the gentiles, and this fact partly balances the negative picture of the life of the Jews in Palestine during this period as depicted in some of the sources and in the writings of historians.

Regulations in Matters of Dress and Jewelry

As a result of the discriminatory laws established by the Moslems against non-Moslems, we find in the Jerusalem regulations a consideration of these matters as well.

During the Mameluke period the authorities were strict only about the color of the turban. According to the sources of the period the Moslems wore white turbans, whereas the Christians and the Jews had yellow or blue ones. The *dhimmis* were also differentiated from the Moslems by the color of the girdle, but this rule was not strictly enforced. Ashtor[202] believed that, except for the matter of the turban and the girdle, the law that demanded different dress for non-Moslems was not kept.

In the beginning of the eighteenth century Rabbi Gedalia of Siemiatycze wrote: "No nationality is allowed to go dressed in green in the Moslem countries except for the believers in Islam."[203] He added that the Jews were differentiated from the Moslems in the color of the turban as well, and that they were not allowed to wear white or green turbans, as the wearing of these colors was a prerogative of the Moslems. They were not so strict about other items of clothing, and the matter was left to the arbitrary decision of the individual rulers.[204] The Jews were even allowed to wear white clothes, especially on the lower part of the body. On the upper part of the body the Sephardim were accustomed to wear black clothes. Aside from the matter of the color green "everyone is equal." The lack of strictness in the enforcement of these and other laws was characteristic of the policies of the Sublime Porte in general. At any rate, at the beginning of the eighteenth century there was not much strictness in the matter of dress.[205]

Later a change occurred in this matter. In the 1730s the immigration to Palestine was renewed, and there was an increase in the population of Jews who knew nothing about the tense relations between the Jews and the Moslems in the wake of the affair of the debts at the beginning of the century. In 1740–41 there were widespread rumors in Istanbul that the Jerusalem Jews were going around in the city streets in magnificent clothing, and that the women were wearing jewelry: "Our ears have heard from people coming from there to here that they have violated the protective regulation established by the earlier sages, both men and women, and they have gone too far in wearing magnificent clothing in the streets of the city, and the residents of the land whistled and gnashed their teeth."[206] From this letter and another letter of the Istanbul Officials one may learn what types of dress the Jerusalem Jews wore: "The males have allowed themselves to wear, in front of the gentiles, two different types of furs and straight hair and a kind of girdle and they go to the synagogue dressed like princes, and the females . . . go out to the bathhouse like prostitutes in gold jewelry and they are always wearing golden clothes, that is, with threads made of expensive metal, as the princesses wear."[207]

When this became known in the capital of the empire, the Istanbul Officials gathered together and demanded that the leaders of the Jerusalem community "agree to the regulation with oaths and stringencies in all force and might."[208] In the opinion of the Istanbul Officials the problem was not only that troubles were in store in relations with the local authorities, as troubles had come upon the Jews in the Diaspora because of their dress—"and if it is so in the Diaspora then how much more so is it in the holy city because of the Arabs within it"[209]—but also that they feared that as a result of these rumors the Jews in the Diaspora would decrease their support for the Yishuv. Indeed, the news about the magnificent clothing worn by the Jerusalem Jews spread rapidly, and when the emissaries from Jerusalem arrived in Istanbul in 1741 they did not succeed in collecting any money, even though they brought letters describing the difficult situation of the Jerusalem community. They particularly complained of false charges by the rulers of the city against the community.[210] The Istanbul Officials argued that the reason for such accusations by the rulers was the magnificent dress of the Jerusalem Jews, and as a first warning they threatened to delay the departure of the boat for the immigrants and pilgrims.[211]

The matter was not corrected, however, and in another letter concerning the problem of dress the Istanbul Officials wrote that they would not merely demand that a regulation be established in Jerusalem, but they were about to send a decision from Istanbul.[212] The next day they sent another letter in which they raised the argument that in Istanbul people were no longer donating money for Palestine, because "for bread they are willing to give but not for magnificent clothing." They again urged the Jerusalem leadership to establish a regulation on the matter, so that they could distribute copies of it in the Jewish communities.[213] About a week later the Istanbul Officials sent another letter, in which they related that at a meeting of the *Maʿamad* (general assembly) in Istanbul, at which emissaries from Jerusalem were present, many people expressed the argument that the difficult situation in the city was a result of the magnificent dress, "and the emissaries returned empty-handed."[214]

We do not know how much the forcefulness of the Istanbul Officials in 1741 helped, but it seems that for several years the situation was improved. However, in 1748 the problem arose again. Emissaries came to Istanbul and complained about the difficult situation in Jerusalem, while the Istanbul community thought that the matter was caused by magnificent dress, and that the rulers were decreeing prohibitions because "Jerusalem was dressing itself up like Istanbul." Therefore the Istanbul Officials renewed the decision in the matter of dress—so that "the sheiks would not consume the Jews"[215]—and they demanded that it be read in all the synagogues of Jerusalem. In 1748 as well many letters on the matter of dress were sent from Istanbul to Jerusalem. In one letter the Istanbul Officials wrote that they were publicizing the regulation in all the Jewish communities in order to improve the collection of donations.[216] They also included the regulation itself,[217] which was similar to the one of 1741.

It is likely that problems arose with the implementation of the regulation of 1748. In the responsa of R. Israel Jacob Algazi, one of the rabbis of Jerusalem at that time, we find:

In the year 5509 [1749] . . . the sages of the city reached a decision and established regulations with all force in the matter of the clothing [following the instructions from Istanbul in 1748] and the jewelry, that the women should not go out into the marketplace with them. And after the establishment of this regulation there were a few women who broke the rule and violated the agreement and the rabbinical court fined them and confiscated their jewelry and it was a wonder to me.[218]

In spite of the problems that arose it seems that this time the regulation was observed for a longer period. In 1767 the Istanbul Officials again sent instructions in the matter of dress, in which there was a demand to renew the regulation and to wear only clothing made from wool and not from silk.[219]

It is surprising that the Jerusalem Jews were not strict about a matter that was likely to endanger their status so greatly. It is possible that the reason for this may be found in the continual turnover of the population in the city. But it is also possible that there were some rulers who were not strict about the matter, and the problem arose again whenever a new ruler arrived in the city who was looking for an excuse to extort money.

Regulations in Matters of Ethics

A regulation of 1730 prohibited marriage for girls under the age of thirteen.[220] Other regulations dealt with the modesty of women: It was prohibited for women to go to the bakery or to the synagogue—except for the High Holy Days—or to the house of a non-Jew.[221] Another regulation dealt with the requirement for women to wear an outer garment.[222]

One of the regulations prohibited the employment of minors—whether gentiles or Jews—in the bakeries. It seems that besides the fear of exploitation, there was also a fear of immoral practices in this case, as bakery work is done at night. In this regulation both the Istanbul Officials and the rabbi of Jerusalem, R. Isaac Hacohen Rapaport, were involved.[223] Another regulation, which prohibited card games, was typical not only of Jerusalem;[224] we have in our possession a similar regulation from Izmir, which was established by R. Haim Abulafia.[225] The officials were given permission to hand over violators to the authorities.

One of the interesting and well-known regulations in this area is the bachelor regulation. This regulation was not new,[226] but it was renewed in 1749 and was enforced during the remainder of the century. The regulation specified that no bachelor between twenty and sixty years of age could live in Jerusalem. [227] It is possible that this regulation was meant to limit the uncontrolled immigration to Palestine, even though there is no doubt that its main purpose was ethical. At any rate, in the same year another regulation was added to this one, which prohibited bachelors from going to midnight *Tikkun* prayers. [228] From a document in the Istanbul Officials' *Pinkas*, it appears that in 1756 Joseph Saban of Izmir tried to immigrate to Jerusalem, but he was not married and not yet sixty years old. The Istanbul Officials tried to ignore the regulation in this case and to send him permission from the Jerusalem leadership, because he was a man of means and they wanted to appoint him as an official in Jerusalem. [229] It seems, then, that the regulation was generally enforced, and the exception proves the rule. Another example is the case of R. Abraham Gerson of Kuty, the brother-in-law of the Baal Shem Tov. His wife died in 1757, while they were in Jerusalem, and he wrote to the Baal Shem Tov that he was planning to go to the Diaspora because the Sephardi sages were pressuring him to get married and he did not want to marry a Sephardi woman. [230] It should be mentioned that at this time the ancient customs concerning the status of women were still in force in the Ottoman Empire and in the Jewish communities there, which may explain the source of these customs.

A *Regulation Concerning the Inheritance of Public Office*

In the matter of the inheritance of the offices of the rabbinate and the lay officers there was a Halakhic controversy. In some of the communities of the Ottoman Empire there was a rule that the rabbinate was an inherited position. [231] Yet in a document of 1797 it appears that "there is a prior agreement that was made in the holy city of Jerusalem . . . that in the holy city of Jerusalem there should not be any presumption or privilege in any appointment for the service of the public, but everything should be done according to the judgment of the judges and rabbis of the time, the holy ones that are in the land." [232] It is thus probable that in Jerusalem the rule of inheritance in public positions was not kept.

12
THE OTHER JEWISH COMMUNITIES AND THEIR LEADERSHIP

THE HEBRON COMMUNITY

In the eighteenth century there was a small Sephardi community in Hebron, which was concentrated in one court and numbered about a hundred people. The number of Ashkenazim in the city was very small. In this small community there was no busy social and spiritual life, and in most areas of life torpor reigned. It is true that two yeshivas established in the seventeenth century still remained, namely Hesed le-Avraham ve-Emeth le-Yaᶜakov and Knesseth Israel, but this does not attest to spiritual activity, as they were mainly a source of income for a few Torah scholars.

The history of this community in the eighteenth century is replete with decrees of the local rulers. The community was required to pay high taxes, and like the Jerusalem community it fell into heavy debt.[1] The community also suffered from the battles between the tribes of the region and from the revolt of Ali Bey.

The Istanbul Officials took care of the Hebron community as well, and starting in the 1730s a special committee for the support of Hebron was active in Istanbul, but in spite of this the community did not develop.

THE TIBERIAS COMMUNITY

In the second half of the seventeenth century Tiberias was almost completely destroyed as a result of the wars in the Galilee. The Jewish settlement in the city dwindled even more in the beginning of the eighteenth century, as is attested by R. Jacob Berav, one of the immigrants to Palestine in 1740: "It is now seventy years that it [Tiberias] is desolate without its sons, there is no synagogue and no study-house and Jews do not live there at all, not a kaddish [prayer] has been heard since the day it was destroyed."[2]

Berav's words are not exactly true, as it cannot be said that there was no one at all in Tiberias. It is true that it was not a central city, but among its ruins there still lived several dozen fishermen, some of whom were Jews. At any rate, in one of his letters R. Haim Ventura said: "For many years . . . the community was less than ten men until 1740."[3]

Berav's mention of seventy years of ruin in Tiberias is also not exact, because Tiberias had actually been destroyed several years before.[4] It seems to me that the reason for this statement is that the rebuilders of the Jewish settlement in Tiberias were trying to draw a parallel with the seventy years of the Babylonian exile in order to give their immigration a messianic flavor.

After he had established his residence in Tiberias and fortified the city, Dahir al-ʿUmar turned to the Jews with the suggestion that they come to live there. He had no doubt that the Jews, whose attitude to Tiberias was surely known to him, would not endanger his rule, and thanks to their connections with their brothers in the Diaspora they would be able to contribute to the development of the place and add money to his coffers.

In 1738[5] he appealed to R. Haim Abulafia in Izmir and suggested that he settle in Tiberias. There are two versions of the story about this suggestion. R. Jacob Berav relates that Dahir al-ʿUmar turned to Abulafia with these words: "Go up and inherit the land—Tiberias, which was the land of your forefathers."[6] R. Moses Yerushalmi, a Jew from central Europe who lived in Palestine in the 1760s and published a travelogue in 1769, relates that for a long time there had been no Jews in Tiberias, until Dahir al-ʿUmar decided to settle it. For this purpose he had consulted with R. Moses Malkhi, the rabbi of Safed, and the latter advised him to ask the Istanbul Officials "to give him Jews to settle in the place."[7] According to Yerushalmi both Dahir al-ʿUmar and R. Malkhi appealed to the Istanbul Officials: "And the sage R. Moses [Malkhi] advised him [Dahir al-ʿUmar] to write letters to the rich men of Istanbul because the Presidents of Eretz Israel resided there."[8] Dahir al-ʿUmar promised the immigrants tax discounts for three years and assistance in the building of houses, synagogues, and study-houses. The Istanbul Officials distributed the appeal in all the Jewish communities in Turkey, and R. Abulafia responded to it. The two sources appear to complement each other.

Around the time that R. Abulafia and his group left for Palestine the Istanbul Officials started to organize support for the settlers in Tiberias. It appears that the main motive for the Istanbul Officials' support of the renewal of the Jewish settlement in Tiberias was their messianic feelings. Thus, for example, we know that R. Abraham Rozanes, one of the heads of the Istanbul community in those days, also immigrated to Palestine. It is plausible that R. Abulafia's status in the Turkish communities also influenced the amount of the support.

R. Haim Abulafia, the man who may be given credit for the renewal of the Jewish settlement in Tiberias, was born in Hebron in 1660 to a family of good lineage, which came from Safed. The forefathers of the family were among those who had given and received the *semikha* (an attempt to renew the Sanhedrin as a messianic act) during the time of the great controversy concerning rabbinic ordination that had occurred in Safed in the middle of the sixteenth century and afterwards.[9] With the decline of Safed at the end of the sixteenth century the family apparently moved to Tiberias. At any rate, Rabbi Haim's grandfather, R. Jacob Abulafia, was the rabbi of Tiberias around 1640.[10] When Tiberias was destroyed in the middle of the seventeenth century, the family moved to Hebron.[11]

During R. Haim Abulafia's childhood, his family moved to Jerusalem, where Haim studied in the Beth Jacob yeshiva founded by the Vega family. In this yeshiva the greatest rabbinical scholars of Jerusalem, such as R. Jacob Hagiz and R. Hezekiah da-Silvia, studied and taught during the second half of the seventeenth century.[12] In 1699 R. Abulafia left for the Diaspora as an emissary for Hebron,[13] and while he was in Salonika he spent time deciding Halakhic questions, among other things. Before 1718 he returned to Palestine and was appointed rabbi in Safed.[14] In a letter to Modena in 1742 he wrote: "I was born in Hebron and grew up in Jerusalem, and I was a rabbi in Safed."[15] After 1721[16] he left again for the Diaspora, but it is not known if he went as an emissary or as a private person. In 1726 he was appointed rabbi in Izmir,[17] where he gained a strong position, as it appears from various sources. In Izmir R. Abulafia established important reforms in the religious and social-welfare areas, which suggests his great sensitivity to the situation of the ordinary people.[18] In many matters he cooperated with R. Isaac Hacohen Rapaport, one of the rabbis of Jerusalem, who had also been a rabbi in Izmir for many years and who immigrated to Palestine in his old age. In Izmir R. Abulafia beame close with a group of Kabbalists, among them R. Jacob Israel Algazi, and he published several books in the fields of Halakha, Midrash, and Kabbala.

In the eighteenth century there were particularly strong ties between the Jewish community in Izmir and those in Palestine.[19] In this city, which was very important economically, there was a large Jewish community, which offered direct assistance to the Yishuv, in spite of the complaints voiced by the Istanbul Officials from time to time. At the head of this community were some of the most important former rabbis of Palestine, some of whom returned there toward the end of their lives. Among these rabbis were—besides R. Abulafia, R. Rapaport, and R. Algazi—also R. Raphael Treves and R. Jacob Saul, the rabbi of Izmir, who was later offered the post of head of one of the yeshivas in Jerusalem.[20]

As was the case with many members of his generation, a fierce anticipation of the redemption inspired R. Abulafia, who was a Kabbalist and an ascetic[21] and believed that he was descended from the Davidic dynasty.[22] In his introductions to his books and in his sermons[23] clear messianic themes can be found. In the twenties he had already preached, "The oath will not be fulfilled unless you will go to the land [of Israel] . . . and I will give you this land for an inheritance . . . and with them My oath is fulfilled."[24] In his introduction to the book *Yashresh Ya'akov* (Jacob Will Take Root), he wrote: "It is now time for redemption, to hear the cry of the poor." And several other introductions express R. Abulafia's anticipation of the redemption:

> And my eyes are directed towards heaven, to heaven, and I pray and entreat that our eyes should look to the East, and the Temple and the redeemer will come to Zion.[25]

> And therefore I will pray to God that he should send His word, saying to the prisoners, "Go out" . . . with the son of David [the Messiah] at the head.[26]

> Send, please, the anointed king [the Messiah] to Israel to light up the land.[27]

> God will build the house [the Temple] with the son of Jesse at the head, the Messiah for Israel.[28]

> And the people of Zion will rejoice with their king, our spirit, the anointed of God [the Messiah] and he will gather together the dispersed people of Israel.[29]

This was the period between the disappointment of the hopes of redemption in the year 1706 (forty years after the first appearance of Sabbetai Zevi) and the anticipation of the year 1740.[30] It is true that R. Abulafia did not mention the year 1740 explicitly, but his immigration to Palestine in that year may have been connected with the mood of the times. At any rate, there were groups in Italy that saw the immigrations of 1740 as the beginning of the redemption. Thus, for example, the proofreader of the book *Zimrath Ha-Aretz* (The Fruit of the Land) wrote about "the last of the ten voyages of the Shekhina that dwells in the dust" and expressed his belief that "This time is the time of redemption and the time of the nightingale has arrived to return to her land . . . and from there she will go up to Mount Moriah with the man Zemach [the Messiah]."[31]

In Rabbi Abulafia's correspondence with members of his family there is also much evidence of messianic tension and calculations of the time of the redemption. His maternal grandfather, R. Nissim ben Jamil,[32] whom R. Abulafia quoted a great deal and some of whose books he printed, discussed the coming redemption at length: "Because He wants your redemption He does not look at your accounts but He leaps over the mountains . . . the mountains and hills are redemption times."[33]

R. Jacob Berav, a son-in-law of R. Abulafia and the author of *Zimrath Ha-Aretz*, made much use of expressions taken from deutero-Isaiah, the prophet of the return to Zion, and from the book of Ezra.[34] Rabbi Berav was convinced that the immigration of 1740 was the beginning of the redemption, and that "He Who has granted us this will also show us the rest in goodness, quickly and in readiness."[35] In calling these events "the day of salvation,"[36] he had recourse to verses of consolation from Lamentations, such as "He will not exile you again" (4:22). The theme of the seventy years of ruin of Tiberias also shows the conceptual connection with the return to Zion in the Babylonian period.

Similar emotions inspired R. Haim Ventura, R. Abulafia's other son-in-law, who was also one of the immigrants who settled in Tiberias. Even before his immigration to Palestine he expressed his fierce longing for the redemption: "The son of Jesse [the Messiah] at the head will come quickly, lightly . . . and Jerusalem [will be] rebuilt, the dwelling place of God from ancient times, those who sit in his protection."[37]

Rabbi Abulafia's deep messianic motives for immigrating to Palestine were accompanied by a personal-familial motive—his strong ties with Tiberias, as the proofreader of *Zimrath Ha-Aretz* also attests: "That he reached his destination in peace . . . the city of the graves of his forefathers."[38] When R. Abulafia reached the age of eighty, he apparently began to consider the possibility of spending the rest of his life in Palestine.[39] An additional factor was undoubtedly the tradition that the Messiah would reveal himself in Tiberias: "From there they will be redeemed"[40] and "From there they will go to the Temple."[41] An Arab source from those days also hinted at this tradition. In this source, which described a debate that took place between R. Abulafia and a Christian who was close to Dahir al-ʿUmar, we find the following: "He [R. Abulafia] told the Jews living there that the Messiah would soon arrive and would emerge from the Sea of Galilee and therefore people would leave food for him on the seashore according to the Rabbi's instructions . . . and he would tell them that the time of the coming of the Messiah was already drawing near."[42]

An anonymous Christian traveler who visited Palestine in 1816–17 also mentions this tradition: "Among the Jews in Tiberias the light in the synagogue burns continuously . . . in the hope of seeing the coming of the Messiah; as their books tell that he is to be revealed in this place."[43]

Rabbi Abulafia and his followers left Izmir by sea, and in June 1740 they arrived in Acre.[44] It seems that the group of R. Abulafia's followers numbered several dozen people. R. Moses Yerushalmi relates that "he and his wife [came] and he brought with him ten students."[45] And the Istanbul Officials wrote: "A very large camp, the honor of the sages . . . because they traveled with their wives and children to immigrate to Palestine."[46] A number of Jews from Safed, some of whom were descendants of people who had left Tiberias, also joined the group.[47]

Rabbi Abulafia's immigration had repercussions in the Diaspora and spurred others to immigrate to Palestine. An excellent example is R. Haim ben Attar, who wrote about R. Abulafia's immigration when the former was still in Italy.[48] In later years additional immigrants joined the new community in Tiberias, mainly from Turkey.[49]

At first a special committee was formed for the support of the Tiberias community, as was accepted in those days. R. Solomon Leon, one of the rich men of Istanbul, donated 5,000 *kurus* for the establishment of a yeshiva, and even before the renewal of the settlement in Tiberias the Istanbul Officials sent emissaries to Turkey, the Balkans, Italy, Germany, and eastern Europe[50] to spread the news about the renewal of the settlement in Tiberias and to collect money for it.

In May 1740, about a month before the immigration of R. Abulafia's group, the Istanbul Officials sent R. Joshua Meir to the European part of Turkey and to Europe,[51] with letters of recommendation that brought news of R. Abulafia's immigration and the renewal of the Jewish settlement in Tiberias. A short while later R. Judah Leib Ashkenazi went as an emissary to Germany and eastern Europe.[52]

When he arrived in Tiberias R. Abulafia was received with great honor by Dahir al-ʿUmar, who put at the disposal of his group, at a low price, a piece of land for building a neighborhood for the Jews. He also assisted them in building their houses and public institutions.[53]

Concerning the development of Tiberias in general we have the following evidence from R. Berav: "And during two years he built houses and courtyards for the Jews and a fine synagogue . . . and he built a fine bathhouse and stores for the market-days and a factory for sesame oil and he began to build roads in the land and he also commanded that fields and vineyards be planted."[54] Rabbi Berav composed a special poem at the occasion of the completion of each step in the following projects: the building of the wall around the Jewish quarter, the founding of the synagogue, and the building of the new houses.[55]

When he arrived in Tiberias R. Abulafia sent a number of emissaries to the Diaspora. One of these was his son-in-law, R. Ventura, who set out in 1741 and founded special funds for Tiberias in Italy.[56] In Mantua he printed the book *Zimrath Ha-Aretz*, from which we have drawn our principal information concerning the renewal of the Jewish settlement in Tiberias.

Rabbi Abulafia founded a yeshiva in Tiberias called Mashmiaʿ Yeshuʿa. He also established some important regulations—such as a regulation concerning the counting of the days of the ʿOmer[57]—in addition to those he had established in Izmir. In 1744 R. Haim Abulafia died in Tiberias at the age of eighty-four. His place at the head of the Jewish settlement was inherited by his son, R. Isaac.[58]

The contributions of the Diaspora Jews thus gave a serious impetus to the renewal of the settlement of Tiberias, and in the city special blessings were recited in honor of the donors in the Diaspora.[59] The donations allowed the small settlement to become somewhat more established, and according to the evidence of contemporaries, residence in Tiberias was safer and more comfortable than in Safed or any other place.[60]

However, it is likely that the collection of money for Tiberias affected the collection of money for the other cities in Palestine and aroused many quarrels. The renewal of the settlement in Tiberias did indeed arouse feelings of joy within extensive circles in the Diaspora, but it also led to quarrels over finances, and even the Istanbul Officials competed with one another for the sake of the Palestine cities under their protection, even though an umbrella organization existed.

In 1742 the economic support for Tiberias encountered further difficulties. In July of that year a huge fire broke out in Izmir, which destroyed many buildings of the Jewish community. Until then the Izmir community had offered much assistance to the settlers in Tiberias, as many of them came from that city. Now it could no longer support them. Moreover, the Izmir community was forced to send emissaries to the countries of Europe and to other communities in Turkey to ask for help in the rebuilding of its houses and synagogues.[61] However, in spite of all the difficulties the Tiberias community continued to develop. The Swedish traveler Hasselquist related that in 1751 about half the residents of Tiberias were Jews, but he does not say how many there were.[62] It is known that in the 1750s about ten Ashkenazim from eastern Europe lived in the city.[63]

The Christian traveler Mariti relates that until 1759, the year of the great earthquake in the Galilee, Tiberias was full of life.[64] In 1769 R. Moses Yerushalmi found about 150 Jewish householders there,[65] apparently in the wake of the immigration of Jews from eastern Europe, among them friends of the Baal Shem Tov.[66]

In the 1770s a group of Hasidim under the leadership of R. Menahem-Mendel of Vitebsk, which had left Safed after quarrels with the Sephardim, settled in the city. The Hasidim established a Hasidic community in Tiberias as well, but very soon quarrels broke out between them and the Ashkenazim and Sephardim in the city.[67] In the 1780s severe economic crises occurred there as in the other parts of Palestine. Prices rose and debts increased.[68]

It may be said that the renewal of the settlement in Tiberias gave a huge impetus to the development of the Jewish community in the Galilee in the second half of the eighteenth century and in the nineteenth century.

The Safed Community

In the first half of the eighteenth century, until the renewal of the settlement in Tiberias in 1740, the Safed community was the only Jewish community in the Galilee. In the beginning of the century a group of Sabbateans, remnants of R. Judah Hasid's group, settled in the city, with R. Jacob Vilna among them.

When he gained control over the Galilee Dahir al-ʿUmar appointed one of his sons to be the ruler of Safed,[69] but in contrast to the policy of his father, who aspired to develop the region and to increase its population, the son oppressed the impoverished community, in which there were a few hundred Sephardim and a handful of Ashkenazim, and forced them to pay heavy taxes.[70]

In 1740 R. Eliezer Rokeach arrived in Safed and stationed himself at the head of the Ashkenazi community in the city. His strong ties with the Council of Four Lands in Poland led to the strengthening of financial support for the Ashkenazim in Safed,[71] but he died a year after his arrival. His death led to a severe crisis among the Ashkenazim, who appealed to the Council of Four Lands with urgent pleas for help. The council met in September 1742 in Tischwitz and published an appeal to support the Ashkenazim in Safed, whose financial condition had worsened since R. Rokeach's death: "And there is not one who cares about them . . . and all the time that the great Rabbi Elazar [Rokeach], who had been the leader of the Amsterdam community, had some vigor, he kept his attention on them to search for food for them from the money for Eretz Israel of the days of the donations, but now that he is dead what can they hope for and to whom can they appeal?"[72] It is plausible that R. Rokeach had taken advantage of his connections in Brody and in Amsterdam to obtain money for the Ashkenazim in Safed, and that after his death this support had ceased.

The Jews of Safed suffered from the battles between Dahir al-ʿUmar and his sons and from his war with the ruler of Damascus, and many of them left the city.[73] Some of them moved to the renewed city of Tiberias.

Some growth took place in the community during the fifties and sixties, with the immigrations from eastern Europe, including those of friends of the Baal Shem Tov. According to the Christian traveler Schultz there were about 200 Jews, a yeshiva, and six synagogues in Safed in 1754.[74]

The community suffered a severe blow at the time of the earthquakes of 1759,[75] which nearly destroyed the city. Thousands of the city's residents died, among them about 150 Jews. The community disintegrated completely, and its members scattered, some to Tiberias and some to the surrounding villages. Only about two years afterwards did the Istanbul Officials rehabilitate the community, and thanks to this effort it became possible for Jews from various parts of the Diaspora, mainly from Europe, to settle there.

In the 1770s a group of Hasidim settled in Safed. There was only a small Ashkenazi community in the city, but very soon the relations between the Hasidim and the other Ashkenazim in the city deteriorated, as the latter were probably influenced by forged letters sent by the Mithnag-dim from Lithuania. At any rate, it was undoubtedly against this back-ground that the letters of R. Menaham-Mendel of Vitebsk were written, in which there were bitter accusations against the Ashkenazim, who "lived there from earlier times, [but] they do not know the proper way [of worshipping God] and they cause trouble for the true worshippers of God."[76]

A short while later the Hasidim were also quarreling with the Sephar-dim,[77] mainly for economic reasons, such as the division of the support money and the income from ritual slaughter. However, it seems that in the background of the quarrels there were also the strange customs of the Hasidim, who had brought with them a new way of worshipping God. In their letters the Hasidim accused the Ashkenazi Mithnagdim of incite-ment of the Sephardim. They also accused the leaders of the Sephardim of having Sabbatean beliefs and of offering them insufficient financial support.[78] In the wake of these quarrels a group of Hasidim led by R. Menaham-Mendel of Vitebsk left the city and settled in Tiberias, as mentioned above.

Substantial growth probably occurred in the seventies, with the great immigration of Hasidim in 1777 and the following immigrations.

JEWS IN OTHER GALILEAN SETTLEMENTS

The development of the Galilee at the initiative of Dahir al-ʿUmar led to the settlement of Jews in the villages as well, such as Shafarʿam, which was fortified in the 1760s, and Kafr Yasif. After the earthquakes of 1759 many Jews from Safed fled to the villages.[79]

Some of the Jews in the villages apparently supported themselves through agricultural plots near their houses; at any rate, in their letters to the Diaspora they praised Dahir al-ʿUmar, at whose mercy they were able "to pray in the name of God in the synagogues and in the study-houses and to live in tents and plant the holy ground."[80]

In the 1740s about ten Jewish householders, led by R. Solomon Ab-badi, settled in Kafr Yasif. The Jews of Kafr Yasif even sent an emissary to the Diaspora.[81] The Jews of Kafr Yasif were mentioned by a member of R. Haim ben Attar's group, who related: "[There are] ten householders and they live well and in great freedom and their work is sowing and reaping and they give the tithe . . . and in this year, the year 5502 [1742], they do not sow because it is the *shemita* year [the seventh year, in which it is not permitted to work the land] and they do not go into exile."[82]

It is known that in some of the Galilean villages—such as Sahnin, Ibillin, Ilabun, and Kafr Manda—there were Jews living at that time who supported themselves in part by selling cotton from the Galilean villages to French merchants in Acre and Sidon.[83]

THE LEADERSHIP IN HEBRON, TIBERIAS, AND SAFED

In contrast to the large amount of material concerning the Jerusalem community, we possess only a small amount on the leadership of the three other holy cities—Hebron, Tiberias, and Safed—and so the following remarks are short and general. Investigation of the few available sources reveals, it seems to me, that there was some difference in the structure of the leadership in the communities of Hebron, Tiberias, and Safed and in the power relations within them. In Hebron and Safed there were small communities that had undergone much hardship, whereas in Tiberias the community had been established only in the middle of the century, which led to a greater centrality. These are the characteristic aspects of the leaderships of these communities in the eighteenth century: (1) the central person was the rabbi;[84] (2) even the small communities received donations and were under the protection of the Istanbul Officials; and (3) it seems that each community was autonomous, without dependence on Jerusalem or any other community.

It is true that Jerusalem had the largest Jewish community in Palestine, but this did not lead to the dominance of Jerusalem over the other cities, whether on the organizational or on the spiritual plane. The reason is clear. The leadership of the Jerusalem community was not autonomous, and so it could not impose its authority on the other communities. At any rate, we do not have enough evidence to determine with certainty whether there were areas in which the spiritual leadership of Jerusalem did nevertheless have authority outside the city. It is likely that the large number of Torah scholars in Jerusalem and the importance of the city in the consciousness of the nation were occasionally the deciding factors in debates that broke out between Jerusalem and Hebron.[85] Jerusalem also may have sent officials to manage the affairs of Hebron,[86] but in the hundreds of customs of Jerusalem that have survived the uniqueness of

Jerusalem stands out. Only in a few cases is it reported that a custom was observed both in Jerusalem and in Hebron.[87] Even when the custom concerned a matter that involved Palestine in general, it is usually mentioned that it was observed only in Jerusalem: "Those who come from the Diaspora to Eretz Israel with the intention of settling in Eretz Israel . . . this is a custom of Jerusalem."[88]

The few instances in which the Jerusalem sages intervened in the affairs of the other communities cannot serve as the basis for generalization, and it may be said that each city with a Jewish community in Palestine had a separate leadership without dependence on Jerusalem. Nevertheless it seems that because of their economic dependence on the Istanbul Officials the communities of Hebron, Tiberias, and Safed also lost their autonomy.

We possess very little information about the leadership of the Hebron community. In the Istanbul *Pinkas* there are no hints at all of a connection between the leaderships of Jerusalem and Hebron from 1741 to 1771. But in other sources we do find such a connection.

At the end of the century the Jerusalem leadership had some influence on what took place in Hebron. Around 1795 R. Yom-Tov Algazi, chief rabbi of Jerusalem, wrote the following:

> For a number of years, for seven and even for eight, the community of Hebron (and this city is close to the community of our holy city) had been under siege and in trouble because of the large number of poor people in one place, and since that time this has been the principle, that the Jerusalem community supervises the Hebron community, to help them pay their debts to the Gentiles and to other Jews, to support them. Now this city is close to our holy city of Jerusalem and so when they were in trouble they appealed to me that I should have mercy on them and appoint supervisors and officials over them from the people of Jerusalem because they have been faithful and for the sake of the love of our forefathers . . . and so I appointed supervisors for them . . . and for a few years they supervised the officials and did business with the leadership of the Hebron community.[89]

It appears that in the 1780s supervisors over the Hebron officials were appointed in Jerusalem and that this was not something new. We do not know when this arrangement began or how long it continued. However, we do have a document from the 1760s in which Rahamim Hacohen, who was an official in Jerusalem, was mentioned: "He is also an official in Hebron and he takes care of their donations and pledges and he did not deal honestly with them."[90]

From the information in our possession it is clear that R. Haim Abulafia was the leader of the Tiberias community and also dealt with the material affairs of the community. His sons inherited the leadership of the community.[91]

We do not know what the structure of the leadership in the city was, and we also have no information about the number of officials and the relationships within the leadership. According to one version, from the time of R. Abulafia the rabbi of Tiberias was also the rabbi of Safed, but there is no documentary evidence for this.[92] It seems that at this time the small community of Acre was subject to the rabbi of Tiberias.[93] Did this perhaps come about because they were part of the same *sancak* (province)?

In Safed the rabbi of the city was also the official. In the first half of the eighteenth century R. Moses Malkhi was the community official and the chief rabbi at the same time.[94] From non-Jewish sources it appears that R. Malkhi was a wealthy man who lent money at interest to gentiles.[95] In the beginning of the 1740s R. Malkhi became ill, and half his body was paralyzed. In his place a leadership of three officials was appointed.[96] In the years 1740–41 R. Elazar Rokeach was at the head of the small Ashkenazi community. Rabbi Simha of Zalozce, one of the immigrants of 1775, tells of "the rabbi, the official . . . whose name is Rabbi Masoud Bounan."[97]

It seems that at the end of the century the positions of rabbi and official were separated, as the Hasidim tell about quarrels with the official in Safed.[98]

The leadership of the Hasidim in the Galilee was completely similar to their leadership in the Diaspora. The *tzaddik* dominated, of course, over the material wealth as well, and it was he who distributed the money that arrived from the Diaspora. At first R. Menahem-Mendel of Vitebsk was the leader of the Hasidim, and after his death R. Abraham of Kalisk took over his position.

The method of organization of the Hasidic communities in Palestine derived directly from the tradition they brought with them from eastern Europe. They did not have an elected leadership or elected patron, but charismatic leaders who made all decisions. The form of their economic support was not different from that of the other Jews in Palestine during the Ottoman period, that is, the sending of emissaries for collecting money, especially in their countries of origin. The organization of the support in the Diaspora also did not differ from that of the other communities in Palestine. At the head of the collection of funds were the Hasidic *tzaddikim* who had remained in the Diaspora.[99]

An interesting episode was the controversy over the leadership of the Hasidim who had remained in White Russia.[100] Before his immigration to Palestine R. Menahem-Mendel of Vitebsk had been the senior leader in White Russia, and R. Shneur-Zalman of Lyady accepted his authority. However, as the years went on R. Menahem-Mendel became estranged from his Hasidim, and the Hasidim in the Diaspora began to seek leaders who were closer to them.

R. Shneur-Zalman of Lyady began to amass power, and even during the time of R. Menahem-Mendel he became "the first spokesman of the generation." In 1788 R. Menahem-Mendel died, and R. Abraham of Koliszki thought that he would inherit his position and would become the leader both of the Hasidim who had immigrated with him to Palestine and of those who had remained in White Russia. However, reality had its own part to play. The status of R. Shneur-Zalman had become stronger, and his new teachings, the teachings of "Habad," were now ascendant in White Russia. From the letters in our possession we get a picture of a sharp conflict. R. Abraham accused R. Shneur-Zalman of distorting the teachings of Hasidism, but it did not do him any good. The Hasidic center in Palestine became more shut in on itself, while the "Habad" Hasidism spread its branches to Palestine as well, and in the beginning of the nineteenth century a group of immigrants from among the "Habad" Hasidim established important centers in Hebron and Jerusalem.[101]

13

OTHER CONGREGATIONS IN PALESTINE

THE ASHKENAZIM IN PALESTINE

At the beginning of the eighteenth century there were a few hundred Ashkenazim living in Palestine, mainly in Jerusalem.[1] With the immigration of R. Judah Hasid and his group the Ashkenazi community in the city grew noticeably, but after the group disintegrated the Ashkenazim dispersed, and some even left the country. Tradition relates that from the time of the destruction of the Ashkenazi court until the renewal of the Ashkenazi community at the beginning of the nineteenth century the Ashkenazim in Jerusalem were forced to dress like the Sephardim so that their Moslem creditors and their descendants would not recognize them and try to collect the Ashkenazi community debt remaining from the early eighteenth century. At any rate, in a document from 1769 R. Moses Yerushalmi related: "And it is forbidden for an Ashkenazi . . . to enter Jerusalem unless he is dressed in Turkish [Sephardi] clothing and speaks the Turkish language so that no one will know that he comes from Europe. And all this is because of the actions of the group of Hasidim that immigrated with the late R. Judah Hasid the second."[2]

It is likely that after the destruction of the Ashkenazi court not all the Ashkenazim left Jerusalem, and a small community, numbering a few dozen souls, remained in the city.[3] With the rehabilitation of the Jerusalem community by the Istanbul Officials attempts were made to renew the activities of the Ashkenazi community, and at the end of the 1720s the few Ashkenazim reorganized themselves into a separate community and elected patrons. They also began to send emissaries on their own behalf to the communities of Europe. Nevertheless a substantial community was not established, since because of past events the Ashkenazim did not have a rabbinical court or a synagogue of their own—"and the Ashkenazi Jews come to pray in the synagogue of the Sephardi Jews"[4]—and so, having no choice, they became part of the Sephardi community.

After the destruction of the Ashkenazi court the number of Ashkenazim in the Galilean communities increased, first in Safed, in which an Ashkenasi core was established, and—beginning in the 1740s—in Tiberias as well. The Ashkenazi communities in the Galilee continued to develop, and by the time of the great immigration of Hasidim in 1777 there was already a basis there for expansion. Ashkenazim who were uprooted from Jerusalem at the time of the destruction of the Ashkenazi court settled in Hebron as well.[5]

In the eighteenth century the entire Jewish population of Palestine numbered between 5,000 and 8,000 people, but it is difficult to know how many of them were Ashkenazim. Nevertheless we do have some data about their numbers. A document from the beginning of the century mentions 400 or more people.[6] In 1735 the Istanbul Officials wrote to the communities of Europe that the number of Ashkenazim in Jerusalem was seventy.[7] A German traveler who visited Jerusalem in 1738 told of 100 Ashkenazim.[8] The signatures of about ten householders are preserved on letters written on behalf of the Ashkenazim of Jerusalem in the 1730s and 1740s.[9] In lists of the recipients of support in 1755–56 about twenty Ashkenazi householders in Jerusalem were mentioned, and more than that number in the other holy cities,[10] but these lists do not include all of the Ashkenazim in Palestine at the time. In 1765 a group of about thirty Ashkenazim from eastern Europe immigrated to Palestine and settled in the Galilee, among them some friends of the Baal Shem Tov.[11] There is reason to believe that this was not the only group that immigrated during this period.[12] In a letter sent from Jerusalem to Metz in 1768 fifty Ashkenazim were mentioned explicitly.[13] In sources from the end of the 1760s forty Jews were mentioned as being in Tiberias and more than twenty in Safed.[14] Data from the years 1720–77 tell of about 130 householders and about twenty women,[15] although they did not all live in Palestine at the same time. If we add the members of their families, it may be said that in the years 1720–77 several hundred Ashkenazim lived in Palestine—a larger number than historians knew about before. With the great Hasidic immigration the number of Ashkenazim increased greatly. In the first wave about 300 people immigrated, and many more came afterwards.

We have very little information about the internal organization of the Ashkenazim. In the 1740s two officials in the Jerusalem community took care of the distribution of the support from the Diaspora. In the fifties R. Abraham Gerson of Kuty was the head of the Ashkenazim. His sons as well were among the heads of the community in Jerusalem. In the seventies R. Yeruham Vilna was the head of the Ashkenazim in Jerusalem. At the head of the Ashkenazim in Safed in 1740–41 was

R. Elazar Rokeach.[16] The Hasidim in Safed and Tiberias were headed by R. Menahem-Mendel of Vitebsk and R. Abraham of Kalisk.

During the entire period there was some immigration of Ashkenazim to Palestine, whether of individuals or of small groups. Many of them came from Brody and its surroundings. Others came from the following places, among others: Kuty, Vilna, Brisk, Shidlov, Posen, Dubnow, Vizhnitz, Lvov, Lublin, Przemyslany, Zalozce, Linetz, Satannov, Miedzyboz, Grodno, Prague, Vienna, and Amsterdam.[17] The immigrants of 1777 came mainly from White Russia. In general, most of them came from eastern Europe, with only a small number from western Europe. It is possible to see a clear connection between the places of origin of the immigrants and the regions where Hasidism flourished: Volhynia and Podolia. Moreover, there was not only a geographical connection. Some of the immigrants were connected to the group of the Baal Shem Tov by family and personal ties, whether directly or indirectly. There is reason to believe that these ties were not coincidental, and that among the early Hasidim there was a widespread trend to immigrate to Palestine.

In spite of the small number of Ashkenazim in Palestine from the time of the destruction of the Ashkenazi court in Jerusalem until the great Hasidic immigration, and in spite of the fact that the Ashkenazim were not organized into separate communities and only sent out emissaries for themselves, great historic importance may be ascribed to their settlement in Palestine, as it constitutes the bridge between Sabbateanism and Hasidism pointed out by Tishbi in his discussion of the development of Hasidism.[18] The Ashkenazim who lived in Palestine during this period were a kind of mixture of the remnants of R. Judah Hasid's group and the remnants of Sabbateanism, on the one hand, and the Kabbalists of the *klaus* (yeshiva) from Brody and the surrounding areas, who presaged the development of Hasidism, on the other.

It is worth emphasizing that most of the Ashkenazim settled in the Galilee, and not in Jerusalem or Hebron. The development of an Ashkenazi core in the Galilee paved the way for the broadening of the Ashkenazi communities in Tiberias and Safed.

THE KARAITES IN JERUSALEM

In the seventeenth century there was a small community of Karaites in Jerusalem,[19] but it dwindled at the beginning of the eighteenth century, and because of the debts that the Karaites owed it the Jerusalem commu-

nity confiscated their houses. Nevertheless a number of Karaites remained in Jerusalem, and at the time of the rehabilitation of the Jewish
community by the Istanbul Officials a rehabilitation of the Karaite community also began. In 1731 the wealthy Karaite R. Joseph Cohen immigrated to Palestine from Damascus, and he settled in Jerusalem and
assisted the Karaites in the city.[20] We have evidence from the beginning
of the 1740s suggesting that at that time there was a small Karaite community in Jerusalem, although there were historians who argued on the
basis of Karaite tradition that the community was renewed only in
1749.[21] In 1745 the Istanbul Officials informed the Jerusalem officials
that they had sent 450 *kurus* to the Karaites in Jerusalem through Joseph
Lutzati.[22] In the same year they also announced that they had paid a debt
of the Karaites that had been sent to Istanbul for payment.[23] The assistance that the Istanbul community extended to the Karaites in
Jerusalem helped to improve the relationship between the Jews and the
Karaites.

Near the end of 1748 a group of several dozen Karaites from
Damascus settled in Jerusalem, led by Samuel ben Abraham Halevi. The
Karaite immigrants demanded that the Jewish community return to them
the houses it had confiscated, and when they encountered a refusal they
brought the matter to the gentile courts, which ruled in their favor.[24]

In all matters relating to taxes and to representation before the authorities the Karaite community was subordinate to the Sephardi community, and against this background quarrels often broke out between the
two communities. In the 1750s this even brought about a rift between the
Karaites and the leadership of the Jewish community.[25] Many apoc-
ryphal motifs are intertwined in the traditions about the quarrel, but we
are able to illuminate the background some on the basis of new sources.

In 1720 the Istanbul Officials wrote in astonishment that it was not
recorded in the account-book of payments for 1749 that the Karaites had
paid their taxes,[26] and they wrote similarly in 1753 about the account-
book of payments for 1752.[27] In these years the Istanbul Officials complained that the Karaites who were immigrating to Palestine through
Istanbul were refusing to pay the immigration tax imposed on immigrants
at that time.[28] This evidence may explain the great quarrel that broke out
around 1755. In that year heavy taxes were imposed on the Jewish community, and the Karaites refused to pay the portion that was imposed on
them.

The Karaites, like the Sephardim and Ashkenazim, used to send emissaries to their communities in the Diaspora.

It is true that there were strained relations between the Karaites and the leadership of the Sephardi community concerning financial matters, but in their daily lives the relations between them were generally normal.[29] The following was written by a Karaite in 1785: "We have about fifteen or sixteen houses in Jerusalem, and Rabbinites [that is, Jews who are not Karaites] are renting all of them."[30] In Hebron the situation was similar: "And we have camped in the houses of the Rabbinites, which were previously housed of the Karaites, and we have given donations to their synagogue and they gave us great honor."[31]

In those days there were good relations between the Rabbanites and the Karaites in Istanbul, in contrast to the strained relations in Egypt.[32] From a responsum of R. Raphael Meyuhas Bechar Samuel, chief rabbi of Jerusalem in the fifties and sixties, it appears that in those days the Jewish community expressed a tolerant attitude to the Karaites, and there was even a trend to befriend them. For example, a marriage between a Jewess and a Karaite man was not treated by Rabbi Samuel as an intermarriage,[33] and he even permitted the Written Torah to be taught to the Karaite children together with the children of the Sephardi community. This responsum of Rabbi Samuel was also approved by R. Mizrahi, one of the rabbis of Jerusalem at that time.[34] In the book of regulations it was written, "It was customary to circumcise the Karaites."[35]

We also have evidence concerning trade between the Jews and the Karaites. Thus, for example, it was mentioned that "a Karaite brought cheeses from a Jew . . . and they were permitted."[36]

It seems, then, that in everyday life—such as trade, education, and circumcision—there was cooperation, and that the quarrels between the two communities broke out because the Karaites did not pay taxes, and the authorities had imposed the responsibility for the payment of all the taxes—from the Sephardim and Ashkenazim as well as from the Karaites—on the Sephardi community.

In the seventies the Karaite community became involved in financial difficulties, as the donations from the Diaspora were delayed because of the war between Turkey and Russia. In 1780 Samuel Halevi, the founder of the community in 1744, was sent as an emissary to the Diaspora.[37] In the eighties the immigration of Karaites to Palestine began again.[38] The financial support was transferred by means of the Greek patriarch in Istanbul and his representatives in Jerusalem.[39] The Karaite community in Jerusalem continued to exist from the middle of the eighteenth century until the twentieth century.

14

THE YESHIVAS

IN THE SECOND HALF of the seventeenth century there were only a few yeshivas in Palestine, but by the middle of the eighteenth century there were already many yeshivas there, with hundreds of Torah scholars. In Jerusalem alone there were more than a dozen yeshivas. From new material found in the archives of the Amsterdam and Jerusalem communities it appears that even more yeshivas were added to these during the rest of the century, although there are some about which we have no details.[1]

In each yeshiva there were about ten Torah scholars or perhaps a few more, and sometimes there were also a few young scholars. The format of the yeshivas was different from that of the eastern European yeshivas of the sort that are commonly found in Israel today. In general they were not educational institutions, but only places for the study of the Torah.

The large number of yeshivas in Palestine in the middle of the eighteenth century stemmed mainly from the rehabilitation of the communities and their administration by the Istanbul Officials, who sought ways to improve the economic support of the Yishuv. They found the solution in the establishment of yeshivas in the name of donors, which led to an increase in the donations and guaranteed a fixed livelihood for hundreds of Torah scholars. The Jews residing in the Diaspora obviously valued the commandment of studying the Torah in Eretz Israel and ascribed great importance to the fact that Jews were living in Eretz Israel and studying the Torah there. The establishment of yeshivas in the period under discussion was thus the outcome of the intertwining of economic and spiritual factors.[2] When one studies the list of yeshivas that were established in Palestine in the eighteenth century, it is difficult not to be impressed by this unique phenomenon. In those days there were indeed Torah scholars in every Jewish community, but they studied in institutions supported by their own communities, whereas in Palestine there were many yeshivas, with a total of hundreds of Torah scholars, all of whose support came from donations from various parts of the Diaspora. It is also worth noting the great concentration of sages who had no other livelihood than the study of the Torah, which was also characteristic of the communities of Palestine. Nevertheless, this great concentration of Torah scholars did not serve as a source of unique spiritual creativity, and the works that were composed by the sages of Eretz Israel generally did not differ from the usual.

Donations for the establishment of the yeshivas generally came from wealthy Jews who wanted to establish memorials for themselves in Eretz Israel, in each of which ten men who were not otherwise employed would study the Torah and benefit from regular support. Thus, for example, an Egyptian Jew donated part of his possessions for the support of ten Torah scholars in Safed.[3] The donors were generally members of rich and famous families, such as the Pereyra, di-Mayo, Rakah, and Agiv families of Holland, Italy, Turkey, Morocco, and other countries. At times they left a legacy for this purpose.

Supervision of the money for the establishment of the yeshivas was generally allotted to the Istanbul Officials or a representative of theirs, who invested the principal. The interest—which was between seven and ten percent at that time—served for the sustenance of the Torah scholars.[4] Sometimes an emissary succeeded in persuading donors to establish a yeshiva and appoint him as its dean.

In many communities of the Diaspora committees were formed for the establishment and support of yeshivas in Palestine. The best-known committee was that called Knesseth Israel in Italy, which was formed by R. Haim ben Attar on his way to Palestine and bore the name of the yeshiva that he established in Jerusalem. The centers of the committee were in Leghorn and Modena, and its branches were spread throughout Italy.[5]

Often a special committee was formed for a specific yeshiva:

> A committee that decided to establish a yeshiva in a particular place and pledged a certain amount of money for the upkeep of the yeshivas, and asked another city that people should join in this good deed, to give 200 *kurus* each year.[6]

> Someone who donated one yeshiva for the sages of Jerusalem . . . in the study-house "Beth Jacob" of the Pereyra [family] that they should study there every day for the peace of his soul . . . in Salonika.[7]

Special committees were set up for other yeshivas as well, such as Yefa'er 'Anavim, Haverim Makshivim, and Damesek Eliezer.

The donors and the Istanbul officials had the authority to appoint the dean of the yeshiva and its sages and to establish their rank. This rank—that is, the order of appearance of the sages of the yeshiva in the list of the appointees—was considered of great importance, because the relative amount of financial support in each yeshiva was determined by it. The income of the dean of a yeshiva was generally twice that of an ordinary member. From various sources we learn that the regular livelihood and honored status led to there being a large number of candidates for each appointment in a yeshiva, and this may be an explanation for the large number of yeshivas in those days. Sometimes there was a struggle for the deanship of the yeshiva, and in the end this struggle led to the establishment of a new yeshiva.

With the establishment of each yeshiva detailed regulations were written concerning the manner of its organization and management and the hours of study. The support was conditional upon the fulfillment of the regulations. We have in our possession regulations of a number of yeshivas, which show us that their dependence upon the donors was absolute.[8]

For each yeshiva officials were appointed in Palestine, and they were responsible for the distribution of money, the renting and furnishing of houses, and the buying of food, books, etc. These officials—as well as the guard and the caretaker of the yeshiva—received a yearly salary from the yeshiva fund. This salary was much smaller than that of the Torah scholars. In general there were two officials for each yeshiva.

A yeshiva had several sources of income. Besides the donors of the fixed fund there were individuals who donated smaller sums for the yeshivas independently of the official funds. Sometimes these were legacies, which were intended for the regular study of portions of the Mishna for the elevation of the souls of the departed donors. Besides this, the yeshivas received ten percent of the profits of the emissaries,[9] and often harsh arguments took place on this topic between the Istanbul Officials and the community leadership.

The large amount of the support for the sages of the yeshivas sometimes led a Torah scholar to enroll in several yeshivas at the same time in order to receive an additional income, or to move to another yeshiva because of the amount of support. Their great wealth even allowed the yeshivas to lend money at interest in order to increase their income.

The good economic situation of the Torah scholars led to the strengthening of their social position. Nevertheless, frequent quarrels broke out between the Torah scholars on the one hand and the householders and officials on the other, because in addition to their high incomes the Torah scholars benefited from reductions in the payment of taxes, and as a result the embittered householders complained to the Istanbul Officials. In general the Torah scholars had the upper hand in these quarrels, as the Istanbul Officials, in spite of their constant intervention in the affairs of the community, were not willing to impose their authority on the yeshiva people, who also enjoyed a great measure of respect in the Diaspora. In the 1760s and 1770s the Torah scholars practically dominated the community leadership in Jerusalem.[10]

There was a strong connection between the yeshivas and the rabbinical courts of the Jerusalem community, and in the eighteenth century a number of rabbinical courts had members who were deans of the yeshivas and senior Torah scholars.

Following is a list of the yeshivas in Palestine in the eighteenth century. In Jerusalem, there were twenty-four: Beth Jacob;[11] the yeshiva of R. Abraham Rovigo;[12] Beth-El;[13] Neveh Shalom—Brith Avraham;[14] Yefaʾer ʿAnavim;[15] Haverim Makshivim;[16] Knesseth Israel;[17] Beth Avraham;[18] Hesed le-Avraham u-Vinyan Shelomo;[19] Gedulath Mordekhai;[20] Damesek Eliezer;[21] Magen David;[22] the Yeshiva of Ashkenazim;[23] Marpe la-Nefesh;[24] Mekor Barukh;[25] Zeraʿ Yitzhak;[26] Beth Gedalia;[27] Beth Aharon;[28] Bnei Moshe;[29] Kedushath Yom-Tov;[30] Rekez;[31] Haim va-Hesed;[32] Kehillath Yaʿakov;[33] and Etz Haim.[34] In Hebron, there were three: Hesed le-Avraham ve-Emeth le-Yaʿakov;[35] Knesseth Israel;[36] and the yeshiva of Elijah Romano.[37] In Tiberias, there was one: Mashmiaʿ Yeshuʿa.[38] In Safed, there was one: the yeshiva of R. Haim Alfandari.[39]

15

DEMOGRAPHIC DATA

DURING THE SEVENTEENTH CENTURY the Jewish settlement in Palestine had dwindled due to internal strife and persecutions. According to the few pieces of evidence in our possession the Yishuv contained between 3,000 and 5,000 people.[1] At the end of the century the Yishuv recovered somewhat.

It is difficult to estimate the number of Jews in Palestine in the eighteenth century. We do not have exact data, as no population census was taken during the entire period under discussion.

There are three types of sources on the Jewish population in Palestine during the eighteenth century. First, there is the evidence of Christian travelers, most of which was published in Ish-Shalom's book, but this evidence is fragmentary and does not enable us to get a complete picture.

Second, there are lists of payers of the poll tax in Ottoman sources. These lists are indeed reliable, but they do not describe the entire picture either, as they include all the non-Moslem residents. Moreover, not all the Jews paid the poll tax. Some of them evaded it, whereas others were exempt because of their poverty. Others—such as the Ashkenazim— were not Ottoman subjects. It is worth adding that the taxes were paid to the Ottoman authorities through the communities or the tax collectors, and so it is difficult to rely on the data.[2] Nevertheless, these lists do tell us about trends of growth or diminution in the population, and from this aspect their data agree with what is recorded in Jewish sources.

Finally, there are Jewish sources, which indeed report data on the number of Jews, except that the sources sometimes contradict one another. We know that the letters of recommendation given to the emissaries and the letters sent to the Diaspora included requests for money, and so they greatly exaggerated the number of people in order to increase the donations. Nevertheless, it is also possible to find some private letters that were written innocently—such as the letter of R. Abraham Gerson of Kuty to his brother-in-law, the Baal Shem Tov—and so their data are more reliable.

At the beginning of the eighteenth century R. Judah Hasid's group arrived in Palestine, and as a result of this immigration and subsequent immigrations the Yishuv grew noticeably, although we are unable to estimate its size.[3] In the wake of the disintegration of the Ashkenazi community in Jerusalem during the first twenty years of the eighteenth century, the Jewish population in the country declined by about twenty percent, as the Ottoman sources attest. In the 1730s and 1740s, after the Istanbul Officials started managing the Jewish communities in Palestine and after the renewal of the settlement in Tiberias, the immigration again increased and the number of Jews grew, especially in Jerusalem, as shown in the following letter from 1744: "There have never been more than a hundred householders gathered together there at one time, and today six or seven hundred householders may be found there. It is well-known today how much the number of householders in Jerusalem has increased, ten times the amount in former times."[4]

In his above-mentioned letter to the Baal Shem Tov, R. Abraham Gerson wrote that there were about one thousand Jewish householders in Jerusalem.[5] In another place the following was written: "There is a danger to the lives of three thousand people living in Jerusalem today."[6] A letter sent from Jerusalem in 1744 said that the number of Jewish residents of Jerusalem was 10,000 but it seems to me that this number is an exaggeration.[7]

It seems that the bachelor regulations of the 1740s,[8] which prohibited the residence of bachelors over the age of twenty in Jerusalem, reflected—alongside the ethical consideration—the wish to limit the number of Jews in Jerusalem. The increase in the number of immigrants at this time also motivated the Istanbul Officials to impose a tax on every immigrant and to establish regulations limiting the number of immigrants.

The growth of the Jewish settlement during this period is also apparent from the tax lists of the Ottoman Empire, most of which point to an increase in the number of Jews beginning in the 1740s. In the following years the number of Jews stabilized, and occasionally there was even a decrease.[9] In 1759 there was an earthquake in Safed, in which 150 Jews died.[10] During the sixties hundreds of Jews fled Jerusalem because of the quarrels within the leadership and the persecutions by the authorities.[11] In 1769 R. Peretz ben Moshe wrote that in all Eretz Israel "there are not even three thousand including all the Sephardi and Ashkenazi Jews."[12] In the seventies the rebellion of Ali Bey broke out, which led to the flight of the residents from Palestine, while the war between Turkey and Russia led to an interruption of the immigration. In a document from 1770 the people of Jerusalem mentioned 5,000 souls.[13] Only when the fighting subsided did the Yishuv grow once more, especially as a result of the great Hasidic immigration of 1777.

It seems that the average number of Jews in Jerusalem during the eighteenth century was about 3,000, out of a total population of 15,000 people. In the other three holy cities—Hebron, Safed, and Tiberias—there were smaller communities, numbering hundreds each, altogether about 1,500–2,000 people. Several hundred Jews also lived in the Galilean villages, while in the other cities—such as Acre, Jaffa, Gaza, and Nablus—there were a few dozen Jews.[14] During the eighteenth century there were thus some 6,000–8,000 Jews in Palestine (see table 1).

It is worth noting that during this period the Jews were a very small percentage of the population of Palestine. There are different estimates of the total number of residents. According to a conservative estimate, the total population of Palestine in the eighteenth century numbered 100,000–250,000 people.[15]

From a demographic standpoint the Jewish settlement thus did not develop in an ordinary manner, and during the eighteenth century there were continual fluctuations in the number of residents. The reasons for this are: (1) the large mortality rate due to the relatively high age of the population. To this must be added the high infant mortality rate and deaths from the plague, phenomena that were prevalent throughout the world at that time;[16] (2) the continual immigration, on the one hand, and the continual emigration, due to the difficult economic conditions and the pressure of the authorities, on the other; and (3) the wars and rebellions that took place in Palestine and along the coasts of the Mediterranean during the eighteenth century.[17]

The lack of stability in the population was a cause of the stagnation of social and spiritual life and the great dependence of the Yishuv on the Istanbul Officials.

TABLE 1. Jewish Population of Palestine in the Eighteenth Century

Year	Number of Jews	Source	Comments
A. All Palestine			
Beginning of century	Decline of 20%	Cohen, *Palestine in the Eighteenth Century*, p. 251	According to Ottoman lists of poll tax payers
1724–41	Growth in tens of percent	Ibid.	
1746–76	No change	Ibid.	
c. 1772	Approx. 3,000	Ya'ari, "Two pamphlets from Palestine," p. 155	
1773	Approx. 1,000 householders (4,000 people)	Ya'ari, *The Emissaries of Palestine*, p. 582	According to an emissary's story
1776–96	Marked growth	Cohen, *Palestine in the Eighteenth Century*, p. 251	
B. Jerusalem			
1690–91	Over 800–900	Heyd, "The Jews of Palestine," p. 177	According to Ottoman lists of taxpayers
c. 1690	Approx. 300 householders (1,000 people)	*Likutim*, vol. 1, p. 12	According to a description of the community
1700	Increase due to arrival of Hasid's group	Benayahu, "The holy Brotherhood of R. Judah Hasid," p. 155	According to various evidence

173

TABLE 1 (Cont.)

Year	Number of Jews	Source	Comments
1706	Mass flight	Shohet, "Three eighteenth-century letters on Palestine," p. 237	According to various evidence
1709	About 1,000 poor people	Benayahu, "The holy Brotherhood of R. Judah Hasid"	
1700–1723	Approx. 2,000	Sefath Emeth, p. 26a	Description for charity purposes
1737	Increase	Ish-Shalom, Christian Travels in the Holy Land, p. 385	Christian's description
1741	10,000	Book of Regulations, p. 46b	Regulation on presumptive ownership
1744	600–700 householders (2,500–3,000 people)	Rivkind, "Documents illustrating Jewish life in Palestine," p. 118	Letter for charity purposes; exaggerated
		Pinkas of Istanbul, letter of 24 Elul 5504 (September 1744), p. 61	Description by Istanbul Officials for charity purposes

174

Year	Figure	Source	Notes
1748	Approx. 1,000 householders	Barnai, *Hasidic Letters from Palestine*, p. 38	Personal letter of R. Abraham Gerson of Kuty; reliable
1748	3,000	*Pinkas* of Istanbul, letter of 17 Iyyar 5508 (May 1748), p. 65	Description by Istanbul Officials for charity
1751	20,000	Ish-Shalom, *Christian Travels in the Holy Land*, p. 401	From responsa
1758	500 pupils in elementary school	S. Marcus, "Documents from Rhodes concerning Palestine," p. 224	Only males
1770	5,000	Rivkind, "Documents illustrating Jewish life in Palestine," pp. 133–34	Letter for charity purposes
1773	About 500 died of hunger	Ben-Yaʿakov, *Jerusalem within Its Walls*, p. 363	
1789(?)	Fewer immigrants and pilgrims	Sharon and Beck, *From Ancient Archives*, pp. 21–22	Firman
1793	Fewer immigrants and pilgrims	Haim, "Sources of Sephardi history," p. 161	Firman

TABLE 1 (Cont.)

Year	Number of Jews	Source	Comments
C. Hebron			
1700	40 householders (approx. 250 people)	Rubashov, *Sha'alu Shelom Yerushalayim*, p. 463	Description by Jewish immigrant
1743	200 people	*Agron*, p. 13	
1765	120 householders (approx. 500 people)	Ya'ari, *The Emissaries of Palestine*, p. 587	According to a letter to an emissary
1765	200 people	Rivkind, "Documents illustrating Jewish life in Palestine," p. 129	Letter of Officials for Hebron in Istanbul
1773	107 householders (approx. 450 people)	Ya'ari, *The Emissaries of Palestine*, p. 582	
1782	300 people	Rivkind, "Documents illustrating Jewish life in Palestine," pp. 137–38	Letter for charity purposes
D. Safed			
1730	200 householders, 150 old people, 50 Torah scholars	Ben-Zvi, *Studies and Documents*, p. 200	Letter for charity purposes
1754	200 people	Kedar, "Information on the Jews of Palestine in eighteenth-century Protestant sources," p. 204	Evidence of Christian traveler

Before 1759	50–60 families (200–240 people)	Mahler, *History of the Jewish People in Modern Times*, vol. 4, p. 273	According to description by Christian traveler
1765	40–50 householders (160–200 people)	Ya'ari, *Travels in Palestine*, p. 399	According to immigrant's description
1777	Marked increase	Halpern, *The Hasidic Immigration to Palestine*, p. 26	Varied evidence from Hasidim
E. Tiberias			
1726	12 families	Ish-Shalom, *Christian Travels in the Holy Land*, p. 393	Description by Christian traveler
1740	Several dozen people	Ya'ari, *Memoirs of Palestine*, vol. 1, p. 74	Evidence of renewers of Tiberias settlement
		Ya'ari, *Travels in Palestine*, p. 440	Evidence of immigrant
1767	Over 100 people	Ish-Shalom, *Christian Travels in the Holy Land*, p. 404	Description by Christian traveler
1769	Over 150 householders (approx. 600 people)	Ya'ari, *Travels in Palestine*, p. 441	Evidence of immigrant
F. Acre			
1742	100 householders	Ya'ari, *Letters from Palestine*, p. 256	Evidence of immigrant

Part V
THE ECONOMIC LIFE
OF THE JEWS IN PALESTINE

THE STRUCTURE OF THE GOVERNMENT in Palestine in the eighteenth century and the economic situation in the country had a decisive influence on the economic life of the Jews. The local rulers generally did not develop the country, but cared only about their own profits and extorted money in various ways. Moreover, the means of transportation in the country were in very bad condition, and because of the lack of security on the roads danger awaited all travelers. Rabbi Azulay wrote the following in his diary:

> And afterwards they came out like the ten sons of Haman from Halhul [a village near Hebron] and they distressed us and brought us back like war prisoners.[1]

> And the shaykhs of Yata and Samóa persecuted us and demanded a large sum of money.[2]

These factors prevented the development of trade and industry, and the country sank into a state of nearly absolute economic degeneration.

The social composition of the population also had a decisive influence on the economic life. Many Jews immigrated to Palestine in the evening of their lives and did not intend to work for their living, but took care in advance to arrange regular support from the Diaspora. Among the rest of the Jews there were also many who only studied the Torah, and so they did not contribute to the development of an economic life. Moreover, the continual turnover in the Jewish population of Palestine during the eighteenth century also prevented the development of an orderly economic life, even in areas such as finance and trade.

In general, in the eighteenth century there were only a few Jews who were engaged in agriculture, industry, trade, agency, and moneylending. Most of the Jews of Palestine lived on donations from the Diaspora or from the charity funds of the communities, and even then in difficult conditions. The following was written by R. Abraham Gerson of Kuty in the letter he sent to the Baal Shem Tov in 1757: "It would be better that my sons should remain in the holy city and I am sure that they will study the Torah and worship diligently all their lives because there is no business here."[3] In the same year the Ashkenazim in Jerusalem wrote to Metz: "And how do the Torah scholars earn a living in the arid land [Eretz Israel] which has nothing of itself and there is no gold in the land it must bring its bread from afar for all the residents of Zion and Jerusalem."[4]

According to Rabbi Yakir, the son of R. Abraham Gerson, the reason for this was connected to the difficult economic situation and the fact that everyone was living on donations from the Diaspora, "and in particular the residents of our country who do not know writing or speaking or customs."[5] We find similar thoughts expressed in letters from the end of the century that were written by Hasidim who from the outset had no intention of working in Palestine, but intended to pray and study the Torah there, as was accepted.[6]

In the Galilee, on the other hand, the situation was different. The legal status of the Galilean communities, and especially that of Tiberias, was better, and so the economic conditions were generally considerably better than those in the communities of Jerusalem and Hebron, as is attested by the following extract from a letter that R. Haim Abulafia sent to Modena in 1742: "I was born in Hebron and grew up in Jerusalem and I lived as a rabbi in Safed, but I did not find satisfaction and quiet and security as in Tiberias. All the residents of the above-mentioned places . . . are very bitter and bothered most of the time by troubles and difficulties . . . because of the informers . . . and especially the inflation of prices . . . while in our holy city of Tiberias there are none of these things."[7]

In the Galilee there was also some development in agriculture, in the export of cotton, and in trade, which led to the development of the coastal cities. In this process the Jews also participated, as they were agents in the cotton trade and worked a little in agriculture, industry, and the retail business.[8] In the Jerusalem area, on the other hand, there were not even these small signs of economic life.

16
THE BUDGETS OF THE COMMUNITIES

THE BUDGET OF THE JERUSALEM COMMUNITY

The data in our possession concerning the budget of the Jerusalem community constitute a very important source of our knowledge about the economic life of the Jews in the eighteenth century. What stands out first and foremost is the drastic increase of the yearly budget of the community during the eighteenth century. This increase derived in part from the decline in the value of the currency (see table 3), but it was mainly a result of the heavy taxes that the authorities imposed on the community. To this must be added the high interest that the Jews were forced to pay on their enormous debts, which also continued to expand.[1]

According to sources from the beginning of the seventeenth century on, it appears that the expenses of the community were about 5,000 *kurus* per year.[2] Until the end of the seventeenth century there was no significant increase in the budget of the Jerusalem community. From the end of the seventeenth century and the beginning of the eighteenth century, R. Raphael Mordecai Malkhi points out that the budget of the Jerusalem community was 5,000–6,000 *kurus*, in contrast to a budget of 10,000 *kurus* for the other communities in Palestine.[3] He suggested that the budget of the Jerusalem community be adjusted to fit reality and that it should be raised to 8,000 *kurus*. For comparison he cited the yearly budget of the Christian communities in Jerusalem during this period: the Catholics—70,000 *kurus*; the Armenians—40,000 *kurus*; and the Greeks—30,000 *kurus*. The budgets of the Christians were also based mainly on contributions from other countries. Incidentally, the ratio between the budgets of the Christians and of the Jews supports what was written in Turkish sources about the number of Christians at the end of the seventeenth century,[4] which was several times larger than the number of Jews. Nevertheless the sums that the Christians received were proportionately larger, and their economic situation was better than that of the Jews.

When he wrote about the budget of the Jerusalem community in 1707, the Jerusalem sage R. Moses Hagiz spoke of a sum of 10,000 *kurus*, and he itemized the sources of income and expenses.[5] He too praised the Christians, who supported their sects in Jerusalem generously.

It is interesting to compare the above-mentioned sums with the sums after the rehabilitation of the community in 1727 and after the renewal of the immigration to Jerusalem beginning in the 1730s. Starting from the early forties we have much information about the enormous increase in the expenses of the community. For example, we find a letter from 1741 that a deficit of 15,000 *kurus* had accumulated in Istanbul.[6] A year later the expenses were doubled due to the robberies of the rulers and the waste of the money on buildings.[7] In a list from 1744 we find that the donations and income had decreased, and that no one cared about the collection of the indirect taxes and the legacies.[8]

In a document from 1747 we find that the expenses of the community were about 12,000 *kurus*.[9] In the year 1749–50 (counting from October to September) the budget was about 28,000 *kurus*. According to the Istanbul Officials there was an increase of 5,000–6,000 *kurus* in contrast to previous years, and the cumulative debts were 31,000 *kurus*. In this year the community spent 2,500 *kurus* on interest payments alone, and a deficit of about 12,000 *kurus* was created.[10] In 1775 the budget had already grown to about 40,000 *kurus*; the deficit was about 10,000 *kurus*.[11] This deficit—which was partly caused, it seems, by embezzlement or disorder in the bookkeeping—brought about a severe crisis in the community leadership. In the year 1756–57 the deficit was 17,838 *kurus*.[12] At the end of February 1758 the Istanbul Officials reprimanded the Jerusalem officials for the waste of 4,800 *kurus* on the building of a synagogue.[13] In the year 1757–58 there was again some disorder in the bookkeeping.[14] In the year 1760–61 the expenses of the community were 26,500 *kurus*, while its income was only 14,015 *kurus*, that is, there was a deficit of about 12,000 *kurus*. In this year the accumulated debts to Jews alone reached 24,502 *kurus*, and as a result the Istanbul Officials demanded that expenses be curtailed and reprimanded the Jerusalem officials for taking loans at high interest from Jews without part of the sum being turned into a donation, as was the accepted practice in order to avoid the prohibition against lending money at interest to other Jews.[15] In 1777, the budget of the Jerusalem community reached 66,696 *kurus* and 7 *paras*, in 1784, 41,365 *kurus*, and in 1796, 108,490 *kurus*.[16]

It appears that the expenses of the community continued to increase, while its income was not able to remain in step. The increase in expenses stemmed from the raising of taxes, the growth of the population, and the high price of food, but mainly from high interest rates. The interest rate was generally about twenty percent, but sometimes it rose and reached as much as forty percent. The decline in the value of the money also affected the financial situation of the Jewish communities in Palestine.

The expenses of the Jerusalem community were mainly for the payment of taxes and debts. The running expenses included the payment of the salaries of the officials and the community workers, rents, and support of the poor people of the community. The other living expenses of the Jerusalem residents did not come from the running budget of the community, but rather from closed budgets. Each yeshiva had its own financial framework, and even individuals lived on money from the Diaspora that was paid according to lists.

In the 1740s there was a clear separation between the fund of the Sephardi community and the funds of the Torah scholars, and the Istanbul Officials pleaded with the people of Jerusalem that there should not be any competition between the two. [17]

THE BUDGET OF THE SAFED COMMUNITY

We have in our possession several pieces of information concerning the budget of the Safed community. At the beginning of the eighteenth century the expenses of the community for taxes and payments to the authorities amounted to 1,000 *kurus*, but the sum increased gradually to 5,000 *kurus*. In 1742 the community spent 10,000 *kurus* for taxes and various payments to the rulers. [18]

SOURCES OF INCOME

The income of the communities from taxes was not very great, as many people were exempt from the payment of the tax, such as the Torah scholars and the people who were supported by the community fund. The collection of taxes from members of the community was not properly organized, and complaints were often heard about the large number of those who evaded tax payments. [19]

Not all the taxes were collected directly, as many immigrants paid their taxes to the Istanbul Officials before their immigration. This payment included both the community taxes and the burial tax, but not the head tax. As an acknowledgment of payment the Istanbul Officials gave an exemption document for life with a standard formula.[20]

Both the Askhenazim and the Karaites paid their taxes to the Sephardi community, as they obtained their services from them. The Sephardi community also collected the head tax, and it was the Sephardim who transferred it to the authorities, as the latter did not distinguish between the communities.

The Income Tax

The established tax of the community was an income tax at a rate of ten percent of one's income. At the end of the 1720s, when the Istanbul Officials were arranging the matter, they became aware "that there is a previous regulation in Jerusalem that every person who receives fifty or a hundred per year, whether his income is from the Diaspora or from within the city, must give the tax to the holy community, ten percent."[21]

On the basis of the amount of the above-mentioned sum it is possible to guess that the regulation mentioned was from the seventeenth century.[22] At the beginning of the eighteenth century new conditions arose in Jerusalem, which necessitated a change in the regulation. On the one hand there had been a sharp decline in the value of the *kurus*, and the fifty *kurus* that had been enough for a livelihood at the end of the seventeenth century were no longer sufficient, while on the other hand all the sources of income and payments of expenses of the Jerusalem community had been transferred to the care of the Istanbul Officials. In 1730 the Istanbul Officials sent, along with other regulations, a regulation about the income tax. It said that whoever received an income of up to eighty *kurus* per year "would negotiate with the officials of the holy community on its evaluation," but whoever received an income of more than eighty *kurus* a year would continue to pay the tax of ten percent.[23] This regulation had a clear social-welfare basis, and it probably stemmed from the great poverty that reigned in Jerusalem.

It seems that another decline in the value of the money and an increase in the number of poor immigrants in the middle of the eighteenth century led to the establishment of a new regulation, which said, among other things: "Women who came to live honorably in the holy city, if they have an income of one hundred *kurus* per year . . . the officials will take five percent, and from two hundred and up . . . eight percent, and [if their income] is less than a hundred they will not take even a small coin."[24] This regulation has no date, but on the basis of the size of the income it is possible to estimate that it is from the second half of the eighteenth century. In this regulation the minimum taxable income was raised from eighty to one hundred *kurus* and the amount of the tax was reduced from eight to five percent. Thus, during the course of the eighteenth century there was a notable decline in the income tax rates. This undoubtedly derived from the difficult situation of many of the Jerusalem Jews, whose income was meager and sufficed only with difficulty for their livelihood.

The Gabela

Another type of community tax was the indirect tax—a kind of purchase tax, called the *gabela*—on various products, mainly food. Whereas the income tax was paid directly to the officials—"the officials will take"[25]—the collection of the indirect taxes was farmed out to people who did their work under the supervision of the officials.[26] At any rate, that is how it was in Jerusalem and in Safed,[27] and it is reasonable to assume that in the other places the collection was not conducted differently. In 1743 the Istanbul Officials demanded that the Jerusalem community be strict about the collection of the *gabela* on meat and that for this purpose they should set up two stores for the selling of meat. They also demanded the collection of the *gabela* on wine and on monuments. The Istanbul Officials demanded that the taxes be collected from everyone, without exception.[28] In 1748 they wrote to the Jerusalem community that the license to collect the community taxes should be sold periodically to the highest bidder and should not be left in the hands of one fixed person.[29] This method of collecting the indirect taxes apparently continued for many years. At any rate, only at the end of the 1760s did the Istanbul Officials demand that the practice of farming out the collection of the indirect taxes be abolished, and that the community itself should collect them.[30] We do not know if this demand was carried out.

The collection of the *gabela* created many difficulties, especially among the Torah scholars. If they were exempt from the payment of external taxes like the head tax, then *a fortiori* they demanded to be exempted from the payment of the community taxes. And indeed, it seems from several documents that there was friction with the Torah scholars concerning the internal taxes as well. In 1751 the Istanbul Officials demanded of the Jerusalem leadership that they insist on the fulfillment of the regulation that had been established in the city concerning the taxes and that they should not give in to anyone.[31] In 1754 they wrote that they were astonished to see, in the account-books of Jerusalem of 1753, that the collection of taxes in the city was not being conducted properly; the community had succeeded in collecting only about one-quarter or one-third of the expected amount. The Jerusalemites explained the matter on the basis of an exemption that the rabbis of the city had granted to various groups. The Istanbul Officials opposed this "rabbinical decision," as everywhere taxes were collected from everyone.[32] At the end of the sixties the controversy concerning the status of the Torah scholars and the taxes they had to pay was renewed. In the framework of the general conflicts in the community at that time[33] several regulations on this matter were again established, with the intention of abolishing some of the reductions and the sources of income of the Torah scholars.

The Burial Tax

One of the important sources of income for the community was the burial tax. From each bereaved family it was customary to collect a burial tax for the community where the cemetery and the road to it were located.[34] These taxes were paid in addition to the burial taxes to the authorities and to the Moslem population. In the eighteenth century changes were made in the tax at the initiative of the Istanbul Officials. The payers of the burial tax were divided into two groups.

The long-time residents of Jerusalem who died in the city. Their bereaved families continued to pay taxes to the community fund. We have many regulations in our possession that deal with this group, mainly from the last quarter of the eighteenth century; there is no doubt that they were based on previous regulations.[35] During the Ottoman period there was no uniform tax, and when there were no heirs the community inherited the legacy according to the legacy regulation. In a regulation that was apparently established between 1776 and 1806,[36] it was written that after the death of a householder the community took ten percent of his assets. If the community's debts were greater than 30,000 *kurus*, then one-third of the above sum was used for the payment of these debts. This regulation had several subsections: (1) before the deduction of the above-mentioned burial tax the debts of the departed were paid; (2) if the person had no money except for a yearly income, then his heirs had to pay the burial expenses according to the amount of this income—one-third of the amount of this income was taken from his other assets to pay the debts of the community; and (3) when someone died who had made an arrangement to pay his burial expenses during his lifetime—that is, he had paid them while he was still alive—his heirs still had to pay the amount of one-third of his income for the repayment of the community debts.

In the middle of the eighteenth century special regulations were established in the matter of the burial tax for Torah scholars. Whoever was able to serve as a teacher paid a burial tax of only five percent and another one-third of this sum for the repayment of the community debts, in addition to the burial tax to the authorities. A Torah scholar who was not able to serve as a teacher, but was among those who received financial support in a yeshiva, paid seven percent of the burial tax, but he paid the other taxes in the same manner as his colleagues who served as teachers. A Torah scholar who had no funds and was supported by charity paid only thirty *kurus* to the community and the burial tax to the authorities. For a poor Torah scholar the yeshiva in which he studied paid the burial tax at a rate of one-quarter of the sum of his support for one year. In 1772 the rate of the burial tax that was imposed on the Torah scholars was decreased, and whoever was able to serve as a teacher paid only three percent, while those who were not able paid five percent.[37]

Additional regulations dealt with women who died childless,[38] with widows who died,[39] with orphans,[40] and with children who died.[41] From most of these a burial tax of about ten percent and the additional fixed payments were collected. A burial tax of thirty *kurus*, in addition to the tax paid to the authorities, was imposed on poor people who died and on those who left an inheritance of not more than 300 *kurus*.[42]

Immigrants to Palestine. The Istanbul Officials attempted to collect from immigrants in advance all taxes that they were supposed to pay in Jerusalem, including the burial tax. This arrangement, concerning which we have a great deal of evidence in our possession,[43] secured relatively large sums of money for the Jerusalem fund in Istanbul. Not only did the Istanbul Officials gain profits from these funds, but in this way they were also able to supervise the sources of income of the immigrants and the budget of the Jerusalem community. This exempted the Jerusalem leadership from having to cope with the large number of immigrants who arrived in Palestine. Occasionally the Jerusalem officials tried to collect the taxes from immigrants who paid these taxes in Istanbul or in other places before their immigration.[44]

In one of the regulations established in Jerusalem the burial tax was raised in order to increase the income of the community, and this increase also applied to those who had signed agreements in the Diaspora.[45] This regulation has no date, but it appears to date from the eighteenth century and suggests a certain amount of freedom of action on the part of the Jerusalem community. It is likely that from time to time the Jerusalem community violated agreements that were made by the Istanbul Officials in order to have some sources of income that were under its direct control.

Estates

In the eighteenth century the communities had a high income from legacies. We have many regulations in our possession on this topic, and this attests to the great importance attached to the matter. Many regulations were collected by Eliezer Rivlin,[46] who prefaced them with an introduction and explained them, but he did not thoroughly understand the principle behind them. The essence of the regulations in their various embodiments is that when a person died in Jerusalem—and it seems that the intention was also for the other cities in Palestine—and he had no heirs in the city, then the community inherited his possessions. In order to enforce the application of the regulation, a complementary regulation was added to it over the course of time, which forbade members of the community from handing over their possessions in their lifetime or writing a will without the presence of the patrons of the community. From the vast amount of material in our possession it appears that the income of the community from the estates was quite large because many of the immigrants came without their families, and so they did not have any heirs in the city. It is therefore not surprising that the community tried with all its might to preserve its share in the assets of the departed.

The investigators who dealt with these regulations, and particularly Rivlin, did not pay attention to the source of the regulation. It was Eliyahu Ashtor who realized the connection between the estate regulations of the Jews and the Moslem inheritance law.[47] This law differs essentially from the inheritance laws of the Jews and the Christians. With the Moslems the property is divided among all the descendants. The sons have preference over the daughters, but the latter also receive part of the inheritance. The state treasury also receives a large share of the inheritance. With the Jews the oldest child is preferred, even if it is a daughter. Shlomo Goitein[48] believes that this derives from the difference between the ancient Jewish society and the Moslem society: the Jews were farmers and were afraid of subdividing their estates, whereas the Moslems were nomads and their property was movable and easy to divide. According to Moslem law in its different variations, the state treasury enjoys a large income from the inheritances, whether of movable property or of real estate.[49] One of the paragraphs of the Moslem law states that the government inherits the property of an alien who dies without heirs in the place of his death.[50]

During the Middle Ages there was continual confrontation between Moslem law, which was intended to increase the income of the government, and Jewish law, which attempted to treat cases of inheritance in the rabbinical courts. During the Fatamid period non-Moslems were already permitted to judge and treat matters of inheritance in their own courts, in spite of debates on this topic in Islamic circles. However, this privilege was not automatic, and it was necessary to fight for it. A judicial opinion from the days of Salah ad-Din (Saladin) recognized the right of non-Moslems to conduct their own inheritance cases.[51] During the Mameluke period the struggle continued, and we have information in our possession about the confiscation of property without heirs from the Jews until it was redeemed by the Jewish community. According to Ashtor, "This was the procedure at the time, that the treating of inheritance cases was in the hands of the Moslem authorities."[52] During the Mameluke period the differences of opinion continued, and changes were made in this law and in the religious hermeneutics that accompanied it.[53] In Jewish sources from the beginning of the Ottoman occupation of Palestine there is also some evidence concerning this law. R. Moses ben Yosef Trani mentions the matter in several of his responsa, and from them it seems that in his time as well the government officials used to appropriate estates without heirs or collect inheritance taxes from estates of this sort. This issue is mentioned more than once in sources from the sixteenth and seventeenth centuries in Palestine and in Egypt.[54]

From what has been said it appears quite clearly that there was a connection between the Moslem inheritance laws, which were satisfied by a monetary redemption of estates by the Jews, and the estate regulation of the Jerusalem Jews. It is clear that the regulation which gave the community the right of inheritance of estates without heirs derived from the Moslem law. In this regulation there was also a paragraph in which it was forbidden to make a will or hand over property without the presence of the patrons. It is likely that the source of this regulation as well was in Moslem law. During the Mameluke and the Ottoman periods the Moslem law permitted the *dhimmis* to establish dedications of funds for various purposes of their communities, and especially for the poor, similar to those of the Moslems (Waqf).[55] Indeed, the Jews took advantage of this privilege to prevent the bequeathing of their property to the government treasury or the Jewish community. The Jews used to register these dedications in the courts of the Moslems in order to give them the legal authority of the state. The complementary regulations of the Jews, which tried to prevent this phenomenon and forbade the dedication of a fund or the making of a will without the presence of the patrons, were established as a reaction to this, with the intention of preventing the loss of money from the province of the community. It appears that there was a clash of interests between the community and its needs, on the one hand, and the dedications of funds, which were mainly set aside for yeshivas and supported a limited and relatively well-to-do class of Torah scholars, on the other hand.

What was the attitude of the Ottoman authorities to the regulations? In the regulations themselves there is no mention of a connection between them and the Moslem law, and there is not even a hint of any payment to the authorities to redeem the estates. However, from one of the letters in the Istanbul *Pinkas* it appears quite clearly that in the eighteenth century as well there was a connection between the regulations and the Moslem law. In a letter that the Istanbul Officials sent in 1762[56] they claimed that from a certain estate[57] in Jerusalem the widow of the departed wanted to donate a part to a yeshiva. The Istanbul Officials objected, "since there is an ancient regulation from many years ago," according to which it was impossible to give a gift or dedicate a fund "because whatever is left over from the departed for whom no heir is found according to the rules of the Ishmaelites [Arabs] is taken by the state treasury." In order to avoid confrontation with the state treasury and the confiscation of the estates, the community paid a fixed sum to the authorities every year, and so it had the right to the estate, "since it is bought by it from the state treasury and they have its authority." In the regulation there were many bans and oaths, and it was forbidden to disobey it. If they compromised on this matter, "this would bring about the destruction of the city." At the conclusion of the letter the Istanbul Officials asked that the promissory note made by the widow of the departed in this matter be torn up.[58]

This document is of great importance because it demonstrates that in the eighteenth century as well the estate regulations continued to derive their authority from the Moslem law and from arrangements with the Ottoman authorities. As far as I know this is the only time it was written explicitly that the authority of the community in this matter "was bought by it from the state treasury." Another hint of the connection of this regulation to the Ottoman law may be found in a composition from the beginning of the seventeenth century. In a Halakhic question that was asked of R. Josiah Pinto, one of the rabbis of Damascus,[59] the following was written: "Reuben died and his wife received the news and because of *the fear of the authorities* they took all the possessions of the house to the house of a neighbor."[60]

It is known that in the Ottoman period there were additional groups that enjoyed privileges in matters of inheritances. The Janissaries had the right to confiscate estates without heirs—that is, they did not have to transfer them to the state treasury—and this was also the case for the non-Jewish Mugrabi in Jerusalem and other communities.[61]

The many Jewish sources that dealt with the estate regulation generally ignored the connection between this regulation and the Moslem law, but it is nevertheless possible to find hints of this in sources from the beginning of the nineteenth century as well. In the great controversy over the estates that broke out in the beginning of the nineteenth century between the Sephardim and the Perushim in Jerusalem, both sides mentioned the connection of the regulation to the Moslem law in their arguments, but scholars have paid no attention to the matter. R. Joseph Hazan, the Rishon Le-Zion of Jerusalem at the beginning of the nineteenth century, wrote the following in his debate with the Perushim: "In the laws of the Gentiles whoever dies and no heir is found in the city, the state treasury inherits his property."[62] R. Israel of Shklov, the spokesman of the Ashkenazim, argued in opposition that the Halakhic ruling "The law of the [secular] government is the [Halakhic] law" did not apply to the Ashkenazim in this case, because they were not Ottoman subjects.[63]

The matter demands a deeper investigation, but it may be said that at the beginning of the nineteenth century as well there was a connection with the Moslem law,[64] although it seems that in the course of time this connection became weaker. At any rate, later in the nineteenth century it was practically not mentioned any more.

An important question is whether it is possible to find evidence of this connection in Ottoman sources. From a recent study by Amnon Cohen it appears that in the sixteenth century the authorities in Jerusalem often leased to the Jews the collection of the taxes on Jewish estates without heirs in the city. It seems that the Jewish community in Jerusalem was thus able to arrange matters so that either the community itself or someone appointed by it leased the collection of the estate taxes and thus succeeded in taking charge of this source of income. Nevertheless, it is known that the Ottoman authorities in Jerusalem collected legal taxes, generally exaggerated, from estates that had heirs, and so it is reasonable to assume that they did the same for estates without heirs as well. In a *firman* of 1743 the Sublime Porte ordered that taxes greater than prescribed by the law should not be collected from estates without heirs.[65]

The many sources in our possession, and particularly the Istanbul *Pinkas*, permit us to understand the application of the regulation in the eighteenth century. It becomes clear that all the instructions sent by the Istanbul Officials in this matter were intended to secure high incomes from estates for the Jerusalem community. In 1730 they wrote, "We have heard it said that there are many men and women in Jerusalem who have received property from the Diaspora or property which had belonged to some of the people who died in Jerusalem, which belongs to the community . . . as the earlier rabbis established . . . these people have caused great ruin to everyone."[66]

During the entire period attempts were made to get around the regulation,[67] and in certain cases the owners of property tried to transfer their property to relatives in the Diaspora by registering it in their names while the true owners were still alive, in order to prevent the community from inheriting it.[68] As a result the Istanbul Officials renewed the second paragraph of the regulation, according to which it was permitted to make a will only in front of an official who was sent from Istanbul for this purpose.[69] The Istanbul Officials also forbade the use of the money from the estates for anything other than the purposes of the community, such as the repayment of debts owed to Jews.[70] In 1737 they again renewed the regulation in Jerusalem itself, and the rabbis and officials of the city signed it.[71] In 1776 they renewed it once more.[72]

The following examples show the difficulties of enforcing the regulation. In 1742 information reached the Istanbul Officials that "they are stealing" the estates in Jerusalem, and as a result they sent a letter accompanied by bans and oaths from the Istanbul rabbis.[73] In 1745 the Istanbul Officials threatened to resign because of the defects in the collection of the estates. In order to improve the situation they suggested that the official Abraham Alhadef should be appointed in Jerusalem to collect the estates, along with a staff of assistants comprising six Torah scholars.[74] They also complained that one sage—Rabbi A. Halevi—had embezzled the estates.[75] In 1748 they protested once more against the neglect in the collection of the estates and demanded the appointment of a "trustworthy person" over the estates, together with some Torah scholars. The latter were to register the property of the departed and take care of the collection of the estates, which were "the mother of all the living."[76] In 1759 the Istanbul Officials transmitted an "agreement" that had been sent from Fez in Morocco, in which it was written that no person in Jerusalem had the right to give presents as he wished.[77] The regulation itself has been lost, but it is reasonable to assume that it was sent from Morocco at the request of the Istanbul Officials and was meant for immigrants from North Africa who came to Jerusalem and did not know about the regulation in force in the city.

In 1761 another problem arose. The Istanbul Officials discovered that the principal of several funds, the interest from which served to sustain the Torah scholars, had been transferred to the yeshiva and not to the community upon the death of the donor, in violation of the estate regulation. As a result the Istanbul Officials again threatened to resign.[78] In 1762 they wrote that they had found out about the sale of the property of estates in one of the Jerusalem courts, and among the buyers there were some non-Jewish merchants. This matter was likely to bring about great trouble and to arouse libels. They advised changing the place of the sale and taking care that the officials in Jerusalem would supervise it.[79] It seems that here as well there was a hint of the connection between the regulation and the Moslem law.

An outstanding example of an attempt to get around the regulation is an affair from the 1750s in which R. Moses Bula, one of the famous rabbis of Jerusalem, gave his property as a "living will" to a person in Sofia, and afterwards the property was returned to him for his use until he died. The Istanbul Officials were furious about the matter. It is likely that this affair, which aroused the Jerusalem community, was connected with the battle over the leadership of the community between Rabbi Bula and the rabbi of the city, R. Isaac Hacohen Rapaport. The sides negotiated a compromise only after the Istanbul Officials intervened and after the affair had reached the knowledge of the authorities and had cost the community a great deal of money.[80]

Donations from the Diaspora

In the eighteenth century the lion's share of the income of the Jewish communities in Palestine came from donations from the Diaspora. Every

year tens of thousands of *kurus* arrived in Palestine from individual donors, estates, funds for Eretz Israel in the Diaspora communities, special
fund-drives, and the collections of the emissaries. This money served
mainly for the payment of taxes to the authorities, for the repayment of
debts, and for the running expenses of the community. Only a small part
was distributed among the people of the community for individual use.

The collection of money was mostly in the hands of the Istanbul Officials, who also arranged special fund-drives in the Jewish communities
and sent emissaries from Palestine to supervise them. The large amount
of the sums led to waste and often to embezzlements and thefts as well.
The supervision of the support money aroused a difficult problem, which
the Istanbul Officials and the leaders of the European Jewish communities tried continually to handle.

TAXES PAYABLE TO CIVIL AUTHORITIES

In the eighteenth century most of the taxes in Palestine were collected
by a leasing (*Iltizam*) system. The Sublime Porte leased the right to collect taxes to a vali, the latter leased it to the pashas, and in the end the
lease was given to third parties. There were certain differences in the
methods of collection between the *vilayets* of Sidon and of Damascus.

In the province of Sidon Dahir al-ʿUmar was the real ruler, and his
subjection to the vali of Sidon was tenuous, whereas in the province of
Damascus the vali himself dealt with the collection of taxes, and for this
purpose he even went around the towns and villages in the area of his
rule.[81] The taxes in the Damascus province were very heavy, and the
Jews and Christians carried most of the burden. In the middle of the
century Jerusalem paid 21,500 *kurus* in taxes to the Sublime Porte, and
of this amount the Jews and the Christians paid eighty percent.[82] At
times the Jews were forced to pay a special tax to the vali of Damascus, in
addition to the regular taxes. In the Sidon province the situation of the
Jews was a little better.

The taxes paid by the Jews to the authorities may be divided into two
types: the poll tax and other fixed taxes. In addition the Jews made one-
time payments on various occasions.

The Poll Tax

In the Ottoman Empire the poll tax (*cizye*) was one of the outstanding
signs that differentiated the Moslems from the non-Moslems. The tax

was imposed on every adult non-Moslem male (*dhimmi*),[83] in three degrees: high, medium, and low. From a document from 1689 we learn that there was a uniform rate for the poll tax—"even the poorest of the poor paid 5.5 *kurus* per year"[84]—but in the eighteenth century varying rates were established in accordance with one's property, and every Ottoman subject of the male sex who had reached adulthood and had any sort of income was required to pay the tax. This is how the tax is described in a letter from Jerusalem of 1741:

> And our country has an added trouble and difficult trait, the poll tax of the king, when the appointed person comes and the proclamation of the king is heard, there is one law for the head of the Jews, one and two and payments of four [three levels of the poll tax, in the ratio 1:2:4], from the great to the small, every one must pass in front of him like sheep to be counted, and even an old man who has reached great age must also pay.[85]

And compare the words of R. Simha of Zalozce:

> When my wife and I were traveling in 1764 . . . from the nearby city of Zalozce . . . to Brody . . . and from there to Galatz . . . and the Jews who live in Galatz are important and generous and give much charity, and they gave me the poll tax for my head, which is called *haraç* [the cizye] in the Ishmaelite language [Arabic and Turkish] and it is the tax to the Ishmaelite king, from each poor person three lions [*kurus*] less a fourth.[86]

The poll tax was collected according to the kada, the region of religious administration, at the head of which was the kadi. This derived, it seems, from the strong connection between this tax and the religious officials. In Palestine there were two regions: the kada of Jerusalem, which included the *sancaks* of Jerusalem (including Hebron), Ramle, Gaza, Jaffa, and Nablus; and the kada of Sidon, which included the *sancaks* of Sidon, Beirut, and Acre.

According to Ottoman and Jewish sources from the eighteenth century the income of the Turkish treasury from the poll tax was thousands of *kurus* per year. In 1741 the Jerusalem Jews reached a compromise with the ruler on the sum of 1,500 *kurus*.[87] In another document it is written that in Jerusalem 7,500 *kurus* poll tax was paid per year.[88] In 1756 1,228 *kurus* were paid for those who had not paid in 1754 and 1,455 *kurus* for those who had not paid in 1755.[89] The poll tax that was collected in Palestine was intended for the financing of the caravan of the hajj to Mecca, which was under the supervision of the pasha of Damascus.

In the eighteenth century the poll tax in Palestine was collected on a personal basis. The Ashkenazim who had settled in the country were also required to pay after they had lived in the country for several years. The tax collectors had lists from Istanbul, but they were not always updated because of the great turnover in the Jewish population, which derived from immigrations, on the one hand, and from the death rate and emigrations, on the other. Many members of the communities were not included in the lists of taxpayers, either because of their poverty or because of their evasion of payment,[90] and so the authorities imposed the collection of the tax on the communities. In many cases it was thus not a poll tax but an additional tax paid by the community, like many other taxes.[91] The community did collect the tax from its members, but because of the difficult economic situation of many of the Jerusalem Jews and as a result of the privileges that were given to groups under stress in the community—such as Torah scholars and the holders of other positions—many people did not pay the tax, and the community fund had to carry the burden.

The Istanbul Officials did not agree to this situation, and from time to time they demanded that the Jerusalem officials stop the faulty practice of paying the poll tax from the community fund. We first encounter this demand in a letter of 1750. The Istanbul Officials ruled that everyone who received a notice from the authorities was required to pay the poll tax, and it was not to be paid from the community fund. This was the kind of regulation established in Istanbul.[92] As a result of the demand of the Istanbul Officials a regulation was formulated in Jerusalem on this matter, but it seems that it was not kept properly. In 1752 the Istanbul Officials asked once again that the Jerusalem officials keep the regulation that was made in Jerusalem in the matter of the taxes and demanded that "the regulation should be upheld without any complaint . . . 'do not be afraid of any man.'"[93] However, the situation became even more severe. In 1753 the Jerusalem community paid 1,500 *kurus* poll tax, probably mainly for individuals who had not paid it. This was quite a large sum, and it suggests the large number of people subject to the poll tax in the city. That year the Istanbul Officials again complained about this practice[94] and came out strongly against the exemption from the poll tax that was given to the Torah scholars.

In the Jewish communities of Palestine and the rest of the Ottoman Empire there was a fierce debate as to whether Torah scholars who did no other work should pay taxes. Gradually, as the economic situation of the empire and the Jewish communities within it worsened, this privilege was almost completely abolished. In the eighteenth century the Torah scholars in Jerusalem still refused to pay taxes, and from time to time they tried to renew the old regulation that was based on a Halakhic ruling which said that they were exempt from the payment of taxes. These attempts aroused the fury of the Istanbul Officials, and in a letter from 1754[95] they wrote sarcastically that there may have been Torah scholars who were exempt from the payment of taxes due to a Halakhic decision, "but the Muteselim and the Pasha do not know what a Halakhic decision is. . . . If we will go according to Halakhic decisions we will not be able to uphold Jerusalem." In their opinion the difficult situation had to override the Halakhic decision, and the Torah scholars also had to pay taxes, including the poll tax.

These demands did not help either. At any rate, at the end of the 1760s the debate on this matter was still going on. As a result of the great expense that was imposed on the Jerusalem community and the new debts that accumulated in the city, a general assembly (*ma'amad*) was held in Istanbul and new regulations were established to improve the difficult situation of the Jerusalem community fund. In these regulations it was established, among other things, that the Jerusalem community would no longer pay the poll tax for anyone, including cantors, caretakers, and sages. Only wealthy people were permitted to pay the poll tax or other taxes for others. In this regulation there was a kind of giving in to the privilege holders. The community was indeed forbidden to pay their taxes, but they were allowed to mobilize the sum from charity donors.

However, in spite of the many regulations and "agreements" in this matter the situation did not improve. The local authorities were not interested in compelling individuals to pay taxes and preferred to collect them from the community, as this was easier to do. Neither the Jerusalem community nor the Istanbul Officials had enough power to compel the collection of the tax.

Other Taxes

The local authorities took advantage of the immigrations and the pilgrimages, both Jewish and Christian, as an opportunity to impose special taxes. At the times of arrival in the departure from Palestine at the ports of Jaffa and Acre they collected a special tax of between seven and twenty-nine *kurus*.[96] Immigrants to Jerusalem were forced to pay a tax for accompaniment by a caravan, which was paid in part to the Bedouins at the sides of the road.[97] A special tax was also collected at the time of entrance to and departure from Jerusalem and at visits to holy places, such as the Western Wall and the Cave of the Patriarchs.[98]

At the time of the appointment of new rulers and government officials in Jerusalem a tax was also collected, and this occurred frequently. Thus, for example, the Jews paid 300 *kurus* at the appointment of a new ruler in the middle of the eighteenth century.[99]

Every month a tax called *muşāhere* was paid to the pasha, and every year a tax called *imdādiye* (assistance) was paid to him. In 1741 the Jerusalem Jews paid 300 *kurus* for the *imdādiye* taxes.[100] Incidentally, these taxes were customary throughout the lands of the Ottoman Empire.[101]

Festival taxes that were called *ʿidiye* and gifts to the government officials on the festivals were a permanent addition to the taxes. Other taxes were: a tax on wood;[102] a tax on wool, sugar, and grapes;[103] a tax on raisins;[104] the burial tax;[105] the estate tax;[106] the tax on fancy dress and jewelry;[107] and a tax for permission to improve or to build buildings. During the 1740s a special tax on the increase in the Jewish population of Jerusalem was imposed, with the argument that this increase was creating a food shortage.[108]

At times fines were imposed on the Jews as punishment for such things as quarrels in the Jerusalem community.[109]

COMMUNITY DEBTS

Because of the difficult economic situation the communities were forced to turn to the rich men of the country, mainly Moslems and Christians, and to borrow large sums from them at high interest. There were also Jews who dealt in loans at interest, but they did not often lend their money to the Jewish communities because they had no guarantee that they would get their money back. The enormous debts that weighed down the Jews brought about very great pressure from the creditors, and the communities had to pay back the debts to the gentiles first, lest they be harmed. This is reflected in a regulation established by the Istanbul Officials in 1730. This regulation was connected in practice with the status of the Jewish *millet*, as it was intended to prevent confrontation between the Jewish community on the one hand, and the authorities and the local population on the other.

One of the first regulations established by the Istanbul Officials was that the Jewish community should not repay its debts to Jews until the debts to the gentiles were repaid. In the first version of the regulation in our possession we find the following: "From now on no man or woman in Jerusalem has the power to repay the smallest part of the debt of the community until all the debts to the Gentiles there have been paid, and afterwards, from the property that God shall give, every Jew shall be repaid from the money of the city."[110] The leaders of the Jerusalem community also signed this regulation: "until all these evil men, sons of miscegenation [the gentiles], shall be repaid, as it is a matter of life and death."[111]

During the eighteenth century this regulation was renewed more than once, and from time to time changes were made in it. In 1742 the Istanbul Officials refused to allow the repayment of debts to Jews because of the difficult situation, aside from the fact that it was also difficult, in their opinion, to find out which debts were still valid. They therefore suggested that Jewish creditors holding promissory notes should send them to Istanbul so that the chief rabbi could investigate the matter of the debts owed to Jews.[112] In 1743 the Istanbul Officials wrote that new debts had been incurred in Jerusalem, and so the force of the regulation, which had originally been established for ten years, had to be extended. The Istanbul Officials also wrote to the Jerusalem community that for the present the debts owed to Jews would not be repaid, and that the force of the regulation would be extended.[113] In 1746 the regulation was strengthened, apparently because it was not being kept. There was a suspicion that the Jerusalem community was unable to withstand the pressure of the Jewish creditors, and so the Istanbul Officials demanded that the creditors in Jerusalem send their promissory notes to Istanbul, as there were some debts whose repayment had priority over others. They also established that the creditors would get their yearly interest from the Istanbul Officials under improved conditions, and no longer from the Jerusalem community.[114] Probably they established this rule in order to persuade the creditors to send their promissory notes to Istanbul. It is also clear that this constituted an additional step in their gaining control over the Jerusalem community.

At the end of the 1740s the Istanbul Officials moderated the regulation somewhat. In 1749 Judah Gomez Pato of Hebron requested the repayment of a debt owed to his father by the Jerusalem community, and since he was in financial difficulties the Istanbul Officials agreed to make an exception to the regulation and arrange a compromise with him.[115] A letter from 1751 states that due to the lessening of the debts the Jerusalem community agreed to arrange compromises with the Jewish creditors and repaid them one-third of the debts. One creditor with an old debt from the Jerusalem community was not satisfied with this and went to Istanbul to demand the repayment of the entire debt. The Istanbul Officials wrote to the rabbi of Jerusalem, R. Isaac Hacohen Rapaport, and expressed surprise that he was ready to give away the community's money in opposition to the regulation: "They had never obligated themselves to repay debts that the people of Jerusalem owed to their brothers and even real debts, while this debt is already invalid."[116] Nevertheless it appears from what was written that occasionally debts to Jews were repaid, and that the regulation was still not fully kept.

During the eighteenth century the Jewish communities in Palestine paid about nine percent interest to Jewish lenders and between twenty and forty percent to gentiles, in accordance with economic and political factors in the country.[117]

Undoubtedly the burden of debt that weighed upon the Jewish communities in Palestine was one of the central causes of the stagnation of the Yishuv. The Jews did not always succeed in repaying their debts, and the cumulative interest increased the amounts so much that even the creditors lost hope of collecting them. From time to time the Istanbul Officials obtained *firmans* that annulled the interest and made arrangements for the repayment of the principal in regular payments. These *firmans* did indeed ease the pressure somewhat, but within a short time a new debt was incurred, and the whole cycle began again. One of the *firmans* was published, and it enables us to learn how the process was actually carried out.[118]

We also have in our possession several sources concerning the difficult economic situation in Hebron in the first half of the eighteenth century. In a letter that the founders of the Committee of Officials for Hebron in Istanbul sent to the Jewish communities in 1733 we find the following: "The debt reached forty-six thousand . . . and those who remain with it are lying in wait for our blood . . . and these Gentiles are threatening and raising their voices."[119]

In the second half of the eighteenth century as well heavy debts oppressed the Hebron community,[120] as one may also learn from Turkish documents, which certainly cannot be considered biased. In 1777 the sultan in Istanbul instructed that the debts be paid back in a convenient arrangement—similar to the arrangement that was made in Jerusalem—

but instructions of this kind were not always carried out by the local authorities. In the last years of the century the debt exploded again, and it is likely that no change for the better occurred in the situation of the Hebron Jews. [121]

Table 2 attests to the difficult situation of the Jewish communities as a result of the debts. There was definitely an enormous increase in the debts at the end of the century, especially at the time of the Napoleonic invasion.

TABLE 2. The Debts of the Jews of Palestine[1]

Year	Debt	Source	Comments
A. Jerusalem			
c. 1690	15,000 *kurus*	*Likutim*, vol. 1, pp. 12, 16	
1695	25,000 *kurus*	Rivkind, "Letters from Jerusalem," p. 226	Interest rate of 20%
1703	32,000 lions[2]	Rivkind, "A collection of writings," p. 322; Ya'ari, *The Emissaries of Palestine*, p. 324	
1704	50,000 lions	Rivkind, "Letters from Jerusalem," p. 230	
1706	15,000 *kurus*	Rivkind, "A collection of writings," p. 322	Only Ashkenazi community
1707	60,000 *kurus*	*Sefath Emeth*, p. 21b	
1709	32,000 *kurus*	Rivkind, "A collection of writings," p. 322	Only Ashkenazi synagogue
c. 1712	60,000 *kurus*	Ya'ari, *The Emissaries of Palestine*, p. 374; Shohet, "Three eighteenth-century letters on Palestine," pp. 240, 241, 248	According to Shohet the value of the *reichstaler* was 2.5 *kurus* at this time

Year	Amount	Source	Remarks
1744	32,000 *kurus*	*Pinkas* of Istanbul, letter of 24 Elul 5504 (September 1744), p. 61	Increased from 11,000 *kurus*, yet 8,000 *kurus* were still lacking for 1744
1748	20,000–25,000 *kurus*	*Pinkas* of Istanbul, letter of Adar I 5508 (February 1748), p. 72	
1748	25,000 *kurus*	*Pinkas* of Istanbul, letter of Adar 5508 (February–March 1748) (?), p. 63	Accumulated debt of eight years
1751	31,000 *kurus*	*Pinkas* of Istanbul, letter of 15 Iyyar 5511 (May 1751), p. 94	Accumulated debt of ten years; yearly interest was 2,500 *kurus*, about 12.5%
1762	24,502 *kurus*	*Pinkas* of Istanbul, letter of 1 Elul 5522 (September 1762), p. 46	Debts owed to Jews only
1767	20,000 *kurus*	*Pinkas* of Istanbul, letter of 25 Av 5527 (August 1767), p. 132	Apparently debt of this year only, not including earlier debts
1769	60,000 lions	Marcus, "Documents from Rhodes concerning Palestine," p. 217	According to Marcus the lion had the value of a *kurus*, but this should be corrected (see note 2)

TABLE 2 (Cont.)

Year	Debt	Source	Comments
1770	70,000 *kurus*	Ya'ari, *The Emissaries of Palestine*, p. 536; Rivkind, "Documents illustrating Jewish life," p. 133	
1774	51,182.25 *kurus* + 5 *paras*	Hirschberg, "Notes on the debts of the Jews," p. 167	Debts to Moslems only
1774	75,000 lions	Ya'ari, *The Emissaries of Palestine*, p. 540; Cohen, "Arabic documents," p. 324; Ben-Ya'akov, *Jerusalem*, p. 363	
1777	98,944	Ben-Zvi Inst. Ms. 1702	
1781	9,000 *kurus*	Rivkind, "Isolated pages," p. 164	For building of synagogue only
1792	70,000 lions	Ya'ari, *The Emissaries of Palestine*, p. 561	According to Ya'ari the lion had the value of a *kurus*, but this should be corrected (see note 2)
1793	50,000 lions	Ya'ari, *The Emissaries of Palestine*, p. 560	Rivkind mistakenly attributes this letter to 1797; see "Isolated pages," p. 153
1796	172,836	Ben-Zvi Inst. Ms. 1706	

Year	Amount	Source	Notes
1799	200,000 lions	Yaʿari, *The Emissaries of Palestine*, p. 566; Gaʾon, *The Jews of the East in Palestine*, vol. 2, p. 42	The year Palestine was occupied
B. Hebron			
1717	12,000 reals	Simonsohn, *History of the Jews in the Duchy of Mantua*, vol. 1, pp. 352–53; Ben-Zvi, *Studies*, p. 190	
1727	19,000 *kurus*	Ben-Zvi, "Emissaries of Palestine in Italy," p. 17	Divided as follows: 15,000 *kurus* at 20% interest to creditors; 3,000 *kurus* at 30% to ruling clans; 1,000 *kurus* at 40% to mayor
1729	46,000 zlotys	Yaʿari, *The Emissaries of Palestine*, p. 496	According to Yaʿari the zloty was equal to the *kurus*, but he was mistaken; see table 3
1744	15,000 reals	Yaʿari, *The Emissaries of Palestine*, p. 499; Yaʿari, "Two documents on the history of the Jewish settlement in Hebron," p. 120.	Remaining debt, perhaps due to founding of committee of Hebron Officials in 1733

TABLE 2 (Cont.)

Year	Debt	Source	Comments
1763	25,000 *pezza*	Rabinowitz, "Scroles," p. 149	
1765	25,000 *pezza*	Rivkind, "Documents illustrating Jewish life in Palestine," p. 128	
1777	Over 40,000 *kurus*	Cohen, *Palestine in the Eighteenth Century,* p. 459	
1795	60,000 *kurus*	Cohen, *Palestine in the Eighteenth Century,* p. 459	
1798	120,000 piasters (= *kurus*)	Rivkind, "Isolated pages," p. 168	80,000 to gentiles in Hebron; 40,000 to gentiles in villages
C. **Safed** 1697	10,000	Simonsohn, "Emissaries from Safed to Mantua," p. 342	Type of coin not mentioned
1736	10,000 *kurus*	Ben-Zvi, *Studies and Documents,* p. 221; Yaʿari, *The Emissaries of Palestine,* p. 432	

Year	Amount	Source	Comments
1742	17,500 lions	Yaʿari, *The Emissaries of Palestine*, p. 437	
1747	10,000 *kurus*	Yaʿari, *The Emissaries of Palestine*, p. 443	
1761	10,000 *kurus*	Yaʿari, *The Emissaries of Palestine*, p. 451; Yaʿari, "The earthquake in Safed," p. 386	Differences result from lack of precision in letter asking for donations from Diaspora
	25,000 *kurus*	Yaʿari, *The Emissaries of Palestine*, p. 453; Simonsohn, "Emissaries from Safed to Mantua," p. 335	
1762	25,000 *kurus*	Rivkind, "Isolated pages," pp. 124–25	
1767	20,000 *kurus*	Yaʿari, *The Emissaries of Palestine*, p. 456	
1774	15,000 *kurus*	Ben-Zvi, *Studies and Documents*, p. 245	
1793	50,000 *kurus*	Yaʿari, *The Emissaries of Palestine*, p. 664	
1795	140,000 *pavels*	Yaʿari, *The Emissaries of Palestine*, p. 667	One-time payment. Type of coin not clear
1800	125,000 *kurus*	Yaʿari, *The Emissaries of Palestine*, pp. 668–69	Payments to rulers during Napoleonic war

TABLE 2 (Cont.)

Year	Debt	Source	Comments
D. Tiberias			
1748	10,000 lions	Ya'ari, *The Emissaries of Palestine*, p. 508	
1749	8,000 *kurus*	Mss. of Letters to the Emissaries, Leeds Library, Roth Collection no. 254, p. 23	Letter from Tiberias to Gibraltar
1774	5,000 lions	Ya'ari, *The Emissaries of Palestine*, p. 517	Apparently a loan
1776	20,000 *kurus*	Toledano, *Treasury of Manuscripts*, p. 74	
1784	15,000 lions	Ya'ari, "Addenda to the book *The Emissaries of Palestine*," p. 231	
1785	15,000 lions	Rivkind, "Isolated pages," p. 160	
1798	20,000 lions	Ya'ari, *The Emissaries of Palestine*, p. 637	

1. The continual decline in the value of the money in the eighteenth century must be taken into account, as the inflation during this period averaged about two percent per annum. At times there was some exaggeration in the sums, especially when a request for donations was presented.

2. It seems that one must distinguish between the Turkish *kurus* and the "lion," which was coined in Holland and was used by the Turks. The *kurus* contained forty *paras*, while the lion contained forty-eight *paras*. After some time the value of the *kurus* declined with respect to the lion; see Lachman, "Numismatic notes," pp. 197–98; Ben-Zvi, *Palestine under Ottoman Rule*, p. 458; Bashan, *Captivity and Ransom*, pp. 317–18.

17

THE STANDARD OF LIVING
OF THE JEWS IN PALESTINE

INCOME LEVEL

The minimal amount necessary for a person to live in the eighteenth century was 75–100 *kurus* per year. This is calculable from the lists of those who received support from the Diaspora, lists which describe tens to hundreds of *kurus* per year.[1] Some sources even give a more detailed picture. When they organized the immigration to Palestine in the middle of the eighteenth century, the Istanbul Officials tried to prevent the immigration of Jews without fixed support from the Diaspora. According to them 150 *kurus* per year were required for a couple to live, 100 *kurus* for a single man, and 75 *kurus* for a single woman.[2] The difference between men and women stemmed, it seems, from payments that were imposed only on men, such as the poll tax. Elsewhere the Istanbul Officials mentioned similar sums of 140 *kurus* for a couple and 70 *kurus* for a woman.[3] Householders received an allowance for a few *kurus*.[4] The allowance of an individual householder was 30 *kurus*.[5] David Ashkenazi of Safed received 72 *kurus*.[6] Widows received 30, 40, or 50 *kurus*,[7] on up to 120 *kurus*.[8] One patron who immigrated in 1745 received an allowance of 250 *kurus*.[9]

Many immigrants did not have a yearly allowance.[10] It is possible that immigrants who arrived in Palestine without permission from the Istanbul Officials did not receive support from the community fund, like the local poor who did not have support from the Diaspora.

The highest incomes were enjoyed, as mentioned, by the Torah scholars. The yeshiva Beth Jacob founded by the Pereyra family—which had ten Torah scholars in 1758—received a yearly allowance of 1,200 *kurus* per year, that is, more than 100 *kurus* for an individual.[11] Besides this the yeshiva men received sums that were not included in the fixed sum, and thus they increased their income. For example, they took ten percent of the income of the emissaries and of the estates.[12]

The yeshiva deans generally received twice the amount that a Torah scholar received. R. Isaac Hacohen Rapaport, who was the dean of the yeshiva Hesed Le-Avraham U-Vinyan Shelomo during the years 1749–55, received a salary of 504 *kurus* per year, in addition to sums that he recevied personally.[13] The chief rabbi Meyuhas Becher Samuel received 450 *kurus* per year.[14] R. Abraham Raphael ben Asher, dean of the yeshiva Yefa'er 'Anavim, received 465 *kurus* together with his wife.[15] In 1744 R. Jacob Saul of Izmir was offered the position of dean of the yeshiva Knesseth Israel in Jerusalem at a salary of 300 *kurus* per year.[16] R. Jekuthiel Gordon, a student of the Ramhal (Luzzatto), who planned to immigrate to Hebron and be the dean of a yeshiva, was supposed to receive 300 *reichstaler*.[17]

The officials of the Jerusalem community received a salary of at least 150–250 *kurus* per year. Besides this some of them received private support from the Diaspora, were owners of businesses, or lent money at interest. R. Joseph Treves recevied 150 *kurus* per year;[18] Abraham Alhadef, 175 *kurus*;[19] and Isaac de-Bilaski, 250 *kurus*.[20] The salary of the official Elijah Rolo was 250 *kurus*, in addition to a private income of 600 *kurus* from the Diaspora and other sums that his wife received.[21] Another source tells of incomes of officials in the amount of 200 *kurus*.[22]

The incomes of the emissaries were also high, as they received one-fourth or one-third of the income of the mission as well as traveling expenses. Moreover, during the period of their mission their families in Palestine received a fixed weekly support, which was not always deducted from the total amount that the emissary received. For example, the emissary R. Ephraim Navon received one-third or one-fourth of the income of the mission and 120 *kurus* for traveling expenses. His family received 250 *kurus* per year in weekly payments.[23] The emissary Jacob Ashkenazi received one-third of the income of his mission in the sum of 4,031 *kurus*. During the years of his stay in the Diaspora his family received 1,000 *kurus* altogether.[24]

Community workers—such as caretakers and ritual slaughterers—had lower salaries, about 50–100 *kurus* per year, according to their status.[25] We have evidence in our possession concerning a "professional conflict" of these workers in order to raise their salaries. It seems that they succeeded fairly often, in spite of the opposition of the Istanbul Officials.[26] The guard and the caretaker of a yeshiva received 12 *kurus* per year.[27]

The Ashkenazim who lived on the support obtained on the basis of the lists received lower sums, and their economic position was particularly difficult.[28]

The Standard of Living

LIVING CONDITIONS

As a result of the increase in the number of immigrants severe problems arose in Jerusalem in the matter of living quarters, and this was the source of many regulations concerning the ownership of houses.[29] In a series of regulations from 1781 we find the following: "With the authority that has been given to us by the community of our congregation in the holy city of Jerusalem and with the authority that has been given to us by the officers and assistants of the Istanbul Officials, we agree . . . that everyone who has a house that he is renting from a gentile and rents it out to others may not add to what he takes even a small coin."[30]

These regulations were established in order to prevent overcharging, unfair competition between men of means and poor people, and the eviction of poor people from their homes. In 1737 a regulation was established in Jerusalem that forbade giving more money to a gentile landlord in order to take the home away from another Jew.[31] In Safed the living conditions were better than in Jerusalem and in Tiberias, as R. Simha of Zalozce wrote in 1765: "There are apartments to rent and to sell cheaply and today the market is such that with the help of God everyone can buy what his heart desires, which is not the case in Tiberias."[32] This was written a short time after the earthquake, and so it is likely that Safed had very few residents.

THE CURRENCY

One of the most difficult problems facing the investigator is determining the value of the currency.[33] In our sources many sorts of coins are mentioned, and it is not always possible to discover their real or equivalent values. Besides the instability in the values of coins there were also differences in the values of the same coins in different places. It is especially important to discuss the real value of the *kurus*, as it was the main coin of the Ottoman Empire. Table 3 presents the sums in *kurus*, accompanied by their value in other coins mentioned in the sources.[34]

During the course of the eighteenth century there was a gradual decline in the value of the money, as is attested by the sources, which frequently mention inflation.[35] In the middle of the eighteenth century R. Isaac Hacohen Rapaport was asked according to which rate the donors should give their yearly contribution to the yeshiva, in the light of the decline in the value of the money.[36]

TABLE 3. Values of the Coins in the Eighteenth Century

Amount in kurus	Amount in another coin	Year	Source
34,000	11,000 reds	1692	Benayahu, "The Ashkenazi community of Jerusalem," p. 132
15,000	5,000 Hungarian reds	1692	Benayahu, "The Ashkenazi community of Jerusalem," p. 132
c. 60,000	87,000 zlotys	1727	Ya'ari, "R. Moses Israel and his mission," p. 160
525	100 whites	1744	Pinkas of Istanbul, letter of 24 Elul 5504 (September 1744), p. 11
1,3 kurus (pattacas)	1 florin	1747	Pinkas of Istanbul, letter of 17 Av 5507 (August 1747), p. 71
300	Somewhat less than 70 Venetian ducats	1750	Pinkas of Istanbul, letter of 1 Adar I 5510 (February 1750), p. 86
864	46.25 pattacas (Dutch coin)[1]	1750	Pinkas of Istanbul, letter of 11 Elul 5510 (September 1750), p. 79
1,140	680 pattacas	1750	Pinkas of Istanbul, letter of 11 Elul 5510 (September 1750), p. 79
581.3	150 venetians	1751	Pinkas of Istanbul, letter of 16 Heshvan 5512 (November 1751), p. 106
370.4	101 gibis	1751	Pinkas of Istanbul, letter of 16 Heshvan 5512 (November 1751), p. 106
37.5	50 zlotys	1751	Pinkas of Istanbul, letter of 16 Heshvan 5512 (November 1751), p. 106

82.2	100 florins	1752	*Pinkas* of Istanbul, letter of 8 Nisan 5512 (April 1752), p. 105
258.39	146.25 pattacas	1753	*Pinkas* of Istanbul, letter of 15 Av 5513 (August 1753), p. 111
429	107 reds	1756	*Pinkas* of Istanbul, letter of 18 Elul 5516 (September 1756), p. 36
1,500	3,012.5 new *kurus*	1757	*Pinkas* of Istanbul, letter of 18 Av 5517 (August 1757), p. 89
600 "black *kurus*"	188 new *kurus*	1757	*Pinkas* of Istanbul, letter of 18 Av 5517 (August 1757), p. 89
861.28	464.75 florins	1757	*Pinkas* of Istanbul, letter from end of Tishrey 5518 (October 1757), p. 24
200	151 florins	1757	*Pinkas* of Istanbul, letter from end of Tishrey 5518 (October 1757), p. 24
8	1 pound sterling	1765	*Pinkas* of Istanbul, letter of 11 Tishrey 5526 (October 1765), p. 90

1. Concerning the pattacas, see Kaplan, "The attitude of the leadership of the Portuguese community in Amsterdam to the Sabbatean movement," p. 199.

Inspection of table 3 reveals that in 1692 there was a ratio of approximately 1:3 between the *kurus* and the gold coin of central Europe, whereas in 1756 there was a ratio of 1:4 between these two coins; that is, during the first half of the eighteenth century there was a decline of approximately twenty-five percent in the value of the *kurus*.

PRICE LEVELS

The study of Turkish documents sheds some light on the prices of a number of products. In 1761 a Jew leased a field that had been planted. His first payment was 250 *kurus*, and afterwards he paid 300 Egyptian *kurus*[37] per year to the fund.[38] In the same year a Jewish patron paid 120 *zlotys*—that is, about 90 *kurus*—for the leasing of a plot in a graveyard. In Jerusalem it cost 100–500 *kurus* to release a prisoner from jail.[39]

To broaden the picture it is worth examining some examples from the Diaspora. In the period under discussion 200 *kurus* were paid for a house in Greece.[40] In Turkey the printing of a book cost hundreds of *kurus*: 600 *kurus* for one volume and 800 *kurus* for two volumes.[41] The printing of R. Moses Hagiz's book cost 800 *kurus*.[42] The renovation of a house in Izmir cost 50 *kurus*.[43]

In the middle of the eighteenth century prices were fairly stable, whereas at the end of the century there was a great rise in prices, first and foremost because of the rebellions in Palestine and the interminable wars between Turkey and the European powers. In letters sent from the Galilee in 1784 the Hasidim wrote that prices rose by a factor of three to four; a "measure" of grain went from 18 *kurus* to 80 *kurus*.[44] In 1799, at the time of Napoleon's conquest of Palestine, a severe economic crisis broke out, and in a letter that he sent from Jerusalem to Edirne, R. Moses Mordecai, son of Joseph Meyuhas, wrote that "the rate has gone up twice in all kinds of things."[45]

CONCLUSION

THE UNIQUENESS OF PALESTINE in the consciousness of the Jews serves as an important touchstone for a scholarly discussion of the history of the Jewish settlement that has existed there throughout the generations. Indeed, this settlement is not just another Jewish community, one whose history can be discussed in isolation. The history of the Jewish settlement in Palestine must also be studied with respect to its connections to the entire Diaspora, which maintained continuous and strong ties with it. In addition, one must consider the Moslem and Christian authorities and populations. During the eighteenth century Palestine was part of the Ottoman Empire and of its Syrian province. What characterized the eighteenth century was the decentralization of the Ottoman Empire, which came about as a result of its weakness and the weakness of its central authority. As a result the importance of the local provincial authorities increased.

Life within the Jewish settlement in Palestine in the eighteenth century was also conducted within this framework of authority. This settlement consisted of several thousand Jews during this period, mostly Sephardi, and included a large proportion of old people. Most of the Jews lived in Jerusalem and the remainder in Hebron, Safed, and Tiberias, which was rebuilt in the eighteenth century by the Galilean ruler Dahir al-ʿUmar. A few Jews lived in some villages in the Galilee. In the second half of the century the Galilee grew in importance, as it was developed by local rulers, and the Jews were included in this trend. Starting in the seventeenth century the patterns of livelihood among the Jews in Palestine had begun to change from trade and handwork to donations from the Diaspora. This trend became even stronger during the eighteenth century.

The first milestone of the eighteenth century occurred at the end of 1699. In this year several hundred Jews from Poland and the Austrian Empire immigrated to Jerusalem, among them Kabbalists and Sabbateans, led by R. Judah Hasid. The entanglement of this group in heavy debts to local Arabs led to its disintegration and to the disintegration of the entire Jerusalem community. Only in the 1720s did the heads of the Jewish community in Istanbul succeed in reaching an arrangement with the Ottoman authorities for the repayment of the debts. As a result, a special committee called the Committee of Officials for Palestine in Istanbul was established in Istanbul in 1726. This committee, which was composed of the most important Jews in Istanbul, continued to take care of the Jews of Palestine throughout the eighteenth century. The committee serves as the fulcrum of our work, and the story of its activities is practically identical with the history of the Jewish settlement in Palestine in the eighteenth century.

The committee of Istanbul Officials concentrated on three main directions of activity: (1) contacts with the Ottoman rulership with its many layers—in Istanbul, in Damascus, and in Sidon (the latter two being the capitals of the *vilayets*, the provinces to which the two parts of Palestine belonged), and with the local authorities in Palestine itself; (2) connections with the Diaspora throughout the world, especially in the areas of collecting money and organizing the immigrations and pilgrimages of Jews to Palestine, and also in the establishment of yeshivas in Palestine by means of donations from the Diaspora; and (3) organizing the Jewish settlement in Palestine and controlling it in all areas of life. This was accomplished by the committee through the appointment of its representatives in the Jewish communities in Palestine, the appointment of rabbis and community leaders, and intervention in the administration of the communities.

With these activities, which were very well organized and quite efficient, the Istanbul Officials became an important factor in uniting Jewish activities on behalf of Palestine throughout the world, and they also became directly responsible for the Jews living in Palestine in the eighteenth century. Thus the Jewish settlement in Palestine became totally dependent on the activities of the Istanbul Officials and completely lost its community autonomy. The activities of the Istanbul Officials also illustrate the great importance attached by Diaspora Jews to the support of the Jewish settlement in Palestine and the high status of the land in their eyes. The institutionalization of financial support for the Jewish settlement in Palestine and the organization of the communities by an external body symbolize a serious change occurring in the character of the Yishuv. This trend was strengthened even more in the nineteenth century, during which the economic support of the Yishuv was transferred from the Jewish communities of the Ottoman Empire to those of Europe.

As a result of the activities of the Istanbul Officials, a renewal of Jewish immigration and pilgrimages was made possible, beginning in the 1730s.

Conclusion

However, in spite of continual immigrations to Palestine during the entire eighteenth century, the Jewish settlement there did not increase significantly. The main reasons for this are grounded in the structure of the Jewish population that immigrated and settled in Palestine, which consisted largely of old people who immigrated without their families. Moreover, the local authorities in Palestine, with their tyranny and extortions of money from the entire population, caused a continuing emigration of Jews from Palestine. Natural disasters and the many plagues that occurred in Palestine during the period caused many deaths and prevented a substantial increase in the population. Significant changes in the history of the Jewish settlement in Palestine began to occur only with Western penetration into the region in the nineteenth century, but that is another topic.

NOTES

INTRODUCTION: THE SOURCES

1. Gil, *Palestine during the First Moslem Period*, vol. 1, p. vii.
2. Lewis, *Notes and Documents*, pp. 1–4; Heyd, *Ottoman Documents on Palestine*; Cohen, *Miqqedem U-Miyam*, pp. 39–48.
3. Hasson, "The penetration of Arab tribes in Palestine," pp. 54–62.
4. Ben-Arieh, "Nineteenth century, Western literature of travel to Palestine," pp. 159–88.
5. Bashan, "Evidence of European tourists," pp. 35–80.
6. Schur, *Pilgrims' and Travellers' Accounts*.
7. Rozen, *The Ruins of Jerusalem*.
8. Manna, "The Farukhids," pp. 196–232.
9. Morgenstern, *Messianism*; Karagila, *Social and Economic Patterns of the Jewish Community in Palestine*.
10. See, e.g., Eliav, *Under Imperial Austrian Protection*; and others.
11. Ashtor, *The Jews and the Mediterranean Economy*.
12. Cohen, "The Jews in northern Palestine."
13. Most of them have been collected in Ya'ari, *Travels in Palestine*; *Memoirs of Palestine*.
14. See, e.g., *Ahavath Zion*; Ya'ari, *Travels in Palestine*, pp. 773–75; Goren, "*Yedey Moshe*," pp. 75–96.
15. *Sefer Hatakanoth*, originally published in Jerusalem in 1842. I have used the better 1883 edition.
16. Ya'ari, *The Emissaries of Palestine*.
17. Bashan, *Bar-Ilan*, pp. 137–65; Tamar, *Studies in the History of the Jews in Palestine*, p. 197; Shmuelevitz, *The Jews of the Ottoman Empire*, pp. 1–9.
18. Gil, "Geniza," pp. 17–29; Cohen and Stillman, "The Cairo Geniza," pp. 3–35.
19. The *Pinkas* of Istanbul, Ms. 4008 (0151), Jewish Theological Seminary, New York.
20. Three volumes taken from this collection have been published in Rivlin and Rivlin, *Letters of the Pekidim and Amarkalim of Amsterdam*.
21. Goldsmith-Lehmann, *Sir Moses Montefiore*.
22. Rozen, *The Jerusalem Community of Jerusalem*, pp. 293–315.
23. Haim, *Documents from the Collection of Elie Eliachar*.

1. HISTORICAL BACKGROUND

1. Epstein, *The Ottoman Jewish Communities*; Shmuelevitz, *The Jews of the Ottoman Empire*.

2. Stillman, *The Jews of Arab Lands*, pp. 22–39; Gerber, *Economic and Social Life*, pp. 9–35.

3. Doubts have been raised recently about the limits of the autonomy; see Hacker, "Jewish autonomy," pp. 349–412.

4. Braude, "Millet system," pp. 69–88; Gerber, *The Economic and Social Life of the Jews in the Ottoman Empire*, pp. 22–24; Cohen, *Jewish Life under Islam*, pp. 1–9.

5. Hirschberg, "Arbitrary tax in Jerusalem," pp. 164–65 (and see there additional references on this topic); *Encyclopaedia Judaica*, s.v. "Jerusalem," vol. 9, p. 1435; Cohen, *Palestine in the Eighteenth Century*, pp. 69–172.

6. Shamir, *A Modern History of the Arabs*, p. 1; Ben-Zvi, *Palestine under Ottoman Rule*, p. 23; Cohen, *Palestine in the Eighteenth Century*, pp. 249–58; Lewis, *The Emergence of Modern Turkey*, pp. 21–40; and especially Heyd, *The Institutions of the Ottoman Empire*, pp. 111–14.

7. See Cohen, *Ottoman Documents of the Jewish Community of Jerusalem*; Cohen, *Jewish Life under Islam*; Barnai, "The leadership of the Jewish community in Jerusalem," pp. 283–84.

8. Here is a list of the Turkish and Arab documents that we know about: Hirschberg, "Notes on the debts of the Jews in Jerusalem in 1775," p. 158; also see Hirschberg, "Arbitrary tax in Jerusalem," p. 161; Haim, "Sources of Sephardi history in Jerusalem," pp. 143–72. Haim's work includes précis of a number of documents from those days that are preserved in the archives of the Committee of the Sephardi Community in Jerusalem, especially these documents: No. 4, p. 153; No. 9, p. 154; No. 17, p. 155; No. 33, p. 157; Nos. 59 and 60, p. 158; Nos. 66 and 77, p. 159; No. 25, p. 160; No. 74, p. 161; No. 75, p. 162; Nos. 78 and 80, p. 162. See also Haim, *Documents from the Collection of Elie Eliachar*; Haim, "Additional documents on the relations of the Sephardi community," pp. 232–34; Cohen, "Arabic documents on the settlement of the debts of the Jewish communities," pp. 317–30; Sharon and Beck, *From Ancient Archives*, pp. 17–26, 67–68; Chayat, "New sources for the history of the Jews in Ottoman Jerusalem."

9. Avitsur, "Safed," pp. 41–70; Cohen, *Jewish Life under Islam*.

10. Ish-Shalom, *Christian Travels in the Holy Land*, p. 354. Concerning the Jewish settlement in Palestine in the seventeenth century, see Rozen, *The Jewish Community of Jerusalem*.

11. Heyd, *Dahir al-ʿUmar*, pp. 12–15.

12. Cohen, *Palestine in the Eighteenth Century*, pp. 1–78; Cohen, "The Jews in northern Palestine," pp. 145–51; Heyd, *Dahir al-ʿUmar*, pp. 79ff.

13. Heyd, *Dahir al-ʿUmar*, p. 20; Barbir, *Ottoman Rule*, pp. 56–64.

14. *Zimrath Ha-Aretz*, p. 34; Heyd, *Dahir al-ʿUmar*, pp. 22–80.

15. *Zimrath Ha-Aretz*, p. 35.

16. Ibid., p. 37.

17. Ibid., p. 47.

18. Ibid., p. 55.

19. Ibid., pp. 68–89.

20. Ibid., p. 69. On these battles, see Cohen, *Palestine in the Eighteenth Century*, pp. 30–42. On the military aspects of the battles, see Nachshon, "The seige of Tiberias according to R. Jacob Beirav's *Zimrath Ha-Aretz*," pp. 55–64.

21. Ben-Zvi, "The emissaries of Palestine in Italy," pp. 15, 20–21.

22. Yaʿari, *The Emissaries of Palestine*, p. 408.

23. Yaʿari, *Letters from Palestine*, p. 265.

24. Klar, *Rabbi Haim ben Attar*, p. 134.

25. *Malkhi Ba-Kodesh*, author's introduction. See also the letter of R. Moses Morporgo of 1747, in which similar events are mentioned: Ben-Zvi, *Studies and Documents*, pp. 232, 236.

26. Yaʿari, "The earthquake in Safed," pp. 349–63; Brilling, "Das Erdbeben von Sefad," pp. 41–58.

27. Yaʿari, "The earthquake in Safed," p. 357; Yaʿari, *The Emissaries of Palestine*, p. 455; Simonsohn, "Emissaries from Safed to Mantua," p. 334.

28. Yaʿari, *Letters from Palestine*, p. 293.

29. Yaʿari, *The Emissaries of Palestine*, p. 441; Toledano, "On the history of the Jewish settlement in Safed," pp. 360–61.

30. *Zimrath Ha-Aretz*, p. 58; Toledano, *Treasury of Manuscripts*, p. 67; Ben-Zvi, *Studies and Documents*, p. 245; Yaʿari, *The Emissaries of Palestine*, pp. 436, 453; Yaʿari, "Addenda to the book *The Emissaries of Palestine*," p. 224.

31. Simonsohn, "Emissaries from Safed to Mantua," p. 335; Cohen, *Palestine in the Eighteenth Century*, pp. 45–56; Toledano, *Treasury of Manuscripts*, p. 74; Yaʿari, *The Emissaries of Palestine*, pp. 586–87, 593–95; Heyd, *Dahir al-ʿUmar*, pp. 46–72; Heyd, *Palestine during the Ottoman Rule*, pp. 40–42.

32. On Jezzār, see Cohen, *Palestine in the Eighteenth Century*, pp. 53–77; Heyd, *Palestine during the Ottoman Rule*, pp. 42–45.

33. Heyd, *Palestine during the Ottoman Rule*, p. 45.

34. See Ben-Zvi, *Palestine under Ottoman Rule*, pp. 319–23, 342–43; Philip, "The Farhi family," pp. 97–114; Schur, "The death of Haim Farhi," pp. 179–91. This Haim Farhi was the nephew of the Haim Farhi who was the adviser to Pasha Süleyman of Damascus in the 1740s, and the theory of the investigators who believed that they were the same person should be corrected.

35. Halpern, *The Hasidic Immigration to Palestine*, p. 28.

36. Yaʿari, "The earthquake in Safed," pp. 349–63; Halpern, *The Hasidic Immigration to Palestine*, p. 29; Brilling, "Das Erdbeben von Safed," pp. 41–58.

37. Rivkind, "Isolated pages," pp. 156–58.

38. Barnai, *Hasidic Letters from Palestine*, p. 74.

39. Elmalech, "From the hidden manuscripts of the past," pp. 321–24. Elmalech was mistaken in the date of the letter. Also see Halpern, *The Hasidic Immigration to Palestine*, p. 29.

40. Rivkind, "Isolated pages," p. 156.

41. See the letter of 1800 in Luncz, "He causes the sleeping ones to speak," *Jerusalem* 7: 213–18.

42. Rivkind, "A collection of writings," pp. 301–31; Rubashov, "Sha'alu Shelom Yerushalayim," pp. 461–93; Benayahu, "Letters of R. Samuel Abuhav, R. Moses Zaccuto and their circle," pp. 136–86; Rozen, "The mutiny of Nakib el Ashraf," pp. 75–90; Manna, "The rebellion of Naqib al-Ashraf," pp. 49–74.

43. *The Shar'i Court of Jerusalem (Sijill)*, vol. 214, p. 142.

44. The *Pinkas* of Istanbul, letters from the following dates: 29 Kislev 5501 (December 1740), p. 48 (four letters); 4 Teveth 5501 (January 1741), p. 55; 1 Teveth 5501 (January 1741), p. 2; 2 Shevat 5501 (February 1741), pp. 2, 3; 25 Iyyar 5501 (May 1741), p. 55; 20 Tammuz 5501 (July 1741), p. 3; 26 Elul 5501 (September 1741), p. 5; 3 Tishrei 5502 (October 1741), p. 5; 1 Heshvan 5502 (November 1741), p. 48; 27 Shevat 5502 (February 1742), p. 37; 12 Iyyar 5502 (May 1742), p. 37 (and see also below, note 45; also see Rivkind, "Documents illustrating Jewish life in Palestine," pp. 118–23; Ya'ari, *The Emissaries of Palestine*, p. 389.

45. See the *Pinkas* of Istanbul, letter of 24 Elul 5504 (September 1744), p. 61. Concerning the difficult condition of the Jerusalem community in those days, see also the letters of 6 Kislev 5506 (December 1745), p. 66; 26 Heshvan 5509 (November 1748), p. 74; 5 Kislev 5509 (December 1748), p. 74; 12 Elul 5513 (September 1753), p. 111; Heshvan 5515 (November 1754), p. 119; 12 Nisan 5522 (April 1762), p. 60; 1 Elul 5522 (September 1762), p. 46; 20 Shevat 5527 (February 1767), p. 91. See also *S'deh Ha-Aretz*, *a*, introduction of the rabbis of Jerusalem; ibid., *c*, approval of R. David Pardo; ibid., *c*, p. 27b; *P'ri Ha-Adama*, *a*, introduction of R. Haim Shalom Hacohen; *Birkhoth Hamayim*, author's introduction; *Mayim Sha'al*, author's introduction; Ya'ari, *The Emissaries of Palestine*, p. 400; Turtshiner, "Letters from Palestine by Simeon de Geldern," p. 106; Rivkind, "Documents illustrating Jewish life in Palestine," pp. 119, 133; Shohet, "The Jews in Jerusalem," *Zion*, pp. 385–86; Hirschberg, "Arbitrary tax in Jerusalem," p. 161.

46. Ya'ari, *The Emissaries of Palestine*, p. 398.

47. The *Pinkas* of Istanbul, letter of 20 Av 5514 (August 1754), p. 116; Haim, "Sources of Sephardi history in Jerusalem," pp. 143–72.

48. Turtshiner, "Letters from Palestine by Simeon de Geldern," p. 110.

49. Rivkind, "Isolated pages," pp. 163–65.

50. Danon, "Seven letters," p. 356, letter 5.

51. *The Shar'i Court of Jerusalem (Sijill)*, vol. 214 (1718), p. 11. Haim, "Sources of Sephardi history in Jerusalem," no. 66, p. 159; no. 77, p. 159; Sharon and Beck, *From Ancient Archives*, pp. 17–25.

52. Rivlin, "The estate regulations of Jerusalem and Palestine," pp. 559–619 (a large collection). Also see below, chap. 16, "Estates."

53. The *Pinkas* of Istanbul, letter of 24 Elul 5504 (September 1744), p. 61; *Sha'ar Yosef*, approval of the rabbis of Hebron; Assaf, "More on the history of the Jews of Kurdistan," pp. 267, 269; Rivkind, "Documents illustrating Jewish life in Palestine," p. 126; Toledano, "The language of sleepers," p. 304. Toledano was mistaken in the date.

54. From *Admath Kodesh, a*, par. 22. The topic is the war between the local tribes in Hebron and Bethlehem.

55. From Ya'ari, "Two documents on the Jewish settlement in Hebron," p. 113; Ya'ari, *The Emissaries of Palestine*, pp. 499–500.

56. From Rivkind, "Documents illustrating Jewish life in Palestine," p. 127; see also Ya'ari, *The Emissaries of Palestine*, p. 587.

57. From Barnai, *Hasidic Letters from Palestine*, p. 39.

58. Toledano, "From manuscripts," pp. 409–13; Benayahu, *Rabbi H. Y. D. Azulay*, p. 449.

2. INFLUENCES ON THE JEWISH SETTLEMENT

1. Anderson, *Europe in the Eighteenth Century*, pp. 1–5.

2. The time arrived for the ship to sail to Palestine: *Batey Kehuna*, vol. 1, p. 82b.

3. Ya'ari, "The 'three weeks' in Palestine," p. 67.

4. *Tzach Ve-Adom*, pp. 41b–42a.

5. *Zichron Yerushalayim* was printed in Istanbul in 1743.

6. See, for example, the edition of Jacob Babani (Amsterdam, 1759), which is slightly different from the Istanbul edition.

7. From *Ahavath Zion*, cited in Ya'ari, *Travels in Palestine*, p. 391.

8. The *Pinkas* of Istanbul, letter of 20 Adar 5509 (March 1749), p. 65.

9. Evidence for the immigration of tens and hundreds per year may be found in ibid., letters of 29 Kislev 5501 (December 1740), p. 48; 26 Elul 5501 (September 1741), p. 5; 18 Av 5505 (August 1745), p. 56; 15 Av 5506 (August 1746), p. 114; 22 Av 5506 (August 1746), p. 69; 1 Elul 5508 (September 1748), p. 73; 15 Av 5509 (August 1749), p. 81; 15 Av 5509 (August 1749)—date uncertain, p. 80 (two letters); 22 Av 5509 (August 1749), p. 81; 5 Iyyar 5510 (May 1750), p. 84; 15 Av 5510 (August 1750), p. 84; 13 Elul 5510 (September 1750), p. 89; 22 Teveth 5511 (January 1751), p. 89; 5 Nisan 5512 (April 1752), p. 99; 10 Tammuz 5512 (July 1752), p. 110; 15 Av 5519 (August 1759), p. 28; 6 Elul 5520

(September 1760), p. 41; end of Elul 5520 (September 1760), p. 41; 4 Elul 5521 (September 1761), p. 45; 26 Iyyar 5522 (May 1762), p. 102; 25 Av 5527 (August 1767), p. 132; Elul (date uncertain) 5528 (September 1768), p. 135.

10. Ibid., letters of 29 Kislev 5501 (December 1740), p. 48; 26 Elul 5501 (September 1741), p. 5; 15 Av 5509 (August 1759), p. 81; 13 Elul 5510 (September 1750), p. 89; 22 Teveth 5511 (January 1751), p. 89; 4 Elul 5521 (September 1761), p. 45; 25 Av 5527 (August 1767), p. 132. The Christians also used to hire ships. On the ship of the "Amalekites"—that is, the Armenians—see ibid., letter of 22 Teveth 5511 (January 1751), p. 89.

11. Bashan, "Contracts for the rental of ships for the bringing of Jews to Palestine since 1775," pp. 291–302.

12. The *Pinkas* of Istanbul, letter of 15 Av 5509 (August 1749), p. 81.

13. Sometimes even two ships arrived from Izmir; ibid., letter of 29 Kislev 5501 (December 1740), p. 48.

14. Ibid., letters of 1 Tammuz 5509 (July 1749), p. 76; 17 Av 5509 (August 1749)—date uncertain, p. 76; 28 Elul 5509 (September 1749), p. 38.

15. Such as, for example, the ship of R. Haim ben Attar and his group.

16. Boats from Amsterdam sailed through Izmir.

17. The *Pinkas* of Istanbul, letter of 29 Kislev 5501 (December 1740), p. 48.

18. Nacht, *From the Hidden Manuscripts of Jerusalem*, pp. 12–13.

19. This calculation is based on the *Pinkas* of Istanbul, letters of 2 Nisan 5503 (April 1743), p. 43; 6 Elul 5520 (September 1760), p. 41; end of Elul 5520 (September 1760), p. 41. It says there that 150 *kurus* are needed. For immigration from Italy the sum of 15–20 *cikini* (i.e., about 100 *kurus*), is mentioned. This is consistent with the words of R. Haim ben Attar, who wrote in 1741 that 24 *cikini* were needed for a couple; see also Klar, *Rabbi Haim ben Attar*, p. 59.

20. The *Pinkas* of Istanbul, letters of 11 Adar 5509 (March 1749), p. 65; 20 Adar 5509 (March 1749), p. 65. For additional sources concerning the immigration of individuals, see *Magen Shaul*, p. 21b; Dinur, *At the Turning-Point of the Generations*, p. 69; Elmalech, "The Rishon Le-Zion Rabbi Jacob Moses Ayash," p. 234; *Hon Rav*, author's introduction; Toledano, *Treasury of Manuscripts*, p. 69.

21. *Admath Kodesh*, a, p. 36b.

22. The *Pinkas* of Istanbul, letters of 15 Av 5509 (August 1749), p. 81; 23 Av 5516 (August 1756), p. 72.

23. Ibid., letter of 25 Av 5527 (August 1767), p. 45.

24. Ibid., letter of Elul 5528 (September 1768), p. 132.

25. From Ben-Ya'akov, *Jerusalem within Its Walls*, p. 361.

26. Ibid.

27. The *Pinkas* of Istanbul, letters of 18 Av 5506 (August 1746), p. 69; 22 Iyyar 5507 (May 1747), p. 71; 22 Tammuz 5509 (July 1749), p. 77; 15 Av 5509 (August 1749)—date uncertain, p. 80.

28. Benayahu, *Rabbi H. Y. D. Azulay*, pp. 19–24.

3. THE BEGINNING OF THE EIGHTEENTH CENTURY

1. These are the important sources for the history of these immigrations: Krauss, "Die Pälastinasiedlung der Polnischen Hasidim und die Wiener Kreise in Jahre 1700," pp. 51–94; Benayahu, "The Holy Brotherhood of R. Judah Hasid and their settlement in Jerusalem," pp. 133–82; Mann, "The settlement of R. Abraham Rovigo and his group in Jerusalem in 1702," pp. 59–84. In the works of Krauss and Mann there are many errors. The historian Ben Zion Dinur even believes that this immigration may be seen as the beginning of the modern age in Jewish history, from a Zionist historiographic viewpoint (see Dinur, *At the Turning-Point of the Generations*, pp. 26–28; also see Barnai, "Trends in the historiography of the medieval and early modern periods of the Jewish community in Palestine," pp. 102–14).

2. Benayahu, "The Holy Brotherhood," p. 141; Benayahu, "Elia Ashkenazi," pp. 69–70; Benayahu, "The Sabbatean movement in Greece," pp. 451–524. On the Sabbatean factor in this immigration many documents have been published; also see Benayahu, "The Holy Brotherhood," p. 149; Benayahu, "The Sabbatean movement in Greece," p. 197; Shazar, *The Hope for the Year 5500 (1740)*, pp. 10–12. The investigators who dealt with the various immigrations in the Ottoman period did not pay sufficient attention to the proximity between the immigrations and the various events in the Ottoman Empire and in Europe. The immigration of Hasid's group did indeed have important investigations—see especially Benayahu, "The Ashkenazi community of Jerusalem," pp. 128–89; Benayahu, "The Holy Brotherhood," pp. 133–82—but a study of these investigations reveals that the treaty of Karlowitz was not mentioned at all. And yet it is clear that it was this treaty, which came after years of war in which the regions that this group came from were captured, that enabled the immigrants to reach Palestine. It is obviously also worth examining the ideological motives for an immigration of this sort, but without the political factor it is impossible to understand all the historical processes associated with this episode.

3. For a very important document in which this immigration is described, see Mann, "The settlement of R. Abraham Rovigo," pp. 59–84. Mann did not accept the view that Rovigo was a Sabbatean, just as he denied the Sabbatean beliefs of Hasid. At present, after many important documents concerning the history of these personalities have been published, there is no longer any reason to doubt the Sabbatean beliefs of Hasid and Rovigo; see especially Scholem, *The Dreams of the Sabbatean R. Mordecai Ashkenazi*; Tishbi, "R. Meir Rofe's letters of 1675–1680 to R. Abraham Rovigo," pp. 71–130; Benayahu, "The Sabbatean movement in Greece," pp. 449–524 (and see the additional bibliography there); Benayahu, "The Holy Brotherhood," pp. 133–82.

4. *Zera'avraham*, *Hoshen Mishpat* section, no. 3; Rozanes, *History of the Jews in Turkey and the Eastern Lands*, vol. 6, p. 114.

5. Rozen, "The mutiny of Nakib el Ashraf"; Manna, "The rebellion of Naqib al-Ashraf in Jerusalem, 1703–1705," p. 53.

4. THE MID-EIGHTEENTH CENTURY

1. Thus, for example, R. Emanuel Hai Riki immigrated in 1717, but he left the country and returned close to 1740.

2. Ya'ari, *Travels in Palestine*, p. 391.

3. Tishbi, *The Paths of Belief and Heresy*, pp. 108–42; Tishbi, "Customs of Nathan of Gaza"; Tishbi, "The 'genealogy' of 'my teacher' and 'my father who is my master and my teacher'"; Barnai, *The "Yishuv,"* pp. 189–200, 248–49.

4. Barnai, "Notes on the immigration of R. Abraham Gerson Kutower to Palestine," pp. 110–19.

5. He is also called R. Eliezer of Cracow or R. Elazar of Brody. In his introduction to his book *Ma'aseh Rokeach*, which was published in 1740, R. Elazar Rokeach wrote that he was planning to immigrate to Palestine in the summer. See *In Praise of the Baal Shem Tov*, pp. 84–85, 185; *Encyclopedia Judaica*, s.v. "Eleazar Rokeach," pp. 313–14; Brilling, "Die Tätigkeit des Jerusalemer Sendboten Petachia," p. 47; Ya'ari, *Travels in Palestine*, p. 433; Ya'ari, *The Emissaries of Palestine*, p. 396; Barnai, "The Ashkenazi community in Palestine," pp. 198–99; Sluys, "The High-German Jewish community in Amsterdam," pp. 106, 111; Halpern, "The attitude of the Jewish councils and communities in Poland to Palestine," p. 87; the *Pinkas* of Istanbul, letter of 1 Heshvan 5511 (November 1750), p. 58; Wurm, *Z Dziejow Zydostwe Brodzkiego*, pp. 50–52; Bartal, "The 'Aliyah' of R. El'azar Rokeach," pp. 7–25.

6. *Hebrew Encyclopedia*, s.v. "Luzzatto, Haim Moses," vol. 21, col. 518; Ginzburg, *R. Moses Haim Luzzatto and His Contemporaries*, vol. 1, pp. 20–23, 135, 167; ibid., vol. 2, pp. 217, 315–17, 321, 401, 500; Ya'ari, *The Emissaries of Palestine*, pp. 143, 169, 435; Tishbi, "Kabbalistic writing in Oxford Ms. 2593," pp. 167–98; Tishbi, "Rabbi Moses David Vale in the circle of Rabbi Moses Haim Luzzatto," pp. 265–302; Tishbi, *The Paths of Belief and Heresy*, pp. 169ff; Benayahu, "The vow of R. Moses Haim Luzzatto," pp. 24–48; Benayahu, "The immigration of R. Haim Moses Luzzatto," pp. 467–74; Klar, *Rabbi Haim ben Attar*, pp. 99, 101; Zohar, "R. Moses Haim Luzzatto in Palestine," pp. 287–93; Ya'ari, "Where is Luzzatto's grave?"

7. Ben-Zion, *Shar'abi*; Benayahu, *Rabbi H. Y. D. Azulay*, pp. 14–18.

8. *Shem Hagedolim*, pt. 1, p. 30; Hirschberg, *A History of the Jews in North Africa*, vol. 2, p. 294; Toledano, *The Candle of the West*, p. 154; Toledano, *Treasury of Manuscripts*, pp. 62–67; Twito, "The immigration of R. Haim ben Attar to Palestine," pp. 52–58; Margoliot, *The life of Rabbi Haim ben Attar*; Klar, *Rabbi Haim ben Attar*; Raphael, "Letters of R. Jacob Paryenti to R. Solomon

Haim Singvineti," pp. 86–91; Raphael, "Letters of R. Solomon Singvineti to R. Haim ben Attar," pp. 271–86; Mann, "The voyage of R. Haim ben Attar and his companions," pp. 74ff. See also *Ohr Hahaim*, author's introduction and approvals; Moyal, "Rabbi Haim ben Attar"; Twito, "The immigration of R. Haim ben Attar," pp. 52–58; Nigal, "In praise of R. Haim ben Attar," pp. 73–93.

9. See Heschel, "R. Gerson Kutower," pp. 17–71 (and see the extended bibliography there). This is the most inclusive paper on the immigration of R. Abraham Gerson, even though it contains some errors and inaccuracies in the appended documents. Also see on this topic Scholem, "Two letters from Palestine," p. 429; Barnai, "The Ashkenazi community in Palestine," pp. 213, 216. Concerning his immigration, see also Barnai, "Notes on the immigration of R. Gerson Kutower to Palestine," pp. 110–19. Also see the following recent works: Stiman-Katz, *Early Hasidic Immigration to Palestine*, pp. 16–20; Barnai, *Hasidic Letters from Palestine*, pp. 33–45; Halpern, *The Hasidic Immigration to Palestine*, pp. 11–19.

5. The Hasidic Immigration

1. This book, which was published in Grodno in 1790, was also called *Ahavath Zion* or *Doresh Zion*. The book describes the immigration of R. Simha and the members of his group from eastern Europe to the Galilee. At the time of its publication, sections about Jerusalem and other places in Palestine that R. Simha had not visited were added to it. These sections were not written by R. Simha, but were copied from other books. Concerning this, see Luncz, "On the book *Ahavath Zion*, its forgery and its forgers," pp. 137–52; Ya'ari, *Travels in Palestine*, pp. 382–423, 773–75; Scholem, "Two letters from Palestine," p. 429. Scholem saw the manuscript of the authentic part of the book. In spite of the great fame of the book and its extensive use by investigators, a critical edition has unfortunately not yet been published.

2. Concerning this immigration, see esp. Halpern, *The Hasidic Immigration to Palestine*, pp. 16–19; Rubinstein, "A possibly new fragment of *Shivhey Habesht?*" pp. 174–91 (and see the detailed bibliography); Alfasi, "Letters of Hasidim from Palestine," p. 285; Stiman-Katz, *Early Hasidic Immigration to Palestine*, pp. 24–27.

3. See Tishbi, "The Messianic idea and Messianic trends in the growth of Hasidism," pp. 1–45.

4. Rubinstein, "A possibly new fragment," pp. 174–91, note 167; *In Praise of the Baal Shem Tov*, pp. 129–30, 182; Barnai, "Some clarifications on the Land of Israel stories," pp. 367–80.

5. Halpern, *The Hasidic Immigration to Palestine*, pp. 21–27.

6. For a proof of this statement, see the recent publication by Stiman-Katz, *Early Hasidic Immigration to Palestine*, p. 27.

7. Dubnow, *The History of Hasidism*, p. 134.

8. Dinur, *At the Turning-Point of the Generations*, pp. 74, 83–227.

9. Halpern, *The Hasidic Immigration to Palestine*, p. 21; Dinur, *At the Turning-Point of the Generations*, p. 72.

10. Halpern, *The Hasidic Immigration to Palestine*, p. 20.

11. Ibid., p. 21. The great majority of the letters that were printed are collected in my book, *Hasidic Letters from Palestine*. Additional letters were published by Wilenski, "The Hasidic settlement in Tiberias," "The Jewish settlement in Tiberias," and *The Hasidic Community in Tiberias*. See also Haran, "The Authenticity of Letters Written by Hasidim in Eretz Israel."

12. Recently several investigators have expressed the opinion that this controversy had no influence on the immigration, and that it also had very little influence on daily life in eastern Europe and on everything connected with the support for Eretz Israel. I thank my colleague Elhanan Reiner for drawing my attention to this matter. Also see Barnai, *Hasidic Letters from Palestine*, pp. 27–29; Halpern, *The Hasidic Immigration to Palestine*, p. 20. Recently a hypothesis was even raised that there was an immigration of the Mithnagdim (the opponents of Hasidism) in the eighteenth century in parallel with the immigrations of the Hasidim. In my opinion this view has no basis. See Hisdai, "Early settlement of *Hasidim* and of *Mithnagdim* in Palestine." See also Wilenski, *The Hasidic Community in Tiberias*.

13. Halpern, *The Hasidic Immigration to Palestine*, p. 20; Etkes, "Rabbi Shneur Zalman of Lyady as a hasidic leader," and "The rise of R. Shneur Zalman of Lyady to the status of leadership."

14. Davison, *Turkey*, pp. 65–66; Lewis, *The Emergence of Modern Turkey*, pp. 23, 37–38, 317.

15. Heyd, *Palestine during the Ottoman Rule*, pp. 38–42; Heyd, *Dahir al-ʿUmar*, pp. 46–72; Cohen, *Palestine in the Eighteenth Century*, pp. 45–52.

6. The Attitude toward Palestine

1. See especially Dinur, *At the Turning-Point of the Generations*, pp. 227–81; Tishbi, "The Messianic idea," pp. 1–45; Scholem, "The Neutralization of the Messianic element in early Hasidism," pp. 25–55.

2. Shazar, *The Hope for the Year* 5500 (1740), pp. 14–36; Scholem, "Contribution to the knowledge about Sabbateanism," pp. 27–38, 84–88; Yaʿari, "Two pamphlets from Palestine," p. 158; Tishbi, "The Messianic idea," pp. 1–45.

3. Scholem, "Contribution to the knowledge about Sabbateanism," p. 27.

4. Tishbi, "The Messianic idea," p. 4.

5. Dinur, *At the Turning-Point of the Generations*, p. 77.

6. *Ohr Hahaim*, commentary to Numbers 25:16; Leviticus 25:25.

7. *Dagul Me-Revava*, p. 8a.

8. *Tzach Ve-Adom*, p. 6a.

9. Ibid., p. 6b.

10. Ibid., p. 5a–b.

11. Benayahu, "The testimony of R. Elia Ashkenazi," p. 70.

12. Publication of sections from this source may be found in Kopf, "A disputation between a Christian and a Jewish rabbi," pp. 272–79.

13. See *Zimrath Ha-Aretz*, pp. 14, 16, 20–29, and elsewhere.

14. Tishbi, *The Paths of Belief and Heresy*, p. 227; Benayahu, *Rabbi H. Y. D. Azulay*, p. 344.

15. *Tzach Ve-Adom*, p. 6a.

16. Ibid.

17. Ibid.

18. Ibid., p. 7b.

19. Ibid.

20. Ibid., author's introduction; *Dagul Me-Revava*, p. 62a.

21. *Ohr Hahaim*, commentary on Leviticus 6:2; Klar, *Rabbi Haim ben Attar*, p. 115.

22. Scholem, *Sabbatai Zevi*, pp. 1–102. For a different view see Gries, *Conduct Literature*, pp. 80–93.

23. Scholem, *Studies and Texts Concerning the History of Sabbateanism and Its Metamorphoses*, p. 28.

24. Echoes of the controversy between them and those who considered the settlement of Eretz Israel to be an obligation may be found in the writings of R. Moses Hagiz, one of the fighters for the settlement of Eretz Israel and a defender of the country's honor, who left Palestine for Europe in the beginning of the eighteenth century in order to strengthen the collection of donations for its residents; see especially the book *Sefath Emeth*. R. Moses Hagiz was also one of the leading persecuters of the Sabbateans, like R. Jacob Emden. Also see Benayahu, "Books composed and edited by R. Moses Hagiz," 2 (1976): 135–52; 3 (1977): 94; 4 (1977): 137. See also the comment of Bauminger, "Notes," p. 170. This episode deserves clarification.

25. Ben-Sasson, *The History of the Jewish People*, p. 744; Shohet, *The Beginnings of the Haskalah among the Jews*, pp. 242–60; Katz, *Tradition and Crisis*, p. 309.

26. *P'ri Ha-Adama*, p. 20b; Luncz, "The customs of our brothers in Palestine," p. 65; Shohet, "The Jews in Jerusalem," *Zion*, p. 396; Shohet, "The Jews in Jerusalem," *Cathedra*, p. 26; Ben-Zvi, *Palestine Under Ottoman Rule*, p. 273; Ben-Zvi, *Remnants of Ancient Jewish Communities in the Land of Israel*, pp. 220, 473.

27. For the text of the letter see Scholem, "Two letters from Palestine," p. 429; Barnai, *Hasidic Letters from Palestine*, pp. 49–52.

28. *Amudey Shamayim*, p. 35a.

29. See Liebes, "The Messianism of R. Jacob Emden," p. 160, according to Emden's introduction to the book *Beth Ya'akov*, p. 14a–b.

30. Ibid. Rabbi Emden cited the words of R. Jonathan Eybeschütz in the book *Eduth Be-Yaʿakov*, p. 44b. Scholem has already commented that this source must be treated with care; see Scholem, *Studies and Texts*, p. 48.

31. Yaʿari, *Letters from Palestine*, p. 306.

32. *Beʾer Mayim Hayim*, author's introduction.

33. *Agan Hasahar*, author's introduction.

34. *Avodath Israel*, author's introduction.

35. *Kol Yaʿakov*, p. 74b.

36. Concerning the problem in its wide historical scope, see Ettinger, *Anti-semitism in Modern Times*, pp. 255–74.

7. Economic Support for the Yishuv from the Diaspora

1. Safrai, *Pilgrimage at the Time of the Second Temple*, p. 8, and according to the entry "half-shekel" in the index.

2. In this discussion I used the following works: Rothschild, *The "Haluka,"* especially pp. 30, 67; Elbaum, "The *Haluka*." I was also assisted by the comments of Prof. Jacob Katz on this work. I thank my friend Jacob Elbaum for permission to read his paper.

3. For letters from Palestine during this period, see Yaʿari, *Letters from Palestine*, pp. 48, 66.

4. Ibid., pp. 53–55; Ben-Sasson, *The History of the Jewish People*, p. 449.

5. See Kedar, "The Jewish community in Jerusalem in the thirteenth century," p. 82; Prawer, *A History of the Latin Kingdom*, vol. 2, p. 386; Prawer, *The Crusaders*, pp. 250–329.

6. Ben-Sasson, *The History of the Jewish People*, p. 466; Yaʿari, *Letters from Palestine*, pp. 75, 83; Kedar, "The Jewish community in Jerusalem in the thirteenth century," pp. 82–94; Ta-Shema, "Palestine studies," pp. 81–96.

7. For letters from Palestine written by R. Ovadiah, by one of his students, and by other immigrants of this period, see Yaʿari, *Letters from Palestine*, pp. 86–88.

8. See Yaʿari, *The Travels of Meshulam of Voltera in Palestine*. In his introduction Yaʿari discusses the immigrations to Palestine in the fifteenth century.

9. See Dinur, "The emigration from Spain to Palestine after the disorders of 1391," pp. 161–74; Hacker, "The connections of Spanish Jewry with Palestine between 1391 and 1492," pp. 105–56; Hacker, "Links between Spanish Jewry and Palestine, 1391–1492," pp. 3–34.

10. See Ben-Sasson, *The History of the Jewish People*, pp. 234–41; Ben-Zvi, *Palestine under Ottoman Rule*, pp. 137–214.

11. Ben-Zvi, *Palestine under Ottoman Rule*, pp. 205–25; Rozen, *The Jerusalem Community of Jerusalem*, pp. 11–20.

12. See Scholem, *Sabbatai Zevi*, pp. 22–43. For a new view, see Idel, "One from a town," pp. 5–30.

13. I will not discuss here the question of messianism and redemption, which arouses controversy among investigators, but rather I will mention only the facts—such as calculations of the date of redemption, remnants of Sabbatean belief, and the immigrations to Palestine—that point to the strengthening of the connection with Palestine. Also see concerning this Dinur, *At the Turning-Point of the Generations*, pp. 9–18. See also chap. 5 above.

14. *Sefath Emeth*, pp. 3–5; see also Ya'ari, *The Emissaries of Palestine*, p. 763; Benayahu, *Rabbi H. Y. D. Azulay*, pp. 25–53; Carlebach, *The Pursuit of Hersey*, pp. 19–44.

15. *Yosef Ometz*, par. 19.

16. Concerning R. Raphael Treves see above, chap. 6, "The intermediate trend."

17. Elbaum, "The *Haluka*," pp. 21–26.

18. *Sefath Emeth*, pp. 2–20.

19. Ha-Yisraeli, *The History of the Prague Community during 1680–1730*, p. 129.

20. Barnai, "The Ashkenazi community in Palestine," pp. 193–230; Heschel, "R. Gerson Kutower," p. 63.

21. Dinur, *The Book of Zionism*, vol. 1, p. 39.

22. Ibid., p. 18.

23. Verete, "The idea of the restoration of the Jews in English Protestant thought, 1790–1840," pp. 145–79.

24. On this episode, see Katz, "Sociological comments on an historical book," pp. 69–72, where there is a criticism of Ya'ari's book, *The Emissaries of Palestine*, and of his approach.

25. Ibid.

26. Dubnow, *The Notebook of the State*, p. 102.

27. Meisel, *The Notebook of the Berlin Community*, p. 153.

28. Brilling, "On the relations of the Jews of Hamburg to Palestine," pp. 87–97.

29. The *Pinkas* of Istanbul, letter of 25 Av 5527 (August 1767), p. 133; letter of 22 Kislev 5501 (December 1740)—date uncertain, p. 1. Concerning "the war of the foreign nations," which delayed the transfer of the money, see the letter of Teveth 5505 (January 1745), p. 16.

30. Cohen, *Palestine in the Eighteenth Century*, pp. 1–29; Shaw, *History of the Ottoman Empire and Modern Turkey*, vol. 1, pp. 217–79.

31. Cohen, *Palestine in the Eighteenth Century*, pp. 30–42; Ben-Zvi, *Palestine under Ottoman Rule*, pp. 265, 276.

32. Braude, "Foundation myths of the millet system"; Benayahu, "The Ashkenazi community of Jerusalem," p. 156.

33. Barnai, "The Jews in the Ottoman Empire," vol. 1, p. 95.

34. The *Pinkas* of Istanbul, four letters of 11 Nisan 5508 (April 1748), pp. 33–34; Hirschberg, *A History of the Jews in North Africa*, vol. 2.

35. See Roth, *The History of the Jews in Italy*, pp. 195–203.

36. Ben-Sasson, *The History of the Jewish People*, pp. 733–35.

37. Benayahu, "The Ashkenazi community of Jerusalem," p. 137; Ya'ari, *The Emissaries of Palestine*, p. 337; Ha-Yisraeli, *The History of the Prague Community*, p. 29; Brilling, "The embargo on the collection of money for Palestine in Austria in 1723," pp. 89–96. The money for Eretz Israel that was frozen by the Austrian government in the eighteenth century was deposited in a foundation in Vienna that still existed in the nineteenth century.

38. Brilling, "Die Tätigkeit des Jerusalemer Sendboten Petachia," pp. 20–49.

39. Personal communication from Dr. Daniel Cohen at a seminar at the home of Prof. Samuel Ettinger on 14 January 1973, on the basis of documentary evidence.

40. The *Pinkas* of Istanbul, letters of 15 Heshvan 5512 (November 1751), p. 58; 12 Kislev 5512 (December 1751), p. 59; end of Kislev 5512 (December 1751), p. 103; 8 Nisan 5512 (April 1752), p. 105; 10 Tammuz 5512 (July 1752), p. 110; 20 Adar 5514 (March 1754), p. 115; Dubnow, *History of the Jews*, vol. 7, p. 157; Rozanes, *History of the Jews in Turkey and the Eastern Lands*, vol. 5, p. 4; Simonsohn, *History of the Jews in the Duchy of Mantua*, vol. 1, p. 354. Concerning Wertheim, see Shohet, "Three eighteenth-century letters on Palestine," pp. 240–48.

41. Halpern, *Eastern European Jewry*, pp. 30–32.

42. Halpern, *The Hasidic Immigration to Palestine*, p. 24.

43. Dubnow, *The History of Hasidism*, pp. 258, 268.

44. Ya'ari, *Letters from Palestine*, pp. 160, 166; Prawer, "On the text of the 'Jerusalem letters' in the fifteenth and sixteenth centuries," pp. 152–53.

45. Sonne, "Neue Dokumente uber Salomon Malcho," p. 134; Carpi, *The Activity of the Italian Synagogue in Venice . . . during 1576–1733*, pp. 12–16.

46. Brilling, "Mahren und Eretz Israel," pp. 237–56.

47. Ya'ari, *The Emissaries of Palestine*, p. 63.

48. Mahler, *The History of the Jews in Poland*, pp. 194, 213.

49. Luncz, "The Jews in the Holy Land," *Jerusalem* 3: 21–24; Frumkin and Rivlin, *The History of the Rabbis of Jerusalem*, vol. 1, p. 115.

50. Pachter, "*Hazut Kasha* of R. Moses Alsheikh," pp. 157–93, where there is a detailed discussion of the activities of R. Moses Alshich on behalf of the Jewish settlement in Safed. On the institutionalization of the support for the Ashkenazim in Safed and in Jerusalem at the beginning of the seventeenth century, see manuscript no. 74 in the Adler Collection, Jewish Theological Seminary, New York.

51. Baron, *The Jewish Community*, pp. 340–41.

52. Ya'ari, *Minha Le-Yehuda*, p. 213; Rozen, *Michael*, pp. 394–430.

53. Schulwass, *Rome and Jerusalem*, p. 105; Simonsohn, *History of the Jews in the Duchy of Mantua*, vol. 1, p. 346; Simonsohn, "The emissaries from Safed to Mantua," p. 327; Benayahu, "Letters of R. Samuel Abuhav, R. Moses Zaccuto and their circle," p. 138.

54. Toledano, "The attitude of the eastern communities to the settlement of Eretz Israel," p. 80.

55. Brilling, "Die frühsten Beziehungen der Juden Hamburgs in Palästina," p. 19.

56. Halpern, "The attitude of the Jewish councils and communities in Poland to Palestine," p. 82; Sonne, "More on the attitude of the councils and communities of Poland to Eretz Israel," p. 252; Halpern, *The Notebook of the Council of Four Lands*, pp. 53, 259, 329, 333, 338, 459, 462, 464; Dubnow, *The Notebook of the State*, pp. 113, 120, 122, 133, 221; Cohen, "The 'Small Council' of the Jewry of Brandenburg-Ansbach," p. 369.

57. Ben-Zvi, *Palestine under Ottoman Rule*, pp. 215–25.

58. See, for example, Ya'ari, *Letters from Palestine*, p. 216; Benayahu, "Letters of R. Samuel Abuhav, R. Moses Zaccuto and their circle," p. 147. This was, for example, the source of the immigration of the SheLaH (R. Isaiah Horowitz) in 1622 with messianic tension, which was expressed in letters; see Ya'ari, *Letters from Palestine*, pp. 210–21.

59. Ben-Zvi, *Palestine under Ottoman Rule*, pp. 250–61; Benayahu, "The Ashkenazi community of Jerusalem," pp. 128–89; Benayahu, "The Holy Brotherhood of R. Judah Hasid," pp. 133–82.

60. Frin, *Charity Funds and Study Societies in Europe in the Sixteenth–Eighteenth Centuries*, pp. 3–4.

61. Assaf, "The Diaspora communities and Palestine," p. 719.

62. Ya'ari, *The Emissaries of Palestine*, p. 573.

63. Ibid., p. 62. Concerning the title "treasurer of Eretz Israel" in Perrera, Italy, see Benayahu, "Letters of R. Samuel Abuhav, R. Moses Zaccuto and their circle," p. 142.

64. Ya'ari, *The Emissaries of Palestine*, p. 65.

65. Ibid.

66. Ibid., p. 66.

67. Benayahu, "Correspondence between the Ashkenazi community in Jerusalem and R. D. Oppenheim," pp. 108–29.

68. Halpern, "The attitude of the Jewish councils and communities in Poland to Palestine," p. 87. Halpern mentions the names of the presidents of Eretz Israel on the Council of Four Lands in Poland according to the monuments in the cemeteries.

69. See the introductions to R. Elazar Rokeach's book, *Arba'ah Turei Even*.

70. Ya'ari, *The Emissaries of Palestine*, pp. 397, 494 and elsewhere.

71. From *Mekitz Ben Hai*, author's introduction. On Solomon Agiv, see also the *Pinkas* of Istanbul, letter of 20 Adar 5509 (March 1749), p. 65. Concerning

the other families, see Nacht, "The letters of the Hida and the emissaries of Palestine," pp. 114–38; Baron, "Towards a history of the Jewish settlement in Tiberias in 1742–1744," p. 80.

72. Brilling, "Die frühsten Beziehungen der Juden Hamburgs in Palästina," p. 19.

73. Mann, "The voyage of R. Haim ben Attar," p. 74.

74. Ben-Zvi, *Studies and Documents*, p. 200; Baron, "Towards a history of the Jewish settlement in Tiberias," p. 80.

75. Benayahu, "The yeshiva of R. Emanuel Hai Riki," p. 29; Benayahu, "On the history of the yeshiva 'Knesset Israel' in Jerusalem," p. 110.

76. Ya'ari, *The Emissaries of Palestine*, p. 502.

77. Ibid.

78. Schulwass, *Rome and Jerusalem*, p. 80.

79. Benayahu, "On the history of the yeshiva 'Knesset Israel,'" p. 110; Schulwass, *Rome and Jerusalem*, p. 150.

80. Brilling, "Die Tätigkeit des Jerusalemer Sendboten Petachia," p. 25, n. 18; see also Benayahu, "The Ashkenazi community of Jerusalem," p. 138; Frumkin and Rivlin, *The History of the Rabbis of Jerusalem*, vol. 3, p. 70.

81. Meisel, *The Notebook of the Berlin Community*, p. 74; Ya'ari, *The Emissaries of Palestine*, p. 397.

82. Brilling, "On the relations of the Jews of Hamburg to Palestine," p. 87.

83. Ya'ari, *The Emissaries of Palestine*, p. 53.

84. Brilling, "On the relations of the Jews of Hamburg to Palestine," p. 87; Ya'ari, "The prayer *Mi-Sheberach*, history and texts," pp. 118, 233; Ya'ari, "Supplements," p. 103.

85. Harkavi, *Ha-Yekev*, p. 75; Ya'ari, *The Emissaries of Palestine*, p. 494; Litvin, "From the Pinkas of Karilicz," p. 168; Nadav, "The minutes book of the Siebież (White Russia) community court," p. 540; Ya'ari, "Two pamphlets from Palestine," p. 143; *Devar Moshe*, vol. 1, p. 76a.

86. Ya'ari, *The Emissaries of Palestine*, p. 52; Ya'ari, "Letters of emissaries from Jerusalem," p. 69; Mahler, *History of the Jewish People in Modern Times*, vol. 4, p. 149; Halpern, "The attitude of the Jewish councils and communities in Poland to Palestine," p. 82; Meisel, *The Notebook of the Berlin Community*, p. 44.

87. Ya'ari, "The Purim money, the half-shekel money and the megilla money," p. 17.

88. Brilling, "On the relations of the Jews of Hamburg to Palestine," p. 88.

89. Ya'ari, "Letters of emissaries from Jerusalem," p. 69; Ya'ari, *The Emissaries of Palestine*, p. 553.

90. Halpern, "The attitude of the Jewish councils and communities in Poland to Palestine," p. 82; Halpern, "The Diaspora and Palestine," p. 719; Dubnow, *The Notebook of the State*, pp. 102, 122.

91. Brilling, "On the relations of the Jews of Hamburg to Palestine," pp. 90–91; Schulwass, *Rome and Jerusalem*, p. 105; Benayahu, "The Ashkenazi community of Jerusalem," pp. 137ff.

92. Shohet, "The Jews in Jerusalem," p. 399.

93. Ya'ari, *The Emissaries of Palestine*, p. 62.

94. Molcho, "The attitude of Salonika to Jerusalem," p. 284.

95. *Devar Moshe*, vol. 1, p. 52b; see also Ya'ari, *The Emissaries of Palestine*, p. 54.

96. Ya'ari, *The Emissaries of Palestine*, p. 466; Brilling, "Die frühsten Beziehungen der Juden Hamburgs in Palästina," p. 25.

97. Ya'ari, *The Emissaries of Palestine*, pp. 396, 402.

98. See Carpi, *The Activity of the Italian Synagogue in Venice*, pp. 50–52.

99. Simonsohn, "Emissaries from Safed to Mantua," p. 332; Ben-Zvi, *Studies and Documents*, p. 182; Benayahu, "Letters of R. Abraham Konaki to R. Judah Briel," p. 308; Shohet, "The Jews in Jerusalem," p. 399; Benayahu, "The Ashkenazi community of Jerusalem," p. 159; Ya'ari, *The Emissaries of Palestine*, pp. 396, 402; Benayahu, "The yeshiva of R. Emanuel Hai Riki," p. 29; Mahler, *History of the Jewish People in Modern Times*, vol. 4, p. 282; Berliner, *The History of the Jews in Rome*, vol. 2, p. 94; Klar, *Rabbi Haim ben Attar*, p. 14; Benayahu, *Rabbi H. Y. D. Azulay*, p. 422; Gelber, *Vorgeschichte des Zionismus*, pp. 30–32.

100. Ya'ari, "The account-book of the HiDA's mission," p. 108; Benayahu, "On the history of the yeshiva 'Knesset Israel,'" p. 104; Baron, "Towards a history of the Jewish settlement in Tiberias," p. 80; Simonsohn, *History of the Jews in the Duchy of Mantua*, p. 350.

101. Brilling, "Die Tätigkeit des Jerusalem Sendboten Petachia," p. 47; Brilling, "New documents on emissaries in Germany in the eighteenth century," p. 37; Ya'ari, "The Pereyra yeshivoth in Jerusalem and Hebron," pp. 185–202; Nahon, "Les Relations Amsterdam et Constantinople au XVIII siècle d'après le copiador de cartas de la nation Juive Portuguise d'Amsterdam," pp. 157–84; Nahon, "Yeshivot Hierosolymites du XVIII siècle," pp. 303–23.

102. Benayahu, "The Ashkenazi community of Jerusalem," p. 140.

103. Malachi, *Studies in the History of the Old Yishuv*, pp. 90–95; Luncz, "He causes the sleeping ones to speak," *Jerusalem* 2: 148–57; Eidelberg, "An eighteenth-century letter from Venice to Metz," pp. 1–6; Barnai, "The Ashkenazi community in Palestine," pp. 197, 199, 203; Shohet, "Three eighteenth-century letters on Palestine," p. 250.

104. Brilling, "On the emissaries from Palestine to Germany," pp. 250–75; Brilling, "The Jewish community of Heidingsfeld and its attitude towards Palestine," pp. 220–31; Brilling, "The Jews of Germany and Palestine," p. 320.

105. Sonne, "More on the attitude of the councils and communities of Poland to Eretz Israel," p. 252.

106. Brilling, "Die frühsten Beziehungen der Juden Hamburgs in Palästina," p. 20; Sonne, "More on the attitude of the councils and communities of Poland to Eretz Israel," p. 252.

107. Brilling, "New documents on emissaries in Germany" pp. 30–42.

108. Zohar, "R. Moses Haim Luzzatto in Palestine," pp. 281–94.

109. For documents concerning this matter, see Brilling, "New documents on emissaries in Germany," pp. 30–42.

110. Halpern, *The Regulations of the State of Mahren*, pp. 8–9.

111. Benayahu, "The Ashkenazi community of Jerusalem," pp. 138, 156; Gelber, "Die Hierosolymitanische Stiftung," pp. 610–24; the *Pinkas* of Istanbul, letters from end of Kislev 5502 (December 1741), p. 103; 8 Nisan 5512 (April 1752), p. 105; 10 Tammuz 5512 (July 1752), p. 110; 20 Adar 5514 (March 1754), p. 115; Brilling, "On the relations of the Jews of Hamburg to Palestine," pp. 87ff; Ya'ari, *The Emissaries of Palestine*, p. 67.

112. Scholem, *Sabbatai Zevi*, p. 347.

113. Simonsohn, *History of the Jews in the Duchy of Mantua*, vol. 1, p. 357; see also note 110 above.

114. Brilling, "The Jews of Germany and Palestine," p. 324; Brilling, "The embargo on the collection of money for Palestine," p. 89.

115. Halpern, *Eastern European Jewry*, pp. 19–22.

116. Dubnow, *The Notebook of the State*, according to the entry "Gaba'ey Eretz Israel" ("Treasurers of Eretz Israel") in the index, notes nos. 462, 523, 559, and 854.

117. Gelber, *Brody*, p. 41; Halpern, "The attitude of the Jewish councils and communities in Poland to Palestine," pp. 82–85.

118. The *Pinkas* of Istanbul, letters of 12 Teveth 5515 (January 1755), p. 121, and 4 Elul 5516 (September 1756), p. 130; Barnai, "The Ashkenazi community in Palestine," pp. 218–24; Halpern, "The attitude of the Jewish councils and communities in Poland to Palestine," p. 82; Weinryb, "Problems of research on the history of the Jews in Palestine and their economic life," p. 64; Sonne, "More on the attitude of the councils and communities of Poland to Eretz Israel," p. 259; Brilling, "The Jews of Germany and Palestine," p. 320; Brilling, "Die frühsten Beziehungen der Juden Hamburgs in Palästina," pp. 19–38; Ya'ari, *The Emissaries of Palestine*, p. 65; Halpern, *The Notebook of the Council of Four Lands*, p. 464, where there is a letter from the rabbis of Egypt from 1673, which includes a request to send them money for the Ashkenazim in Jerusalem, as was accepted.

119. Halpern, *The Notebook of the Council of Four Lands*, p. 338.

120. Ibid., p. 329.

121. Ibid., p. 333.

122. Ibid., pp. 333, 459.

123. Dubnow, *The Notebook of the State*, regulation of 5399 (1639), p. 72.

124. Ibid., regulation of 5415 (1655), p. 122.

125. Ibid., regulation of 5447 (1687), p. 211; Assaf, *The Rabbinical Courts*

and Their Arrangements, p. 114; Assaf, "The Diaspora communities and Palestine," p. 913; Dubnow, *The Notebook of the State*, regulation of 5483 (1623), p. 11.

126. Yaʿari, *The Emissaries of Palestine*, pp. 608–29; Halpern, *The Hasidic Immigrations to Palestine*, pp. 18–21; Nadav, "The minutes book of the Siebiez (White Russia) community court," pp. 410, 555; Gelber, *Brody*, pp. 45, 53.

127. *Likutim*, pp. 12–16; Rozen, "The mutiny of Nakib el Ashraf," pp. 75–90.

128. Concerning the identification of the Armenians with the Amalekites, see *Likutim*, p. 56; the *Pinkas* of Istanbul, letters of 7 Teveth 5503 (January 1743), p. 12, and 12 Shevat 5503 (February 1743), p. 13. The term was already in use in the Byzantine period.

129. Kalaydjian, "The correspondence (1725–1740) of the Armenian Patriarch Gregory the chain-bearer," pp. 562–67.

8. THE DISTRIBUTION OF SUPPORT MONEY

1. Benayahu, "A treatise on the distribution of the money for Eretz Israel collected in Germany," p. 103; Yaʿari, *The Emissaries of Palestine*, p. 23.

2. Yaʿari, *The Emissaries of Palestine*, p. 23.

3. Ibid., pp. 24 (n. 1), 605, 722. In the 1660s the Sephardi community in Hamburg established a different key; see Brilling, "On the relations of the Jews of Hamburg to Palestine," p. 89; Frumkin and Rivlin, *The History of the Rabbis of Jerusalem*, vol. 3, p. 152.

4. Concerning this agreement, see Yaʿari, *The Emissaries of Palestine*, p. 312. In 1743 the emissary of Jerusalem in Italy complained angrily about the violation of the agreement and claimed that the money was being divided equally between the three communities; see Yaʿari, *The Emissaries of Palestine*, p. 391.

5. Benayahu, *Rabbi H. Y. D. Azulay*, p. 305, on the basis of a manuscript in his private collection.

6. Yaʿari, *The Emissaries of Palestine*, pp. 132, 459.

7. Harkavi, *Ha-Yekev*, pp. 28–31.

8. At the beginning of the eighteenth century the Mantua community established a new distribution of the money, and the emissaries of Palestine in Venice distributed the donations from Mantua among the Ashkenazim, the Jews of Italian origin, and the Sephardim in Palestine; see Simonsohn, *History of the Jews in the Duchy of Mantua*, vol. 1, p. 356.

9. Meisel, *The Notebook of the Berlin Community*, p. 44.

10. Concerning the special donations for Hebron in the period under discussion, see Alfasi, "Documents on the history of the old Yishuv," pp. 213–14; Yaʿari, *The Emissaries of Palestine*, pp. 363–64; Dubnow, *The Notebook of the State*, par. 348.

11. Ya°ari, *The Emissaries of Palestine*, p. 587.

12. Ibid., p. 587.

13. Ibid., p. 494.

14. Concerning the committees for Tiberias in Leghorn and Ancona, see Baron, "Towards a history of the Jewish settlement in Tiberias," p. 80. In Mantua yearly sums were donated to Tiberias; also see Simonsohn, *History of the Jews in the Duchy of Mantua*, vol. 1, p. 358; Ya°ari, *The Emissaries of Palestine*, pp. 503–4. With the renewal of Tiberias, Solomon Leon, one of the rich men of Istanbul, donated 500 *kurus* (Turkish *piasters*) for the support of ten Torah scholars in Tiberias; see *Mekitz Ben Hai*, end of the book; Ya°ari, *The Emissaries of Palestine*, p. 503.

15. Manuscript of Letters to the Emissaries, Roth Collection no. 254, Leeds Library, p. 23; Ya°ari, *The Emissaries of Palestine*, p. 508.

16. Toledano, *Treasury of Manuscripts*, pp. 67–68; Ya°ari, *The Emissaries of Palestine*, p. 432; Ben-Zvi, *Studies and Documents*, pp. 202, 239.

17. In 1742 the Istanbul Officials donated 5,000 *kurus* to ease the burden of the taxes in Safed, which added up to 17,500 *kurus* in that year; see Ya°ari, *The Emissaries of Palestine*, p. 437.

18. The *Pinkas* of Istanbul, letter of 27 Iyyar 5502 (May 1742), p. 9.

19. Ibid., letter of 21 Shevat 5504 (February 1744), p. 31.

20. Ibid., pp. 31, 61.

21. Ben-Ya°akov, *Jerusalem within Its Walls*, p. 311.

22. Ya°ari, *The Emissaries of Palestine*, p. 312; Halpern, "The attitude of the Jewish councils and communities in Poland to Palestine," p. 84; Halpern, *The Notebook of the Council of Four Lands*, p. 465.

23. The *Pinkas* of Verona, Manuscript Department, Jewish National and University Library, Jerusalem, no. 4°553, p. 61.

24. Ya°ari, *The Emissaries of Palestine*, p. 314.

25. *Ginath Veradim*, p. 126a; Ya°ari, *The Emissaries of Palestine*, p. 316; Benayahu, "A treatise on the distribution of the money for Eretz Israel," p. 103; Benayahu, "The letters of R. Abraham Konaki," pp. 305–7, 316. Concerning the important date of 1691, see Halpern, "The attitude of the Jewish councils and communities in Poland to Palestine," p. 84; Sonne, "More on the attitude of the councils and communities of Poland to Eretz Israel," p. 252; Tauber, "A section of my book *Minhath Yehuda Va-Yerushalayim*," p. 261.

26. Halpern, *The Notebook of the Council of Four Lands*, p. 465; Sonne, "More on the attitude of the councils and communities of Poland to Eretz Israel," p. 252; Ya°ari, *The Emissaries of Palestine*, p. 319.

27. Smid, "The deeds of the fathers," pp. 258–60; Brilling, "The Jewish community of Heidingsfeld," p. 225; Ya°ari, *The Emissaries of Palestine*, pp. 530–34; Benayahu, "A treatise on the distribution of the money for Eretz Israel," p. 104.

28. Ya°ari, *The Emissaries of Palestine*, pp. 520–34; Barnai, "The Ashkenazi

community in Palestine," p. 198; Brilling, "Die Tatigkeit des Jerusalemer Send-boten Petachia," pp. 20–49.

29. Barnai, "The Ashkenazi community in Palestine," p. 225.

30. Ibid., pp. 203, 225.

31. *Ma'agal Tov*, pp. 15–17.

32. Barnai, "The Ashkenazi community in Palestine," p. 227.

33. *Ma'agal Tov*, pp. 15–17.

34. Barnai, *Hasidic Letters from Palestine*, p. 47.

35. Ibid., p. 48; Benayahu, "The Ashkenazi community of Jerusalem," pp. 160, 170–83.

36. Ya'ari, *The Emissaries of Palestine*, p. 528; *Melekh Shalem*, p. 62; Luncz, "He causes the sleeping ones to speak," *Jerusalem*, 2: 148–51.

37. The *Pinkas* of Istanbul, letter from the end of Adar 5523 (March 1763), p. 52; Ya'ari, *The Emissaries of Palestine*, p. 397.

38. Brilling, "On the emissaries from Palestine to Germany," pp. 250–75; Smid, "The deeds of the fathers," p. 258; Ya'ari, *The Emissaries of Palestine*, pp. 258–60.

39. Benayahu, "A treatise on the distribution of the money for Eretz Israel," p. 105; Luncz, "A letter from Jerusalem of 1782," p. 45; Ya'ari, *The Emissaries of Palestine*, p. 550.

40. Mehlman, "Eighteen Hebrew books and isolated pages," p. 102.

9. The Jewish Community of Istanbul

1. See Ya'ari, *The Emissaries of Palestine*, pp. 221–32.

2. See Ya'ari, *Hebrew Printing in Constantinople*, p. 172; Ya'ari, *The Emissaries of Palestine*, p. 390; Mehlman, "Eighteen Hebrew books and isolated pages," p. 102; Halpern, *The Hasidic Immigration to Palestine*, p. 57, document 7.

3. See Rozanes, *History of the Jews in Turkey and the Eastern Lands*, vol. 1, pp. 43–90; Hirschberg, *Mimizrach U-Mima'arav*, pp. 9–35; Goodblatt, *Jewish Life in Turkey in the XVIth Century as Reflected in the Legal Writings of Samuel de Medina*, pp. 1–23.

4. Heyd, "The Jewish communities of Istanbul in the XVIIth century," pp. 299–314.

5. Rozanes, *History of the Jews in Turkey and the Eastern Lands*, vol. 3, pp. 339–46; Heyd, "The Jewish communities of Istanbul," p. 308.

6. See, for example, the approvals of the Istanbul rabbis to various books; Ya'ari, *Hebrew Printing in Constantinople*, pp. 159–223. Also see the appointment documents of the Istanbul Officials below. And see Barnai, "On the history of the Jewish community of Istanbul in the eighteenth century," pp. 53–66.

7. Benayahu, "The Ashkenazi community of Jerusalem," pp. 141–42. Benayahu writes that the "compromise" was not carried out "for reasons that are not clear." However, the ramified activities that the Austrian authorities conducted in the 1720s in an attempt to achieve the "compromise" (see below) show, in my opinion, that it was political motives that led to the failure of the first "compromise." See also Simonsohn, *History of the Jews in the Duchy of Mantua*, vol. 1, p. 351, where the efforts that were made in 1711–12 in the Italian communities to save the Jerusalem community are described.

8. Ya⁽ari, "R. Moses Israel and his mission for Palestine," p. 153; Agron, Ms. Mic. 4034/1, Jewish Theological Seminary, New York, p. 9.

9. Concerning this mission, see Ya⁽ari, *The Emissaries of Palestine*, p. 362; Elmalech, *Harishonim Le-Zion*, p. 85; Ben-Ya⁽akov, *Jerusalem within Its Walls*, p. 87.

10. See Kaufmann, "Towards a history of the Ashkenazi community in Jerusalem," pp. 25–40; and see there especially the letter that Simon Wolf Wertheimer sent to his brother-in-law in 1729 (pp. 40–50). In this letter are described the ramified connections that Wertheimer had with the Austrian ambassadors in Istanbul and the influence of these connections on the activities of the Austrians on behalf of the Jews of Jerusalem. See also Shohet, "Three eighteenth-century letters on Palestine," pp. 235ff; Gelber, "Die Hierosolymitanische Stiftung," pp. 610–24. I have in my possession documents from the government archives in Vienna concerning this episode and I hope to publish them in the future.

11. Agron, p. 1; and see there also pp. 9–10.

12. From Ya⁽ari, "R. Moses Israel and his mission," p. 161. Incidentally, this is another similarity with the episode of the debts of the Armenian community. The Turkish title means "gatekeeper" and Sabbetai Zevi also attained it.

13. *Sefer Hatakanoth*, p. 25a; Ya⁽ari, "R. Moses Israel and his mission," p. 160; Benayahu, "The Ashkenazi community of Jerusalem," p. 156; Kaufmann, "Towards a history of the Ashkenazi community in Jerusalem," pp. 40–42; Shohet, "The Jews in Jerusalem," *Zion* 1: 405–10.

14. Especially the above-mentioned letter of the Istanbul Officials from 5487 (1727) to R. Moses Israel: Ya⁽ari, "R. Moses Israel and his mission," pp. 149–63. See also Ya⁽ari, *The Emissaries of Palestine*, pp. 376–80.

15. From Ya⁽ari, *The Emissaries of Palestine*, p. 385.

16. From Agron, p. 9.

17. Ya⁽ari, "R. Moses Israel and his mission," pp. 153–63; Ya⁽ari, *The Emissaries of Palestine*, pp. 376–80.

18. The communities of Istanbul and Izmir had already paid the allotted amount for 1727; see Ya⁽ari, "R. Moses Israel and his mission," p. 161. In the other communities this applied only from 1728; see the *Pinkas* of Istanbul, letter of 3 Adar 5507 (March 1747), p. 84.

19. Ya'ari, *The Emissaries of Palestine*, p. 377.

20. The *Pinkas* of Istanbul, letter of 12 Tammuz 5606 (July 1746), p. 122.

21. One of the rabbis of Istanbul.

22. One of the rabbis of Istanbul. For information about him, see Ben-Ya'akov, *Jerusalem within Its Walls*, pp. 35–44.

23. He too was one of the rabbis of Istanbul. See Rozanes, *History of the Jews in Turkey and the Eastern Lands*, vol. 5, p. 13.

24. The *Pinkas* of Istanbul, letter of 23 Tammuz 5506 (July 1746), p. 67, emphasis added.

25. These are the seven authorized persons that are listed in the document.

26. From Agron, p. 15; see also Ya'ari, *The Emissaries of Palestine*, pp. 494–96, 499, 574–75, 584–87; Ben-Zvi, "The emissaries of Palestine in Italy," pp. 14, 21–24; Toledano, "The language of sleepers," p. 309.

27. Agron, pp. 13–17.

28. Agron, p. 17. It is true that the appointment document is undated, but there are two reasons to assume that it is from 1733. First, in the manuscript it is attached to the letter of mission of R. Gedalia Hayyun. Second, at the head of the Hebron Officials in Istanbul who signed the appointment document is the name of R. Abraham Rozanes, which is also at the head of the signers of the letter of R. Gedalia Hayyun.

29. Rivkind, "Documents illustrating Jewish life in Palestine," p. 129.

30. Agron, pp. 13–17; Ya'ari, *The Emissaries of Palestine*, pp. 495–97.

31. Agron, p. 21; Ya'ari, *The Emissaries of Palestine*, pp. 437–38; Simonsohn, "Emissaries from Safed to Mantua," p. 334.

32. Ya'ari, *The Emissaries of Palestine*, p. 437.

33. See Simonsohn, *History of the Jews in the Duchy of Mantua*, vol. 1, pp. 355–56; Baron, "Towards a history of the Jewish settlement in Tiberias," p. 80; *Zimrath Ha-Aretz*, p. 68; Ya'ari, *The Emissaries of Palestine*, pp. 501, 516.

34. The *Pinkas* of Istanbul, two letters from 23 Teveth 5509 (January 1749), p. 34. In one the signers are "The Officials of all Eretz Israel" and in the other one the signers are "the Officials of the Four Lands in Istanbul."

35. Ibid., letter of 23 Tammuz 5506 (July 1746), p. 68; Ya'ari, *The Emissaries of Palestine*, p. 382.

36. For example, R. Abraham Rozanes, the rabbi of Istanbul, and David Kimhi.

37. The *Pinkas* of Istanbul, letter of 26 Teveth 5513 (January 1753), p. 108.

38. Ibid., letter of 17 Kislev 5531 (December 1770), p. 136.

39. Ya'ari, *The Emissaries of Palestine*, pp. 537, 546, 555, 594, 609, 634, 663.

40. Ibid., pp. 537, 555.

41. Rivlin and Rivlin, *Letters of the Pekidim and Amarkalim of Amsterdam*, vol. 1, letters 79, 82, 87, 107, 120; vol. 2, letters 183, 219, 249, 260.

42. Concerning the immigration of the Perushim, see, for example, Malachi, *Studies in the History of the Old Yishuv*, pp. 9–21, 90–97.

43. Cohen, *Palestine in the Eighteenth Century*, introduction.

44. Anderson, *The Eastern Question*, pp. 30–70.

45. Avitsur, *Daily Life in Palestine in the Nineteenth Century*, pp. 299–310.

46. Verete, "The idea of the restoration of the Jews in English Protestant thought," pp. 145–79.

10. ACTIVITY OF THE ISTANBUL OFFICIALS

1. See, for example, the *Pinkas* of Istanbul, letters from the following dates: 10 Shevat 5505 (February 1745), p. 51; 22 Elul 5505 (September 1745), p. 51; 23 Tammuz 5506 (July 1746), p. 52; 1 Av 5506 (August 1746), p. 63; 12 Adar I 5508 (February 1748), p. 72; 5 Kislev 5509 (December 1748), p. 74; 22 Teveth 5511 (January 1751), p. 89; 8 Nisan 5512 (April 1752), p. 105; 12 Elul 5513 (September 1753), p. 111; 20 Adar 5519 (March 1759), p. 27.

2. The title of a judge, that is, the *kadi*.

3. The ruler of Jerusalem.

4. See, for example, the *Pinkas* of Istanbul, letters of 15 Tammuz 5503 (July 1743), p. 14; 22 Elul 5505 (September 1745), p. 19; 10 Tammuz 5512 (July 1752), p. 110; 1 Elul 5518 (September 1758), pp. 15–26; 16 Adar 5519 (March 1759), p. 27; end of Shevat 5516 (February 1756), p. 125.

5. Ibid., letters of 12 Iyyar 5502 (May 1742), p. 37; 7 Teveth 5503 (January 1743), p. 12; 6 Nisan 5503 (April 1743), p. 66; 11 Tishrei 5505 (October 1744), p. 16; 5 Kislev 5509 (December 1748), p. 74; 10 Tammuz 5512 (July 1752), p. 110; 20 Av 5514 (August 1754), p. 115; 1 Elul 5518 (September 1758), p. 26.

6. Ibid., letters of 1 Elul 5502 (September 1742), p. 11; 3 Tishrei 5510 (October 1749), p. 82; 15 Av 5510 (August 1750), p. 87; 3 Iyyar 5512 (May 1752), p. 105; 19 (date uncertain) Kislev 5512 (December 1751), p. 104; 8 Nisan 5513 (April 1753), p. 109; 12 Elul 5513 (September 1753), p. 111; 20 Av 5514 (August 1754), p. 116; 3 Iyyar 5515 (May 1755), p. 123; end of Adar I 5518 (February 1758), p. 24; 25 Elul 5519 (September 1759), p. 28; 18 Adar 5520 (March 1760), p. 40; 1 Heshvan 5523 (November 1762), p. 50; Elul 5528 (September 1768), p. 135.

7. Ibid., letters of 1 Elul 5502 (September 1742), p. 11; 27 Elul 5502 (September 1742), p. 12; 6 Shevat 5504 (February 1744), p. 32; 22 Elul 5505 (September 1745), p. 19; 23 Tammuz 5506 (July 1746), p. 52; 26 Heshvan 5509 (November 1748), p. 74; 1 Sivan 5509 (June 1749), p. 75; 15 Av 5509 (August 1749), p. 81; 15 Av 5510 (August 1750), p. 87.

8. Ibid., letters of 29 Kislev (date uncertain) 5501 (December 1740), p. 48; 22 Elul 5505 (September 1745), p. 51; 11 Av 5502 (August 1746), p. 57; 3 Tishrei 5510 (October 1749), p. 82; 8 November 1751, p. 99.

9. Ibid., letter of 8 Nisan (April 1752), p. 105.

10. When he was in Istanbul Joseph Lutzati conducted negotiations with the Istanbul Officials and with the Sublime Port; see the *Pinkas* of Istanbul, letter of 25 Shevat 5503 (February 1743), p. 31. In another letter the Istanbul Officials reported the appointment of a new vali for Damascus and the good relationship between him and David Zonana, one of the rich men of Istanbul, who managed to get a letter of recommendation for Lutzati and for the Jews of Jerusalem; see ibid., letter of 18 Heshvan 5501 (November 1740), p. 1. For additional letters of the Istanbul Officials in which Lutzati was asked to use his influence on behalf of the Jews of Jerusalem, see ibid., letters of 22 Elul 5505 (September 1745), p. 51; 23 Tammuz 5506 (July 1746), pp. 52, 67.

11. Ibid., letters of 18 Heshvan 5501 (November 1740), p. 1; 27 Heshvan 5509 (November 1748), p. 74; 19 Kislev 5512 (December 1751), p. 105; 8 Nisan 5512 (April 1752), p. 105.

12. Ibid., letter of 7 Teveth 5512 (January 1752), p. 12.

13. Concerning David Zonana, see Heschel, "R. Gerson Kutower," p. 41.

14. In addition to the appointment documents cited above, see, for example, the *Pinkas* of Istanbul, letter of 20 Adar 5519 (March 1759), p. 27.

15. See for example, the appointment of Solomon Rekah as official in Venice: ibid., letter of 6 Kislev 5506 (December 1745), p. 66. Concerning the appointment of officials in the communities of Candia and Cania, see ibid., letters of 3 Adar 5507 (March 1747), p. 84; 28 Teveth 5510 (January 1750), p. 85.

16. Ibid., letter of 23 Tammuz 5506 (July 1746), p. 68.

17. Ibid., letter of 28 Av 5502 (August 1742), p. 10; compare with the letter of 24 Elul 5504 (September 1744), p. 61, in which 3,000–4,000 householders are mentioned.

18. Ibid., letters of 1 Adar 5508 (March 1748), p. 63; 17 Iyyar 5508 (May 1748), p. 65; 15 Tammuz 5508 (July 1748), p. 67; 15 Elul 5508 (September 1748), p. 98; 17 Elul 5509 (September 1749), p. 82; 10 Nisan 5510 (April 1750), p. 82.

19. Ibid., letters from the first third of Teveth 5509 (January 1749), p. 101; 22 Elul 5518 (September 1758), p. 101.

20. Ibid., letters of 18 Av 5505 (August 1745), p. 56; 24 Iyyar 5509 (May 1749), p. 75; 10 Tammuz 5509 (July 1749), p. 76.

21. Ibid., letter of 17 Elul 5509 (September 1749), p. 38.

22. Ibid., letters from Sivan 5509 (June 1749), p. 34; 10 Nisan 5510 (April 1750), p. 35.

23. Ibid., letter of Tammuz 5510 (July 1750), p. 35.

24. Ibid., letter of 29 Kislev 5501 (December 1740), p. 48.

25. Ibid., letter of 10 Shevat 5505 (February 1745), p. 51.

26. Ibid., letters of 4 Shevat 5502 (February 1742), p. 49; 28 Tishrei 5503 (October 1742), p. 50.

27. Ibid., letter of 4 Shevat 5502 (February 1742), p. 49; see also Tobi, "A letter from the 'Constantinople Officials' to R. Shalom Iraqi," p. 257.

28. The *Pinkas* of Istanbul, letter of 6 Kislev 5506 (December 1745), p. 66.

29. Ibid., letters of 1 Elul 5502 (September 1742), p. 11; 18 Av 5517 (August 1757), p. 89; 15 Heshvan 5512 (November 1751), p. 58; 12 Kislev 5512 (December 1751), p. 59.

30. Ibid., letters of 12 Elul 5513 (September 1753), p. 111; Heshvan 5515 (November 1754), p. 119; 1 Elul 5518 (September 1758), p. 25.

31. Ibid., letter of 8 Heshvan 5490 (November 1729), p. 130. This is the earliest letter in the *Pinkas* of Istanbul.

32. Ibid., letter of 10 Iyyar 5502 (May 1742), p. 37.

33. Ibid., letter of 12 Iyyar 5502 (May 1742), p. 37.

34. Ibid., letter from 5512 (1752)—date uncertain, p. 137.

35. Ibid., letters of 8 Heshvan 5510 (November 1749), p. 85; the first third of Teveth 5515 (January 1755), p. 101.

36. Ibid., letter of Sivan 5509 (June 1749), p. 75.

37. Ibid., letter of 8 Heshvan 5510 (November 1749), p. 85.

38. Ibid., letter of 28 Teveth 5510 (January 1750), p. 85.

39. See Barnai, "The Ashkenazi community in Palestine," pp. 139–230.

40. The *Pinkas* of Istanbul, letter of 16 Teveth 5510 (January 1750), pp. 82–83.

41. The *para* was the smallest coin in the Ottoman Empire, and its value was one-fortieth of a *kurus*.

42. The *Pinkas* of Istanbul, letter of 8 Heshvan 5490 (November 1729), p. 130. Chronologically, this letter is not only the first one in the *Pinkas*, but also the only one of that year. The other letters are from the years 5501–33 (1740–73). This letter tells about the establishment of the *para* fund-drive. See also *Sefer Hatakanoth*, p. 25a; Ya'ari, "R. Moses Israel and his mission," pp. 152–63.

43. Ya'ari, *The Emissaries of Palestine*, p. 343. Concerning the *para* fund-drive, in Yemen in 1730, see Ya'ari, "The emissaries of Palestine in Yemen," p. 404; Assaf, "The selling of Hebrew books in Yemen through envoys from Palestine," p. 493. Concerning the *para* fund-drive in Mantua in 1727–30, see Simonsohn, *History of the Jews in the Duchy of Mantua*, vol. 1, p. 354. Even in 1797 the Jerusalem leaders demanded the *para* fund-drive; see Rivkind, "Isolated pages," p. 153.

44. The *Pinkas* of Istanbul, letter from between 5502 and 5507 (1742 and 1747), p. 139. R. Isaac Rozanes, one of the signers of the decree, immigrated to Palestine in May 1747, and thus it is clear that the regulation is from before that date. For the complete formulation of the document, see Barnai, "The regulations (*taqanot*) of Jerusalem," pp. 311–12.

45. The *Pinkas* of Istanbul, letter of 21 Adar 5502 (March 1742), p. 7; compare with the letter of 24 Elul 5504 (September 1744), p. 61.

46. Ibid., letter from the end of Sivan 5509 (June 1749), p. 76; see also *Nehpa Bakesef*, p. 97a. Concerning the failure of the *para* fund-drive, see Shohet, "The Jews in Jerusalem," p. 407. Concerning the amounts of the *para* fund-drive and the allotment, see also Ya'ari, "R. Moses Israel and his mission," p. 161.

47. Concerning the regulation of the allotment, see the *Pinkas* of Istanbul, letter of 8 Heshvan 5490 (November 1729), p. 130.

48. For example, the allotment of Izmir was established in ibid., letter of 21 Adar 5502 (March 1742), p. 7; the allotment of Edirne, in a letter of 4 Teveth 5501 (January 1741), p. 55; and the allotment of Salonika, in a letter of 15 Av 5510 (August 1750), p. 39.

49. For arguments with the communities of Izmir and Edirne about the size of the allotment, see, for example, ibid., letters of 4 Av 5506 (August 1746), p. 63; 18 Av 5505 (August 1745), p. 56.

50. *Zechor Le-Avraham*, p. 60b. There was no change in the size of the sum for thirty years, which attests to the relative decline in the donations to Palestine, as there was a decline in the value of the money. Nevertheless it was a respectable amount, considering the difficult situation of the Istanbul community during the 1770s and its heavy debts.

51. The *Pinkas* of Istanbul, letters from Adar 5508 (March 1748)—date uncertain, p. 64; 17 Iyyar 5508 (May 1748), p. 65.

52. Ibid., letters of 1 Elul 5502 (September 1742), p. 11; 15 Heshvan 5512 (November 1751), p. 58.

53. Ibid., letter of 24 Iyyar 5509 (May 1749), p. 75.

54. Ibid., letter of 10 Tammuz 5509 (July 1749), p. 77.

55. Ibid., letters of 27 Shevat 5502 (February 1742), p. 37; Av 5510 (August 1750)—date uncertain, p. 88.

56. Ibid., three letters of 3 Adar 5507 (March 1747), p. 85.

57. Ibid., letter of 25 Av 5527 (August 1767), p. 132.

58. Ibid., letters of 4 Teveth 5501 (January 1741), p. 55; 25 Iyyar 5501 (May 1741), p. 55; 18 Av 5505 (August 1745), p. 56; 24 Iyyar 5509 (May 1749), p. 75.

59. Ibid., letter from the end of Sivan 5509 (June 1749), p. 76.

60. Ibid., three letters of 8 Heshvan 5510 (November 1749), p. 85.

61. Ibid., letter of 4 Shevat 5502 (February 1742), p. 49.

62. Ibid., letter of 17 Iyyar 5508 (May 1748), p. 65. In this letter the Istanbul Officials accuse R. Isaac Hacohen Rapaport of negligence. See also the letters of 21 Adar 5502 (March 1742), p. 7; 27 Iyyar 5502 (May 1742), p. 9; 24 Elul 5504 (September 1744), p. 61; 13 Heshvan 5505 (November 1744), p. 62; 4 Av 5506 (August 1746), p. 63; 17 Iyyar 5508 (May 1748), p. 64; 8 Heshvan 5509 (November 1748), p. 65; 13 Sivan 5509 (June 1749), p. 76.

63. Ibid., letter of 1 Elul 5502 (September 1742), p. 11.

64. Ibid., letters of 12 Shevat 5503 (February 1743), p. 13; 25 Shevat 5503 (February 1743), p. 31.

65. Ibid., letters of 25 Shevat 5503 (February 1743), p. 31; 1 Elul 5502 (September 1742), p. 11.

66. Concerning the problems of the collection in Italy, see Ya'ari, "The account-books of the HiDA's mission," pp. 110–26; Ben-Zvi, *Studies and Documents*, p. 242.

67. *Ma'agal Tov*, pp. 13–20 and elsewhere.

68. The *Pinkas of Istanbul*, letters of 10 Iyyar 5502 (May 1742), p. 37; 10 Tammuz 5509 (July 1749), p. 77; 1 Elul 5522 (September 1762), pp. 46–47.

69. Concerning the debate about the consecrated funds from Egypt, see ibid., letter of Sivan 5509 (June 1749), p. 34.

70. Ben-Ya'akov, *Jerusalem within Its Walls*, p. 157.

71. For an extensive description of the institution of the missions, see Ya'ari, *The Emissaries of Palestine*, pp. 1–188. For criticism of this book, see Katz, "Sociological comments on an historical book," pp. 69–72; Benayahu, "Review of Abraham Ya'ari, *The Emissaries of Palestine*, pp. 16–35 (where there are many corrections of errors in Ya'ari's description).

72. The *Pinkas* of Istanbul, letter from 5501 (1741), p. 126.

73. Ya'ari, *The Emissaries of Palestine*, pp. 179–80.

74. According to Ya'ari, *The Emissaries of Palestine*.

75. Ya'ari, "R. Moses Israel and his mission," pp. 149–63.

76. Benayahu, *Rabbi H. Y. D. Azulay*, pp. 273–74 (where there are maps of his mission).

77. *Ma'agal Tov*, pp. 1, 47, 49.

78. Wilensky, "Notes on the biography of Rabbi R. E. H. Riki," pp. 311–14; Benayahu, "The yeshiva of R. Emanuel Hai Riki," p. 31.

79. *Ma'agal Tov*, pp. 1–2.

80. The *Pinkas* of Istanbul, letters of 22 Kislev 5501 (December 1740)—date uncertain, p. 1; 4 Teveth 5503 (January 1743), p. 54; 5512 (1752)—date uncertain, p. 92; Ya'ari, *The Emissaries of Palestine*, pp. 376–77, 451; Benayahu, *Rabbi H. Y. D. Azulay*, pp. 31, 40–41; Ya'ari, "The ledger of an eighteenth-century emissary of Palestine," p. 239; Ben-Zvi, *Studies and Documents*, p. 184.

81. The *Pinkas* of Istanbul, letter of 11 Tishrei 5526 (October 1765), p. 90.

82. Ibid., letter of 20 Tammuz 5501 (July 1741), p. 13.

83. Ibid., letter of 15 Elul 5520 (September 1760), p. 74.

84. Ibid., letter of 25 Av 5527 (August 1767), p. 132. He is also known by the name De-Corona.

85. Ibid., letters of 25 Av 5503 (August 1743), p. 111; 15 Av 5513 (1753), p. 111; compare also the letter of 18 Av 5526 (August 1766), p. 90.

86. Ibid., letter of 4 Teveth 5503 (January 1743), p. 6; compare also the letter of 5512 (1752) (date uncertain), 92.

87. *Luhoth Eduth*, p. 41.

88. Ibid., pp. 57–58; Ya'ari, *The Emissaries of Palestine*, p. 171; Ya'ari, "Letters of emissaries from Jerusalem," p. 61; *Ma'agal Tov*, pp. 6, 71, 76–77, 79,

108, 111–12, 121; Brilling, "The 'Pinkas' of the emissaries," in Benayahu, *The Book of the HIDA*, p. 142; Benayahu, "The Ashkenazi community of Jerusalem," p. 144; Ben-Zvi, *Studies and Documents*, p. 204.

89. The *Pinkas* of Istanbul, letters of 6 Elul 5520 (September 1760), pp. 40–41; end of Elul 5520 (September 1760), p. 41.

90. Ibid., letters of 15 Av 5506 (August 1746), p. 114; 22 Av 5509 (August 1749), p. 81; 12 Nisan 5522 (April 1762), p. 45.

91. Ibid., letter of 2 Nisan 5503 (April 1743), p. 43. See, for example, letters of 16 Tammuz 5503 (July 1743), p. 14; 16 Iyyar 5511 (May 1751), p. 94; 17 Iyyar 5513 (May 1753)—date uncertain, p. 110; 25 Adar 5517 (March 1757), p. 22; end of Adar 5523 (March 1763), p. 52.

92. Ibid., letters of 6 Nisan 5511 (April 1751), p. 82; 10 Iyyar 5511 (May 1751)—date uncertain, p. 95; 6 Elul 5520 (September 1760), pp. 40–41; 26 Iyyar 5522 (May 1762), p. 102; 20 Elul 5522 (September 1762), p. 102.

93. We have preserved several agreements of this type; see ibid., letters of 22 Av 5506 (August 1746), p. 69; Av 5506 (August 1746)—date uncertain, p. 114. Concerning the immigration of R. Joseph Samnun, a rich man of Salonika, see ibid., for example, letter of 1 Tammuz 5509 (July 1749), p. 76.

94. Ibid., letters of 28 Av 5502 (August 1742), p. 10; 27 Elul 5502 (September 1742); 15 Av 5506 (August 1746), pp. 114, 122; 17 Av 5506 (August 1746), p. 114; 12 Av (date uncertain) 5509 (August 1749), p. 79; Tammuz 5512 (July 1752), p. 110; 25 Elul 5519 (September 1759), p. 28; 12 Nisan 5522 (April 1762), p. 45.

95. For the complete version of the agreement, see Barnai, "The regulations of Jerusalem," pp. 310–11.

96. The *Pinkas* of Istanbul, letters of 10 Iyyar 5501 (May 1741), p. 37; Sivan 5509 (June 1749), p. 34; 10 Tammuz 5509 (1749), p. 76; 1 Elul 5522 (September 1762), p. 47.

97. For a list of this sort, see ibid., letter of 28 Tammuz 5501 (July 1741), p. 4. Also see letters of 22 Av 5509 (August 1749), p. 81; 6 Elul 5520 (September 1760), p. 41; end of Elul 5520 (September 1760), p. 41; also see Barnai, "The Ashkenazi community in Palestine," pp. 219–24; concerning the yearly allotment from Edirne for Eliezer Nahum, the chief rabbi of Jerusalem, see the *Pinkas* of Istanbul, letter of 18 Av 5505 (August 1745), p. 56.

98. Concerning the method of establishing and publishing the regulation, see the *Pinkas* of Istanbul, letters of 6 Nisan 5511 (April 1751)—date uncertain, p. 82; 10 Iyyar 5512 (May 1752), p. 95; 6 Elul 5520 (September 1760), pp. 40–41; 26 Iyyar 5522 (May 1762), p. 102; 6 Elul 5522 (September 1762), p. 102.

99. Ibid., letter of 8 Iyyar 5510 (May 1750), p. 84.

100. Ibid., two letters of 15 Av 5510 (August 1750), p. 39.

101. Ibid., letter of 12 Elul 5510 (September 1750), p. 58.

102. Ibid., letter of 6 Elul 5520 (September 1760), p. 41.

103. Ibid., letters of 15 Av 5510 (August 1750), p. 39; end of Tammuz 5512 (July 1752), p. 39; 17 Iyyar 5514 (May 1754), p. 115.

104. Ibid., letter of 22 Av 5506 (August 1746), p. 115.

105. Ibid., letter of 20 Av 5512 (August 1752), p. 106, where there is a detailed listing of the immigration payments collected in Istanbul and a mention of the fact that many of the immigrants were poor people, but that it was impossible to prevent their immigration, because they would simply immigrate via some other route. See also letter of 1 Elul 5518 (September 1758), p. 26.

106. Ibid., letter of 20 Av 5514 (August 1754), p. 115.

107. Ibid., letter of 26 Teveth 5515 (January 1755), p. 101.

108. Ibid., letter of 6 Elul 5520 (September 1760), pp. 40–41.

109. Ya'ari, *Travels in Palestine*, p. 391, where there is a detailed description of the leasing of the ship in Istanbul and the organization of the immigration.

11. The Jewish Community of Jerusalem

1. See Ben-Zvi, *Palestine under Ottoman Rule*, pp. 205–63; Pachter, "*Hazut Kasha* of R. Moses Alsheikh," pp. 157–94; Heyd, *Palestine during the Ottoman Rule*, pp. 31–34; Ya'ari, *The Emissaries of Palestine*, pp. 262–321, 408–500; Rosen, *The Jewish Community of Jerusalem*.

2. See Benayahu, "A key to the understanding of the sources on the Sabbatean movement in Jerusalem," pp. 35–45; Benayahu, "The status of the Sabbatean movement in Jerusalem," pp. 41–69.

3. Benayahu, "The status of the Sabbatean movement in Jerusalem," p. 57.

4. From Ms. no. 4°31, Manuscript Dept., Jewish National and University Library, Jerusalem, p. 235b. See also Benayahu, "The holy Brotherhood of R. Judah Hasid," p. 156, n. 98; Havlin, "Jerusalem yeshivot," p. 131.

5. Havlin, "Jerusalem yeshivot," p. 131.

6. Benayahu, "The Ashkenazi community of Jerusalem," pp. 128–89.

7. From the introduction to *Zera' Avraham*, vol. 2.

8. From Rivkind, "Letters from Jerusalem," pp. 226–27. My attention was called to this paper by my friend Rabbi S. Z. Havlin. The letter mentioned has two interesting aspects: first, the mission was not known about; and second, the son of the known persecutor of Sabbateans R. Jacob Sasportas was sent precisely to R. Benjamin Hacohen, one of the important Sabbateans at the end of the seventeenth century, whose home was a meeting place for the Sabbatean sages of his period; see Benayahu, "The Sabbatean movement in Greece," pp. 449–524.

9. Concerning the number of immigrants in the caravan, there is a difference of opinion among the investigators. Benayahu believed that only about 150 people arrived in Jerusalem; see "The holy Brotherhood of R. Judah Hasid," p. 156. The historical sources Benayahu cited (ibid., p. 155, n. 9) tell of many hundreds that started out, even more than a thousand. According to Dinur a thousand immigrants actually arrived; see *At the Turning-Point of the Genera-*

tions, p. 70; also see Ya'ari, *Travels in Palestine,* p. 321; Ya'ari, *The Emissaries of Palestine,* p. 322. The opinion that seems reasonable to me is that of Shohet, who concluded that more than 150 people immigrated; see "Three eighteenth-century letters on Palestine," p. 237.

10. Feld, "A letter from R. David Oppenheim to the rabbis of Jerusalem," pp. 39–53. The author ignores the modern research on the Sabbateanism of R. Judah Hasid. Concerning additional letters that describe the difficult situation of Jerusalem in those years, see Benayahu, "Contribution to the dating of two letters from Jerusalem," pp. 324–32 (where there is an additional bibliography); Rivkind, "Towards a history of the Ashkenazi settlement after the immigration of R. Judah Hasid," pp. 248–56; Benayahu, "Correspondence between the Ashkenazi community in Jerusalem and R. D. Oppenheim," pp. 108–29.

11. In a responsum to a question of R. Raphael Mordecai Malkhi of 1696, R. Abraham Israel Ze'evi wrote that the young rabbis do not know how to act; see *Orim Gedolim,* p. 59b.

12. Benayahu, "The Ashkenazi community of Jerusalem," p. 139.

13. Ya'ari, *The Emissaries of Palestine,* pp. 262–321; Benayahu, "The Ashkenazi community of Jerusalem," pp. 150–55; Ben-Ya'akov, *Jerusalem within Its Walls,* pp. 81–89; Rozen, "The mutiny of Nakib el Ashraf," pp. 75–90.

14. Benayahu, "The holy Brotherhood of R. Judah Hasid," p. 136.

15. See Rivkind, "Letters from Jerusalem," pp. 226–27; Ya'ari, *The Emissaries of Palestine,* pp. 347–51.

16. See Ya'ari, *The Emissaries of Palestine,* pp. 322–407; Benayahu, "The Ashkenazi community of Jerusalem," pp. 142–49; Agron; Ms. Mic. 3623, Jewish Theological Seminary, New York. I thank my friend Dr. A. David for calling my attention to this last manuscript.

17. See Benayahu, "The Ashkenazi community of Jerusalem," p. 138; Rivkind, "A collection of writings towards a history of the Jews in Palestine," pp. 322–23; Shohet, "Three eighteenth-century letters on Palestine," p. 239.

18. From *Zera' Avraham,* vol. 1, introduction of R. Yedidia Hacohen.

19. From Agron, p. 9.

20. Ibid.

21. From a letter that has not yet been published, Ms. no. 255, 56–B, Berlin-Staatsbibliothek. Concerning the study-house mentioned in the letter and the connection between this study-house and R. Judah Hasid's group, see Benayahu, "The holy Brotherhood of R. Judah Hasid," p. 169.

22. So far four letters have reached us on this matter. Three of them were published by Rivkind, Whereas the fourth was published by Shohet; see Rivkind, "A collection of writings," pp. 309–17; Shohet, "Three eighteenth-century letters on Palestine," pp. 246–48. Also see Benayahu, "The Ashkenazi community of Jerusalem," pp. 187–88.

23. Shohet, "Three eighteenth-century letters on Palestine," pp. 246–48.

24. From Agron, p. 1.

25. From Ms. no. 255, 56-B, Berlin-Staatsbibliothek. Concerning the size of the debts of the Sephardim, see also table 2.

26. Ya'ari, *The Emissaries of Palestine*, pp. 361–62.

27. Ibid.; Ben-Ya'akov, *Jerusalem within Its Walls*, pp. 86–96. For a complete description of this mission, see *Megilath Yuhasin*; for other editions, see Ya'ari, *The Emissaries of Palestine*, p. 362, n. 94; Elmalech, *Harishonim Le-Zion*, pp. 76–80.

28. Ben-Ya'akov, *Jerusalem within Its Walls*, pp. 95–97.

29. A regulation of 1760 states that the rebels are "black-haired"; see *Sefer Hatakanoth*, p. 47b; also see Benayahu, *Rabbi H. Y. D. Azulay*, pp. 379–420; Turtshiner, "Letters from Palestine by Simeon de Geldern," p. 110.

30. Benayahu, *Rabbi H. Y. D. Azulay*, pp. 389–92.

31. Ben-Zvi, *Palestine under Ottoman Rule*, pp. 226–32; Rozen, *The Jewish Community of Jerusalem*, pp. 64–74.

32. Benayahu, "The status of the Sabbatean movement in Jerusalem," pp. 57–59; Benayahu, "Towards a history of the study houses in Jerusalem in the seventeenth century," pp. 1–28; Havlin, "Jerusalem yeshivot," p. 131.

33. Ya'ari, *The Emissaries of Palestine*, p. 262.

34. Benayahu, "The Ashkenazi community of Jerusalem," p. 131; Benayahu, "Correspondence between the Ashkenazi community in Jerusalem and R. D. Oppenheim," pp. 108–29.

35. Benayahu, "The Ashkenazi community of Jerusalem," pp. 135, 139–41; Shohet, "Three eighteenth-century letters on Palestine," p. 240.

36. Only during the 1730s did the Ashkenazim begin to reorganize; see Ya'ari, *The Emissaries of Palestine*, pp. 520–34; Benayahu, "The Ashkenazi community of Jerusalem," pp. 159ff.

37. For this purpose R. Raphael Meyuhas Becher Samuel was sent there in 1723; see Elmalech, *Harishonim Le-Zion*, pp. 84–94.

38. From *Admath Kodesh*, vol. 1, p. 132b; see also the author's introduction.

39. *Zera' Avraham*, introduction of R. Yedidia Hacohen.

40. *Sefer Hatakanoth*, p. 28a.

41. The *Pinkas* of Istanbul, letter from the end of Elul 5506 (September 1746), p. 21.

42. This arises from the signatures on the letters that were sent from Jerusalem in those years; see, for example, Rivkind, "Letters from Jerusalem," pp. 226–28.

43. The *Pinkas* of Istanbul, letter of 12 Tammuz 5506 (July 1746), p. 122; and see also three letters of 23 Tammuz 5506 (July 1746), pp. 52, 68.

44. Ibid., letters of 4 Kislev 5501 (December 1740), p. 29; 27 Iyyar 5502 (May 1742), p. 9; 10 Shevat 5505 (February 1745), pp. 16–17; 15 Av 5509 (August 1749), p. 80; 6 Av 5519 (August 1759), p. 27; 15 Iyyar 5521 (May 1761), p. 43. For complaints about faulty procedures, see letters of 22 Teveth 5502 (January

1742), pp. 29–30; Adar I 5508 (February 1748), p. 72; end of Nisan 5510 (April 1750), p. 83; end of Shevat 5514 (February 1754), p. 115; end of Teveth 5517 (January 1757), p. 21; 15 Av 5519 (August 1759), p. 28.

45. Ibid., letters from the end of Adar I 5518 (February 1758), p. 24; 4 Nisan 5518 (April 1758), p. 25.

46. The matter has not been sufficiently clarified. It is certain that the Istanbul Officials demanded that Elijah Samnun repay the sum from his pocket; see ibid., letter of 27 Av 5516 (August 1756), p. 129.

47. Ibid., letters of 16 Adar 5519 (March 1759), p. 27; 15 Av 5516 (August 1756), p. 28.

48. Ibid., letter of 15 Av 5510 (August 1750), p. 87.

49. Ibid., letter of 10 Shevat 5521 (February 1761), p. 42.

50. Ibid., letters of Adar II 5505 (March 1745), p. 18; Adar II 5505 (March 1745), p. 19; Adar I 5508 (February 1748), p. 72; 22 Adar II 5508 (March 1748), p. 73; *Sefer Hatakanoth*, p. 28a.

51. The *Pinkas* of Istanbul, letters of 6 Nisan 5502 (April 1742), p. 7; 6 Shevat 5504 (February 1744), pp. 14–15; 1 Sivan 5504 (June 1744), p. 15; 15 Iyyar 5521 (May 1761), p. 42; 25 Av 5527 (August 1767), pp. 133–34.

52. Ibid., letters of 1 Sivan 5509 (June 1749), p. 75; 26 Teveth 5513 (January 1753), pp. 107–8; 17 Iyyar 5514 (May 1754), p. 115.

53. Ibid., letters of 4 Kislev 5501 (December 1740), p. 29; 27 Iyyar 5502 (May 1742), p. 9; 1 Sivan 5504 (June 1744), p. 15; 14 Shevat 5512 (February 1752), p. 105; 1 Adar II 5516 (March 1756), p. 126; end of Shevat 5516 (January 1756), p. 125; 27 Av 5516 (August 1756), p. 129; end of Adar I 5518 (February 1758), p. 24; 29 Teveth 5519 (January 1759), p. 26; 1 Elul 5522 (September 1762), p. 46.

54. Ibid., letters of 27 Iyyar 5502 (May 1742), p. 9; 1 Adar II 5516 (March 1756), p. 126.

55. Ibid., letter from the end of Tishrei 5518 (October 1757), p. 24. Also see letters of 25 Sivan 5511 (June 1751), p. 97; 12 Teveth 5515 (January 1755), p. 120.

56. Concerning the deficit of about 10,000 *kurus* in 1755, see letter of 23 Av 5516 (August 1756), p. 128; see also letters of 12 Teveth 5515 (January 1755), pp. 120–21; 27 Av 5516 (August 1756), p. 129.

57. Ibid., letters of 1 Elul 5508 (September 1748), p. 73b; 16 Iyyar 5511 (May 1751), p. 94; end of Iyyar 5511 (May 1751), p. 96; 25 Adar 5517 (March 1757), p. 22.

58. Ibid., letters of 4 Nisan 5518 (April 1758), p. 25; 1 Elul 5518 (September 1758), pp. 25–26.

59. Ibid., letter of 16 Iyyar 5511 (May 1751), pp. 94–95.

60. *Ma‘agal Tov*, p. 47; Benayahu, *Rabbi H. Y. D. Azulay*, p. 379.

61. "Joshua Kalev, an official of Jerusalem, . . . asked of me in 1730"; see *Hut Hameshulash*, responsa, p. 17b; also see *Sefer Hatakanoth*, p. 26a; Shohet, "The Jews in Jerusalem," p. 406.

62. The *Pinkas* of Istanbul, letter of 21 Iyyar 5507 (May 1757), p. 71.

63. Ibid., letter of 12 Teveth 5515 (January 1755), p. 120.

64. Ibid., letter of 25 Av 5527 (August 1767), p. 132.

65. Ibid., letter of 20 Av 5514 (August 1754), p. 118.

66. Ibid., pp. 117–18; Benayahu, *Rabbi H. Y. D. Azulay*, pp. 381–85.

67. Benayahu, *Rabbi H. Y. D. Azulay*, p. 384.

68. The *Pinkas* of Istanbul, letters of 18 Heshvan 5501 (November 1740), p. 1; 28 Tammuz 5501 (July 1741), p. 4; 1 Elul 5502 (September 1742), p. 11; 7 Teveth 5503 (January 1743), p. 12; 13 Teveth 5503 (January 1743), p. 7; Teveth 5505 (January 1745), p. 16; 23 Tammuz 5506 (July 1746), p. 68; 15 Teveth 5507 (January 1747), p. 71; 1 Elul 5508 (September 1748), p. 73b.

69. Ibid., letter of 12 Teveth 5515 (January 1755), pp. 120–21.

70. Ibid., letters of 20 Av 5514 (August 1754), p. 118; 12 Nisan 5522 (April 1762), p. 60.

71. Ibid., letters of 1 Tammuz 5509 (July 1749), p. 76; 22 Tammuz 5509 (July 1749), p. 77; 3 Av 5509 (August 1749), p. 79; 6 Av 5509 (August 1749), pp. 78–79; Av 5509 (August 1749), p. 79.

72. Ibid., letter of 4 Kislev 5510 (December 1740), p. 29.

73. Ibid., letters of 12 Teveth 5502 (January 1742), p. 7; 9 Iyyar 5502 (May 1742), p. 8; 27 Iyyar 5502 (May 1742), p. 9.

74. Ibid., four letters of 26 Teveth 5513 (January 1753), pp. 107–8.

75. Ibid., two letters of 20 Shevat 5513 (February 1753), pp. 108–9.

76. Ibid., letter of 22 Av 5506 (August 1746), p. 69.

77. Ibid., letters of 4 Kislev 5501 (December 1740), p. 29; 11 Shevat 5505 (February 1745), p. 17; 26 Teveth 5513 (January 1753), p. 108; 20 Av 5514 (August 1754), pp. 117–18.

78. Ibid., letters of 1 Elul 5502 (September 1742), p. 11; 12 Teveth 5515 (January 1755), p. 120; 12 Nisan 5522 (April 1762), p. 60; 1 Elul 5522 (September 1762), p. 46; 20 Shevat 5527 (February 1767), p. 91.

79. Ibid., letter of 4 Kislev 5501 (December 1740), p. 29.

80. Ibid., letter of 11 Shevat 5505 (February 1745), p. 17.

81. Ibid., letter of Adar II 5505 (March 1745), pp. 18–19.

82. Ibid., letters of 17 Iyyar 5515 (May 1755), p. 122; the end of Shevat 5516 (February 1756), p. 125.

83. Ibid., letter of 20 Av 5519 (August 1759), p. 28; see also Benayahu, *Rabbi H. Y. D. Azulay*, pp. 381–90.

84. The *Pinkas* of Istanbul, letter of 12 Teveth 5515 (January 1755), p. 120.

85. Ibid., letter of 1 Adar II 5516 (March 1756), p. 126.

86. Concerning the division of authority among the officials, see also ibid., letters of 4 Kislev 5501 (December 1740), p. 29; Adar 5505 (March 1745), p. 18; 1 Adar II 5516 (March 1756), p. 126.

87. Ibid., letter from the end of Teveth 5517 (January 1767), pp. 21–22.

88. Ibid., letters of 21 Kislev 5515 (December 1754), p. 119; 12 Teveth 5515

(January 1755), p. 121; last third of Teveth 5515 (January 1755), p. 101; end of Tammuz 5515 (July 1755), p. 101; 23 Av 5516 (August 1756), p. 128; 27 Av 5516 (August 1756), p. 129.

89. Benayahu, *Rabbi H. Y. D. Azulay*, pp. 382–85.

90. The *Pinkas* of Istanbul, letter of 2 Shevat 5501 (February 1741), p. 2.

91. Ibid., letter of 27 Iyyar 5502 (May 1742), p. 9.

92. Ibid., letters of 22 Teveth 5506 (January 1746), p. 20; 22 Av 5506 (August 1746), p. 69; end of Elul 5506 (September 1746), p. 21.

93. Ibid., letter of 1 Adar 5509 (March 1749), p. 75.

94. Ibid., letter of 22 Kislev 5514 (December 1753), p. 112; two letters from the end of Kislev 5514 (December 1753), pp. 112–13.

95. Ibid., letters from end of Shevat 5516 (February 1756), p. 125; 23 Av 5516 (August 1756), p. 128; 27 Av 5516 (August 1756), p. 129; 4 Elul 5516 (September 1756), p. 130; 12 Nisan 5522 (April 1762), p. 60; Nisan 5522 (April 1762), p. 60; 1 Elul 5522 (September 1762), p. 46; Benayahu, *Rabbi H. Y. D. Azulay*, pp. 379–81.

96. The *Pinkas* of Istanbul, letters of Adar II 5505 (March 1745), p. 19; 12 Teveth 5515 (January 1755), p. 120; 1 Elul 5518 (September 1758), p. 25.

97. Concerning the appointment of Judah Pizanti and his two assistants for this position, see the letter in the *Pinkas* of 12 Teveth 5515 (January 1755), pp. 120–21.

98. *Responsa of Algazi*, p. 50b.

99. Ibid.

100. The *Pinkas* of Istanbul, letter of 22 Av 5506 (August 1746), p. 69.

101. Ibid.; see also letter from the end of Shevat 5516 (February 1756), p. 125.

102. Concerning the title "Rishon Le-Zion" and its history, see Barnai, "The leadership of the Jewish community," p. 297, n. 134; Barnai, "The status of the 'General Rabbinate' in Jerusalem in the Ottoman period," pp. 54–65.

103. *Mizbeah Adama*, p. 18a.

104. The HIDA (Rabbi Azulay), for example, wrote the following: "And I, the youth, wrote the document of the rabbinate of the community of the holy city [Jerusalem]" (*Shem Hagedolim, Maʿarekheth Gedolim*, s.v. "Isaac Hacohen," p. 52a).

105. The *Pinkas* of Istanbul, letters of 12 Teveth 5503 (January 1743), p. 13; 18 Av 5505 (August 1745), p. 56; 22 Teveth 5506 (January 1746), p. 20.

106. Ibid., letters of 20 Adar 5509 (March 1749), p. 65; 1 Adar 5509 (March 1749), p. 75.

107. See, for example, ibid., letter of 20 Adar 5509 (March 1749), p. 65.

108. The Istanbul Officials paid 300 *kurus* for his traveling expenses to reach Palestine (ibid.).

109. Ibid., letter of 1 Adar 5509 (March 1749), p. 75.

110. Elmalech, *Harishonim Le-Zion*, p. 80. According to Elmalech, R. Ab-

raham Itzhaki retired voluntarily in 1722 and died in 1729, but he does not bring any support for his opinion. Could this be connected with the difficult events that were occurring in the community at that time? The matter is still in need of clarification.

111. *Sefer Hatakanoth*, p. 2a. The words of Elmalech (*Harishonim Le-Zion*, p. 103) are based on an error.

112. Ben-Ya'akov, *Jerusalem within Its Walls*, p. 364.

113. *Sefer Hatakanoth*, p. 29b. Benayahu believes that in 1782 the proposal was offered to the HIDA to return to Palestine from Leghorn and accept the position of chief rabbi of Jerusalem; see Benayahu, *Rabbi H. Y. D. Azulay*, p. 73. It is possible that the position was offered to him because R. Algazi had not returned from the Diaspora.

114. See *Hama'aloth Le-Shelomo*, p. 102b; Frumkin and Rivlin, *The History of the Rabbis of Jerusalem*, vol. 3, p. 44; the *Pinkas* of Istanbul, letters of 25 Av 5527 (August 1767), p. 133; Elul (date uncertain) 5528 (September 1768), p. 136. Support for this opinion may be found in Turkish documents: Hirschberg, "Notes on the debts of the Jews," p. 165 ("the person appointed over the funds of the Jews"); Cohen, "Arabic documents," p. 328 ("Afterwards the Rabbi (Hakham) Tzemah attested that he was appointed *vekil* over the community of the Sephardim and was their secretary for funds and estates").

115. Elmalech, *Harishonim Le-Zion*, p. 118; Frumkin and Rivlin, *The History of the Rabbis of Jerusalem*, vol. 3, p. 183.

116. The *Pinkas* of Istanbul, letter of 29 Av 5514 (August 1754), p. 118.

117. Ibid., letters of 27 Av 5516, p. 129; 4 Elul 5516 (September 1756), p. 128.

118. Ibid., letter of Nisan 5522 (April 1762), p. 60.

119. Concerning R. Eliezer Nahum, see ibid., letter of 22 Teveth 5506 (January 1746), p. 20.

120. Concerning R. Raphael Meyuhas Becher Samuel, see ibid., letter of 9 Elul 5523 (September 1763), p. 53.

121. Concerning R. Isaac Hacohen Rapaport, see ibid., letters of 11 Adar 5509 (March 1749), p. 65; 20 Adar 5509 (March 1749), p. 65; 22 Adar 5509 (March 1749), p. 75.

122. *Hama'aloth Le-Shelomo*, p. 102b.

123. The *Pinkas* of Istanbul, letters from the end of Iyyar 5511 (May 1751), p. 96; Nisan 5522 (April 1762), p. 60.

124. *Hama'aloth Le-Shelomo*, p. 102b.

125. The *Pinkas* of Istanbul, letter of 25 Av 5527 (August 1767), pp. 133–34.

126. Ibid., letters of Adar II 5505 (March 1745), p. 19; Adar I 5508 (February 1748), p. 73.

127. *Hama'aloth Le-Shelomo*, p. 102b.

128. Ibid.

129. Benayahu, *Rabbi H. Y. D. Azulay*, pp. 19–20.
130. *Haim Sha'al*, vol. 1, p. 43a; Benayahu, *Rabbi H. Y. D. Azulay*, pp. 19, 347. Nevertheless, it is not absolutely certain that all of these rabbinical courts existed simultaneously.
131. It seems to me that this is Haim Solomon Mizrahi, the seventh sage in the Pereyra yeshiva; see *Hama'aloth Le-Shelomo*, p. 102b.
132. Benayahu, "Matters of the HiDA," p. 28.
133. Toledano, "Two documents from Jerusalem dated 5480 (1720) and 5520 (1760)," pp. 218–19.
134. Benayahu, *Rabbi H. Y. D. Azulay*, p. 19.
135. *Sefer Hatakanoth*, p. 47b.
136. For examples, see Bornstein, *The Jewish Communal Leadership*, and "The structure of the Rabbinate in the Ottoman Empire," pp. 223–58.
137. *Admath Kodesh*, vol. 1, author's introduction.
138. *Sefer Hatakanoth*, p. 28b.
139. Ibid., p. 47a.
140. Ibid., p. 41b.
141. Ibid., p. 44b.
142. *Hama'aloth Le-Shelomo*, p. 103a.
143. *Sefer Hatakanoth*, p. 29b.
144. Ibid., p. 40b.
145. Benayahu, *Rabbi H. Y. D. Azulay*, p. 20.
146. *Birkhoth Hamayim*, p. 85a–b.
147. *Admath Kodesh*, vol. 1, author's introduction.
148. The *Pinkas* of Istanbul, letter of 1 Elul 5502 (September 1742), p. 11.
149. Ibid., letter of 25 Av 5527 (August 1767), pp. 133–34. The letter was sent to the rabbis R. Tzemah ben Simon—who was apparently the chief official—and R. Yom-Tov Algazi, and to the officials Abraham ben Menahem and Isaiah Shani. Rabbi Tzemah is also mentioned as leader of the Jerusalem community in several Turkish documents of this period; see, for example, Cohen, "Arabic documents," p. 328.
150. The *Pinkas* of Istanbul, letter of 20 Av 5514 (August 1754), pp. 118–19.
151. Ibid., letters from end of Elul 5506 (September 1746), p. 21; 1 Adar II 5516 (March 1756), p. 126; 27 Av 5516 (August 1756), p. 129; *P'ri Ha-Adama*, vol. 3, p. 43b; *Sha'ar Hamayim*, p. 42b.
152. The *Pinkas* of Istanbul, letters of 8 Nisan 5512 (April 1752), p. 105; 20 Av 5514 (August 1754), p. 118; Benayahu, *Rabbi H. Y. D. Azulay*, pp. 379, 388.
153. The *Pinkas* of Istanbul, letter of 20 Av 5514 (August 1754), p. 118.
154. Benayahu, *Rabbi H. Y. D. Azulay*, p. 379.
155. Bornstein, *The Jewish Communal Leadership*, pp. 125–26.
156. Ibid., pp. 196–200.
157. The *Pinkas* of Istanbul, letter of 6 Iyyar 5510 (May 1750), p. 83.

158. *Likutim*, vol. 1, p. 53.

159. Hacker, "The payment of *Djizya* by scholars in Palestine in the sixteenth century," pp. 63–118.

160. The *Pinkas* of Istanbul, letter of 19 Kislev 5512 (December 1751), p. 104.

161. Ibid., letter from the end of Shevat 5514 (February 1754), p. 114.

162. Ibid., letter of 17 Iyyar 5514 (May 1754), p. 115; compare with letter of 25 Av 5527 (August 1767), pp. 133–34.

163. Ibid., letter of 20 Av 5514 (August 1754), p. 117.

164. Ibid., letter of 25 Av 5527 (August 1767), pp. 133–34.

165. Ibid., letter of 17 Kislev 5531 (December 1770), p. 136. Concerning the quarrel in 1776, see *Ma'agal Tov*, pp. 114–15. Concerning additional quarrels, see, for example, the *Pinkas* of Istanbul, letters of 22 Av 5506 (August 1746), p. 69; first third of Av 5510 (August 1750), p. 86; 15 Av 5510 (August 1750), p. 87; 17 Iyyar 5514 (May 1754), p. 115.

166. See, for example, Danon, "La communate juive de Salonique," pp. 98–177, 249–65; Molcho and Amarilio, "A collection of communal regulations in Ladino from Salonika," pp. 26–60.

167. Rozanes, *History of the Jews in Turkey and the Eastern Lands*, vol. 3, pp. 339–46; *Ginath Veradim*, vol. 2, p. 154b.

168. *Avodath Massa; Hanan Elohim*, end of the book.

169. For examples, see Bashan, *Community regulations*; Rackover and Hildesheimer, *The Community*, esp. pp. 10–13 (the book also contains an extensive bibliography on this topic).

170. See Badhav, *The Jerusalemite*; Freimann, *Matters concerning Sabbetai Zevi*, p. 207. For other sources, mainly on the responsa literature, see Lavsky, *By-Laws (Takanot Ve-Haskamot) Prevailing in Jerusalem during the Ottoman Period*, pp. 114–20. See also Barnai, "The leadership of the Jewish community," pp. 280–83.

171. *Sefer Hatakanoth*, first published in Jerusalem in 1842.

172. *Sefer Hatakanoth* (Jerusalem, 1883). For the purposes of this study I have used this edition.

173. *Sha'ar Hamifkad.*

174. Ya'ari, *Hebrew Printing in Constantinople*, p. 37.

175. *Sefer Hatakanoth*, p. 25b.

176. *Lev Shelomo*, p. 95a.

177. From Agron, p. 19. Also see Benayahu, "The great fires in Izmir and Edirne," pp. 144–54. Concerning the great fire in Izmir and its significance, see Barnai, "On the Jewish community of Izmir in the late eighteenth and early nineteenth centuries," pp. 65–76; Barnai, "The development of links between the Jews of Izmir and the Jews of Palestine in the seventeenth and eighteenth centuries," pp. 111–12.

178. Benayahu, "The great fires in Izmir and Edirne," p. 144.

179. Concerning the earthquake in 1759, see Ya'ari, "The earthquake in Safed," pp. 349–63; Brilling, "Das Erdbeben von Sefad," p. 41. Concerning the great earthquake in 1837, see Malachi, *Studies in the History of the Old Yishuv*, pp. 22–64.

180. Molcho and Amarilio, "A collection of communal regulations," p. 26.

181. See, for example, Frumkin and Rivlin, *The History of the Rabbis of Jerusalem*, vols. 2–3.

182. *Likutim*, p. 39.

183. *Birkhoth Hamayim*, p. 85a–b.

184. Concerning the Halakhic and legal aspects, see Elon, *Jewish Law*, vol. 2.

185. *Sefer Hatakanoth*, p. 301. For additional examples, see pp. 28a, 40a of the same source.

186. Cohen, *Palestine in the Eighteenth Century*, pp. 16–17, 28–31; Sharon and Beck, *From Ancient Archives*, pp. 17–26.

187. Shohet, "The Jews in Jerusalem," pp. 378–87.

188. For a comparison of this sort with respect to the Mameluke period, see Ashtor, *History of the Jews in Egypt and Syria under the Rule of the Mamelukes*, vol. 2, pp. 200–35.

189. See, for example, Gerber, "Archives of the Shari court of Bursa as a source for the history of the Jews in the city," pp. 31–38; Cohen, *Jewish Life under Islam*. See also *Account-Book of Court*, which includes many documents concerning the business connections in the eighteenth century (manuscript Mic. 3149/1, Emc. 2226, Jewish Theological Seminary, New York). I thank the Jewish Theological Seminary of New York and the Department of Photostatted Manuscripts at the National and University Library of Jerusalem for permission to use the manuscript. For some documents from this manuscript, see Barnai and Gerber, "Jewish guilds in Istanbul in the late eighteenth century," pp. 206–26.

190. Hirschberg, "Arbitrary tax in Jerusalem," pp. 161–68; Haim, "Sources of Sephardi history," document 9, p. 154; documents 17, 19, p. 155; document 33, p. 157; and others.

191. Ya'ari, *Travels in Palestine*, p. 333; *Admath Kodesh*, vol. 1, p. 149b; Shohet, "The Jews in Jerusalem," p. 381.

192. Ya'ari, *Travels in Palestine*, p. 333.

193. *Sefer Hatakanoth*, p. 45b.

194. Ya'ari, *Travels in Palestine*, p. 333.

195. *Admath Kodesh*, vol. 1, p. 149b.

196. For a collection of sources concerning this matter, see Ettinger, *The Hasidic Movement in Its First Generations*, pp. 25–35; also see Halpern, *Eastern European Jewry*, pp. 30–33.

197. See *Account-Book of Court*, p. 5. Concerning regulations in this area in North Africa, see Ankawa, *Kerem Hemed*, vol. 2, secs. 42, 49, 93; and see there also the words of S. Bar-Asher, p. 8.

198. *Shaʿar Hamifkad*, p. 87a.

199. Ibid., p. 42b.

200. *Birkhoth Hamayim*, p. 15b.

201. *Sefer Hatakanoth*, pp. 27a–28a.

202. Ashtor, *History of the Jews in Egypt and Syria*, vol. 2, pp. 210–14.

203. Yaʿari, *Travels in Palestine*, p. 538; Rozen, "The mutiny of Nakib el Ashraf," p. 82.

204. Yaʿari, *Travels in Palestine*, pp. 361, 538–39. Compare Shohet, "The Jews in Jerusalem," p. 381. Shohet quotes these words in a fragmentary way and leaves out what was said about the wickedness of the ruler toward the Moslems as well, which changes the significance of what was written.

205. Rozanes, *History of the Jews in Turkey and the Eastern Lands*, vol. 5, pp. 7, 18, 75, 178. Nevertheless there was no uniformity in the application of the law in the Ottoman Empire. In 1748 R. Abraham Gerson of Kuty wrote to his brother-in-law, the Baal Shem Tov, that the Jews in Hebron "walk about here wearing green and all sorts of colors and no one opens his mouth" (Barnai, *Hasidic Letters from Palestine*, p. 39).

206. The *Pinkas* of Istanbul, letter of 14 Tammuz 5501 (July 1741), p. 30. Compare the letter of 22 Teveth 5501 (January 1741), p. 29; Rozanes, *History of the Jews in Turkey and the Eastern Lands*, vol. 5, p. 438, according to Marcus, "From old manuscripts," no. 18.

207. The *Pinkas* of Istanbul, letter of 22 Teveth 5501 (January 1741), p. 29.

208. Ibid.

209. Ibid.

210. Also see ibid., letter of 2 Shevat 5502 (February 1742), p. 38; Rozanes, *History of the Jews in Turkey and the Eastern Lands*, vol. 5, p. 38; see also Yaʿari, *The Emissaries of Palestine*, pp. 389–92.

211. The *Pinkas* of Istanbul, letter of 15 Tammuz 5501 (July 1741), p. 3.

212. Ibid., letter of 20 Tammuz 5501 (July 1741), p. 3.

213. Ibid., letter of 21 Tammuz 5501 (July 1741), p. 31.

214. Ibid., letter of 28 Tammuz 5501 (July 1741), p. 4.

215. Ibid., letter from Adar I 5508 (February 1748), p. 73.

216. Ibid., letter of 1 Adar II 5508 (March 1748), p. 64.

217. Ibid., letter of 2 Adar II 5508 (March 1748), p. 139. The regulation was first published by Marcus ("From old manuscripts," no. 18) and again by Rozanes, *History of the Jews in Turkey and the Eastern Lands*, vol. 5, pp. 439–40. For similar regulations concerning the clothing that was customary in that period in North Africa, see Ankawa, *Kerem Hemed*, vol. 2, secs. 81, 92, and others.

218. *Responsa of Algazi*, p. 35a.

219. See the *Pinkas* of Istanbul, letter of 20 Shevat 5527 (February 1767), p. 91.

220. The regulation was established by the rabbinical court of R. Solomon Abdallah, one of the sages of Jerusalem at the beginning of the eighteenth century; see *Sefer Hatakanoth*, p. 69b. Incidentally, at the end of the nineteenth century the historian Heinrich Graetz was already protesting vigorously against this phenomenon in his report on his visit to Jerusalem; see Graetz, *Essays, Memories, Letters*, p. 279.

221. This regulation is from 1754; see *Sefer Hatakanoth*, p. 45b.

222. Ibid., p. 45a–b.

223. Ibid., p. 45b; the *Pinkas* of Istanbul, letter of 20 Av 5514 (August 1754)—date uncertain, p. 118.

224. *Sefer Hatakanoth*, p. 45a.

225. *Hanan Elohim*, end of the book.

226. Shohet, "The Jews of Jerusalem," p. 396.

227. *Sefer Hatakanoth*, p. 41a; see also Badhav, *The Jerusalemite*, p. 51b; *P'ri Ha-Adama*, vol. 4, p. 20b, where there is a discussion about the danger foreseen for the Jerusalem community because of the increase in the population.

228. *Sefer Hatakanoth*, p. 41b.

229. The *Pinkas* of Istanbul, letter of 23 Av 5516 (August 1756), p. 128.

230. See his letter of 5517 (1757) in *Birkath Ha-Aretz*, p. 64a–b. It is not clear whether he actually left for the Diaspora. See concerning this: Barnai, "Notes on the immigration of R. Gerson Kutower to Palestine," pp. 115–16.

231. *Batey Kenesiyoth*, p. 21b; see also Barnai, "The Jews in the Ottoman Empire," pp. 91–92.

232. Ben-Yaʿakov, *Jerusalem within Its Walls*, p. 310.

12. OTHER JEWISH COMMUNITIES

1. *Admath Kodesh*, vol. 1, *Hoshen Mishpat*, sec. 62; Yaʿari, *The Emissaries of Palestine*, pp. 496, 499, 574, 586, 587, 593, 733; Rivkind, "Documents illustrating Jewish life in Palestine," pp. 126, 134; Toledano, "From manuscripts," p. 409; Nacht, "The letters of the Hida," p. 114; Assaf, "Towards a history of the Karaites in the Eastern countries," p. 208; Brillings, "Embargo on the collection of money," p. 89; Rivkind, "Isolated pages," p. 154; Rivkind, "The society *Hadashim La-Bekarim* in Hebron," p. 215; Weinryb, "The Jews in Poland and Lithuania," p. 107; Ben-Zvi, *Palestine under Ottoman Rule*, p. 291.

2. From *Zimrath Ha-Aretz*, p. 31.

3. From a letter of R. Moses Haim Morporgo of 1742; see Baron, "Towards a history of the Jewish settlement in Tiberias," p. 83; see also Heyd, *Dahir al-ʿUmar*, p. 18; Ish-Shalom, *Christian Travels in the Holy Land*, pp. 362–63, 393, 398.

4. Concerning the destruction of Tiberias at least eighty years before the

renewal of the settlement in 1740, see Rozen, *The Jewish Community of Jerusalem*, p. 342.

5. "And when he was a rabbi in Izmir two years before he came to Eretz Israel"; see *Zimrath Ha-Aretz*, p. 32.

6. Ibid.

7. Ya'ari, *Travels in Palestine*, p. 440; Ya'ari, *The Emissaries of Palestine*, pp. 432–38.

8. From Ya'ari, *Travels in Palestine*, p. 440.

9. The first R. Jacob Berav was, as is well known, the one who renewed the *semikha* (the rabbinical ordination) in Safed in 1538. R. Haim Abulafia's great-grandfather, R. Jacob Abulafia, received *semikha* at the end of the sixteenth century from the second R. Jacob Berav, the grandson of the first R. Jacob Berav. His grandfather, the elder R. Haim Abulafia, received *semikha* from his father, R. Jacob Abulafia. It is worth mentioning the marriage relationships between the Berav and the Abulafia families, which had already begun in the sixteenth century: The above-mentioned R. Jacob Abulafia was the son of the daughter of the first R. Jacob Berav. On this topic and on the sages mentioned here, see Benayahu, "The revival of ordination in Safed," pp. 248–69. According to one tradition brought by R. Azulay, R. Haim Abulafia traced his descent to the tribe of Judah and was a descendant of the Davidic dynasty; see *Shem Hagedolim*, A, p. 57a, s.v. "Etz Hahayim." Could there be a hint here of the affair of the *semikha*? At any rate, this tells us about the importance of this family in those generations. In 1718 R. Haim Abulafia wrote an approval, together with the rabbis of France, for the book *Hon Ashir* by R. Emanuel Hai Riki, which was published in Amsterdam in 1731. Here, in the heading of the approval, the following is written: "The approval of the sages and rabbis of Safed and at their head the great rabbi, the president of the court and the rabbi of the city of the dynasty of the rabbis with *semikha* like R. Haim Abulafia."

10. See *Zimrath Ha-Aretz*, p. 32; *Shem Hagedolim, Ma'arekheth Gedolim*, 10, par. 22; *Eshkol Encyclopedia*, s.v. "Abulafia Haim," vol. 1, pp. 79–80; Rozanes, *History of the Jews in Turkey and the Eastern Lands*, vol. 2, p. 172.

11. See Ben-Zvi, *Palestine under Ottoman Rule*, p. 213; Heyd, *Palestine during the Ottoman Rule*, pp. 31–34.

12. See Benayahu, "Towards a history of the study houses," pp. 1–28; Havlin, "Jerusalem yeshivot and sages in the late seventeenth century," pp. 113–92.

13. "I heard from the perfect sage . . . Haim Abulafia, the emissary of Hebron in the year 5459 [1699]"; *Tzeror Hakesef*, p. 106b.

14. Also see the above-mentioned approval (note 9) to Riki's book *Hon Ashir*.

15. In Klar, *Rabbi Haim ben Attar*, p. 66. It is thus likely that during his lifetime Abulafia lived in all four holy cities.

16. In 1721 the sages of Safed tried to send R. Moses Israel, the rabbi of Rhodes, as an emissary on their behalf, and they even provided him with a letter

of recommendation; also see *Hamaʿaloth Le-Shelomo*, p. 58b. However, this mission was not actually carried out; see also Yaʿari, "R. Moses Israel and his mission," p. 151. One of the signers of the letter was Abulafia, and so it is likely that he was still in Safed in 1721. Possibly he had already left Safed in 1722, as a letter from Safed in that year did not have his signature; see also Yaʿari, *The Emissaries of Palestine*, p. 429.

17. In 1736 Abulafia wrote: "And now . . . it is ten years since I was accepted here"; also see *Hanan Elohim*, regulation 11, at the end of the book.

18. *Hanan Elohim*, regulation 11. The thirty-two regulations do not appear in all the editions of the book that I have seen. The complete edition is preserved in the Ben-Zvi Institute in Jerusalem.

19. Barnai, "The development of links between the Jews of Izmir and the Jews of Palestine," pp. 95–114.

20. See Benayahu, "The history of the yeshiva Knesset Israel," pp. 110–11.

21. In a Christian manuscript of this period written in Arabic the following is written: "Most of his days were fasts"; also see Kopf, "A disputation between a Christian and a Jewish rabbi," p. 275; Wasserstein, "Jewish Christian relations," pp. 42–69.

22. In R. Isaac Hacohen Rapaport's approval for the book *Hemdath Yamim*, vol. 2, which appears next to Abulafia's approval, is written: "the dynasty of the princely house," but possibly there is a hint here of his being of the family of those who received the *semikha* in Safed (see above, note 9).

23. Written as a commentary to Lamentations in *Etz Hahaim*, pp. 105a–106b (second numbering); written as a commentary to Psalms 89 in *Etz Hahaim*, pp. 87a ff. The theme of the redemption after seventy years was widespread. Thus, for example, it had already appeared many years before the renewal of Tiberias, in the book *Beʾer Lahai* by R. Haim Abulafia's grandfather, R. Isaac Nisim Ibn Jamil, which was added to his grandson's book *Yashresh Yaʿakov*, p. 168b.

24. In *Yosef Lekak*, vol. 3, p. 13a.

25. In *Mikraʾei Kodesh*, author's introduction.

26. In *Shevuth Yaʿakov*, author's introduction.

27. *Yosef Lekah*, vol. 1, author's introduction.

28. Ibid., vol. 2, author's introduction.

29. Ibid., vol. 3, author's introduction.

30. Shazar, *The Hope for the Year 5500 (1740)*, p. 11–12; Scholem, "Contribution to the knowledge about Sabbateanism," pp. 27–38, 84–88.

31. In *Zimrath Ha-Aretz*, pp. 15–16.

32. See concerning him, Frumkin and Rivlin, *The History of the Rabbis of Jerusalem*, vol. 2, p. 33.

33. In *Beʾer Lahai*, pp. 148a, 161a. There is reason to assume that these words are from the time of Sabbetai Zevi. The second book of R. Nissim Ibn

Jamil, *Haim Va-Hesed*, is also full of calculations of the date of the redemption and other matters concerning the redemption; see, for example, p. 10a–b. From this book several interesting things emerge: (1) the author lived in Istanbul before he immigrated to Hebron (see p. 34a–b); and (2) at the beginning of the seventeenth century there was an Ashkenazi community in Istanbul (ibid). According to Frumkin (Frumkin and Rivlin, *The History of the Rabbis of Jerusalem*, vol. 2, p. 33), Rabbi Nissim also lived in Jerusalem. Some of his sermons are from the actual time of Sabbetai Zevi—one from 1667 and one from September 1668; see *Haim Va-Hesed*, pp. 58b, 106b. It would be worthwhile to study this book and this personality.

34. *Zimrath Ha-Aretz*, p. 29. The book opens with a sentence written in the phrasing of the opening of the book of Ezra: "And it was in the days of the sultan Mahmud . . . In the year 5500 of the creation that God awakened the holy spirit of our teacher."

35. Ibid., p. 22.

36. Ibid., p. 24; after Isa. 49:5.

37. From the introduction of R. Ya'akov Ventura to *Etz Hahaim*.

38. *Zimrath Ha-Aretz*, p. 14.

39. Ibid., p. 32.

40. Babylonian Talmud, Rosh Hashana 31b.

41. Maimonides, *Mishneh Torah*, Sanhedrin, chap. 14, par. 12; *Yalkut Shimoni*, portion of *Vayehi*, sec. 161.

42. In Kopf, "A disputation between a Christian and a Jewish rabbi," p. 275.

43. In Ish-Shalom, *Christian Travels in the Holy Land*, p. 423.

44. Concerning their arrival at the port of Acre in 1740, see Agron, p. 5; on p. 3 of that book it says that this event occurred at the end of May; see also *Zimrath Ha-Aretz*, p. 31. At that time R. Elazar Rokeach set sail for Palestine.

45. Ya'ari, *Travels in Palestine*, p. 440.

46. Agron, pp. 2–4.

47. Ya'ari, *Letters from Palestine*, p. 260.

48. In Klar, *Rabbi Haim ben Attar*, p. 19.

49. The *Pinkas* of Istanbul, letter of 26 Elul 5502 (September 1742). This letter tells about the immigration of the daughter of R. Haim Alfandari.

50. Ya'ari, *The Emissaries of Palestine*, pp. 501–2; Agron, pp. 2–6.

51. Ya'ari, *The Emissaries of Palestine*, pp. 502–3.

52. Ibid., p. 503.

53. *Zimrath Ha-Aretz*, p. 14.

54. Ibid., p. 32.

55. Ibid., pp. 22–27.

56. Baron, "Towards a history of the Jewish settlement in Tiberias," p. 83; Ya'ari, *The Emissaries of Palestine*, p. 504.

57. Luncz, "The customs of our brothers in Palestine," p. 48.

58. Agron, p. 6.

59. Ya'ari, "The prayer *Mi-Sheberach*," p. 248; Fried, "Notes on A. Ya'ari's studies on the *Mi-Sheberach* prayers," p. 511; Cohen, "Notes and Supplements to Ya'ari's paper, 'The *Mi-Sheberach* prayers,'" p. 542.

60. Klar, *Rabbi Haim ben Attar*, pp. 62–70.

61. Agron, p. 19. In 1772 as well fires broke out in these two communities; see concerning this, Benayahu, "The great fires in Izmir and Edirne," pp. 144–54.

62. Ish-Shalom, *Christian Travels in the Holy Land*, p. 401.

63. Barnai, "The Ashkenazi community in Palestine," pp. 193–213.

64. Ish-Shalom, *Christian Travels in the Holy Land*, p. 404.

65. Ya'ari, *Travels in Palestine*, p. 469.

66. Barnai, "The Ashkenazi community in Palestine," pp. 194–96, 206–10.

67. Ibid., pp. 104–9.

68. Rivkind, "Isolated pages," pp. 160–62.

69. Cohen, *Palestine in the Eighteenth Century*, pp. 30–52.

70. Ya'ari, *The Emissaries of Palestine*, pp. 453, 455; Ish-Shalom, *Christian Travels in the Holy Land*, p. 386; Ben-Zvi, *Studies and Documents*, p. 198.

71. Halpern, *The Notebook of the Council of Four Lands*, p. 433.

72. Ibid., p. 334.

73. Ya'ari, *The Emissaries of Palestine*, p. 437.

74. Kedar, "Information on the Jews of Palestine in eighteenth-century Protestant sources," p. 204.

75. Ya'ari, "The earthquake in Safed," pp. 349–63; Brilling, "Das Erdbeben von Safed," p. 41.

76. Halpern, *The Hasidic Immigration to Palestine*, p. 32.

77. Barnai, *Hasidic Letters from Palestine*, pp. 84–85, 98–103.

78. Ibid., pp. 84–85.

79. Ya'ari, "The earthquake in Safed," pp. 349–63; Ben-Zvi, *Palestine under Ottoman Rule*, p. 313; Ben-Zvi, *Remnants of Ancient Jewish Communities*, p. 151; Luncz, "The Jews in the Holy Land," *Jerusalem* 5, 189.

80. Ya'ari, *Letters from Palestine*, p. 273.

81. Ibid., p. 256; Ben-Zvi, *Remnants of Ancient Jewish Communities*, p. 139.

82. Ibid.; see also Ben-Zvi, *Remnants of Ancient Jewish Communities*, pp. 132–47; Ben-Zvi, *Palestine under Ottoman Rule*, p. 312.

83. Cohen, "The Jews in northern Palestine," p. 150.

84. *Zimrath Ha-Aretz*, as it appears from the content of the book.

85. *S'deh Ha-Aretz*, vol. 3, p. 16a.

86. Elmalech, *Harishonim Le-Zion*, p. 110.

87. See, for example, *Sefer Hatakanoth*, pp. 51a, 66a.

88. Ibid., p. 57a.

89. For the text of the document, see Rivlin, "The Gaon R. Yom-Tov Algazi et al.," p. 135.

90. Ben-Yaʿakov, *Jerusalen within its Walls*, p. 145.

91. Toledano, "The secret scrolls," p. 41.

92. Avissar, *The Book of Tiberias*, p. 262. I do not know what Avissar relies on.

93. The Christian traveler Schultz, who visited Palestine in 1754–55, attests to this; also see Scholem, "Contribution to the knowledge about Sabbateanism from the eighteenth century," p. 87. For additional information concerning his tour in Palestine, see Kedar, "Information on the Jews of Palestine in eighteenth-century Protestant sources," pp. 203–6.

94. Yaʿari, *The Emissaries of Palestine*, p. 438.

95. Cohen, "The Jews in northern Palestine," p. 148.

96. Agron, p. 21.

97. Yaʿari, *Travels in Palestine*, p. 406.

98. See, for example, Barnai, *Hasidic Letters from Palestine*, pp. 98–103.

99. Also see Halpern, *The Hasidic Immigration to Palestine*, pp. 35–36.

100. Ibid., p. 36.

101. Shapira, "The Habad congregation in Hebron (1816–1929), its history and main features," pp. 67–116.

13. OTHER CONGREGATIONS IN PALESTINE

1. For an extended treatment of this topic, see Barnai, "The Ashkenazi community in Palestine," pp. 193–227 (and see there also appendixes and new documents).

2. From Yaʿari, *Travels in Palestine*, p. 448. This source is generally reliable, but in this instance it exaggerates. Also see *Tevuʾoth Ha-Aretz*, p. 471.

3. See "The Ashkenazi community in Palestine," p. 194; Ben-Zvi, "The Ashkenazi settlement in Jerusalem after the immigration of R. Judah Hasid," pp. 38–42; Shohet, "Comments on the paper of Y. Ben-Zvi, 'The Ashkenazi settlement in Jerusalem,'" pp. 127–28.

4. Benayahu, "The Ashkenazi community of Jerusalem," p. 171.

5. In the few documents concerning the Ashkenazim in Hebron not more than two are mentioned; see Barnai, "The Ashkenazi community in Palestine," pp. 220–24. Shohet believes that the expression "the holy community of the Ashkenazi Jews in Hebron" in a letter signed by only two Ashkenazim proves that there was an Ashkenazi community in the city; see Shohet, "Three eighteenth-century letters from Palestine," p. 248. This does not seem likely to me, both in the light of what is written in other documents—such as R. Abraham Gerson of Kuty's letter of 1748 (Barnai, *Hasidic Letters from Palestine*, p. 26)—and in the light of what is written in the letter published by Shohet.

6. Benayahu, "The Ashkenazi community of Jerusalem," pp. 128–32.

7. Ibid., p. 171, document 5.

8. Bashan, "A German source on the Ashkenazi community in Jerusalem in the 1830's," p. 321.

9. Ya⁽ari, *The Emissaries of Palestine*, pp. 522–23; Ben-Zvi, "The Ashkenazi settlement in Jerusalem," pp. 41–42.

10. Barnai, "The Ashkenazi community in Palestine," pp. 199–227.

11. See *Ahavath Zion* in Ya⁽ari, *Travels in Palestine*, pp. 382–423; Halpern, *The Hasidic Immigration to Palestine*, pp. 16–18; Rubinstein, "A possibly new fragment of *Shivhey Habesht?*" pp. 174–91.

2. This arises from the evidence of R. Simha of Zalozce concerning the group of people from Stanov, which already existed in Palestine when he arrived there; see Ya⁽ari, *Travels in Palestine*, p. 397.

13. Luncz, "Three letters," p. 156, letter no. 3.

14. Shohet, "Three eighteenth-century letters from Palestine," pp. 255–56.

15. Barnai, "The Ashkenazi community in Palestine," pp. 206–10.

16. Ibid., pp. 194–96.

17. Ibid., p. 206.

18. Tishbi, *The Paths of Belief and Heresy*, pp. 204–26.

19. Assaf, "Towards a history of the Karaites," pp. 228–51; Ya⁽ari, *Travels in Palestine*, pp. 221–66, 305–22.

20. Assaf, "Towards a history of the Karaites," p. 233, document 8.

21. Luncz, "On the history of the Karaites in Jerusalem," p. 252. On the basis of this Ben-Zvi considered the date of the renewal of the community to be 1749; see Ben-Zvi, *Studies and Documents*, p. 42. Ya⁽ari wrote 1749 in several places and 1744 in several places; see Ya⁽ari, *The Emissaries of Palestine*, p. 26 (1749), p. 548 (1744), and *Travels in Palestine*, p. 224 (1744). See also Sonne, "On a Karaite letter," pp. 222–24. Here, according to what Luncz copied from the Karaite document of Samuel Halevi, the year is 1745. It seems to me that the date should be read without the five thousand years, and then there is no contradiction with the *Pinkas* of Istanbul.

22. The *Pinkas* of Istanbul, letter of 10 Shevat 5505 (February 1745), p. 51.

23. Ibid., letter of Adar II 5505 (March 1755), p. 18.

24. Assaf, "Towards a history of the Karaites," p. 233; see also his story about the Karaite Moses Halevi: Luncz, "On the history of the Karaites in Jerusalem," pp. 239–51.

25. Assaf, "Towards a history of the Karaites," p. 233.

26. The *Pinkas* of Istanbul, letter of 15 Iyyar 5510 (May 1750), p. 84.

27. Ibid., letter of 20 Shevat 5513 (February 1753), p. 109.

28. Ibid., letter of 10 Tammuz 5512 (July 1752), p. 110.

29. Ibid., letter of 20 Av 5514 (August 1754), pp. 116–17; Ya⁽ari, *Travels in Palestine*, pp. 468, 474; Ya⁽ari, *The Emissaries of Palestine*, pp. 548ff.

30. Ya⁽ari, *Travels in Palestine*, p. 468.

31. Ibid., p. 474.
32. Assaf, "Towards a history of the Karaites," pp. 218, 224.
33. *Mizbeah Adama*, p. 22b.
34. *P'ri Ha-Adama*, pp. 7a–9a.
35. *Sefer Hatakanoth*, p. 65a, sec. 58.
36. Ibid., p. 63a, sec. 35.
37. Ya'ari, *The Emissaries of Palestine*, pp. 26, 548.
38. Ya'ari, *Travels in Palestine*, pp. 549–78.
39. Ibid., p. 461.

14. The Yeshivas

1. *Hama'aloth Le-Shelomo*, p. 102b; Nahon, "Yeshivot Hierosolymites du XVIII siècle"; Mss. nos. 1701–1706, Ben-Zvi Institute, Jerusalem.
2. *P'ri Ha-Adama*, vol. 2, p. 76b.
3. *Admath Kodesh*, vol. 1, p. 80a.
4. The *Pinkas* of Istanbul, letters from the following dates: 22 Av 5506 (August 1746), p. 69; 15 Teveth 5507 (January 1747), p. 71; 18 Av 5507 (August 1747), p. 72; Adar I 5508 (February 1748), pp. 72–73; 11 Nisan 5508 (April 1748), pp. 33–34; 1 Elul 5522 (September 1762), p. 47; 1 Heshvan 5523 (November 1762), p. 50; 9 Elul 5523 (September 1763), p. 53; 11 Tishrei 5526 (October 1765), p. 90; 25 Av 5527 (August 1767), p. 132; 5528 (1768), p. 135.
5. Benayahu, "On the history of the yeshiva 'Knesset Israel,'" pp. 103–31.
6. From *Batey Kehuna*, sec. 25, p. 56a; see also Benayahu, "The yeshiva of R. Emanuel Hai Riki," pp. 29–37; Shisha, "The status of the yeshiva 'Haverim Makshivim' in Jerusalem," pp. 20–28; Schulwass, *Rome and Jerusalem*, p. 110.
7. *Admath Kodesh*, vol. 1, sec. 68, p. 142b.
8. These are the regulations that were published: of the yeshiva Haverim Makshivim, see Shisha, "The status of the yeshiva 'Haverim Makshivim,'" p. 20; of the yeshiva Knesset Israel in Hebron, see Ya'ari, "Two documents on the history of the Jewish settlement in Hebron," p. 113; of the Pereyra yeshivas in Jerusalem and Hebron, see Ya'ari, "The Pereyra yeshivoth," p. 185; of the yeshiva Damesek Eliezer, see Barnai, *The "Yishuv,"* pp. 247–48.
9. The *Pinkas* of Istanbul, letters from end of Av 5508 (August 1748), p. 73; 25 Av 5513 (August 1753), p. 111; 3 Heshvan 5527 (November 1766), p. 131; 25 Av 5527 (August 1767), p. 134.
10. Thus, for example, R. Raphael Tzemah ben Simon was both the dean of a yeshiva and the chief official in Jerusalem, and for some time he even fulfilled the role of chief rabbi of the city, until the return of R. Yom-Tov Algazi from his mission to the Diaspora. Also see Cohen, "Arabic documents," p. 328.
11. See Ya'ari, "The Pereyra yeshivoth," pp. 185–202; the *Pinkas* of Istanbul,

letters of 17 Av 5507 (August 1747), p. 71; 18 Av 5507 (August 1747), p. 72. We have in our possession a copy of the account-book of this yeshiva for the last quarter of the eighteenth century (Ms. no. 4°1037, Manuscript Department, Jewish National and University Library, Jerusalem).

12. For details about this yeshiva, see Mann, "The settlement of R. Abraham Rovigo," pp. 63–70; Scholem, *The Dreams of the Sabbatean Mordecai Ashkenazi*, pp. 5–6; Rivkind, "Letters from Jerusalem," p. 225.

13. Ya῾ari, *The Emissaries of Palestine*, pp. 496–97; concerning this group see especially Kook, *Readings and Studies*, vol. 2, p. 153 (where there is a detailed bibliography). The group was connected by special documents, three of which have survived; see Benayahu, *Rabbi H. Y. D. Azulay*, pp. 14–18; Tamar, *Studies in the History of the Jews*, pp. 95–100; Barnai, "On the history of the Sabbatean movement," p. 59.

14. Frumkin and Rivlin, *The History of the Rabbis of Jerusalem*, vol. 3, p. 43; *Shama Ya῾akov*, p. 98b; Havlin, "Jerusalem yeshivot and sages," p. 183; the *Pinkas* of Istanbul, letter of 4 Teveth 5503 (January 1743), p. 54; Ya῾ari, *The Emissaries of Palestine*, p. 382. The Tzuntzin family gave a substantial donation for the settlement in Palestine; see Ya῾ari, *Studies in Hebrew Booklore*, pp. 307–22; Havlin, "Jerusalem yeshivot and sages," pp. 183–84.

15. Ya῾ari, *The Emissaries of Palestine*, pp. 389–92, 401; the members of the Franco family lived in Italy, England, Holland, and other countries and donated a great deal of money for the Yishuv and for the founding of yeshivas. See Benayahu, "The yeshiva of R. Emanuel Hai Riki," p. 29; Katsh, "R. Abraham Ben Asher's mission to Italy," pp. 323–35.

16. Wilensky, "Notes on the biography of Rabbi R. E. H. Riki," p. 311; Benayahu, "The yeshiva of R. Emanuel Hai Riki," pp. 29–37; Shisha, "The status of the yeshiva 'Haverim Makshivim,'" pp. 17–21. Riki's personality and works are still in need of extensive investigation; see *Hazeh Zion*, author's introduction; *Adereth Eliyahu*, author's introduction, pp. 27b, 56b; the *Pinkas* of Istanbul, letter of 6 Nisan 5503 (April 1743), p. 66; Benayahu, "The yeshiva of R. Emanual Hai Riki," pp. 33–34.

17. According to Twito, R. Haim ben Attar decided to found the yeshiva Knesseth Israel under the influence of the immigration of R. Haim Abulafia, but the idea of founding a yeshiva preceded Abulafia's immigration; see Twito, "R. Haim ben Attar (when he was in Italy)," pp. 37, 41–42; Benayahu, "On the history of the yeshiva 'Knesset Israel,'" p. 104; Raphael, "Letters of R. Solomon Singvineti to R. Haim Ben Attar," pp. 271–86; Frenkel, "More documents for a history of the immigration of the author of *Ohr Hahaim* to Palestine," pp. 125–30; Ya῾ari, *Letters from Palestine*, p. 268; Klar, *Rabbi Haim ben Attar*, pp. 60–96.

18. Benayahu, *Rabbi H. Y. D. Azulay*, p. 410; Ben-Ya῾akov, *Jerusalem within Its Walls*, pp. 35–44; *Hama῾aloth Le-Shelomo*, p. 102b.

19. See above, note 1; Frumkin and Rivlin, *The History of the Rabbis of Jerusalem*, vol. 3, p. 40. Frumkin is mistaken concerning R. David Pardo. The latter was the dean of the yeshiva in 1785, and not at the time of its founding. See *Derekh Yeshara*, author's introduction; Havlin, "Some important dates in the biography of R. David Pardo," pp. 503–6; the *Pinkas* of Istanbul, letters of 27 Nisan 5508 (April 1748), p. 127; 9 Adar I 5508 (February 1748), p. 72; Adar I 5508 (February 1748), p. 73; Nisan 5508 (April 1748)—date uncertain, p. 127; 12 Adar I 5508 (February 1748)—date uncertain, p. 72; 9–12 Adar I 5508 (February 1748), p. 72; 12 Adar I 5508 (February 1748)—date uncertain, p. 72; 27 Nisan 5508 (April 1748), p. 127; 20 Adar 5509 (March 1749), p. 65; letter to R. Isaac Hacohen Rapaport of 20 Adar 5509 (March 1749), p. 65. It is worth comparing this list with the list of members of the yeshiva of 1758: *Hama'aloth Le-Shelomo*, p. 102b. See also the *Pinkas* of Istanbul, letter of 11 Tishrey 5526 (October 1765), p. 90; Hirschberg, "Notes on the debts of the Jews," p. 158; Cohen, "Arabic documents," p. 328. See also above, note 10; Benayahu, *Rabbi H. Y. D. Azulay*, pp. 72, 75, 339–40, 422, 520–21; Havlin, "Some important dates in the biography of R. David Pardo," p. 505.

20. *Hama'aloth Le-Shelomo*, p. 102b; Ya'ari, *The Emissaries of Palestine*, pp. 386, 500, 580; Benayahu, "On the history of the yeshiva 'Knesset Israel,'" p. 111; the *Pinkas* of Istanbul, letters of 10 Iyyar 5511 (May 1751)—date uncertain, p. 95; 5511 (1751)—date uncertain, p. 92; 5511 (1751)—date uncertain, p. 33; Benayahu, "On the history of the yeshiva 'Knesset Israel,'" p. 109. The information in the *Pinkas* of Istanbul supports Benayahu's hypothesis that R. Jonah Navon actually transferred at that time from the yeshiva Knesset Israel to the deanship of the new yeshiva; the *Pinkas* of Istanbul, letter of 5511 (1751)—date uncertain, p. 93. According to the list of yeshivas of 1758 R. Shem-Tov Gabbai and R. Jonah Navon were still members of the yeshiva Knesset Israel; see *Hama'aloth Le-Shelomo*, p. 102b.

21. *Hama'aloth Le-Shelomo*, p. 103a; Haim, *Documents from the Collection of Elie Eliachar*, document 21, p. 33; document 43, p. 40; document 93, p. 46; document 92, p. 53; document 96, p. 59 (summary of the document). I have a copy of the document whose number in the Eliachar collection is 93. See also ibid., document 97, p. 76; document 98, p. 59; document 106, p. 60; document 99, p. 60; document 8, p. 23; document 8a, p. 24; document 67, p. 47; the *Pinkas* of Istanbul, letter of 1 Elul 5522 (September 1762), p. 47.

22. The *Pinkas* of Istanbul, letters from the end of Tammuz 5521 (July 1761), p. 45; 4 Elul 5521 (September 1761), p. 45; 12 Nisan 5522 (April 1762), p. 45; Nahon, "Yeshivot Hierosolymites du XVIII siècle." In *Shivhey Yerushalayim* by R. Baruch Haim the author lists eleven yeshivas in Jerusalem in 1782, nine of which he specifies by name, among them the yeshiva Magen David. Rozanes and Ben-Ya'akov, who cite an additional list of yeshivas in Jerusalem in the eighteenth century, write that the yeshiva Magen David was founded by David de-Pinto of Amsterdam.

23. Ya'ari, *The Emissaries of Palestine*, p. 554.

24. Ibid., p. 770. It is possible that Raphael Picciotto was the Austrian consul in one of the cities of Palestine at the beginning of the nineteenth century; see Eliav, *Palestine and Its Yishuv in the Nineteenth Century*, p. 94; Barnai, "Towards changes in Jerusalem in the nineteenth century," pp. 151–55; Ga'on, *The Jews of the East in Palestine*, vol. 2, p. 547. For the conditions of the establishment of the yeshiva, see Haim, *Documents from the Collection of Elie Eliachar*, document 101, p. 61; document 71, p. 48.

25. Ben-Ya'akov, *Jerusalem within Its Walls*, pp. 62–63.

26. Ibid.

27. Ibid.

28. Ibid.

29. Ibid.

30. Nahon, "Yeshivot Hierosolymites du XVIII siècle."

31. Ibid.

32. Ibid.

33. Ms. no. 1704, Ben-Zvi Institute, Jerusalem.

34. Ibid.

35. Abraham Pereyra, the founder of the yeshiva, was one of the important members of the Amsterdam community and a supporter of Sabbetai Zevi. It seems that after Sabbetai Zevi's conversion Pereyra left the movement; see Kaplan, "The attitude of the leadership of the Portuguese community in Amsterdam to the Sabbatean movement," p. 207; the *Pinkas* of Istanbul, letters of 17 Av 5507 (August 1747), p. 71; 18 Av 5505 (August 1747), p. 72; Ya'ari, "The Pereyra yeshivoth," pp. 185–202; Ya'ari, *The Emissaries of Palestine*, p. 584; *Sefath Emeth*, p. 26b.

36. In a letter that an emissary wrote in 1788 we find that the yeshiva had already existed for thirty years, and its yearly support was 1,000 florins; see Rivkind, "Documents illustrating Jewish life in Palestine," pp. 139–40; Ya'ari, *The Emissaries of Palestine*, p. 593; Ya'ari, "Two documents on the history of the settlement in Hebron," p. 113.

37. *Responsa of Algazi*, p. 52b.

38. *Zimrath Ha-Aretz*, pp. 14, 15, 19; Ya'ari, *The Emissaries of Palestine*, pp. 502, 507; Klar, *Rabbi Haim ben Attar*, pp. 61–62.

39. Havlin, "Jerusalem yeshivoth and sages," p. 184; Ish-Shalom, *Christian Travels in the Holy Land*, pp. 388, 400; Ya'ari, *The Emissaries of Palestine*, pp. 423, 507; Ben-Zvi, *Studies and Documents*, p. 239; Toledano, *Treasury of Manuscripts*, p. 67. For additional evidence concerning donations to the yeshiva in Safed, see *Mekitz Ben Hai*, author's introduction; *Admath Kodesh*, p. 80a; Kedar, "Information on the Jews of Palestine in eighteenth-century Protestant sources," p. 204.

15. DEMOGRAPHIC DATA

1. According to a letter of 1622 there were 2,500–3,000 Jews in Jerusalem; see Ya'ari, *Letters from Palestine*, p. 220. According to a document of 1625 there were 2,000 souls in Jerusalem. On the basis of a list of poll-tax payers Heyd concludes that at the end of the seventeenth century there were about 1,000 Jews in Jerusalem; see Heyd, "The Jews of Palestine in the late seventeenth century," p. 173. See also *Likutim*, vol. 1, p. 12. Also, on the number of Jews in Jerusalem in the seventeenth century, see the table in Rozen, *The Jewish Community of Jerusalem*, pp. 15–16.

2. Cohen, *Palestine in the Eighteenth Century*, pp. 249–55.

3. According to Dinur, about a thousand immigrants arrived in this immigration; see *At the Turning-Point of the Generations*, p. 26. Benayahu believes that only about 150 people immigrated; see "The holy Brotherhood of R. Judah Hasid," p. 155. Shohet objected to this stipulation and argued that there were more than 150 immigrants in the group; see "Three eighteenth-century letters on Palestine," p. 237. Also see Mann, "The settlement of R. Abraham Rovigo," pp. 59–84. In this article there are many errors; see especially Benayahu, "The holy Brotherhood of R. Judah Hasid," pp. 133–82.

4. The *Pinkas* of Istanbul, letter of 24 Elul 5504 (September 1744), p. 61. One cannot accept the exact number from this source, only the trend.

5. Barnai, *Hasidic Letters from Palestine*, p. 38.

6. The *Pinkas* of Istanbul, letter of 17 Iyyar 5508 (May 1748), p. 65.

7. Rivkind, "Documents illustrating Jewish life in Palestine," p. 119.

8. *Sefer Hatakanoth*, p. 41a.

9. Cohen, *Palestine in the Eighteenth Century*, p. 251. Concerning the decrease in the number of Jerusalem residents in 1756, see *P'ri Ha-Adama*, vol. 4, p. 20b.

10. Ya'ari, "The earthquake in Safed," pp. 349–63; also see Brilling, "Das Erdbeben von Safed," pp. 41–58.

11. Benayahu, *Rabbi H. Y. D. Azulay*, pp. 391–92.

12. See *Shevah U-Tehila*, p. 1. Concerning R. Peretz ben Moshe and the pamphlet mentioned, see Ya'ari, "Two pamphlets from Palestine," pp. 155–59.

13. Rivkind, "Documents illustrating Jewish life in Palestine," p. 133.

14. Ben-Zvi, *Palestine under Ottoman Rule*, pp. 281–326; Cohen, "The Jews in northern Palestine," pp. 145–51; Kedar, "Information on the Jews of Palestine," p. 204.

15. Mahler summarized the opinions of various investigators on this topic and included a table of all the populations of Palestine in the eighteenth and nineteenth centuries according to various sources (*History of the Jewish People in Modern Times*, vol. 4, pp. 271–73). According to the estimates of several other investigators, the number of residents of Palestine at the end of the eighteenth century was about 300,000.

16. There were epidemic plagues in 1702, 1729, 1740, 1741, 1746, 1748, 1757, and other years; see *P'ri Ha-Adama*, vol. 1, p. 42b; vol. 4, p. 111a–b; Ya'ari, *Letters from Palestine*, pp. 282–86; *P'ri Ha-Aretz*, vol. 3, sec. 11; *Admath Kodesh*, vol. 1, pp. 83a, 111b; Mann, "The settlement of R. Abraham Rovigo," p. 83; Mann, "The voyage of R. Haim ben Attar," p. 82; *Haim Sha'al*, vol. 2, p. 22b. Concerning the famine in 1773, see Ben-Ya'akov, *Jerusalem within Its Walls*, pp. 139, 363.

17. Cohen, *Palestine in the Eighteenth Century*, part I.

INTRODUCTION TO PART V: ECONOMIC LIFE

1. From the list of 1753, the complete *Ma'agal Tov*, p. 1; see also p. 3.

2. From the list of 1773, ibid., p. 50; see also p. 47. It thus seems probable that for twenty years there was no change in the situation.

3. From Barnai, *Hasidic Letters from Palestine*, p. 45.

4. Ibid., p. 47.

5. Ibid., p. 51.

6. Luncz, "The Jews in the Holy Land," *Jerusalem* 5, p. 165.

7. From Klar, *Rabbi Haim ben Attar*, p. 66. Also see the writings of R. Moses Yerushalmi in Ya'ari, *Travels in Palestine*, p. 399. Concerning the difficult economic situation in Jerusalem, see also the *Pinkas* of Istanbul, letters from the following dates: 4 Teveth 5501 (January 1741), p. 55; winter 5502 (1741–42)—date uncertain, p. 6; 13 Iyyar 5502 (May 1742), p. 8; 28 Nisan 5502 (April 1742), p. 56; 6 Shevat 5504 (February 1744), pp. 14–15; 1 Sivan 5504 (June 1744), p. 15; 17 Iyyar 5508 (May 1748), p. 64; 1 Adar I (date uncertain) 5508 (February 1748), p. 63; 2 Adar II 5508 (March 1748), p. 139; 6 Kislev 5510 (December 1750), p. 66. These letters contain information about the increase in the number of residents of Jerusalem, about the high prices of food, drought and famine, high taxes, bribery to the authorities, and expenses of the community.

8. Cohen, "The Jews in northern Palestine," p. 145. Concerning the sources of income see below, chap. 17.

16. BUDGETS OF THE COMMUNITIES

1. Hirschberg, "Notes on the debts of the Jews," p. 158.

2. We have much evidence in our possession on this matter; see Rozen, *The Jewish Community of Jerusalem*, pp. 181–85; *Hurvoth Yerushalayim*, pp. 50–67.

3. *Likutim*, vol. 1, pp. 12–16 (where there are details of the budget).

4. Heyd, "The Jews of Palestine," p. 173.

5. *Sefath Emeth*, p. 21b.

6. The *Pinkas* of Istanbul, letter of 4 Kislev 5501 (December 1740), p. 29. This deficit also included debts.

7. Ibid., letter of 12 Teveth 5502 (January 1742), p. 7. This letter could be referring to Riki's yeshiva.

8. Ibid., letter of 6 Shevat 5504 (February 1744), p. 15.

9. Ibid., letter of 17 Kislev 5507 (December 1746), p. 70.

10. Ibid., letter of 16 Iyyar 5511 (May 1751), p. 95.

11. Ibid., letters of 23 Av 5516 (August 1756), p. 127; end of Teveth 5517 (January 1757), p. 21; 27 Av 5516 (August 1756), p. 129.

12. Ibid., letter of 4 Nisan 5518 (April 1758), p. 25.

13. Ibid., letter from the end of Adar I 5518 (February 1758), p. 24.

14. Ibid., letters of 29 Teveth 5519 (January 1759), p. 26; 15 Av 5519 (August 1759), p. 28.

15. Ibid., letter of 1 Elul 5522 (September 1762), p. 46.

16. Ms. no. 1702, 1706, Ben-Zvi Institute, Jerusalem.

17. The *Pinkas* of Istanbul, letter of 3 Tishrey 5502 (October 1741), p. 5.

18. Agron, pp. 20, 25, 27.

19. For complaints from the beginning of the eighteenth century, see *Sefath Emeth*, p. 20b. For complaints from the middle of the century, see the *Pinkas* of Istanbul, letter of 1 Sivan 5504 (June 1744), p. 15.

20. For an example of such a document, see ibid., letter of 15 Av 5506 (August 1746), p. 114; *Account-Book of Court*, p. 5. See also the complaint of the Istanbul Officials that the Jerusalem community had ignored an exemption document of this type and collected the tax in the *Pinkas* of Istanbul, letter of 8 Elul 5510 (September 1750), p. 88.

21. *Sefer Hatakanoth*, p. 26a–b. It seems that this was the accepted percentage in the communities of the Ottoman Empire at this time. See, for example, the Izmir regulations of the seventeenth century in *Avodath Massa*, p. 23a.

22. According to R. Mordecai Malkhi the minimum income at the end of the seventeenth century was 50 *kurus* per person; see *Likutim*, vol. 1, p. 12.

23. *Sefer Hatakanoth*, p. 26a–b.

24. Ibid., p. 33b.

25. Ibid.

26. The *Pinkas* of Istanbul, letters of Adar I 5508 (February 1748), p. 73; the end of Shevat 5516 (February 1756), p. 125.

27. Ya'ari, *The Emissaries of Palestine*, p. 456; *Mayim Sha'al*, p. 56a.

28. The *Pinkas* of Istanbul, letter of 25 Shevat 5503 (February 1743), p. 31.

29. Ibid., letter of Adar I 5508 (February 1748), p. 72.

30. Ibid., letter of Av 5527 (August 1767)—date uncertain, p. 131.

31. Ibid., letter of 17 Kislev 5512 (December 1751), p. 104.

32. Ibid., letter from the end of Shevat 5514 (February 1754), p. 114.

33. See Barnai, "The leadership of the Jewish community in Jerusalem," pp. 302–9.

34. Cohen, *Palestine in the Eighteenth Century*, p. 256; Sharon and Beck, *From Ancient Archives*, p. 25.

35. In some of the regulations a precise date is not mentioned, and their date is estimated (see discussion that follows).

36. *Sefer Hatakanoth*, p. 30a. The expression "and now we are explaining since God has given us latitude" attests, in my opinion, to the date of the regulation. The reference is apparently to a previous regulation that dates from 1776; from the material there in parentheses it clearly appears that the regulation at hand is from before 1807 (p. 31a). Concerning the nature of the parentheses, see introduction, p. 24b.

37. Ibid., p. 32a–b.

38. Ibid., p. 33a.

39. Ibid., p. 32b.

40. Ibid., p. 32a.

41. Ibid., p. 31b.

42. Ibid.

43. See, for example, the *Pinkas* of Istanbul, letters of 17 Av 5506 (August 1746), p. 114; Iyyar 5507 (May 1747)—date uncertain, p. 71; *Account-Book of Court*, p. 5.

44. The *Pinkas* of Istanbul, letters of 15 Iyyar 5510 (May 1750), p. 84; 11 Tammuz 5510 (July 1750), p. 86; 8 Elul 5510 (September 1750), p. 88.

45. *Sefer Hatakanoth*, p. 30a.

46. Rivlin, "The Estate regulations of Jerusalem and Palestine," pp. 559–619.

47. Ashtor, *History of the Jews in Egypt and Syria*, vol. 2, 221–35; Lavsky, *By-Laws (Takanot Ve-Haskamot) Prevailing in Jerusalem during the Ottoman Period*, pp. 70–73. Both authors cite additional sources for this issue. Also see Tamar, *The Book "Lekah Tov,"* introduction, p. 30.

48. Goitein, *A Mediterranean Society*, vol. 2, pp. 394–99.

49. See *Encyclopaedia of Islam*, s.v. "Bayt Al Māl," vol. 1, pp. 1143–48; see also Gibb and Bowen, *Islamic Society and the West*, vol. 2, pp. 119–25.

50. Goitein, *A Mediterranean Society*, vol. 2, p. 398.

51. Ibid.

52. Ashtor, *History of the Jews in Egypt and Syria*, vol. 2, pp. 223–24.

53. Ibid., p. 225.

54. *Responsa of Hamabit*, pt. 3, sec. 183 and sec. 10; *Kehilath Ya'akov*, p. 58b. Compare Tamar, *The Book "Lekah Tov,"* p. 30; Ya'ari, *Letters from Palestine*, pp. 128–29. For additional sources on this topic from the end of the Mameluke and the beginning of the Ottoman period see: Lavsky, *By-Laws Prevailing in Jerusalem*, pp. 70–73; Ashtor, *History of the Jews in Egypt and Syria*, pp. 221–35. Probably the law concerning the inheritance of estates without heirs by the government was a general law and was practiced in other parts of Turkey; see, for example, Gerber, *Economics and Society in an Ottoman City: Bursa*,

1600–1700; and compare Shpitsan, "Jewish charitable trusts in late nineteenth-century Jerusalem," p. 74.

55. Ashtor, *History of the Jews in Egypt and Syria*, vol. 2, pp. 228–30; see also Goitein and Ben Shemesh, *Islamic Law in the State of Israel*, pp. 140–72; Haim, "Sources of Sephardi history in Jerusalem," p. 145. Concerning several consecrations of funds of Jerusalem Jews in the eighteenth century that were listed in the Shara'ite court, see Shpitsan, "Jewish charitable trusts."

56. The *Pinkas* of Istanbul, letter of 5522 (1762)—date uncertain, p. 47. At the beginning of the letter it is written that it was not sent out, but this does not negate what is written in it about the estate regulation. For the text of the letter, see Barnai, "The regulations of Jerusalem," pp. 313–16.

57. This was the estate of Eliezer Ashkenazi, from which the yeshiva Damesek Eliezer was founded in the end.

58. The *Pinkas* of Istanbul, letter of 1 Elul 5522 (September 1762)—date uncertain, p. 46. This document refutes the statement of Lavsky (*By-Laws Prevailing in Jerusalem*, p. 82) that the source of the regulation was not known during the Ottoman period.

59. See concerning him, *Nivhar Mi-Kesef*, introduction of R. Abraham Hatufa to the facsimile edition.

60. Ibid., p. 127b.

61. *Encyclopaedia of Islam*, s.v. "Bayt Al Māl," vol. 2, p. 1148.

62. *Hikrey Lev, Even Ha-Ezer*, sec. 42, pp. 89–90.

63. Rivlin, "The estate regulations," pp. 605–9. For discussion about these sources, see Kaniel, "Organizational and economic contentions between communities in Jerusalem in the nineteenth century," pp. 113–16. Kaniel did not deal with the connection between the regulation and Moselm law.

64. For a veiled hint about this, see *Sefer Hatakanoth*, introduction of Rishon le-Zion Rabbi Moses Suzin, pp. 22b–23a.

65. Cohen, *Jewish Life under Islam*, p. 59; Haim, "Sources of Sephardi history in Jerusalem," document 78, p. 162.

66. *Sefer Hatakanoth*, p. 25b.

67. The *Pinkas* of Istanbul, letter of Adar I 5505 (February 1745), p. 32. In previous periods it often happened that Jews turned to the gentile courts in matters of inheritance because they knew that the Moslem law would decide in their favor; see Goitein, *A Mediterranean Society*, vol. 2, p. 399.

68. That is what R. Moses Bula, one of the rabbis of Jerusalem, did; see the *Pinkas* of Istanbul, three letters from the end of Nisan 5510 (April 1750), p. 83.

69. *Sefer Hatakanoth*, p. 26a–b.

70. Ibid., p. 26a.

71. Ibid., p. 28a–b.

72. Ibid., p. 29a–b.

73. The *Pinkas* of Istanbul, letter of 28 Av 5502 (August 1742), p. 10.

74. Ibid., letter of Adar II 5505 (March 1745), p. 19.

75. Ibid., letter of Adar I 5505 (February 1745), p. 32.

76. Ibid., p. 73.

77. Ibid., letter of 21 Teveth 5519 (January 1759), p. 27.

78. Ibid., letter of 15 Iyyar 5521 (May 1761), p. 43.

79. Ibid., letter of 1 Elul 5522 (September 1762), p. 46.

80. Ibid., three letters from the end of Nisan 5510 (April 1750), p. 84; letter of 8 Nisan 5510 (April 1750), p. 84.

81. Ibid., letter of 24 Elul 5504 (September 1744), p. 61.

82. Concerning the topic of the taxes, see especially Cohen, *Palestine in the Eighteenth Century*, pp. 249–59. According to Cohen the ratio between the tax payments of the Moslems, Christians, and Jews in the eighteenth century was 11:5:3 (p. 250).

83. Ibid., pp. 249–56.

84. Rivkind, "Letters from Jerusalem," p. 226. It is possible that the writer of the letter, R. Moses Malkhi, calculated the average sum of the three levels.

85. From Rivkind, "Documents illustrating Jewish life in Palestine," p. 119.

86. From Yaʿari, *Travels in Palestine*, p. 386.

87. Ibid.

88. The *Pinkas* of Istanbul, letter of 12 Nisan 5522 (April 1762), p. 45.

89. Ibid., letter from the end of Shevat 5516 (February 1756), p. 125; see also Cohen, *Palestine in the Eighteenth Century*, p. 249 (where there is a table).

90. Incidentally, it appears from Ottoman documents that at the end of the seventeenth century as well many of the Jews of Jerusalem avoided paying the poll tax; see Heyd, "The Jews of Palestine," p. 177.

91. See Cohen, *Palestine in the Eighteenth Century*, pp. 256–59.

92. The *Pinkas* of Istanbul, letter of 15 Av 5510 (August 1750), p. 87.

93. Ibid., letter of 19 Kislev 5512 (December 1751), p. 104.

94. Ibid., letter of 17 Iyyar 5514 (May 1754), p. 115.

95. Ibid., letter of 20 Av 5514 (August 1754), p. 117.

96. Sharon and Beck, *From Ancient Archives*, pp. 17–24; Cohen, *Palestine in the Eighteenth Century*, p. 258; also see the evidence of R. Moses Yerushalmi in Yaʿari, *Travels in Palestine*, pp. 393, 449.

97. Cohen, *Palestine in the Eighteenth Century*, p. 259; *Maʿagal Tov*, pp. 1, 47.

98. Yaʿari, *Travels in Palestine*, pp. 449, 451; Sharon and Beck, *From Ancient Archives*, pp. 17–18, 20–21, 23–24; Haim, "Sources of Sephardi history in Jerusalem," p. 161.

99. Cohen, *Palestine in the Eighteenth Century*, p. 249.

100. Rivkind, "Documents illustrating Jewish life in Palestine," p. 119.

101. Concerning the *imdādiye* and the *muşāhere* that the Jews of Turkey paid, see, for example, *Lev Shelomo*, p. 84a.

102. Cohen, *Palestine in the Eighteenth Century*, p 256.

103. The *Pinkas* of Istanbul, letter of 22 Sivan 5505 (June 1745), p. 19; see also Cohen, *Palestine in the Eighteenth Century*, pp. 256–57.

104. The *Pinkas* of Istanbul, letters of 24 Elul 5504 (September 1744), p. 61; 8 Nisan 5512 (April 1752), p. 105.

105. Ibid., letter of 24 Elul 5504 (September 1744), p. 61; Haim, "Sources of Sephardi history in Palestine," pp. 159–60; Sharon and Beck, *From Ancient Archives*, pp. 25–26.

106. The *Pinkas* of Istanbul, letter of 1 Elul 5522 (September 1762), p. 47; Haim, "Sources of Sephardi history in Palestine," p. 162.

107. The *Pinkas* of Istanbul, letter of Adar I 5508 (February 1748), p. 73; Rozanes, *History of the Jews in Turkey and the Eastern Lands*, vol. 5, p. 438.

108. Shohet, "The Jews in Jerusalem," *Zion* 1: 379–89.

109. The *Pinkas* of Istanbul, letter from the end of Nisan 5510 (April 1750), p. 83.

110. *Sefer Hatakanoth*, p. 26a.

111. Ibid., p. 25b.

112. The *Pinkas* of Istanbul, letter of 9 Iyyar 5502 (May 1742), p. 8.

113. Ibid., letter of 2 Nisan 5503 (April 1743), p. 38.

114. Ibid., letter of Tammuz 5510 (July 1750), p. 68.

115. Ibid., letter of Av (date uncertain) 5509 (August 1749), p. 78.

116. Ibid., letter from the end of Iyyar 5511 (May 1751), p. 96.

117. Ibid., letters of 5501 (1741), p. 5; Av–Elul (date uncertain) 5502 (August–September 1742), p. 6; 5 Teveth 5507 (January 1747), p. 70; 15 Av 5510 (August 1750), p. 87; 4 Nisan 5518 (April 1758), p. 25; 10 Shevat 5521 (February 1761), p. 42; 12 Nisan 5522 (April 1762), p. 45; also see Ya'ari, *Travels in Palestine*, p. 518; Rivkind, "Letters from Jerusalem," pp. 226–28; Klar, *Rabbi Haim ben Attar*, p. 80; *Likutim*, p. 20; Simonsohn, "Emissaries from Safed to Mantua," pp. 342, 344.

118. Hirschberg, "Notes on the debts of the Jews," p. 158; see also Cohen, "Arabic documents," p. 317; Shohet, "The Jews in Jerusalem," *Zion* 1: 400–402. For an additional *firman* for the debt of the Ashkenazim, see the *Pinkas* of Istanbul, letter of 15 Tammuz 5503 (July 1743), p. 14. For a *firman* on the debt of the Ashkenazim from the beginning of the eighteenth century, see Benayahu, "The Ashkenazi community of Jerusalem," p. 156. Concerning the compromise on the debts in Safed in 1767, see Ya'ari, *The Emissaries of Palestine*, p. 456.

119. From Ya'ari, *The Emissaries of Palestine*, p. 496.

120. Ibid., pp. 595–603.

121. Concerning the episode of the debts, see Cohen, "Arabic documents," pp. 324–25, 329–30.

17. THE STANDARD OF LIVING

1. The *Pinkas* of Istanbul, letters from the following dates: 28 Tammuz 5501 (July 1741), p. 4; 22 Av 5506 (August 1746), p. 69; 15 Teveth 5507 (January 1747), p. 71; end of Elul 5520 (September 1760), p. 41; 20 Elul 5522 (September 1762), p. 102; end of Adar 5523 (March 1763), p. 52.

2. Ibid., letter of 6 Elul 5520 (September 1760), p. 40.

3. Ibid., letter of 15 Av 5506 (August 1746), p. 122.

4. Ibid., letters of 20 Av 5514 (August 1754), p. 117; Heshvan 5509 (November 1748), p. 119.

5. Ibid., letter of 26 Elul 5502 (September 1742), p. 11.

6. Ibid., letter of 22 Kislev 5514 (December 1753), p. 112.

7. Ibid., letter of Elul 5528 (September 1768), p. 135.

8. Ibid., letter of 25 Av 5508 (August 1748), p. 73.

9. Ibid., letter of 33 Elul 5505 (September 1745), p. 19.

10. Ibid., letter of 6 Elul 5520 (September 1760), p. 40.

11. *Hamaʿaloth Le-Shelomo*, p. 102b.

12. The *Pinkas* of Istanbul, letters from end of Av 5508 (August 1748), p. 73; 25 Av 5513 (August 1753), p. 111; 3 Heshvan 5527 (November 1766), p. 131; 25 Av 5527 (August 1767), p. 133.

13. Ibid., letter of 20 Adar 5509 (March 1749), p. 65.

14. Ibid., letter of 12 Nisan 5522 (April 1762), p. 45.

15. Ibid., letter of 6 Elul 5520 (September 1760), p. 41.

16. See Benayahu, "On the history of the yeshiva 'Knesset Israel,'" p. 125.

17. Tishbi, "The spreading of Ramhal's Kabbalistic writings in Poland and Lithuania," p. 141; see also Benayahu, "The immigration of R. Haim Moses Luzzatto," p. 470.

18. The *Pinkas* of Istanbul, letter of 5 Tishrey 5502 (October 1741), p. 5.

19. Ibid., letter of 13 Elul 5502 (September 1742), p. 89.

20. Ibid., letter of 4 Nisan 5518 (April 1758), p. 25. Concerning the private business of the official Rahamim Hacohen, see letter of 12 Teveth 5515 (January 1755), p. 121.

21. Ibid., letter of 22 Teveth 5506 (January 1746), p. 20. Concerning the affairs of Rolo, see letter of 13 Teveth 5503 (January 1743), p. 7.

22. Ibid., letter of 25 Av 5527 (August 1767), p. 133.

23. Ibid., letter of Elul 5528 (September 1768), p. 135.

24. Ibid.

25. Ibid., letters of 22 Av 5506 (August 1746), p. 69; end of Shevat 5516 (February 1756), p. 125.

26. Ibid., letters of 5 Teveth 5507 (January 1747)—date uncertain, p. 70; 12 Teveth 5515 (January 1755), p. 120; 1 Adar II 5516 (March 1756), p. 126; 27 Av

5516 (August 1756), p. 129; 4 Elul 5516 (September 1756), p. 130; 25 Elul 5527 (September 1767), p. 132.

27. Ibid., letter of 27 Nisan 5508 (April 1748), p. 127.

28. See Barnai, "The Ashkenazi community in Palestine," pp. 219–24.

29. Lavsky, *By-Laws Prevailing in Jerusalem*, pp. 107–14; Rivlin, "Rights of possession of courts and houses in Jerusalem," pp. 149–62.

30. *Sefer Hatakanoth*, pp. 39a–46a.

31. Ibid., pp. 46b–47a.

32. From Ya'ari, *Travels in Palestine*, p. 399.

33. Extensive investigations have not yet been undertaken in this matter. In this section I was assisted by information given to me by Prof. Nahum Gross, for which I thank him. See also Gerber, *Economy and Society in an Ottoman City: Bursa, 1600–1700*; this book makes an important contribution to the study of the economy of the Ottoman Empire.

34. In addition to table 3, see also Luncz, "Preise der Lebensmittel," pp. 11–14; Ben-Zvi, *Palestine under Ottoman Rule*, appendix of coins at the end of the book. Concerning the difficulties in comparing the values of Turkish and European coins, see Flemming, "Drei Türkische Chronisten in Osmanische Kairo," p. 229.

35. See Tobi, "A letter," pp. 257–69; Rivkind, "Documents illustrating Jewish life in Palestine," p. 111; Ya'ari, "R. Moses Israel and his mission," p. 153; Klar, "New writings for a history of the immigration of the author of *Ohr Hahaim* to Palestine," p. 46; Ben-Zvi, *Studies and Documents*, p. 245; Ya'ari, *The Emissaries of Palestine*, pp. 352, 586–87, 593–95; *Get Mekushar*, author's introduction.

36. *Batey Kehuna*, vol. 2, *Beth Din* section, p. 56a. Concerning the decline in value of the *kurus* as a result of the wars between Turkey and Russia in the years 1768–74, see Rozanes, *History of the Jews in Turkey and the Eastern Lands*, vol. 5, p. 82.

37. I do not know the exact value of the Egyptian *kurus*.

38. Haim, "Sources of Sephardi history in Jerusalem," document 4, p. 153.

39. *Nehpa Bekesef*, vol. 1, p. 141a.

40. *Magen Shaul*, p. 21a.

41. *Batey Kehuna*, vol. 1, author's introduction.

42. See Benayahu, "Books composed and edited by R. Moses Hagiz," vol. 2, p. 132.

43. *Batey Kehuna*, vol. 1, p. 68b. Concerning the prices of basic foods in Egypt in 1716, see Flemming "Drei Türkische Chronisten," p. 230. It should be noted that the Egyptian money was not always identical to the Turkish money; see Gibb and Bowen, *Islamic Society and the West*, vol. 2, pp. 3–69.

44. Halpern, *The Hasidic Immigration to Palestine*, p. 19.

45. From Danon, "Seven letters by Jerusalem rabbis during 1591–1801," p. 356.

BIBLIOGRAPHY

MANUSCRIPTS

Jewish Theological Seminary, New York

The *Pinkas* of Istanbul, Ms. 4008 (0151) [Ben-Zvi Institute, Jerusalem, Mic. 1857]

Agron = Mic. 4034/1 (Acc. 0231) [Institute of Microfilmed Hebrew Manuscripts (IMHM), The Jewish National and University Library, Jerusalem, Mic. 29186]

Account-Book of Court = Mic. 3149/1 (Emc. 2226) [IMHM, Mic. 29839]

Adler Collection no. 74, Mic. 3541 [IMHM, Mic. 39346]

Mic. 3623 (1Mc. 2265) [IMHM, Mic. 29428]

Leeds Library, Leeds

Mss. of Letters to the Emissaries, Roth Collection no. 254 [IMHM, Mic. 15391]

The Shari Court of Jerusalem

Vol. 214

Jewish National and University Library, Jerusalem, Manuscript Department

No. 4°31

No. 4°553 (the *Pinkas* of Verona)

No. 4°1037

Ben-Zvi Institute, Jerusalem

Mss. nos. 1701–1706

Bibliography

RABBINICAL SOURCES

Adereth Eliyahu   R. Emanuel Hai Riki. *Adereth Eliyahu*. Leghorn, 1742.
Admath Kodesh   R. Nissim Haim Moses Mizrahi. *Admath Kodesh*, vols. 1–2. Istanbul, 1742. Salonika, 1756.
Agan Hasahar   R. David Hazan. *Agan Hasahar*. Salonika, 1750.
Ahavath Zion   R. Simha ben R. Yehoshu‘a. *Ahavath Zion*. Grodno, 1790.
Amudey Shamayim   R. Jacob Emden. *Amudey Shamayim*. Koretz, 1818.
Arba‘ah Turei Even   R. Elazar Rokeach. *Arba‘ah Turei Even*. Lwow, 1789.
Avodath Israel   R. Israel Kimchi. *Avodath Israel*. Izmir, 1737.
Avodath Massa   R. Abraham Yehoshu’a Yehuda. *Avodath Massa*. Salonika, 1846.
Babylonian Talmud, Rosh Hashana.
Batey Kehuna   R. Isaac Hacohen Rapaport. *Batey Kehuna*, vols. 1–2. Izmir, 1736. Reprint. Salonika, 1754.
Batey Kenesiyoth   R. Abraham Ben Ezra. *Batey Kenesiyoth*. Salonika, 1806.
Be’er Lahai   R. Isaac Nissim ben Jamil. *Be’er Lahai*. Izmir, 1728.
Be’er Mayim Hayim   R. Isaac Halevi. *Be’er Mayim Hayim*. Salonika, 1786.
Beth Ya‘akov   R. Jacob Emden. *Beth Ya‘akov*. Lemberg, 1904.
Birkath Ha-Aretz   Baruch David Kahane, ed. *Birkath Ha-Aretz*. Jerusalem, 1904.
Birkhoth Hamayim   R. Moses Mordecai Meyuhas. *Birkhoth Hamayim*. Salonika, 1789.
Dagul Me-Revava   R. Raphael Treves. *Dagul Me-Revava*. Istanbul, 1743.
Derekh Yeshara   R. Reuven Ben Abraham. *Derekh Yeshara*. Salonika, 1785.
Devar Moshe   R. Moses Amarilio. *Devar Moshe*, vols. 1–3. Salonika, 1742–50.
Eduth Be-Ya‘akov   R. Jacob Emden. *Eduth Be-Ya‘akov*. Altona, 1752.
Etz Hahaim   R. Haim Abulafia. *Etz Hahaim*. Izmir, 1729.
Get Mekushar   R. Moses Bula. *Get Mekushar*. Leghorn, 1785.
Ginath Veradim   R. Abraham Halevi. *Ginath Veradim*, vols. 1–2. Istanbul, 1716–17.
Haim Sha’al   R. Haim Joseph David Azulay. *Haim Sha’al*, vols. 1–2. Leghorn, 1792–95.
Haim Va-Hesed   R. Isaac Nissim ben Jamil. *Haim Va-Hesed*. Izmir, 1736.
Hama‘aloth Le-Shelomo   R. Solomon Hazan. *Hama‘aloth Le-Shelomo*. Alexandria, 1899.
Hanan Elohim   R. Haim Abulafia. *Hanan Elohim*. Izmir, 1736.
Hazeh Zion   R. Emanuel Hai Riki. *Hazeh Zion*. Leghorn, 1742.
Hemdath Yamim   R. Jacob Israel Algazi et al., eds. *Hemdath Yamim*, vols. 1–3. Izmir, 1731–32.
Hikrey Lev   R. Yosef Hazan. *Hikrey Lev*. Salonika, 1818.
Hon Ashir   R. Emanuel Hai Riki. *Hon Ashir*. Amsterdam, 1731.

Bibliography

Hon Rav   R. Raphael El'azar Nahmias. *Hon Rav*, vols. 1–2. Salonika, 1777–84.

Hurvoth Yerushalayim   Minna Rozen, ed. *The Ruins of Jerusalem.* Tel Aviv, 1981.

Hut Hameshulash   R. Yehuda Diwan. *Hut Hameshulash.* Istanbul, 1739.

In Praise of the Baal Shem Tov   *In Praise of the Baal Shem Tov*, trans. and ed. Dan Ben-Amos and Jerome R. Mintz. Bloomington, 1970.

Kehilath Ya'akov   R. Moses Galante. *Kehilath Ya'akov.* Safed, 1578.

Kol Ya'akov   R. Jacob Shaul. *Kol Ya'akov.* Izmir, 1760.

Lev Shelomo   R. Solomon Halevi. *Lev Shelomo.* Salonika, 1808.

Likutim   R. Raphael Mordecai Malkhi. *Chapters of commentary*, ed. A. Rivlin, vol. 1. Jerusalem, 1923.

Luhoth Eduth   R. Jonathan Eibeschutz. *Luhoth Eduth.* Altona, 1755.

Ma'agal Tov   R. Haim Joseph David Azulay. *Ma'agal Tov Hashalem.* Berlin, 1921.

Ma'aseh Rokeach   R. El'azar Rokeach. *Ma'aseh Rokeach.* Amsterdam, 1740.

Magen Shaul   R. Hananya Shaul. *Magen Shaul.* Salonika, 1747.

Malkhi Ba-Kodesh   R. Ezra Malkhi. *Malkhi Ba-Kodesh.* Salonika, 1749.

Mayim Sha'al   R. Moses Mordecai Meyuhas. *Mayim Sha'al.* Salonika, 1799.

Megilath Yuhasin   R. Raphael Meyuhas Behar Samuel. *Megilath Yuhasin.* Jerusalem, 1875.

Mekitz Ben Hai   R. Abraham Kanyeti. *Mekitz Ben Hai.* Istanbul, 1746.

Melekh Shalom   R. Samuel Shalom. *Melekh Shalom.* Salonika, 1769.

Mikra'ei Kodesh   R. Haim Abulafia. *Mikra'ei Kodesh.* Izmir, 1729.

Mizbeah Adama   R. Raphael Meyuhas Behar Samuel. *Mizbeah Adama.* Salonika, 1777.

Nehpa Bekesef   R. Jonah Navon. *Nehpa Bekesef*, vols. 1–2. Istanbul, 1748. Reprint. Jerusalem, 1843.

Nivhar Mi-Kessef   R. Yoshiya Pinto. *Nivhar Mi-Kessef.* Allepo, 1869.

Noda Be-Yehuda   R. Ezekiel Landau. *Noda Be-Yehuda.*

Ohr Hahaim   R. Haim ben Attar. *Ohr Hahaim.* Venice, 1790.

Orim Gedolim   R. Abraham Israel Ze'evi. *Urim Gedolim*, Izmir, 1758.

P'ri Ha-Adama   R. Raphael Meyuhas Behar Samuel. *P'ri Ha-Adama*, vols. 1–4. Salonika, 1752–63.

Responsa of Algazi   R. Jacob Israel Algazi. *Responsa.* Jerusalem, 1977.

Responsa of Hamabit   R. Moses ben Yose Trani. *Responsa*, vols. 1–2. Venice, 1629.

Sam Hayey   R. Haim Asael. *Sam Hayey.*

S'deh Ha-Aretz   R. Abraham Meyuhas. *S'deh Ha-Aretz*, vols. 1–4. Salonika, 1784–98.

Sefath Emeth   R. Moses Hagiz. *Sefath Emeth.* Amsterdam, 1707.

Sefer Hatakanoth   *Sefer Hatakanoth.* Jerusalem, 1883. Originally published in Jerusalem in 1842.

Bibliography

Sha'ar Hamayim   R. Mordecai Joseph Meyuhas. *Sha'ar Hamayim*. Salonika, 1778.
Sha'ar Hamifkad   R. David ben-Simon. *Sha'ar Hamifkad*. Alexandria, 1908.
Sha'ar Yosef   R. Haim Joseph David Azulay. *Sha'ar Yosef*. Leghorn, 1757.
Shema Ya'akov   R. Jacob Israel Algazi. *Shama Ya'akov*. Istanbul, 1745.
Shem Hagedolim   R. Haim Joseph David Azulay. *Shem Hagedolim*. Vilna, 1853.
Shevah U-Tehila   R. Peretz ben Moshe. *Shevah U-Tehila Le-Eretz Israel*. Metz, 1772.
Shevuth Ya'akov   R. Haim Abulafia. *Shevuth Ya'akov*. Izmir, 1734.
Shivhey Yerushalayim   R. Baruch Haim. *Shivhey Yerushalayim*. Leghorn, 1782.
Tevu'oth Ha-Aretz   R. Yehosef Schwarz. *Tevu'oth Ha-Aretz*. Jerusalem, 1900.
Tzach Ve-Adom   R. Raphael Treves. *Tzach Ve-Adom*. Istanbul, 1740.
Tzeror Hakesef   R. Haim Abraham Getenyu. *Tzeror Hakesef*. Salonika, 1756.
Yashresh Ya'akov   R. Haim Abulafia. *Yashresh Ya'akov*. Izmir, 1728.
Yosef Lekah   R. Haim Abulafia. *Yosef Lekah*, vols. 1–2. Izmir, 1730–32.
Yosef Ometz   R. Haim Joseph David Azulay. *Yosef Ometz*. Leghorn, 1798.
Zechor Le-Avraham   R. Abraham Behar Avigdor. *Zechor Le-Avraham*. Istanbul, 1847.
Zera' Avraham   R. Abraham Yitzhaki. *Zera' Avraham*, vols. 1–2. Istanbul, 1732.
Zichron Yerushalayim   R. Judah Poliastro. *Zichron Yerushalayim*. Istanbul, 1743. Reprint. Amsterdam, 1759.
Zimrath Ha-Aretz   R. Jacob Berav. *Zimrath Ha-Aretz*, ed. A. Benayahu. Jerusalem, 1946.

PUBLISHED SOURCES AND STUDIES

Alfasi, Isaac. "Documents on the history of the old Yishuv." *Bar-Ilan* 3 (1965): 213–24. (Heb.)
———. "Letters of Hasidim from Palestine." *Sinai* 88 (1981): 285–87. (Heb.)
Anderson, Matthew Smith. *Europe in the Eighteenth Century 1713–1783*. New York, 1961.
———. *The Eastern Question*. London, 1966.
Ankawa, David. *Kerem Hemed*, ed. S. Bar-Asher. Facsimile ed. Jerusalem, 1977. (Heb.)
Ashtor (Strauss), Eliyahu. *History of the Jews in Egypt and Syria under the Rule of the Mamelukes*, vols. 1–3. Jerusalem, 1946–70. (Heb.)
———. *The Jews and the Mediterranean Economy, 10th–15th Centuries*. London, 1983.

Bibliography

Assaf, Simha. *The Rabbinical Courts and Their Arrangements*. Jerusalem, 1924. (Heb.)

———. "The Diaspora communities and Palestine." *Ha-ʿOlam*, 1930, p. 719. (Heb.)

———. "More on the history of the Jews in Kurdistan." *Kiryat Sefer* 13 (1936): 266–71. (Heb.)

———. "Towards a history of the Karaites in the Eastern countries." *Zion* 1 (1936): 208–51. (Heb.)

———. "The selling of Hebrew books in Yemen through envoys from Palestine." *Kiryat Sefer* 16 (1939–40): 493–95. (Heb.)

Avissar, Oded. *The Book of Tiberias*. Jerusalem, 1973. (Heb.)

Avitsur, Shmuel. "Safed: Center of the Manufacture of Woven Woolens in the 16th Century." *Sefunoth* 6 (1962): 41–70. (Heb.)

———. *Daily Life in Palestine in the Nineteenth Century*. Tel Aviv, 1973. (Heb.)

Badhav, Yitzhak. *The Jerusalemite*. Jerusalem, 1930. (Heb.)

Barbir, Karl K. *Ottoman Rule in Damascus, 1708–1758*. Princeton, 1980.

Barnai, Jacob. "The leadership of the Jewish community in Jerusalem in the mid-eighteenth century." *Shalem* 1 (1974): 271–316. (Heb.)

———. *The "Yishuv" in Palestine during 1740–1777 and Its Connections with the Diaspora*. Ph.D. diss., Hebrew University of Jerusalem, 1975. (Heb.)

———. "The Ashkenazi community in Palestine, 1720–1777." *Shalem* 2 (1976): 193–230. (Heb.)

———. "Notes on the immigration of R. Abraham Gerson Kutower to Palestine." *Zion* 42 (1977): 110–19. (Heb.)

———. "Towards changes in Jerusalem in the nineteenth century." *Sinai* 81 (1977): 151–55. (Heb.)

———. "The regulations *(taqanot)* of Jerusalem." *Jerusalem in the Early Ottoman Period*, ed. A. Cohen, pp. 271–316. Jerusalem, 1979. (Heb.)

———. "The status of the 'General Rabbinate' in Jerusalem in the Ottoman period." *Cathedra* 13 (1979): 47–70. (Heb.)

———. *Hasidic Letters from Palestine*. Jerusalem, 1980. (Heb.)

———. "On the history of the Jewish community of Istanbul in the eighteenth century." *Miqqedem U-Miyam* 1 (1981): 53–66. (Heb.)

———. "The Jews in the Ottoman Empire." In *History of the Jews in Islamic Countries*, vols. 1–3, ed. S. Ettinger. Jerusalem, 1981–86. (Heb.)

———. "On the Jewish community of Izmir in the late eighteenth and early nineteenth centuries." *Zion* 47 (1982): 56–76. (Heb.)

———. "The development of links between the Jews of Izmir and the Jews of Palestine in the seventeenth and eighteenth centuries." *Shalem* 5 (1987): 95–114. (Heb.)

———. "Some clarifications on the Land of Israel stories of *In Praise of the Baal Shem Tov*." *Revue des Etudes Juives* 146 (1987): 367–80.

Bibliography

————. "Trends in the historiography of the medieval and early modern periods of the Jewish community in Palestine." *Cathedra* 42 (1987): 87–120. (Heb.)

Barnai, Jacob, and Haim Gerber. "Jewish guilds in Istanbul in the late eighteenth century." *Michael* 7 (1982): 206–46. (Heb.)

Baron, Salo W. *The Jewish Community.* Philadelphia, 1942.

————. "Towards a history of the Jewish settlement in Tiberias in 1742–1744." *Jubilee Volume for Alexander Marx*, pp. 79–88. New York, 1943. (Heb.)

Bartal, Israel. "The 'Aliyah' of R. El'azar Rokeach (1740)." *Studies on the History of Dutch Jewry* 4 (1984): 7–25. (Heb.)

Bashan, Eliezer. *Community regulations.* Bar-Ilan University, 1973. (Heb.)

————. "The names of towns in Palestine as appellations of foreign towns in the responsa literature of the Ottoman period. *Bar-Ilan* 12 (1974): 137–65. (Heb.)

————. "A German source on the Ashkenazi community in Jerusalem in the 1830's." *Jerusalem in the Early Ottoman Period*, ed. A. Cohen, pp. 317–22. Jerusalem, 1979. (Heb.)

————. *Captivity and Ransom.* Bar-Ilan University, 1980.

————. "Evidence of European tourists as a source for the economic history of the Jews in the Mediterranean area in the Ottoman period." In *The Sephardi and Oriental Jewish Heritage*, ed. I. Ben-Ami, pp. 35–80. Jerusalem, 1982. (Heb.)

————. "Contracts for the rental of ships for the bringing of Jews to Palestine since 1775." *Studies in the Memory of R. Yitzhak Nissim*, vol. 4, pp. 291–302. Jerusalem, 1985. (Heb.)

————. "Notes." *Aley Sefer* 3 (1977): 169–70. (Heb.)

Ben-Arieh, Joshua. "Nineteenth century Western literature of travel to Palestine: A historical source and a cultural phenomenon." *Cathedra* 40 (1966): 159–88. (Heb.)

Benayahu, Meir. "The great fires in Izmir and Edirne." *Reshumoth*, n.s. 2 (1946): 144–54. (Heb.)

————. "Towards a history of the study houses in Jerusalem in the seventeenth century." *Hebrew Union College Annual* 21 (1948): 1–28. (Heb.)

————. "On the history of the yeshiva 'Knesset Israel' in Jerusalem." *Jerusalem* 2 (1949): 103–31. (Heb.)

————. "The yeshiva of R. Emanuel Hai Riki in Jerusalem and his murder on a mission in Italy." *Jerusalem* 2 (1949): 29–37. (Heb.)

————. "Correspondence between the Ashkenazi community in Jerusalem and R. D. Oppenheim." *Jerusalem* 3 (1950): 108–29. (Heb.)

————. "Review of Abraham Ya'ari, *The Emissaries of Palestine*." *Kiryath Sefer* 28 (1952–53): 16–35. (Heb.)

————. "Letters of R. Abraham Konaki to R. Judah Briel." *Sinai* 32 (1953): 300–319. (Heb.)

————. "A treatise on the distribution of the money for Eretz Israel collected in Germany." *Sura* 1 (1954): 103–55. (Heb.)

————. "Contribution to the dating of two letters from Jerusalem." *Jerusalem* 5 (1955): 324–32. (Heb.)

————. "Letters of R. Samuel Abuhav, R. Moses Zaccuto and their circle concerning Palestine." *Jerusalem* (quarterly) 5 (1955): 136–86. (Heb.)

————. "The Ashkenazi community of Jerusalem 1647–1747." *Sefunoth* 2 (1958): 128–89. (Heb.)

————. "Matters of the HiDA." *The Book of the HiDA*, ed. M. Benayahu, pp. 28–44. Jerusalem, 1959. (Heb.)

————. *Rabbi H. Y. D. Azulay*. Jerusalem, 1959. (Heb.)

————. "The Holy Brotherhood of R. Judah Hasid and their settlement in Jerusalem." *Sefunoth* 3–4 (1960): 133–82. (Heb.)

————. "The revival of ordination in Safed." *Yitzhak F. Baer Jubilee Volume*, pp. 248–69. Jerusalem, 1960. (Heb.)

————. "The immigration of R. Haim Moses Luzzatto to Palestine." *Mazkereth*, pp. 467–74. Jerusalem, 1962. (Heb.)

————. "A key to the understanding of the sources on the Sabbatean movement in Jerusalem." *Studies in Mysticism and Religion: Volume Presented to Gershom Scholem*, pp. 35–46. Jerusalem, 1967. (Heb.)

————. "The testimony of R. Elia Ashkenazi of Safed concerning the Sabbateanism of R. Haim Malach and R. Judah Hasid." *Eretz Israel* 10 (1971): 67–71. (Heb.)

————. "The Sabbatean movement in Greece." *Sefunoth* 14 (1971–77). (Heb.)

————. "The status of the Sabbatean movement in Jerusalem." *Salo Wittmayer Baron Jubilee Volume* (Hebrew section), pp. 41–70. Jerusalem, 1975. (Heb.)

————. "Books composed and edited by R. Moses Hagiz." *Aley Sefer* 2 (1976): 121–62; 3 (1977): 94–120; 4 (1978): 137–55. (Heb.)

————. "The vow of R. Moses Haim Luzzatto to abstain from writing works 'dictated by a *magid*.'" *Zion* 42 (1977): 24–48. (Heb.)

Ben-Sasson, Haim Hillel. *The History of the Jewish People*. Cambridge, 1979.

Ben-Ya'akov, Abraham. *Jerusalem within Its Walls*. Jerusalem, 1976. (Heb.)

Ben-Zion, Ariel. *Sar Shalom Shar'abi*. Jerusalem, 1939. (Heb.)

Ben-Zvi, Yitzhak. "The Ashkenazi settlement in Jerusalem after the immigration of R. Judah Hasid." *Jerusalem* 1 (1948): 38–42. (Heb.)

————. "The emissaries of Palestine in Italy." *Sinai: Jubilee Book*, pp. 13–27. Jerusalem, 1958. (Heb.)

————. *Remnants of Ancient Jewish Communities in the Land of Israel*. Jerusalem, 1965. (Heb.)

————. *Studies and Documents*. Jerusalem, 1966. (Heb.)

————. *Palestine under Ottoman Rule*. Jerusalem, 1968. (Heb.)

Berliner, Abraham. *The History of the Jews in Rome*. Vilna, 1973. (Heb.)

Bornstein, Leah. "The structure of the Rabbinate in the Ottoman Empire." *East and Maghreb* 1 (1974): 233–58. (Heb.)

————. *The Jewish Communal Leadership in the Near East from the end of the*

15th century through the 18th century. Ph.D. diss., Bar-Ilan University, Israel, 1978. (Heb.)

Braude, Benjamin. "Foundation myths of the millet system." In *Christians and Jews in the Ottoman Empire,* ed. B. Braude and B. Lewis, vol. 1, pp. 69–88. New York and London, 1982.

Brilling, Bernard (Dov). "Die frühsten Beziehungen der Juden Hamburgs in Palästina." *Jahrbuch der Jüdisch Literarischen Geselschaft* 21 (1030): 19–38.

———. "Mähren and Eretz-Israel." *Zeitschrift für die Geschichte der Juden in der C.S.R.* 3 (1932): 237–56.

———. "The Jews of Germany and Palestine." *Sinai* 6 (1940): 320–35. (Heb.)

———. "The embargo on the collection of money for Palestine in Austria in 1723." *Zion* 12 (1947): 89–96. (Heb.)

———. "On the relations of the Jews of Hamburg to Palestine." *Jerusalem* 3 (1950): 87–97. (Heb.)

———. "The Jewish community of Heidingsfeld and its attitude towards Palestine." *Jerusalem* 4 (1953): 220–31. (Heb.)

———. "New documents on emissaries in Germany in the eighteenth century." *Sinai* 42 (1958): 30–42. (Heb.)

———. "The 'Pinkas' of the emissaries R. Abraham Azulay and R. Asher Ashkenazi," in *The Book of the HiDA,* ed. M. Benayahu, pp. 141–77. Jerusalem, 1959. (Heb.)

———. "On the emissaries from Palestine to Germany." *Sura* 4 (1964): 250–75. (Heb.)

———. "Die Tätigkeit des Jerusalemer Sendboten Petachia b. Jehuda Wahl Katzenellenbogen in Westeuropa (1735–1750)." *Festschrift I. E. Lichtigfeld,* pp. 20–49. Frankfurt, 1964.

———. "Das Erdbeben von Sefad." *Zeitschrift für die Geschichte der Juden* 8 (1971): 41–58.

Carlebach, Elisheva. *The Pursuit of Hersey.* New York, 1990.

Carpi, Daniel. *The Activity of the Italian Synagogue in Venice . . . during 1576–1733.* Tel Aviv, 1978. (Heb.)

Chayat, Shimon. "New sources for the history of the Jews in Ottoman Jerusalem." *Hebrew Union College Annual* 51 (1980): 1–8. (Heb.)

Cohen, Amnon. "The Jews in northern Palestine in the 18th century." *Proceedings of the Fifth World Congress of Jewish Studies,* vol. 5, pp. 145–51. Jerusalem, 1973. (Heb.)

———. *Palestine in the Eighteenth Century.* Jerusalem, 1973.

———. "Arabic documents on the settlement of the debts of the Jewish communities of Jerusalem and Hebron in the 18th century." *Shalem* 1 (1974): 317–30. (Heb.)

———. *Ottoman Documents of the Jewish Community of Jerusalem in the 16th Century.* Jerusalem, 1976. (Heb. and Turkish)

Bibliography

———. "Turkish and Arabic archives as a source for the history of the Jews in Palestine during the Ottoman period." *Miqqedem U-Miyam* 1 (1981): 39–48. (Heb.)

———. *Jewish Life under Islam*. Cambridge, 1984.

Cohen, Daniel J. "The 'Small Council' of the Jewry of Brandenburg-Ansbach." *Yitzhak F. Baer Jubilee Volume*, pp. 351–73. Jerusalem, 1960. (Heb.)

———. "Notes and supplements to A. Ya'ari's paper, 'The *Mi-Sheberach* prayers.'" *Kiryat Sefer* 40 (1965): 542–59. (Heb.)

Cohen, M., and Y. Stillman. "The Cairo Geniza and the custom of geniza among Oriental Jewry: An historical and ethnographic study." *Pe'amim* 24 (1985): 3–35. (Heb.)

Danon, Abraham. "La communauté juive de Salonique." *Revue des études juives* 41 (1901): 98–177, 249–65.

———. "Seven letters by Jerusalem rabbis during 1591–1801." *Jerusalem* 7 (1906): 345–60. (Heb.)

Davison, Roderic H. *Turkey*. Englewood Cliffs, N.J., 1968.

Dinur (Dinaburg), Ben Zion. *The Book of Zionism*, vol. 1. Tel Aviv, 1932. (Heb.)

———. *At the Turning-Point of the Generations* (Historical writings, vol. 1). Jerusalem, 1955. (Heb.)

———. "The emigration from Spain to Palestine after the disorders of 1391." *Zion* 32 (1967): 161–74. (Heb.)

Dubnow, Simon. *The Notebook of the State*. Berlin, 1925. (Heb.)

———. *History of the Jews*, vol. 7. Tel Aviv, 1940. (Heb.)

———. *The History of Hasidism*. Tel Aviv, 1962. (Heb.)

Eidelberg, Shlomo. "An eighteenth-century letter from Venice to Metz." *Salo Wittmayer Baron Jubilee Book* (Hebrew section), pp. 1–6. Jerusalem, 1975. (Heb.)

Elbaum, Jacob. "The *Haluka*." Unpublished ms., The Hebrew University of Jerusalem, 1969. (Heb.)

Eliav, Mordecai. *Palestine and Its Yishuv in the Nineteenth Century, 1777–1917*. Jerusalem, 1978. (Heb.)

———. *Under Imperial Austrian Protection*. Jerusalem, 1985.

Elmalech, Abraham. "From the hidden manuscripts of the past." *East and West* 3 (1929): 321–24. (Heb.)

———. "The Rishon Le-Zion Rabbi Jacob Moses Ayash." *Sinai* 49 (1961): 234–49. (Heb.)

———. *Harishonim Le-Zion* (The chief rabbis of Jerusalem). Jerusalem, 1970. (Heb.)

Elon, Menahem. *Jewish Law*. Jerusalem, 1973. (Heb.)

Encyclopaedia Judaica. Jerusalem, 1971.

Encyclopedia of Islam, vol. 1. Leiden and London, 1960.

Epstein, Mark A. *The Ottoman Jewish Communities and Their Rule in the 15th and 16th Centuries*. Freiburg, 1980.

Bibliography

Etkes, Emanuel. "Rabbi Shneur Zalman of Lyady as a hasidic leader." *Zion* 50 (1985): 321–54. (Heb.)

————. "The rise of R. Shneur Zalman of Lyady to the status of leadership." *Tarbitz* 51 (1985): 429–39. (Heb.)

Ettinger, Samuel. *The Hasidic Movement in Its First Generations*. Jerusalem, 1965. (Heb.)

————. *Antisemitism in Modern Times*. Tel Aviv, 1979. (Heb.)

Feld, Y. D. "A letter from R. David Oppenheim to the rabbis of Jerusalem." *Hamaʿayan* 16 (1976): 39–53. (Heb.)

Flemming, Barbara. "Drei Turkische Chronisten in Osmanische Kairo." *Harvard Ukrainian Studies* 3–4 (1979–80): 227–35.

Freimann, Aaron. *Matters concerning Sabbetai Zevi*. Berlin, 1912. (Heb.)

Frenkel, David. "More documents for a history of the immigration of the author of *Ohr Hahaim* to Palestine." *Jubilee Book presented to Alexander Marx*, pp. 125–30. New York, 1943. (Heb.)

Fried, Nathan. "Notes on A. Yaʿari's studies on the *Mi-Sheberach* prayers." *Kiryat Sefer* 37 (1961): 511–14. (Heb.)

Frin, A. *Charity Funds and Study Societies in Europe in the Sixteenth–Eighteenth Centuries*. Master's thesis, Tel-Aviv University, 1963. (Heb.)

Frumkin, Aryeh Leib, and Eliezer Rivlin. *The History of the Rabbis of Jerusalem*, vols. 1–4. Jerusalem, 1928–30. (Heb.)

Ga'on, Moses David. *The Jews of the East in Palestine*, vol. 2. Jerusalem, 1938. (Heb.)

Gelber, Nathan Michael. *Vorgeschichte des Zionismus*. Vienna, 1921.

————. "Die Hierosolymitanische Stiftung." *Menorah* 4 (1926): 610–24.

————. *Brody*. Jerusalem, 1955. (Heb.)

Gerber, Haim. "Archives of the Shari court of Bursa as a source for the history of the Jews in the city." *Miqqedem U-Miyam* 1 (1981): 31–38. (Heb.)

————. *The Economic and Social Life of the Jews in the Ottoman Empire in the Sixteenth and Seventeenth Centuries*. Jerusalem, 1982. (Heb.)

————. *Economy and Society in an Ottoman City: Bursa, 1600–1700*. Jerusalem, 1988.

Gibb, Hamilton A. R., and Harold Bowen. *Islamic Society and the West*, vol. 2. Oxford, 1967.

Gil, Moshe. *Palestine during the First Moslem Period (634–1099)*, vol. 1–3. Tel Aviv, 1983. (Heb.)

————. "On the research of the Geniza." *Yedion Ha-Igud Ha-Olami Le-Madáey Ha-Yahaduk* 22 (1983): 17–29.

Ginzburg, Shimon. *R. Moses Haim Luzzatto and His Contemporaries*, vols. 1–2. Tel Aviv, 1937. (Heb.)

Goitein, Shlomo Dov. *A Mediterranean Society*, vol. 2. Berkeley, 1977.

Goitein, Shlomo Dov, and Aaron Ben Shemesh. *Islamic Law in the State of Israel*. Jerusalem, 1958. (Heb.)

Bibliography

Goldsmith-Lehmann, Ruth P. *Sir Moses Montefiore*. Jerusalem, 1984.

Goodblatt, M. S. *Jewish Life in Turkey in the XVIth Century as Reflected in the Legal Writings of Samuel de Medina*. New York, 1952.

Goren, Haim. "An eighteenth century geography: *Sefer Yedey Moshe* by R. Moshe Yerushalmi." *Cathedra* 34 (1985): 75–96.

Graetz, Heinrich. *Essays, Memories, Letters*. Jerusalem, 1969. (Heb.)

Gries, Ze'ev. *Conduct Literature*. Jerusalem, 1989. (Heb.)

Hacker, Joseph. "The connections of Spanish Jewry with Palestine between 1391 and 1492." *Shalem* 1 (1974): 105–56. (Heb.)

———. "The payment of *Djizya* by scholars in Palestine in the sixteenth century." *Shalem* 4 (1984): 63–118. (Heb.)

———. "Links between Spanish Jewry and Palestine, 1391–1492." *Cathedra* 36 (1985): 3–34. (Heb.)

———. "Jewish autonomy in the Ottoman Empire: Its scope and limits." *Transition and Change in Modern Jewish History*, pp. 349–88. Jerusalem, 1987. (Heb.)

Haim, Abraham. "Sources of Sephardi history in Jerusalem during the Ottoman period." *Shevet Va'am*, 2d ser., 2 (1973): 143–72. (Heb.)

———. "Additional documents on the relations of the Sephardi community with the Ottoman authorities and the Arab population of Jerusalem." *Chapters in the History of the Jewish Community in Jerusalem* 2 (1976): 216–38. (Heb.)

———. *Documents from the Collection of Elie Eliachar*. Tel Aviv, 1977. (Heb.)

Halpern, Israel. "The Diaspora and Palestine." *Ha-'Olam* 36 (1930): 719. (Heb.)

———. "The attitude of the Jewish councils and communities in Poland to Palestine." *Zion* 1 (1936): 82–88. (Heb.)

———. *The Notebook of the Council of Four Lands*. Jerusalem, 1945. (Heb.)

———. *The Hasidic Immigration to Palestine during the Eighteenth Century*. Jerusalem and Tel Aviv, 1946. (Heb.)

———. *The Regulations of the State of Mahren*. Jerusalem, 1952. (Heb.)

———. *Eastern European Jewry*. Jerusalem, 1969. (Heb.)

Harkavi, Abraham Elijah. *Ha-Yekev*. Petersburg, 1894. (Heb.)

Haran, Raya. "The Authenticity of Letters Written by Hasidim in Eretz Israel." *Cathedra* 55 (1990): 22–58. (Heb.)

Hasson, Isaac. "The penetration of Arab tribes in Palestine." *Cathedra* 32 (1984): 54–65.

Havlin, Shlomo Zalman. "Some important dates in the biography of R. David Pardo." *Tarbitz* 42 (1975): 503–6. (Heb.)

———. "Jerusalem yeshivot and sages in the late seventeenth century." *Shalem* 2 (1976): 113–92. (Heb.)

Ha-Yisraeli, Reuven. *The History of the Prague Community during 1680–1730*. Master's thesis, Tel Aviv University, 1965. (Heb.)

Hebrew Encyclopedia, vol. 21.

Bibliography

Heschel, Abraham Joshua. "R. Gerson Kutower." *Hebrew Union College Annual* 23, no. 2 (1950–51): 17–71. (Heb.)

Heyd, Uriel. *Dahir al-ʿUmar*. Jerusalem, 1942. (Heb.)

———. "The Jewish communities of Istanbul in the XVIIth century." *Oriens* 6 (1953): 299–314.

———. "The Jews of Palestine in the late seventeenth century." *Jerusalem* 4 (1953): 173–84. (Heb.)

———. *Ottoman Documents on Palestine 1552–1615*. Oxford, 1960.

———. *Palestine during the Ottoman Rule*. Jerusalem, 1969. (Heb.)

———. *The Institutions of the Ottoman Empire*. Jerusalem, 1974. (Heb.)

Hirschberg, Haim Zeʾev. "Notes on the debts of the Jews in Jerusalem in 1775." *Eretz Israel* 1 (1951): 158–68. (Heb.)

———. "Arbitrary tax in Jerusalem and its abrogation." *Mazkereth Levi*, pp. 161–68. Tel Aviv, 1954. (Heb.)

———. *A History of the Jews in North Africa*, vols. 1–2. Jerusalem, 1965. (Heb.) English edition. Leiden, 1974.

———. "Between East and West." *Mimizrach U-Mimaʿarav* 1 (1974): 9–35.

Hisdai, Yaakov. "Early settlement of *Hasidim* and of *Mithnagdim* in Palestine— immigration of religious obligation and of mission." *Shalem* 5 (1984): 231–70. (Heb.)

Idel, Moshe. "One from a town and two from a family: A new look at the problem of dissemination of Lurianic Kabbala and the Sabbatean movement." *Peámim* 44 (1990): 5–30.

Ish-Shalom, Michael. *Christian Travels in the Holy Land*. Tel Aviv, 1965. (Heb.)

Kalaydjian, A. "The correspondence (1725–1740) of the Armenian Patriarch Gregory the chain-bearer." *Studies on Palestine during the Ottoman Period*, ed. M. Maoz, pp. 562–67. Jerusalem, 1975.

Kaniel, Joshua. "Organizational and economic contentions between communities in Jerusalem in the nineteenth century." *Chapters in the History of the Jewish Community in Jerusalem*, vol. 2, pp. 97–126. Jerusalem, 1976. (Heb.)

Kaplan, Joseph. "The attitude of the leadership of the Portuguese community in Amsterdam to the Sabbatean movement." *Zion* 39 (1974): 198–216. (Heb.)

Karagila, Zvi. *Social and Economic Patterns of the Jewish Community in Palestine during the Egyptian Rule (1831–1839)*. Ph.D. diss., Tel Aviv University, 1980. (Heb.)

Katsh, Abraham I. "R. Abraham Ben Asher's mission to Italy." *Sefunot* 9 (1964): 321–36. (Heb.)

Katz, Jacob. "Sociological comments on an historical book." *Behinoth* 2 (1952): 69–72. (Heb.)

———. *Tradition and Crisis*. Jerusalem, 1958. (Heb.)

Kaufmann, David. "Towards a history of the Ashkenazi community in Jerusalem." *Jerusalem* 4 (1892): 25–40. (Heb.)

Bibliography

Kedar, Benjamin Ze'ev. "The Jewish community in Jerusalem in the thirteenth century." *Tarbitz* 41 (1971–72): 82–94. (Heb.)

———. "Information on the Jews of Palestine in eighteenth-century Protestant sources." *Eretz Israel* 12 (1975): 203–6. (Heb.)

Klar, Benjamin. "New writings for a history of the immigration of the author of *Ohr Hahaim* to Palestine." *Alim* 3 (1930): 37–52. (Heb.)

———. *Rabbi Haim ben Attar.* Jerusalem, 1959. (Heb.)

Kook, Shaul Hone. *Readings and Studies*, vols. 1–2. Jerusalem, 1963. (Heb.)

Kopf, L. "A disputation between a Christian and a Jewish rabbi, held at Tiberias in the eighteenth century." *Kiryath Sefer* 39 (1963–64): 272–79. (Heb.)

Krauss, Samuel. "Die Palästinasiedlung der Polnischen Hasidim und die Wiener Kreise in Jahre 1700." *Abhandlungen zur Erinnerung an Hirsch Perez Chajes*, pp. 51–94. Vienna, 1973.

Lachman, Samuel. "Numismatic notes." *Cathedra* 8 (1978): 197–98. (Heb.)

Lavksy, Abraham. *By-Laws (Takanot Ve-Haskamot) Prevailing in Jerusalem during the Ottoman Period.* Master's thesis, Bar-Ilan University, 1974. (Heb.)

Lewis, Bernard. *Notes and Documents.* Jerusalem, 1952.

———. *The Emergence of Modern Turkey.* Oxford, 1966.

Liebes, Judah. "The Messianism of R. Jacob Emden and his attitude toward Sabbateanism." *Tarbitz* 49 (1980): 122–65. (Heb.)

Litvin, A. "From the Pinkas of Karalicz 1784–1839." *Reshumoth*, n.s. 1 (1946): 162–70. (Heb.)

Luncz, Abraham Moses. "The customs of our brothers in Palestine in religion and in national life." *Jerusalem* 1 (1882): 1–70. (Heb.)

———. "Preise der Lebensmittel." *Jerusalem* 1 (Vienna, 1882): 11–16.

———. "Three letters from the Ashkenazi leaders." *Jerusalem* 2 (1887): 148–57. (Heb.)

———. "The Jews in the Holy Land." *Jerusalem* 3 (1889): 1–52. (Heb.)

———. "On the book *Ahavath Zion*, its forgery and its forgers." *Jerusalem* 4 (1892): 137–52. (Heb.)

———. "The Jews in the Holy Land." *Jerusalem* 5 (1901): 189–239. (Heb.)

———. "A letter from Jerusalem of 1782." *Jerusalem* 6 (1903): 43–47. (Heb.)

———. "On the history of the Karaites in Jerusalem." *Jerusalem* 6 (1904): 237–54. (Heb.)

———. "He causes the sleeping ones to speak." *Jerusalem* 7 (1907): 213–18. (Heb.)

Mahler, Raphael. *The History of the Jews in Poland.* Merhavia, 1946. (Heb.)

———. *History of the Jewish People in Modern Times*, vol. 4. Merhavia, 1956. (Heb.)

Maimonides, Moses. *Mishneh Torah*, ed. M. Hyamson, Jerusalem, 1962. (Heb.–Eng.)

Malachi, Elazar, *Studies in the History of the Old Yishuv.* Tel Aviv, 1971. (Heb.)

Bibliography

Mann, Jacob. "The settlement of R. Abraham Rovigo and his group in Jerusalem in 1702," *Zion* 6 (1934): 59–84. (Heb.)

———. "The voyage of R. Haim ben Attar and his companions to Palestine and their temporary settlement in Acre." *Tarbitz* 7 (1936): 74–101. (Heb.)

Mannà, Ádel, "The Farukhids and their relations with the Beduins." *Jerusalem in the Early Ottoman Period*, pp. 196–232. Jerusalem, 1979.

———. "The rebellion of Naqib al-Ashraf in Jerusalem, 1703–1705." *Cathedra* 42 (1989): 49–74.

Marcus, R. "From old manuscripts." *Hamevasser* 2 (1911): 210–11. (Heb.)

Marcus, Simon. "Documents from Rhodes concerning Palestine." *Jerusalem* 5 (1955): 214–32. (Heb.)

Margoliot, Reuben. *The Life of Rabbi Haim ben Attar*. Lvov, 1928. (Heb.)

Mehlman, Israel. "Eighteen Hebrew books and isolated pages." *Aley Sefer* 1 (1975): 101–8. (Heb.)

Meisel, Joseph. *The Notebook of the Berlin Community*. Jerusalem, 1962. (Heb.)

Molcho, Michael. "The attitude of Salonica to Jerusalem." *Sinai* 49 (1961): 284–87. (Heb.)

Molcho, Isaac Raphael, and Abraham Amarilio. "A collection of communal regulations in Ladino from Salonika." *Sefunoth* 2 (1958): 26–60. (Heb.)

Morgenstern, Aryeh. *Messianism and the Settlement of Palestine*. Jerusalem, 1985. (Heb.)

Moyal, Eli. "Rabbi Haim ben Attar." *Oroth* 1 (1978). (Heb.)

Nachshon, Benny. "The siege of Tiberias according to R. Jacob Beirav's *Zimrath Ha-Aretz*." *Cathedra* 14 (1980): 55–64. (Heb.)

Nacht, Jacob. *From the Hidden Manuscripts of Jerusalem*, vol. 25, pp. 12–13. 1932. (Heb.)

———. "The letters of the Hida and the emissaries of Palestine." *Zion* 6 (1934): 114–38. (Heb.)

Nadav, Mordecai. "The minutes book of the Siebiez (White Russia) community court." *Kiryat Sefer* 36 (1961): 410–16, 535–41. (Heb.)

Nahon, Gerard. "Les Relations Amsterdam et Constantinople au XVIII siècle d'après le copiador de cartas de la nation Juive Portuguise d'Amsterdam." *Dutch Jewish History*, pp. 157–84. Jerusalem, 1984.

———. "Yeshivot Hierosolymites du XVIII siècle." *Les Juifs au regard de l'Histoire: Mélanges a l'honneur de Bernard Blumenkranz*, pp. 300–323. Paris, 1985.

Nigal, Gedalia. "In praise of R. Haim Ben Attar." *Kav Lakav*, 1983: 73–93. Jerusalem. (Heb.)

Pachter, Mordecai. "*Hazut Kasha* of R. Moses Alsheikh," *Shalem* 1 (1974): 157–94. (Heb.)

Philip, Thomas. "The Farhi family and the changing position of the Jews in Syria and Palestine, 1750–1860." *Cathedra* 34 (1985): 97–114. (Heb.)

Prawer, Joshua. "On the text of the 'Jerusalem letters' in the fifteenth and sixteenth centuries." *Jerusalem* 1 (1948): 139–59. (Heb.)

———. *A History of the Latin Kingdom of Jerusalem*, vols. 1–2. Jerusalem, 1963. (Heb.)

———. *The Crusaders, a Colonial Society*. Jerusalem, 1976. (Heb.)

Rabinowitz, Michel. "Scroles." *Mizrah U-Maʿarov* 3 (1929): 148–56.

Rackover, Nahum, and Esriel Hildesheimer. *The Community*. Jerusalem, 1977. (Heb.)

Raphael (Werfel), Isaac. "Letters of R. Jacob Paryenti to R. Solomon Haim Singvineti." *Sinai* 70 (1972): 86–91. (Heb.)

———. "Letters of R. Solomon Singvineti to R. Haim Ben Attar." *Temirin* 1 (1972): 271–86. (Heb.)

Rivkind, Isaac. "A collection of writings towards a history of the Jews in Palestine." *Reshumoth* 4 (1926): 301–44. (Heb.)

———. "Documents illustrating Jewish life in Palestine in the eighteenth century." *Yerushalayim* (dedicated to the memory of A. M. Luncz), pp. 111–85. Jerusalem, 1928. (Heb.)

———. "Isolated pages." *Zion* 5 (1933): 148–74. (Heb.)

———. "Towards a history of the Ashkenazi settlement after the immigration of R. Judah Hasid." *Bitzaron* 27 (1953): 248–56. (Heb.)

———. "Letters from Jerusalem." *A Present to Isaiah*, pp. 225–33. Tel Aviv, 1956. (Heb.)

———. "The society *Hadashim La-Bekarim* in Hebron." *Zion* 6 (1974): 218–19. (Heb.)

Rivlin, Eliezer. "The Gaon R. Yom-Tov Algazi et al." *Zion* 5 (1933): 131–48. (Heb.)

———. "The estate regulations of Jerusalem and Palestine." *Azkara* 5, (1937): 559–619. (Heb.)

———. "Rights of possession of courts and houses in Jerusalem." *Emeth Le-Yaʿakov* (jubilee volume in honor of Dr. Jacob Freimann), pp. 149–62. Berlin, 1937. (Heb.)

Rivlin, Joseph Joel, and Benjamin Rivlin. *Letters of the Pekidim and Amarkalim of Amsterdam*, vols. 1–3. Jerusalem, 1965–79. (Heb.)

Roth, Cecil. *The History of the Jews in Italy*. Tel Aviv, 1962. (Heb.)

Rothschild, Meir Menahem. *The "Haluka."* Jerusalem, 1969. (Heb.)

Rozanes, Solomon. *History of the Jews in Turkey and the Eastern Lands*, vols. 1–6. Tel Aviv and Jerusalem, 1930–46. (Heb.)

Rozen, Minna. *The Ruins of Jerusalem*. Tel Aviv, 1981. (Heb.)

———. "The mutiny of Nakib el Ashraf in Jerusalem (1702–1706) and its impact on the *dhimmis*." *Cathedra* 22 (1982): 75–90. (Heb.)

———. "Influential Jews in the Sultan's court in Istanbul in support of Jerusalem Jewry in the 17th century." *Michael* 7 (1982): 394–430. (Heb.)

Bibliography

————. *The Jewish Community of Jerusalem in the Seventeenth Century.* Tel Aviv, 1984. (Heb.)

Rubashov (Shazar), Shneur Zalman. "Sha'alu Shelom Yerushalayim." *Reshumoth* 2 (1927): 461–93. (Heb.)

Rubinstein, Abraham. "A possibly new fragment of *Shivhey Habesht?*" *Tarbitz* 35 (1966): pp. 174–91. (Heb.)

Safrai, Samuel. *Pilgrimage at the Time of the Second Temple.* Tel Aviv, 1965. (Heb.)

Scholem, Gershom. *The Dreams of the Sabbatean R. Mordecai Ashkenazi.* Tel Aviv, 1938 (Heb.)

————. "Contribution to the knowledge about Sabbateanism from the eighteenth century." *Zion* 9 (1944): 27–38, 84–88. (Heb.)

————. "Two letters from Palestine." *Tarbitz* 25 (1955): 429–40. (Heb.)

————. "The neutralization of the Messianic element in early Hasidism." *Journal of Jewish Studies* 20 (1969): 25–55.

————. *Sabbatai Zevi, the Mystical Messiah.* Princeton, N.J., 1973.

————. *Studies and Texts Concerning the History of Sabbateanism and Its Metamorphoses.* Jerusalem, 1974. (Heb.)

Schulwass, Moses A. *Rome and Jerusalem.* Jerusalem, 1944. (Heb.)

Schur, Nathan. *Jerusalem in Pilgrims' and Travellers' Accounts.* Jerusalem, 1980.

————. "The death of Haim Farhi as it appears from travelers' reports." *Cathedra* 39 (1986): 179–91. (Heb.)

Shamir, Shimon. *A Modern History of the Arabs in the Middle East.* Ramat Gan, 1971. (Heb.)

Shapira, Moses. "The Habad congregation in Hebron (1816–1929), its history and main features." *Vatiqin*, pp. 67–116. Ramat Gan, 1975. (Heb.)

Sharon, Moses, and Isaac Beck, eds. *From Ancient Archives*, collected by Pinhas Ben Zvi Grajewsky. Jerusalem, 1977. (Heb.)

Shaw, Stanford J. *History of the Ottoman Empire and Modern Turkey*, vol. 1. Cambridge, 1976.

Shazar, Salman. *The Hope for the Year 5500 (1740).* Jerusalem, 1970. (Heb.)

Shisha, Abraham. "The status of the yeshiva 'Haverim Makshivim' in Jerusalem." *Jerusalem* 3 (1950): 20–28. (Heb.)

Shmuelevitz, Arieh. *The Jews of the Ottoman Empire in the Late Fifteenth and the Sixteenth Centuries.* Leiden, 1984.

Shohet, Azriel. "The Jews in Jerusalem in the eighteenth century." *Zion* 1 (1936): 177–410. (Heb.)

————. "Comments on the paper of Y. Ben-Zvi, 'The Ashkenazi settlement in Jerusalem.'" *Jerusalem* 1 (1948): pp. 127–28. (Heb.)

————. *The Beginnings of the Haskalah among the Jews.* Jerusalem, 1960. (Heb.)

————. "Three eighteenth-century letters on Palestine." *Shalem* 1 (1974): 235–56. (Heb.)

Bibliography

―――. "The Jews in Jerusalem in the eighteenth century." *Cathedra* 13 (1979): 3–46. (Heb.)

Shpitsan, Aryeh. "Jewish charitable trusts in late nineteenth-century Jerusalem." *Cathedra* 19 (1981): 73–82. (Heb.)

Simonsohn, Solomon. "Emissaries from Safed to Mantua in the seventeenth and eighteenth centuries." *Sefunoth* 6 (1962): 327–54. (Heb.)

―――. *History of the Jews in the Duchy of Mantua,* vols. 1–2. Jerusalem, 1962–65. (Heb.)

Sluys, D. M. "The High-German Jewish community in Amsterdam from 1635 to 1795." *Studies on the History of Dutch Jewry,* pp. 69–122. Jerusalem, 1975. (Heb.)

Smid, Mordecai. "The deeds of the fathers." *Gilyonoth* 11 (1941): 258–60. (Heb.)

Sonne, Isaiah. "Neue Dokumente uber Salomon Malcho." *Monatschrft fur die Geschichte und Wissenschaft des Judentums* 75 (1931): 127–35.

―――. "On a Karaite letter." *Zion* 6 (1934): 222–24.

―――. "More on the attitude of the councils and communities of Poland to Eretz Israel." *Zion* 1 (1936): 252–55. (Heb.)

Stillman, N. *The Jews of Arab Lands.* Philadelphia, 1979.

Stiman-Katz, Haya. *Early Hasidic Immigration to Palestine.* Jerusalem, 1986. (Heb.)

Tamar, David. *The Book "Lekah Tov."* Jerusalem, 1977. (Heb.)

―――. *Studies in the History of the Jews in Palestine and the East.* Jerusalem, 1981. (Heb.)

Ta-Shema, Israel. "Palestine studies." *Shalem* 1 (1974): 81–96. (Heb.)

Tauber, Aryeh. "A section of my book *Minhath Yehuda Ve-Yerushalayim.*" *Jerusalem* 13 (1919): 257–78. (Heb.)

Tishbi, Isaiah. "R. Meir Rofe's letters of 1675–1680 to R. Abraham Rovigo." *Sefunoth* 3–4 (1960): 71–130. (Heb.)

―――. *The Paths of Belief and Heresy.* Ramat Gan, 1964. (Heb.)

―――. "The Messianic idea and Messianic trends in the growth of Hasidism." *Zion* 32 (1967): 1–45. (Heb.)

―――. "The spreading of Ramhal's Kabbalistic writings in Poland and Lithuania." *Kiryat Sefer* 45 (1970): 127–54. (Heb.)

―――. "Kabbalistic writing in Oxford Ms. 2593: A collection of hidden works by R. Moses Haim Luzzatto." *Kiryat Sefer* 53 (1973): 167–98. (Heb.)

―――. "Customs of Nathan of Gaza, letters of R. Moses Zaccuto and *takkannoth* of R. Haim Abulafia in *Hemdath Yamim.*" *Kiryat Sefer* 54 (1979): 598–610. (Heb.)

―――. "Rabbi Moses David Vale in the circle of Rabbi Moses Haim Luzzatto." *Zion* 44 (1979): 265–302. (Heb.)

―――. "The 'genealogy' of 'my teacher' and 'my father who is my master and my teacher' as pseudonymous quotations in *Hemdath Yamim.*" *Tarbitz* 50 (1980–81): 463–514. (Heb.)

Tobi, Yosef. "A letter from the 'Constantinople Officials' to R. Shalom Iraqi." *Shalem* 1 (1974): 257–70. (Heb.)

Toledano, Baruch. "On the history of the Jewish settlement in Safed." *Mizrah U-Ma'arav* 5 (1932): 359–62. (Heb.)

Toledano, Jacob Moses. "He causes the sleeping ones to speak." *Jerusalem* 7 (1907): 343–45. (Heb.)

———. *The Candle of the West.* Jerusalem, 1911. (Heb.)

———. "The language of sleepers." *Jerusalem* 10 (1914): 301–10. (Heb.)

———. "From manuscripts." *Hebrew Union College Annual* 5 (1928): 403–13. (Heb.)

———. "The secret scrolls." *Mizrah U-Ma'arav* 4 (1930): 40–48. (Heb.)

———. "Two documents from Jerusalem dated 5480 (1720) and 5520 (1760)." *Jerusalem* 4 (1954): 218–19. (Heb.)

———. "The attitude of the eastern communities to the settlement of Eretz Israel." *Shevet Va-Am* 1 (1954): 80–83. (Heb.)

———. *Treasury of Manuscripts.* Jerusalem, 1960. (Heb.)

Turtshiner, N. H. "Letters from Palestine by Simeon de Geldern." *Yerushalayim* (dedicated to the memory of A. M. Luncz), pp. 106–10. Jerusalem, 1928. (Heb.)

Twito, Elazar. "The immigration of R. Haim ben Attar to Palestine: Practical aspects and theoretical aspects." *The Jews of North Africa and Palestine,* pp. 52–58. Tel Aviv, 1981. (Heb.)

———. "R. Haim ben Attar (when he was in Italy)." *Zechor Le-Avraham,* pp. 36–46. Jerusalem, 1972. (Heb.)

Verete, Meir. "The idea of the restoration of the Jews in English Protestant thought, 1790–1840." *Zion* 33 (1968): 145–79. (Heb.)

Wasserstein, David. "Jewish Christian relations in 18th century Tiberias." *Cathedra* 56 (1989): 42–69. (Heb.)

Weinryb, Dov. "Problems of research on the history of the Jews in Palestine and their economic life." *Zion* 3 (1938): 58–83. (Heb.)

———. "The Jews in Poland and Lithuania and their relations to Breslau in 16–19 centuries." *Tarbiz* 9 (1938): 65–107. (Heb.)

Wilenski, Mordecai. "The Hasidic settlement in Tiberias at the end of the eighteenth century." *Hado'ar* 53 (1978): 661–62. (Heb.)

———. "The Jewish settlement in Tiberias at the end of the eighteenth century." *AJS Revue* 48 (1981): 1–17. (Heb.)

———. *The Hasidic Community in Tiberias.* Jerusalem, 1988. (Heb.)

Wilensky, Michael. "Notes on the biography of Rabbi R. E. H. Riki." *Kiryat Sefer* 25 (1949): 311–14.

Wurm, David. *Z Dziejow Zydostwe Brodzkiego za Czasow.* Brody, 1935.

Bibliography

Ya'ari, Abraham. "Where is Luzzatto's grave?" *Moznayim* 4 (1932): 3–11. (Heb.)
———. "The emissaries of Palestine in Yemen." *Sinai* 4 (1939): 392–430. (Heb.)
———. "Two pamphlets from Palestine." *Kiryat Sefer* 23 (1946): 140–59. (Heb.)
———. "Letters of emissaries from Jerusalem." *Jerusalem* 2 (1949): 61–73. (Heb.)
———. "R. Moses Israel and his mission for Palestine." *Sinai* 25 (1949): 149–63. (Heb.)
———. *The Travels of Meshulam of Voltera in Palestine*. Jerusalem, 1949. (Heb.)
———. "Two documents on the history of the Jewish settlement in Hebron." *Kiryat Sefer* 25 (1949): 113–25. (Heb.)
———. "The emissaries of Palestine in Tire." *Minha Le-Yehuda*. Jerusalem, 1950, pp. 212–15. (Heb.)
———. *The Emissaries of Palestine*. Jerusalem, 1951. (Heb.)
———. "The earthquake in Safed in 1759/60." *Sinai* 28 (1951): 349–63. (Heb.)
———. "The Pereyra yeshivoth in Jerusalem and Hebron." *Jerusalem* 4 (1954): 185–202. (Heb.)
———. "The ledger of an eighteenth-century emissary of Palestine." *Sura* 3 (1958): 235–57. (Heb.)
———. "The prayer *Mi-Sheberach*, history and texts." *Kiryat Sefer* 33 (1958): 118–30, 233–50. (Heb.)
———. *Studies in Hebrew Booklore*. Jerusalem, 1958. (Heb.)
———. "The account-book of the HiDA's mission." *The Book of the HiDA*, ed. M. Benayahu, pp. 105–40. Jerusalem, 1959. (Heb.)
———. "Hebrew printing in Izmir." *Aresheth* 1 (1959): 97–222. (Heb.)
———. "The 'three weeks' [between 17 Tammuz and the Ninth of Av] in Palestine throughout the generations." *Mahanayim* 47 (1960): 67–72. (Heb.)
———. "The Purim money, the half-shekel money and the *megilla* money." *Mahanayim* 54 (1961): 17–29. (Heb.)
———. "Supplement to my article 'The Prayer Mi-Sheberach.'" *Kiryat Sefer* 36 (1961): 103–18. (Heb.)
———. "Addenda to the book *The Emissaries of Palestine*." *Sura* 4 (1964): 223–49. (Heb.)
———. *Hebrew Printing in Constantinople*. Jerusalem, 1967. (Heb.)
———. *Letters from Palestine*. Ramat Gan, 1971. (Heb.)
———. *Memoirs of Palestine*, vols. 1–2. Ramat Gan, 1976. (Heb.)
———. *Travels in Palestine*. Ramat Gan, 1976. (Heb.)
Yalkut Shimoni, ed. Isaac Shiloni, Jerusalem, 1973. (Heb.)
Zohar, Haim. "R. Moses Haim Luzzatto in Palestine." *Sinai* 30 (1952): 281–94. (Heb.)

INDEX

Index

Benayahu, Meir, 7, 131
Benveniste, Meir, 122–24, 126
Berakha, Nissim, 102, 131
Berav, Jacob, 43, 147–48, 151, 153, 260 (n. 9)
Berlin, 58, 65, 69, 74
Beth Aharon (yeshiva), 169
Beth Avraham (yeshiva), 169
Beth-El (yeshiva), 36, 46, 89, 169
Beth Gedalia (yeshiva), 169
Beth Jacob, Pereyra (yeshiva), 167, 169, 209
Beth Jacob, Vega (yeshiva), 109–10, 149
Bnei Moshe (yeshiva), 169
Bohemia, 68, 70
Borgaz, 97
Bosnia, 97
Buda, 99
Bula, Moses, 21, 128, 130–31, 193
Burial Tax, 186–88
Bounan, Masoud, 159
Byelorussia. See White Russia

Cairo, 66
Cairo geniza, 5
Calev, Joshua, 122
Cammondo, 95
Cantarini, 44
Catholics, 71, 181
Cave of the Patriarchs, 198
Chief Rabbi, 83, 117, 127, 129–35, 137, 145. See also Rishon Le-Zion
Christians, 1–4, 7, 11, 22–23, 27, 57, 64, 71–72, 82, 87, 91, 112, 121, 141–42, 152, 154–55, 170, 181–82, 188, 194, 197–98, 215, 264 (n. 93)
Cizye (poll tax), 19, 184, 194–96
Cohen, Amnon, 8, 191
Cohen, Joseph, 164
Cohen, Moses, 77
Council of Lithuania, 70
Council of the Four Lands, 62, 67, 70, 77, 155, 233 (n. 68)
Crusaders, 2, 7, 53

D'Aguilar, Baron, 57, 62, 66, 70, 97

Dahir al-ʿUmar, 15–17, 19, 38–39, 59, 90, 94, 148, 152–56, 194, 215
Damascus, 12, 15–17, 20, 22, 54, 81, 93–94, 96, 155, 164, 191, 194–95, 216, 221 (n. 34)
Damesek Eliezer (yeshiva), 131, 167, 169
David, Isaac Behar, 98
David, Yekutiel, 114
De-Bilasco, Dr. Isaac, 122–23, 125, 210
De-Boton, Moses, 123
De-Gilderin, Simon, 21
Derjavine, 62
De-Silva, Hezekiah, 109, 116, 149
Dhimmis, 11–12, 140, 142, 190, 195
Di-Mayo, Isaac, 133, 167
Dinur, Ben Zion, 40, 42, 225 (n. 1)
Dirling, Von (Austrian ambassador), 94
Dömme, 46
Dubnow, 163

Earthquake, 17–18, 32–33, 99, 154–56, 171, 211
Edirne, 54, 59, 96, 99, 137, 212, 247 (n. 97)
Egypt, 17, 28, 66, 77, 82, 96, 101, 126, 165, 167, 189, 212
Elyashar, Jacob, 19
Emden, Jacob, 48–49, 57, 102
Emissary, 61, 64, 68, 75–76, 78–80, 101, 103, 237 (n. 8)
England, 267 (n. 15)
Estates, 188
Ettinger, Samuel, 232 (n. 39)
Etz Haim (yeshiva), 169
Eybeschütz, Jonathan, 48–49, 57, 102

Farhi, Eliezer, 125
Farhi, Haim, 15–16, 18, 94, 221 (n. 34)
Fatamid, 189
Ferrara, 66
Fintz, Abraham, 123
Firmans, 13, 19, 21, 72–73, 78, 85, 94, 192, 200
France, 16, 68–69, 71
Franco family, 66, 97, 267 (n. 15)
Frankfurt-am-Main, 64–65, 69–70

Index

Index

Index

Romaniotes, 11, 83
Romano, Elijah (yeshiva), 169
Rome, 63–64
Rovigo, Abraham, 41, 112, 169
Rozanes, Abraham, 36, 42, 87, 89, 149,
    249 (n. 28)
Rozanes, Isaac, 36, 98
Rumelia, 87, 95
Russia, 17, 29, 31, 38–39, 58, 62, 171

Sabbatean, 12, 34–36, 40–43, 45–46,
    49, 55–57, 64, 102, 109–12, 156, 163,
    225 (n. 2)
Sabbetai, Zevi, 12, 41, 43, 46, 109, 150
    240 (n. 12), 262 (n. 33), 269 (n. 35)
Sahnin, 157
Salah ad-Din, 189
Salonika, 12, 14, 30–32, 54, 59, 65, 67,
    96, 99, 104, 123, 133, 136–37, 167
Samnun, Elijah, 122–23, 125
Samóa, 179
Sancak, 12, 20, 93, 159, 195
Saporta, Moses, 125
Sasportas, Jacob, 248 (n. 8)
Sasportas, Moses, 110
Saul, Jacob, 49, 96, 150, 210
Scholem, Gershom, 40, 47
Schlesia, 70
Schultz, 155, 264 (n. 93)
Segal, Berman (Lehman Berend), 113
Semikha, 149
Shafarʿam, 156
Shani, Isaiah Isaac, 122, 255 (n. 149)
Sharʿabi-Mizrahi, Shalom, 36
Sharʿi archives, 3
Sharʿi court, 1, 13
Shemita, 157
Shidlov, 163
Shklov, 191
Shohet, Azriel, 7
Sidon, 12, 15, 17, 22, 71, 81, 94, 157,
    194–95, 216
Sijill, 1
Simha of Zalozce, 28, 37, 41, 44, 105,
    159, 195, 211
Singuineti, Abraham Ishmael Hai, 17, 65

Skopje, 99
Sofer, Joseph, 48
Sofer, Moses, 55
Sofia, 99, 193
Spain, 11, 54
Spanish Exile, 54–55, 59, 60, 63–64, 82
Sublime Porte, 59, 82, 93, 95, 140, 143,
    192, 194
Süleyman al-ʿAẓm, 15–16, 94, 221
    (n. 34)
Suzin, Solomon Moses, 137
Syria, 11–12, 14, 18, 29, 58, 82

Tarnopol, 97
Tikun, 146
Tischwitz, 155
Tishbi, 40, 163
Tokat, 97
Trani, Moses, 189
Treves, Joseph, 126, 210
Treves, Raphael, 22, 35, 41–44, 55, 57,
    150
Tzach Ve-Adom (book), 27–28, 43
Tzaddik, 42, 159–60
Tzalmona, Joseph, 122

Ulema, 2

Vali, 15, 18, 20
Vega family, 109
Venice, 3, 60, 63, 65, 67–68, 77, 96,
    113, 237 (n. 8)
Ventura, Haim, 76, 148, 151
Vienna, 60, 62, 65–66, 69–70, 97, 113,
    163, 240 (n. 10)
Vilayets, 194, 216
Vilna, 70, 91
Vilna, Jacob, 102, 163
Vilna, Yeruham, 78, 102
Vitebsk, 154, 156, 159–60, 163
Vizhnitz, 163
Volhynia, 163

Waqf, 190
Wertheim, Samson, 62, 65, 67, 84–85,
    113

304

Index

ABOUT THE AUTHOR

JACOB BARNAI is Senior Lecturer in the Department of Jewish History and Palestine Studies at Haifa University and Visiting Professor at Hebrew University, Jerusalem. He received his master's degree and doctorate from The Hebrew University of Jerusalem. For the academic year 1991–92 he is a member of the Institute for Advanced Studies at The Hebrew University of Jerusalem.